Powell's   Our Rival the Rascal (NoDJ)

OP/6.98   **NDJ** (H)

Social Science   103982

OUR RIVAL, THE RASCAL

PATTERSON SMITH REPRINT SERIES IN
CRIMINOLOGY, LAW ENFORCEMENT, AND SOCIAL PROBLEMS

A listing of publications in the SERIES *will be found at rear of volume*

PUBLICATION NO. 166: PATTERSON SMITH REPRINT SERIES IN
CRIMINOLOGY, LAW ENFORCEMENT, AND SOCIAL PROBLEMS

Our Rival the Rascal

BENJAMIN P. ELDRIDGE & WILLIAM B. WATTS

•

REPRINTED
WITH A
NEW
INTRODUCTION
BY
ROGER LANE

•

MONTCLAIR, NEW JERSEY
PATTERSON SMITH
1973

First published 1897 by the Pemberton Publishing Company
Reprinted 1973 by Patterson Smith Publishing Corporation
Montclair, New Jersey 07042
New material copyright © 1973 by
Patterson Smith Publishing Corporation

Library of Congress Cataloging in Publication Data

Eldridge, Benjamin P. 1838–
  Our rival, the rascal.

  (Patterson Smith reprint series in criminology, law enforcement, and social problems. Publication no. 166)
  Reprint of the 1897 ed. with a new introduction.
  1. Crime and criminals—U. S. 2. Police—U. S.
I. Watts, William B., 1852– joint author. II. Title.
HV6783.E3 1973   364'.973   79–172578
          ISBN 0–87585–166–5

This book is printed on
permanent/durable paper

INTRODUCTION

Our Rival the Rascal, by Benjamin Eldridge and William B. Watts, is the finest example of its genre, the "anatomy of roguery," ever published in the United States. The "anatomy," as a specialized subcategory of criminal literature, is distinguished by a detailed concern with the structure, operations, language, and life-style of the professional criminal underworld. And it has a long and honorable history. A fascination with various villainies was strong enough in Elizabethan England to inspire several authors to crib and expand upon the seminal "Conny-Catching" pamphlets of Robert Greene. Today, and over the past decade, readers of such staid publications as *Harper's* and *The New York Times Magazine* have found edification in the habits and methods of burglars, prostitutes, and car thieves. But it is the nineteenth century which was the golden age of criminal literature of all types.

There are many reasons for this, chiefly the fact that a variety of new institutions had by this time combined with mass literacy to engage the public imagination, and to keep it engaged. The second quarter of the century, in particular, set the stage. Perhaps the most obvious contribution was the establishment of urban police departments, in England and the United States, beginning with the London Metropolitan force in 1829. But there were many others. The 1820s brought important penal reforms on both sides of the Atlantic, as the criminological theories of Jeremy Bentham and the Utilitarians began to bear fruit. It was the building of the first true penitentiaries, during the same decade, that was responsible for bringing Alexis de Tocqueville to the United States. Another and very different Frenchman,

Eugène François Vidocq, began publishing his "memoirs" in 1827. This most famous of criminals-turned-cop had founded the first modern detective bureau, in Paris, and as his gaudy adventures went through several editions, they found an eager audience in English. It was entirely natural, in 1841, for Edgar Allan Poe to place his pioneering "Murders in the Rue Morgue" in a Gallic setting; by the 1850s and 1860s, the detective story was a well-established form in the two languages. And an even wider audience was captured by the American "penny press," which, beginning in the 1830s, based much of its mass appeal on sensationalized crime and court reporting. By about mid-century, then, the list was complete: humanitarians and philosophers were struggling to explain crime, policemen to control it, and newspapers to exploit it. These and other developments contributed to a growing mountain of written material on the subject.

The forms and media involved were almost as varied as the works themselves: they included Sunday supplements, scientific treatises, statistical reports, pamphlet accounts of major murders, police histories, the memoirs of famous cops and crooks, and several levels of detective literature, from Deadwood Dick to Sherlock Holmes. Watts and Eldridge, writing in 1897, were able to draw on all these sources, as well as on their own experience—and their experience was impressive. Benjamin Eldridge, a policeman for more than thirty years, was at the time head not only of the prestigious Boston department but also of the National Union of Chiefs of Police. William B. Watts had equally sound credentials; later founder of the private agency which still bears his name, he was in 1897 Boston's Chief Detective. Their collaboration reflects a union of the experienced policeman's common sense with a wide knowledge of printed sources, and is animated throughout by a confidence in the progressive virtues of the period. It is this combination which makes the book stand first in its class—a more accurate, more characteristic, more sophisticated "anatomy" than such earlier efforts as *Professional Criminals of America,* by the celebrated Thomas F. Byrnes.

The nineteenth century's interest in criminality was at once romantic and realistic, represented on the one hand by a fascination with gothic horrors and dashing detectives, and on the other by masses of undigested statistics, hard-boiled police reportage, and scientific theorizing. *Our Rival the Rascal* appeals mainly to the latter set of appetites. The book does have its share of the literary language and references almost mandatory in an age when the word "genteel" was still a compliment; one crowded stretch (pp. 11–14) manages to touch on Dickens and Charles Lamb, Wordsworth and Shakespeare. But generally the tone is restrained, and Watts and Eldridge explicitly warn against the diabolical criminal portraits and flamboyant detectives of more fanciful writers. Their purpose is practical, even scholarly: to advise their readers how to protect themselves against theft and fraud, to serve as guides to the hard world of criminal behavior, and to survey the latest theories.

The sections of preventive advice go well beyond the usual injunctions to carry wallets well-buttoned, and to beware of strangers with intriguing plans for getting rich in a hurry. There is, in particular, nowhere a better survey of the history and techniques of nineteenth-century burglary. Three chapters and nearly two dozen technical illustrations are devoted to the schemes, tools, and devices used in the contest between those who have wealth and those who would take it. The picture is that of an ancient and ongoing game, with the advantage belonging now to the offense and now to the defense, as each set of contestants stretches its wits to find new uses for the mechanical, metallurgical, and chemical advances of the Age of Invention.

But these sections, however interesting, are outweighed in bulk and importance by the "anatomy" proper, the heart of the book. Here the rascals are classified by type, but they are also quite specific antagonists with personal histories, men and women who stare at us from over a hundred photographs.

Nothing conveys the sense of realism better than these grim images, four to a page, mostly from Boston's own files. The authors describe the use of this rogues' gallery and of the Bertillon measurement system, together with some medical and laboratory technology used in cases of murder and forgery. These aids, rarely used, were all the nineteenth-century detective could count on. His work, as never since, was based on firsthand experience not only with the methods of crime but also with the individuals involved. The necessary intimacy was often acquired in shady ways. The maxim was still, as in the days of Jonathan Wild and Eugène Vidocq, "It takes a thief to catch a thief." The career lines of most detectives were not the same as those of other policemen; many of them simply stepped into their jobs over the blurred line between hunter and hunted. Watts himself never served the usually obligatory time on the beat, and Eldridge owed his promotion, in 1891, to a messy detective scandal: his predecessor's chief lieutenant was accused of masterminding a series of burglaries. The prevailing system of thief-taking clearly involved collusion, at worst, and at best illegal bullying, spying, and harassment. But it did produce policemen who knew their way around.

The underworld that Watts and Eldridge describe was flourishing. Its halcyon years, in the United States, had a definite beginning and end. The traditional underworld did not encompass all those who committed crime, certainly not violent or passionate crime. Its full-time membership, perhaps a few thousand in the nation, comprised men with carefully developed skills, many of them ancient. Access to their world was limited—although by no means organized, thieves did have a sort of loose fraternal society of their own, tied by the bonds of necessity, familiarity, and common interest. They were distinguished, and graded, by their possession of specialized arts and talents, they went to the same places, used the same language, and shared the same links —crooked politicians and lawyers—to the world above. They depended on a loose, anonymous, and complex urban society in which to live and work. The necessary conditions were not met, on this side of the Atlantic, until shortly before the Civil War, when a criminal underworld very like the English one began to make itself felt. Importation, as with other skilled crafts, was often direct, as many old masters sought these shores both to clip provincial sheep and to educate provincial talent. The British origins of the fraternity may in fact have been one of its bonds—it seems significant that there is only a single black face in the gallery of photographs, and few names to suggest southern or eastern European descent. And it was in part the pressure of new ethnic groups, together with radically different criminal techniques and means of organization, that ended its heyday in the 1920s and 1930s. The year 1897, in any case, falls almost precisely in the middle, the time of full maturity.

The date is significant for another reason. Part of the interest in the traditional underworld lies in its continuity, the fact that its ploys, stratagems, and language were—and with diminishing vigor still are—passed on in subterranean fashion from Elizabethan times and earlier. Watts and Eldridge are aware of this heritage and its development. Sometimes they refer directly to earlier scholars, villains, and techniques; in other places their description of, say, the art of picking pockets recalls the eighteenth century. But they were writing in a period of rapid change, when thieves as well as others had constantly to adapt to new conditions. With quick wits as their principal stock in trade, criminals on the whole did better than most, often in fascinating ways.

No group of practitioners illustrates the need for progressive thinking better than burglars, and especially bank burglars. These were the aristocrats of the criminal social hierarchy, but their status was by no means traditional. It was all right for "church-workers" such as "Funeral Wells" to go on picking pockets on holy occasions in much the same fashion as their predecessors of generations back; the only changes they had to

our present vantage-point. So does the wider world of nineteenth-century confidence and faith in progress. The peculiar virtue of *Our Rival the Rascal* is that it manages to capture the one and reflect the other at almost the last moment possible, before they both began to pass away.

ROGER LANE

Haverford College
February 1972

OUR · RIVAL · THE · RASCAL

A · FAITHFUL · PORTRAYAL · OF THE · CONFLICT · BETWEEN · THE CRIMINALS · OF · THIS · AGE · AND THE · DEFENDERS · OF · SOCIETY — THE · POLICE.

BY

BENJ. P. ELDRIDGE   and   WILLIAM B. WATTS
Superintendent of Police.   Chief Inspector of the Detective Bureau

OF THE CITY OF BOSTON.

PEMBERTON - PUBLISHING - COMPANY, - 287
CONGRESS - STREET, - BOSTON, - MASS., - 1897.

Copyright, 1896, by Pemberton Publishing Co. All Rights Reserved.

[*facsimile of the original title page*]

BENJAMIN P. ELDRIDGE.

BENJAMIN P. ELDRIDGE, Superintendent of Police, of the city of Boston, was born in the seashore town of Truro, Mass., in 1838. When he was four years old, his parents moved to Dorchester, then a suburban town bordering on Boston. He was educated in the Dorchester public schools and after graduation entered the office of the Dorchester Fire Insurance Company, first as a clerk and subsequently undertaking the duties of a special policeman.

Shortly after his entry into the field of service to which his life has since been devoted, he was elected a constable by the choice of the town and discharged all the duties of this post until his enlistment in the state police force of Massachusetts in 1867. He served on this force till 1875, working in all parts of the Commonwealth, and at times in the discharge of his duties in other states of the Union.

Upon the abolition of the institution of the state police in 1875 he was appointed to the Boston police force and three years later promoted to the rank of Lieutenant. In 1885, upon the organization of the Boston Board of Police Commissioners, Lieut Eldridge served as deputy at headquarters to the acting superintendent and in October of the same year was raised to the rank of Captain and assigned to the charge of one of the city stations.

On July 14, 1888, Captain Eldridge was promoted to the rank of Chief Inspector, and on November 9, 1891, he became by appointment Superintendent of Police, which position he has since held. His long and wide ranging service in police circles has given him the intimate experience with crime and criminals requisite to the preparation of Our Rival, The Rascal. He is the present head of the association of the Massachusetts Chiefs of Police and also President of the National Union of Chiefs of Police, embracing the representatives of all the leading cities of the country.

CHIEF INSPECTOR WILLIAM B. WATTS is the present head of the detective branch of the Boston Police Department officially designated as the Bureau of Criminal Investigation. In this position he has at the present time under his command thirty skilled detectives. He was born in Cambridge, Mass., June 19, 1852, his parents moving to Boston while he was very young. He was educated in the Boston public schools from which he was graduated during the time of the war.

He became a member of the Boston Police Department in December, 1877. Early in 1881 he was appointed an Assistant Inspector of Police and assigned to duty at the Detective Bureau at Police Headquarters. He was promoted to the rank of Inspector of Police December 24, 1884. He served in this capacity until November 9, 1891, when he was promoted to the rank of Captain in which capacity he served for three years in charge of a city station.

In August, 1894, upon the reorganization of the Detective Bureau he was transferred by the Board of Police to his former field of duty and promoted to the office of Assistant Chief Inspector. Two months later upon the promotion of the former Chief Inspector to the post of Deputy Superintendent he was advanced to the rank of Chief Inspector in the same branch of the service, which position he has since held.

In his nearly twenty years of service he has become necessarily familiar with every type of criminal and his constant study of their character, habits and ways of operation has been unremitting and minute. He feels that he may with propriety state that the conclusions of his years of experience are frankly presented in the following pages.

WILLIAM B. WATTS.

PREFACE.

AS we sit in our office chairs, our rival, the rascal, leers down at us through a thousand masks. He is reckless, gay, demure, stolid, dogged, sullen, surly, threatening, desperate. He has the smirk of the confidence man, the furtive glance of the sneak thief, the scowl of the burglar, the menace of the murderer. The moulds of every vice and crime which the world knows are ranged before us in a single group of pictures— the photographs which compose the Rogues' Gallery.

Our rival, the rascal, was born before the beginning of history. He has existed ever since knavery sought to outwit honesty and villainy attacked by force or fraud the natural right of man to life, liberty and the pursuit of happiness. In the earliest conditions of society the honest man fought the rascal single-handed or with the chance help of his neighbors. With the advance of civilization, came the institution of the standing safeguards of watchmen and constables, culminating at length in the great disciplined forces of our city police.

From the farthest stretch of tradition down to the present hour society has been fighting our rival, the rascal, day and night, with all its accumulating powers of defence and suppression, and yet the rascal has not been subdued and for ages to come he will doubtless continue to defy the law and infest the earth. Still the advancing experience, organization and determination arrayed against him have succeeded, at least, in making his path in life a painful tramp over rocks and thorns with traps and pitfalls threatening his feet at every step. Between him and the grand organization of the defenders of society, simply summed up in the term, the police, there is an undying rivalry and an incessant contest, the one striving by every hook and crook to blind the eyes or escape the clutch of the other which in turn is constantly spurred on to meet craft with craft and foil every new shift of resourceful villainy by redoubled alertness in detection and capture.

In the following pages we have designed to show the rascal of to-day in his multiform bodies and faces. We have distinguished, as sharply, and vividly as we can, the varying types in our Rogues' Gallery. We have depicted the bunco man, the sneak thief, the burglar, the forger—the trickster and ruffian of every known stripe. We have shown what conditions make or mould them, how they plan, how they work, what covers they seek, and how the police in turn plan and work to forestall, deter, detect and capture them.

For the sake of illustration and interest, we have sketched in the life dramas of typical rascals, in which no stroke of fancy is added to distort or impair the truth of the pictures. If they do not appear like the heroes or principals in the lurid yellow covered fiction of our time, they have at least the merit of being true portraits of real men.

Accompanying these sketches we have given also photographs of distinctive criminals who have made their mark in the crime of this century, together with cuts illustrating the latest improvements in the instruments and weapons used for the perpetration of crimes.

It has been our aim in the preparation of this book to make not only a graphic and faithful portrayal of the criminal classes and the police of to-day, but also to supply a work of practical every day service to the public at large in the suggestion of precautions for the better security of life and property. It has further been of heartfelt satisfaction to us that we have the opportunity here of offering a just tribute to the ability, zeal, fearlessness and unflagging devotion to duty of our brother officers in the police service and to the admirable administration of the boards of direction of our police throughout the country.

What we have written is the product of many years of actual service on the police force of Boston in various capacities, during which we have been brought into intimate personal contact with the range of criminals whom we have depicted. To our personal experience we have been enabled to add also the co-operation of friends, expert in the police service, and the comprehensive official records of the police departments of this and other countries. Supplementing these official sources of information we have also a personal collection of memoranda touching crimes and criminals, which we have been making for many years for the purpose of reference and identification. This collection we have now found of much value in preparing the work which we have entitled, Our Rival, The Rascal.

CONTENTS.

CHAPTER I.

THE SWINDLING BEGGAR 1

A master in tricks of disguise—Tramps' unions—Methods of recruiting—The manufacture of cripples—The daily life of a tramp—A convenient mask for a burglar—How to provide for mendicants and vagabonds.

CHAPTER II.

BY SLEIGHT OF HAND 15

The pickpocket and his methods—The amateur and professional—Favorite haunts of the pickpocket—Representative rogues—How to guard against them—The shoplifter—Guarding stores in the shopping districts—The cloak of kleptomania—"Morning hoisters" and "Penny-weight thieves"—Representative shoplifters and their methods—Safeguards against their operations.

CHAPTER III.

FROM JIMMIES TO DYNAMITE 35

Bank burglars, old-fashioned and modern—Their tools—Evolution in burglary—Selection of a "mark"—Famous bank robberies—"Max Shinburn" and other foremost craftsmen—The introduction of explosives—Coöperating defences—Electricity applied to safe breaking—Best precautions and safeguards.

CHAPTER IV.

THROUGH WALLS OF STEEL 64

Extensions of common law burglary—"Safe blowers" and store breakers—Insecurity of old and cheap safes—How store robberies are planned and executed—Burglars' correspondence—Old-fashioned and modern "kits"—Typical safe breakers and their operations—The vigilance of the police—Coöperative methods of defence suggested.

CHAPTER V.

UNDER COVER OF NIGHT 93

Different classes of house breakers—The "second story worker"—Some representative "climbers"—Raids of the "flat worker"—Necessary precautions—House sneaks and how to foil them—The professional burglar—Typical house breakers and their undertakings—Essential safeguards for the protection of householders.

CHAPTER VI.

A SLIPPERY AND SUBTLE KNAVE 120

The "bank sneak"—A connecting link between burglar and forger—The foremost American "bank sneaks" and their ways of working—The "invalid" trick and the "drop game"—Characteristics and habits—Recruiting—Useful precautions.

CHAPTER VII.

THE STROKE OF THE QUILL 144

The forger's craft—The development of counterfeiting—Dangerous current counterfeits and how to detect them—"Sweating," "plugging" and "filling"—Counterfeit paper money—Raised bank notes—Means of detection of forgery—Characteristics of forged handwriting—Celebrated cases of forgery—Sketches of the most notorious forgers—Organization for protection.

CHAPTER VIII.

SHARPERS AND DUPES 185

Origin of "Bunco"—Curious exhibit of the game—The "gold brick" and its variations—Buried treasures and sunken galleons—"Green goods" and "sawdust" games—The "horse sharp"—"Confidence men"—Swindling land agents, lightning rod men and commission agents—Bogus business investments and publishing frauds—Overdrafts and worthless checks—How immigrants are swindled—Detection and capture.

CHAPTER IX.

IN THE CLOAK OF A GUEST 223
The hotel thief—His tricks to gain entrance to rooms—Typical rogues and their arts—The professional hotel "beat"—Precautions for landlord and guest.

CHAPTER X.

"KNIGHTS OF THE ROAD" 248
The rise of the train robber—The celebrated Reno gang—Other noted gangs of outlaws—"Sleeping car workers"—Safeguards for travellers—Pilferers from express wagons.

CHAPTER XI.

THE ROVING FOOTPAD 280
The modern highwayman—Weapons, old and new—Palioly's "choke-pear"—Modern knock-out drops—Representative ruffians—The need of stringent legislation.

CHAPTER XII.

THE RECEIVER 291
The "Fence"—How stolen goods are disposed of—Marks of identification destroyed—The receiver's share—Representative receivers—Masks of professional "fences."

CHAPTER XIII.

THE INCENDIARY 299
The rise of arson—Commercial incendiarism—Reckless over-insurance—The pyromaniac—An advanced system of fire inquests—Duties and services of a fire marshal—The duty of the State.

CHAPTER XIV.

ARREST AND IDENTIFICATION 306

Organization and operation of police and detective forces—Progress in discipline and service—A typical city police department—How detectives and patrolmen cover and guard a city—Methods of identification—The Bertillon system—The Rogues Gallery—Tracing and capturing criminals.

CHAPTER XV.

THE MAKING OF CRIMINALS 337

Causes of crime—Opinions of experts—Lombroso's theory—Proal's rejoinder—Indications of criminality—Application of photography to the study of criminal types—Composite photographs of criminals—The spread of crime.

CHAPTER XVI.

THE CRIMINAL WOMAN 357

Proportionally few women are criminals—Characteristics observed by experts—Resources of pretence—Habits and methods illustrated by typical instances—Remarkable criminals.

CHAPTER XVII.

THE TREATMENT OF CRIMINALS 376

Advances during the present century—European and American methods—Habitual criminal acts—For discrimination in treatment—Plan of the Abbé Moreau—Progressive classification—Requisites for reform—For diminution of crime—Care of discharged convicts—An indelible brand.

CHAPTER XVIII.

SAFEGUARDS 391

The evolution of the modern burglar-proof safe—Safe deposit vaults and locks—Chrome steel jail cells—Electric burglar alarm systems—Insurance against burglary—The "Yale" lock—Safety paper—Watchmen's clocks—Police signal systems.

INDEXES 421

OUR RIVAL, THE RASCAL

THE SWINDLING BEGGAR.

IN the dim, old traditional days when every tree had a nymph as a tenant and every fountain was the bath of a naiad, there lived an old fellow called Proteus. He made his living as the herdsman of Neptune, god of the sea, and it was his custom to tell over his herds of sea calves at noon and then to go to sleep on the floor of his cave. The only way of catching him was to pounce upon him suddenly in his sleep and bind him fast, for otherwise he could change his shape in an instant to any form he chose and slip away beyond the reach of pursuit.

There is a curious likeness between this shifty old fellow of ancient fable and the artful rascal of our day who is wandering up and down through this country as a swindling beggar. Like Proteus he is a master of every trick of disguise. He veils his cunning eyes behind patches and gropes through the crowded streets of our cities with his pattering staff. He stuffs up a monstrous hump on his back and invokes a shuddering pity for his dreadful deformity. He counterfeits every imaginable distortion of body or limb. He swathes himself in filthy bandages as a victim of every wounding, maiming and shattering agency on earth, from a cyclone to a trolley car. He paints the most loathsome sores on his face, neck or hands, or by the use of chemicals actually makes eruptions of the flesh that may well pass for the surface show of incurable diseases. In the ingenuity of his devices and variety of his masks he is really an artist whose works might be studied with profit by the character actors of our modern stage.

If he is persistently hunted from cover to cover by the police or other agencies of the law, he will slip away like old Proteus to some other place of refuge from which he can later return to his favorite haunts, in some novel mask, after all scent of him has grown cold. Even when arrested, he is never at a loss for some plausible tale of woe to palliate his offences and shorten his sentence, if he cannot escape conviction as an impostor and vagrant. With his tricks of disguise and his shifts of pretence he is certainly one of the most bothersome rascals with whom our police has to deal.

Commonly this strolling beggar is a member of a little confederacy or gang of tramps whose field of imposition stretches from the Atlantic to the Pacific and from northern Canada to the Gulf of Mexico. In their swindling practice, these tramps go about usually singly or in pairs, but the gangs are bound together by pledges which are rarely broken and are subject to the direction of a chosen leader or captain. Their favorite pastures are the cities and larger towns where they can beg most successfully and meet by appointment at night in some low dive or cheap lodging house to plan for the next day and confide their spoils to their leader who serves as the treasurer of the joint collection.

A considerable share of the booty is often left to accumulate in the hands of the captain as a fund to be used as bail money or in payment of fines when any of the gang are arrested. It serves also as a means of support in weeks when the pastures yield little or when the beggars are driven from the streets by the bitter cold or the blasts of wintry storms. This reserve fund is kept in some secret hiding place or, it may be, regularly deposited in a bank by the leader who can readily put on the dress and manner of a thrifty working man.

It may seem strange that so much confidence is reposed in the head of the gang, by the associated rogues, but it is a very rare instance when this trust is abused. An absconding or defaulting treasurer would be branded as a treacherous thief by the men whom he robbed and blacklisted by every gang of beggars throughout the country as fast as the tale could travel. There is honor among these rascals to this extent, at least, that no one can swindle another without being barred out of the united order of American beggars and exposed to every device of vindictive resentment. Doubtless the assurance of this penalty is a fine buttress for a shaky conscience and a better shield for a trust fund than any combination of locks and bars.

When the day's collection is put in the hands of the captain, he divides all except the reserve among the members of the gang equally or in regularly stipulated proportions, without regard to the actual amount turned in by each as the proceeds of his day's beggary. This distribution is accepted without complaint and it is a matter of fact that there is rarely any attempt to hold back a cent secretly of the full amount which each beggar is expected to put in the common purse.

These beggars are of every age and nationality under the sun. They make up their gangs from chance association in the same district, or from personal liking, or the shrewd appreciation of the peculiar knack in imposition which each knave possesses to a greater or less extent. In this association a combination may be made that will successfully impose on every class in the community or in the beggar's parlance "work the whole town at once."

For the recruiting of the gangs, keen-witted young boys of a wayward disposition are the ones preferred as a rule. These boys are dissatisfied with their homes or life for some reason or other. Some lack moral training, some have harsh or abusive parents or none at all, some are naturally of a vicious disposition and all may be led to follow a tempter who lures them on with tales of pockets jingling with silver, of the free and easy life of the rover, and of the curious and interesting sights to be seen in his rambling over the country from ocean to ocean.

When a boy is enlisted by the captain, he is introduced to every member of the gang and regularly adopted as a confederate with a fixed allowance of the joint booty. He is warned and trained to obey the directions of his chief implicitly and continue faithful to his obligations to his companions. How he advances in roguery may well be illustrated by a typical instance, in the person of a young fellow who not long ago fell into the hands of the Boston police.

This lad was an orphan boy who wandered away from his home in Connecticut and drifted into the company of "Frisco Slim," one of the most notorious of the "knights of the road." This remarkable beggar was no slender stripling as his sobriquet might suggest, but a strapping young rogue from California, weighing over 200 pounds and towering above his confederates as one of the giant firs on the slopes of his native Sierras overtops the mass of the forest. He had lost by some accident or gambling squabble part of the fingers of his left hand and this mutilation was a handy corner stone for a fabric of imposition in the rôle of a cripple. His strength and arrogance had won for him a certain preëminence in the company of his fellow beggars and he was then the recognized chief of a gang which was plaguing Boston particularly.

He was on the lookout for serviceable young recruits and by adroit pumping he soon perceived that the Connecticut boy might readily be turned into a useful tool. So he began to fill the lad's mind with the enticements of life on the road and the ease of imposition on the credulous public.

"Why should you rub along as a common bum," he said, "when you might go up to the top of the profession and easily make from three to ten dollars a day?" Then he showed the boy how his arm had been chemically treated to counterfeit closely the appearance of a frightful burn. "With that arm," said Frisco, waving it proudly, "I collar many a dollar every day of my life. I can fix up your arm in another style that will catch on just as well and you can make money enough to burn if you come with me." With this kind of talk, he soon won over the boy to join the gang which he headed and the lad was duly enrolled under the name of "Kid Johnson."

THE SWINDLING BEGGAR. 5

As soon as he was enlisted Johnson was taken to a resort of the gang where his arm was set in a plaster cast as if it had been recently broken. In outward seeming the counterfeit was complete and nobody would be likely to suppose that it was the cover of a cheat. Even if there was a suspicion of humbug, no examination that could be made by the ordinary observer would detect the trick.

Then the novice was sent out to beg on the streets with his arm in a sling. His face was made up to show pitiful traces of pain, hunger and weariness. He had no coat on his back. His scanty clothing was thin and ragged. His naked toes peeped through the tatters of his shoes. From head to heel he was an image of woe cunningly fashioned to melt a heart of ice and he had at his tongue's end a distrustful tale composed by his mentor, the artful Slim.

The pains expended on his make-up and training were richly rewarded. "Kid Johnson" proved to be a little silver mine on legs. Over and over again his pockets were filled with dimes and quarters and even round dollars by compassionate people in the shops and on the streets. Good, kindly housewives fed him on the fat of the land in their warm, cosy kitchens and big-hearted servant girls took their mites from hard-earned wages to comfort the poor little orphan, with a broken arm, who was forced to beg his bread from door to door.

When night came, the young beggar went with overflowing pockets to the rendezvous of his gang, which, in Boston, was a room in the West End of the city. Here he was warmly welcomed by his chief, "Frisco Slim," and his mates, numbering nearly a dozen in all, and the booty of the day was counted and divided. The chief lieutenants, so to speak, of "Frisco Slim" were the rogues, "English Harry" and "Sheeny Si," whose portraits appear in illustration of this class of impostors in a group with their chief. "Harry" was by profession or pretence a bartender and "Si" a brakeman, but like their captain, the stalwart Slim, who called himself a painter, both had a rooted aversion

washed and unkempt from their litter, taking perhaps a few cheap pencils or shoestrings to distinguish themselves from common tramps.

So "Kid Johnson" spent his first night with his new mates and went out like the rest to cheat the city with his woe-begone face and plaster cast. Day after day he returned with jingling pockets to slide down the pit of vice lower and lower. The wayward boy was changing fast to a debased and hardened rogue like his comrades.

As he grew more expert and his first city pasture ground was well grazed over he was sent out to neighboring towns to beg. He brought back several dollars a day but the avarice of "Frisco Slim" grew faster than his pupil could appease it, and, as his control over his young accomplice increased, he treated the lad little better than a slave. The boy was driven to beg without resting by the threat of a beating if his day's collection did not exceed the stint fixed by his bully and such was the craft of this master beggar that the poor, ignorant boy grew more and more abject under his thumb.

He was freed from his bondage by a resolute dash of the Boston police who captured the whole gang of beggars at one swoop in the winter of 1894–95. "Kid Johnson" was sifted out of the incorrigible tramps and pains were taken to reform and place him in a good position as a clerk where he could earn a comfortable living with hope of advancement. But the contamination of his fellow beggars had been fatal to him. He ran away after a short time of honest work to resume his life in the streets. When he left his place, he sent a grateful letter to the Boston police department thanking his friends on the force for their kindly care and regretting that their hope for him should be disappointed. The latest report of him records that he is a tramp like his vicious companions, "Frisco Slim," "English Harry," and "Sheeny Si," now scattered over the country or serving terms as vagrants and impostors.

With natural variations, that may be easily imagined, the

experience of this young boy is the experience of thousands like him and the habits and practices of "Frisco Slim's" gang are fairly representative of hundreds of others infesting our country. Besides these organized gangs there are many of the fraternity also who beg independently, preferring to be their own masters or thinking this course more safe and profitable. These are apt to be the cleanest of their order and the least dependent on any artificial cheat or counterfeit of bodily ailment or deformity. These are the mendicants who meet us on the street with tales of recently lost situations and hunts for employment. These beggars are continually anticipating promised remittances from their parents and friends, that never arrive. Some have the promise of employment the next day and want a trifle to tide over the night or buy a meal or make a more decent appearance when they go to work. How familiar too is that plea for another five cents to put with the five which the beggar has in hand for the hire of a bed! And who has not been besought by the beggars that hang about the railroad stations for the price of a ticket to carry them home?

This class of beggars is commonly known to the police as "lodging house tramps," because they usually aim to keep out of the station houses and save enough to pay for a cheap cot in the tenements where lodgings for the night are furnished at ten cents and upward.

Below this class comes the rough, drunken, brutalized and filthy tramp, who prefers rum any time to a bed, and only keeps a nickel on winter nights for the cost of a shelter in the vilest dens in lofts or cellars. There they lie packed together on the floor like rats in their holes, a frightful, reeking, lousy mass of human kind that has fallen below the level of brutes. Sometimes even the wretched ease of a stretch at full length on the filthy boards is denied to them and men pass the nights hanging in lines on thick ropes that are carried from wall to wall a few feet above the floor. In the morning one end of the rope is unfastened and dropped, flinging the weary tramps on the floor as the easiest method of rousing and notifying them to get up and go.

The continuance of life after years in these vile slums can only be accounted for by the extraordinary ruggedness of bodies inured to every form of hardship and refreshed by the pure outdoor air in which the days of the tramp are spent. The coarse food eaten is also generally wholesome, and probably less enervating than the luxuries on the table of Dives. Certainly it is rare that the police see a sickly professional tramp or find a dead one unless he has been killed by accident.

The country is the tramp's paradise in summer. He sometimes travels in gangs but generally in parties of two or three. Idling about from one farm or village to another, sleeping under a hay stack, in a barn or in the lockup, is his usual life. He seldom works but begs persistently for money and for food when he can get nothing else. Petty thieving is his recreation. He keeps a sharp eye on the clothes lines and steals the farmer's poultry, eggs, fruit and vegetables. If he wants to cross a comparatively barren pasture he secretes himself in an empty freight car or makes as comfortable berth as possibly on the trucks under the car. Freight trains are frequently stopped by conductors to drive out the tramps and it is not uncommon to dislodge a dozen or more at one time.

There is only a gauzy veil of division between the patent professional beggar and the thinly covered kind that goes from door to door and especially seeks an entrance to business offices with a tale of misfortune and a handful of cheap pencils, or penholders or useless knick-knacks. Some of them simply present a few printed stanzas of doggerel, reciting their claim to compassion and closing with the plea to buy the poor handbill. A few of these petty pedlars may be really deserving of pity or actually trying to keep themselves above the level of beggars, but the vast majority are particularly crafty and annoying impostors who resort to this device to evade the statutes against undisguised vagrancy and gain access to places from which the ordinary tramp is shut out. Among these swindling beggars are many really desperate characters, burglars and ruffians of the vilest stripe, who have purposely sought the disguise of a mendicant to cover their designs or evade pursuit and the strong arm of the law. When arrested as suspicious characters, such rascals profess to be merely vagabonds and serenely accept light sentences for vagrancy as an assurance against more formidable indictments.

A fair representative example of this imposture was given by the gang of tramps and burglars which was arrested by the Boston police, a year ago, in a cheap lodging house in the North End of the city where the tramps were sleeping three in a bed. One of the worst of the lot was William Carroll, alias Hayes, alias Carpenter, alias Cole, whose portrait is given on our page of typical impostors. He was convicted in the superior court at Dedham, in December, 1887, of breaking and entering a shop and sentenced to the state prison for five years. Before the expiration of his term he was released only to be re-arrested a few days later in the act of "piping" a residence in Brighton, as the preliminary survey for burglary is styled by the craft. A revolver and burglar tools were found upon him when searched, and for this offence he was sent back to prison to serve out the remainder of his sentence.

When the gang was captured by a raid of the police, a lad of fourteen, the brother of Carroll or Cole, was acting as a spy or advance agent for them, in the disguise of a crippled beggar whose lameness was a mere counterfeit produced by a shoe with a built-up sole. In a heavy valise under the bed in their sleeping room a loaded revolver and a complete outfit of giant powder, fuse and burglar tools were stowed together with bundles of begging cards, covered with doggerel like this extract:

A CRIPPLE'S APPEAL.

Don't cast this from you, reader,
But read my story through;
I, like many other unfortunates,
Must ask the aid of you.
Misfortune has befallen me,
Like many more before,
My appeal, I wish to tell you,
Is to keep hunger from the door.

With this plaintive petition, the little beggar extracted a good many silver coins from compassionate pockets and it probably served also as a passport admitting a spy to "pipe" off tempting marks for his brother and his fellow burglars in the guise of tramps. The elder Carroll was convicted in the court of Worcester, in the following May, of breaking and entering and robbery, aggravated by the carrying of arms, and was sentenced to a term of twenty-two years in the Massachusetts state prison.

It would be vain and wearisome to attempt to distinguish all the multiform phases of beggary or the current pretexts with which the compassionate or the careless or the gullible are cajoled into almsgiving by the professional beggar of every stripe. There is, however, one really notable line of distinction between what may be termed the invisible and the too visible beggar whom we have so far sketched. Our invisible beggar has already been depicted by Charles Dickens with masterly vividness and the bitterness of experience in his sketch of the Begging Letter Writer.

"He has besieged my door," writes the vivacious Boz, "at all hours of the day and night; he has fought my servant; he has lain in ambush for me, going out and coming in; he has followed me out of town into the country, he has written to me from immense distances, when I have been out of England. He has fallen sick; he has died and been buried; he has come to life again, and again departed from the transitory scene; he has been his own son, his own mother, his own baby, his idiot mother, his uncle, his aunt, his aged grandfather. He has wanted a great-coat to go to India in; a pound, to set him up in life forever; a pair of boots to take him to the coast of China; a hat to get him a permanent situation under Government. He has frequently been just seven and six pence short of independence; he has had such openings at Liverpool—posts of great trust and confidence in merchants' houses which nothing but seven and six pence was wanting to him to secure—that I wonder he is not mayor of that flourishing town at the present moment."

So Dickens runs on with graphic pen for page after page of lively portraiture and what he has written of the invisible English beggar will fit neatly with a few trivial changes his brother beggar of America. Every millionaire and prominent public man in this country has doubtless a stack of correspondence on hand from this begging letter writer unless he has thrown their letters into the fire. The judgment of Dickens in regard to such beggars is perhaps somewhat too harsh and sweeping. "The poor never write these letters. Nothing could be more unlike their habits. The writers are public robbers and we who support them are parties to their depredations. They trade upon every circumstance within their knowledge, that affects us, public or private, joyful or sorrowful; they pervert the lessons of our lives; they change what ought to be our strength and virtue into weakness and encouragement of vice. There is a plain remedy and it is in our own hands. We must resolve at any sacrifice of feeling, to be deaf to such appeals, and crush the trade."

It is certain, however, that in the main this stern condemnation is justified and it should be observed that the impassioned writer had been suffering for years from an extraordinary plague of importunity and imposition. There is fortunately less of this kind of begging in this country than in Great Britain but there is too much here for the credit of our republic.

THE SWINDLING BEGGAR.

In some cases real and unavoidable misfortunes impel honest men and women to beg indiscriminately of strangers by piteous appeals in writing or in person, but ninety-nine times in a hundred the beggar is a professional mendicant and money given by the ordinary citizen in the ordinary way is not charity but an encouragement of fraud and indolence,—the blackmail levied by rascals who bleed sentimentality, heedlessness and the desire to be rid of a provoking interruption or person.

No deserving applicant will be denied food or lodging in this great republic, if the appeal is made to the proper authorities. Public ordinances and private charities have made provision for the destitute and homeless to this extent at least. Even the inveterate loafer, beggar and tramp can secure food and shelter if he seeks them at the expense of the city or town which he infests, for the time. But the ordinary swindling beggar and tramp wants no such assistance except in days of the direst necessity. He shuns the police and has a well rooted dread of the investigation conducted by well organized charities. Petty thieving would be his favorite resort, if he were not checked at every step by the watchfulness of the police and the public and the dread of capture and punishment. If an enticing opportunity is presented to him he will eagerly pounce upon an unprotected house or store and even break open an old-fashioned safe. In the city or country, the prudent American will keep out of touch with these rascals as far as possible and, when he cannot avoid them, curtly notify them to apply to the proper local authorities for all the attention their needs demand.

We may read with a smile Charles Lamb's whimsical lament upon the decay of beggars and acknowledge the tenderness and poetic beauty of Wordsworth's plea for license for the old Cumberland beggar but, in view of the actual conditions of American society, especially in our larger cities, plain common sense must not be suffered to yield to illogical and fanciful sentimentality. The conjunction of a good heart with a weak or heedless head is chiefly responsible to-day for the pest of the swindling beggar.

Thirty years ago a committee of the Boston Overseers of the Poor made a careful study of the question of street begging. One of the conclusions of this committee's report expressly enforces the point which we have sought to drive home. "By a thorough coöperation of all well-disposed citizens in the reference of all applicants for alms at the door or on the street to the officers or local charities instituted for their relief, an effectual check can be put to street begging." When this intelligent counsel is generally heeded, the swindling beggar will cry with Othello that his occupation's gone.

THE PICKPOCKET.

BY SLEIGHT OF HAND.

Did you ever cling to a strap in a street car? Yes? You remember then riding home at nightfall in a car packed to the doors and overflowing at both ends? No doubt you recall that you probably gave up your seat to a gentle woman who took it with hesitation and grateful thanks. Then you stood up or tried to stand in the aisle, in the midst of an uneasy mass that rolled to and fro, whenever the car stopped and started, like one of those rocking figure toys that wabble about so comically without losing their balance.

As you were gripping the strap by your right hand with the clutch of a drowning man, you recollect that somebody behind you tipped your hat over your eyes with his elbow, in one of the galvanic starts of the car. Of course you put up your left hand instinctively to settle your hat back on your head. The gentleman with the awkward elbow filled your ear with his flow of apology. A minute or two later, there was a little lull in the pressure of the pack in the car. You had room to draw a full breath of relief and to shrug your shoulders like a pilgrim whose burden has dropped from his back.

The next moment a gentleman sitting near you pulled your sleeve lightly.

"Did you notice, sir," said he, "that your watch chain is hanging down?"

"Oh no, much obliged!" you replied, glancing down in surprise and fumbling for the chain.

You found the hanging chain but, when you clapped your hand on your waistcoat pocket with a start of suspicion, your gold watch was gone. Naturally your next thought was to look for the thief. Everybody about you seemed to share in your concern but nobody was more sympathetic and indignant at the impudent theft than the gentleman behind you who had accidentally tipped over your hat.

You recollected dully that somebody at the same instant had given you an uncommonly hard shove with his shoulder, and began to suspect that he might have been the thief. But who was the rude pusher and where was he? Did you call out "Stop thief!" at once and get the conductor or a policeman to overhaul everybody on the car in search of your missing watch? If so, you made yourself universally disagreeable to no purpose. Your watch was not on the car. It was nearly half a mile away in the pocket of a man who had hopped off from the car platform several blocks farther up town, and fused himself with the crowd on the sidewalk until he darted down a side street.

What, did you say that you never lost your watch in this way? Well, you are to be congratulated, for too many good gentlemen have had this experience in crowded cars or in the vestibules of theatres or at race tracks or great public celebrations or even on the steps of our city churches. Particular watchfulness is needed in entering or leaving a car, for the doorways and platforms of cars are the favorite places for the execution of this thievish trick. Pickpockets are constantly hanging about city railroad stations and watching, if they can, the purchase of tickets. If a large roll of bills or a well-filled pocket book is shown at the ticket-seller's window, a signal is likely to be given to confederates and the gang will contrive to push through the doorway of a car at the moment when their victim is entering. For this reason these railroad stations are always watched and guarded by detectives and any persons acting suspiciously are keenly looked after. Known thieves are not suffered to stand in the stations.

The mode of picking your pocket has shifting details but

its back-bone is the same. The essentials are a crowd, a jam and a sudden distraction of attention. Usually one man knocks your hat over your eyes, another jostles you rudely and a third picks your pocket, twisting off your watch with a quick turn of his wrist, as is illustrated by our artist. Sometimes the gang is larger and your pocket is picked while you are shoved along by a sudden rush of the thieves. It is usual, however, for these knaves to consort in pairs or knots of three and they are more apt to rely on dexterity and nimbleness than on rude shoving.

The difficulty of catching the pickpocket is greatly increased by his practice of giving the watch to a confederate without an instant of delay. The receiver then slips out of the crowd as quickly as possible, or he may slyly pass along the plunder to a third who can slink away with less risk than either of the others. After the actual holder of the watch has slipped off undetected, it is comparatively easy for his confederates to follow him in turn, and, even if they are arrested, they may escape conviction because no stolen property can be found on their persons when searched.

Has anybody who reads these lines ever lost a diamond or fine pearl shirt stud in making a landing from a ferry boat, or in the course of a harbor excursion, or in leaving a crowded theatre? We think we hear a chorus of ayes. Some of you, no doubt, remember that a man carrying a long linen duster or an overcoat on his arm suddenly turned around in front of you and began to push you back, crying indignantly: "Come now, let up! Stop this crowding! What are you climbing on me for! Can't you let me have a little room to breathe in! What do you want—the earth!"

All the while he was protesting, he was shoving his arm under your chin and you were resentfully pushing back or trying to convince him that you were not to be blamed for pressing behind him. After the little fracas was over and you had passed out of the crowd, you happened in some

trives to press close to his chosen victim and bear down on his right shoulder with sufficient weight to bend his body slightly and open the left hand pocket a little. Then his confederate slily pulls out the lining of the pocket until the coveted watch or money is brought within the nip of his fingers. This can be done by an expert in this knavish sleight of hand so delicately and quickly that the booty may be abstracted and carried off while the suspicious owner is patting his pocket and pluming himself on his phenomenal caution and smartness.

It is somewhat more difficult to extract a pocket book from an inside coat pocket, especially when the coat fits closely and is carefully buttoned. The first attempt of a pickpocket in this case is to unfasten the upper button or preferably two in the press of a crowd, as slyly as possible. Then the attention of the victim is distracted by some sudden jostling or other device and his pocket is picked while his head is momentarily turned away from the darting hand of the thief. When a purse or roll of bills is carried in the inside pocket of a waistcoat, the upper buttons of this coat are loosened in the same sly way, for the thief knows that this opening will often be unnoticed while the unfastened lower buttons hold the waistcoat in place with no marked change in the pressure of the cloth on the body.

Some of the most dexterous pocket picking is effected while the victim is seated in a car or on a bench in a railway station or in a crowded theatre or some great popular gathering. Many ladies among our readers will sorrowfully bear witness to their losses from this mode of robbery. Few may understand clearly, however, how they were robbed and for their satisfaction and the sake of the wide-spread warning that should be given for the protection of all exposed to this thievish device, we shall fully uncover it.

Let us question one of the sufferers to bring to mind more exactly the situation in which her pocket was picked.

You remember, do you not, placing your purse carefully in the skirt pocket of your dress, before leaving home? Then you went down town for two hours of delightful bargain hunting through the aisles of our city stores, bordered by rows of enticing goods displaying every hue and cut of the latest fashion. You could not fail to profit by some chances to get prizes that were almost gifts in the depth of their sacrifice. Still your purse was so lavishly filled by your devoted husband and you were so prudent in your purchases that you finally put temptation behind you and started for home with a plump little roll of bills and some silver packed in your wallet.

It was late in the afternoon, was it not, when you passed through the crush into a street car and fortunately succeeded in getting the last vacant seat? Some moments later the faithful conductor struggled through the car taking the fares and you promptly took out your purse and extracted a nickel, so that you might be ready to pay without taxing his patience. A well-dressed man, standing in front of you, politely offered to hand your fare to the conductor and you were pleased by his courtesy. You may have recalled later that he glanced quickly and impertinently into your open wallet but the chances are a hundred to one that you didn't catch his eye in this operation. At any rate you thought little of this glance, for he was careful not to annoy you further, and you shut your purse at once discreetly and slid it back into your pocket in the folds of your dress.

You were living then in the suburbs and the crowd in the car melted away through the city until there was a vacant seat beside you which was taken by your polite fellow-passenger. He was wearing a long light overcoat stylishly cut, and, as he sat down beside you, the flaps of his coat fell naturally over a fold of your dress. You did not remark this particularly at the time, for it is too common to attract special notice. He took out an evening newspaper, unfolded it and was soon absorbed apparently in its news of the day. After riding in this way for ten or twelve minutes he quietly looked up from his paper, nodded to the conductor to stop the car and stepped off without even the flattering impertinence of a farewell glance at the attractive lady who had been sitting beside him.

It was not until you reached home and were vivaciously telling over the triumphs of your bargains to your enraptured husband that you chanced to think of your pocket book again. You slid your hand into your pocket and were horrified to find a slit in it cut through the skirt of your dress. Your purse was gone and you were indeed fortunate if the thief was arrested before he had time to spend or hide your money or turn it over to some waiting confederate. There was the usual pocket opening in his coat but, when he was caught by the police, it was shown that the coat had no side pockets. He had slily thrust his hand through the slit in his own coat which lapped over your dress, and cut a slit in your skirt from which he extracted your pocket book.

Sometimes this same trick is performed under the cover of a folded duster or overcoat carried on the arm of the thief and women who have become expert pickpockets will cut a dress under the fold of a shawl. When a wallet is put in a little hand bag, instead of the dress pocket, a coat or shawl is easily laid over the bag if it is placed on the seat beside the owner, as is too often the case. Of course a sharp knife will cut through the light leather of such a bag almost as quickly as a pair of scissors will make a slit in a dress. Sometimes the bag can be opened in the ordinary way by the catch and a pocket book extracted, or the bag itself may be carried off with all its contents when the owner lays it down carelessly on a seat or store counter and forgets to keep an eye upon it. This opening or stealing of bags is so regular a pursuit that the pickpockets who make a specialty of it are known as "bag openers."

Pickpockets range in age from mere children to white-haired veterans in larceny. They are of both sexes and some of the women can give points to most of the men. The theft of a handkerchief or a scarf or veil or opera-glass or any other light article, frequently carried in an outside coat or sack pocket, is one of the primary school lessons in crime and young boys and girls may master it without any teacher, or they may have old thieves as tutors. Everybody will recall the familiar instance of Fagin and his hopeful pupils, and the like instruction is still given to boys and girls who have been led astray, and, sad to say, too often by fathers to their sons and by mothers to their daughters. But it is a satisfaction to note that by far the greater portion of the children who steal in this way are only wayward boys and girls, tempted by chance opportunities which come in their way and not regularly engaging in theft as a means of making a living.

As they advance in age they are apt to seek for pocket books and other things of greater value than handkerchiefs, and, if they escape detection, these thefts grow bolder and more frequent. But thieves of this class, amateurs in their line, are generally within the range of possible reformation, if they can be properly guarded and directed. In large cities, where they chiefly live and roam, they are apt to be very seriously annoying, but the provisions for their repression and reformation are constantly advancing and no class of offenders receives more anxious care and humane consideration from the police and the courts.

In the case of a first offence the child is usually discharged on probation with good counsel and warning in words which even the youngest can understand and take home. Every effort is made to shield such children from the shame and injury of public exposure, and parents are urged to watch

PHILIP START.

THOMAS B. WILLS.

SAMUEL STRAEHLER.

FRANK DUFFY.

their conduct with all possible care. When it is judged best to take them out of the hands of their parents, they are sent to reform schools where they are trained to live honestly and usefully. For the prevention of the spread of crime nothing is more important than the proper treatment of the wayward children of our great cities, and this truth is every day gaining a fuller recognition and more complete advancement.

Between these youthful amateurs and the true professional pickpocket, or "dip" as he is styled by his craft, there is a wide and deep gulf of distinction, although this may be crossed if the passage is not blocked in some way. These "dips" usually travel in gangs from city to city and sometimes from one end of the country to the other. A gang is made up of three or four, commonly, and known as a "mob." There are expert thieves, however, who prefer to work with only one confederate and some will accept no companion. Female "dips" are accustomed to work alone or in pairs, though they may be members of a "mob" partly composed of men.

These "mobs" haunt railroad stations, steamship wharves and all crowded thoroughfares and, if practicable, they never miss attendance upon great conventions or celebrations or popular gatherings of any description. Frequently diagrams and lists have been taken from these thieves, when arrested, that marked the precise locations and dates of all the important celebrations that would occur for six months to come, together with notes of all regular and excursion trains to and fro, so far as arranged. Unless they were stopped at the railway stations and arrested or sent back, there would be a swarm of thieves at every great popular gathering, and, if they were not intercepted at the start by detectives, the excursion trains would surely be plundered even if the conventions were safely guarded. Of recent years the necessity of proper protection has grown so apparent that it is usual in our larger cities for the police to arrest and confine every known pickpocket, who haunts the streets on the eve of any great assembly, until the meeting is over and the people in attendance are safe at home. At the time of great political conventions or other notable assemblies, the best detectives are detailed from all the leading cities of the country to watch the arriving trains and arrest the thieves flocking from every quarter to the prospect of plunder.

If let alone, the travelling gangs will usually proceed in regular circuits from one convention or fair or dedication or mass meeting of any kind to another and, as might be expected, the thief follows a circus as devotedly as the small boy hangs on the heels of the elephants or giraffes. There is always a harvest of silver and small bills to be picked out of the pockets of the festive citizen or countryman, who delights in this perennial institution almost as much as his rapturous children. If the "mobs" that go around with the circus were not warned off or arrested by the police, it is very probable that the "thieves" would net as much as the average showman, to say the least.

Fashionable weddings in churches are another favorite and productive field for this thief and even funerals are not respected by his elastic conscience. One of the most noteworthy pickpockets in America, James Wells, made such a specialty of attendance at obsequies that he became known throughout the country as "Funeral Wells." His portrait is given on one of our pages depicting thieves of his order, and it may readily be seen that his doleful visage would naturally fit into the ranks of the mourners. He rarely consorted with other thieves and it was no effort for him to keep his face in harmony with his customary suit of solemn black. James McCaffrey, alias "James Peters," who has a place beside him on our portrait page, was also a distinguished "church worker," as the constant attendants at marriages and funerals are called by the fraternity of "dips." George (alias "Kid") Hennessey has gained notoriety as an accomplished "worker" in spite of the loss of one of his hands by an accident, and Joshua, better known as "Josh" Hines, his companion on the page, has earned his place as a remarkably expert "stone getter," as the pluckers of diamonds from shirt fronts are professionally styled.

Philip Start, Frank Duffy, alias "Pete McCormack," Thomas B. Wills, alias "Watt Jones" and Samuel Straehler, alias "Dayton Sammy," make up another quartette of rogues, representing the species pickpocket as well as any that could be selected. All four have travelled in professional mobs from Maine to California and all whose hands are free cannot keep them out of the pockets of other people. Wills was sentenced, this year, for larceny, to a term of three years in the Pennsylvania State Penitentiary and, if any of the others are at present out of jail, it is because they have kept out of states where theft is punished under an habitual criminal act.

When the more notorious of these thieves are arrested, they have, almost always, recourse to the "fences" or receivers of stolen goods, with whom they are in league, and they can usually obtain their bail or "fall money," as it is termed, from these backers. As they commonly intend to run off and forfeit their "fall money," it is of obvious importance for the protection of the public that the bail demanded from these thieves should be too high for their escape in this way.

After making a successful theft or series of thefts, they seek cover commonly in cheap boarding houses or third rate hotels and, to shun suspicion, are apt to scatter and live singly. They are more likely to be uncommunicative and sly than social in their habits though they usually spend their plunder in low dissipations.

The detectives of our city police know hundreds of these

thieves by sight and reputation and are constantly alert in watching for their appearance and preventing their thefts. But it would be prudent for good citizens to coöperate for their own protection by making the picking of pockets and the taking of jewelry more difficult to effect. One easy and clearly safe precaution is to leave watches and valuable scarf pins at home before going into places where great crowds are gathered or are certain to assemble.

When watches are carried they can be well secured by passing the chain through a little button hole cut in the waistcoat pocket before fastening the end of the chain in the usual way. A pickpocket extracts a watch by a gentle pluck on the chain which lifts it out of the pocket before he takes it in his hand and twists it from the chain. Obviously, he cannot pull the watch through a button hole and this simple little device would save many watches if it were generally adopted, for pickpockets plunder slyly as a rule and not by rude robbery.

Wallets can be kept much more safely in pockets which are buttoned and cannot be easily reached by nipping fingers than they are in the usual open pockets. The location of such pockets may well be varied by individual judgment and we shall offer no suggestions which may serve as guides for a thief. It is, however, a matter of some relevant interest to note that thieves are quite commonly accustomed to protect their own money or plunder from the disloyal fingers of their fellow pickpockets by lining the sleeves of their undershirts with their bank notes. As they sleep without removing these shirts, it is hard to steal their money from them even when their eyes are closed in slumber.

There is another branch of the upas tree of theft which is closely allied to the pickpocket and may well be sketched in the same chapter. This is the "shop-lifter," the thief who filches from store counters in broad daylight or while

THE SHOPLIFTER.

the store is open to customers. Many professional pickpockets are also professional shop-lifters but the mass of the petty thieves who plague our retail merchants would not venture so far as the bolder ones.

There are doubtless thousands of dabblers in shop-lifting in our country as in the countries of the old world,—boys who slyly pocket an apple or a handful of candy or even a knife or a necktie when the shop-keeper's head is turned,— and girls who pick up a handkerchief or a bottle of cheap perfumery from the heaps on a counter. These little pilferers would commonly shrink from any considerable theft and, probably, most of them learn to be more honest as they grow older. But these first slips on the crust of crime are demoralizing and dangerous and most of our veteran thieves can trace their downfall from such a start.

Undoubtedly many of these little ones are sorely tempted by the show of luxuries which they have no money to buy, and many really feel the pinch of hunger or of cold impelling them to the theft of food and clothing. All the palliating circumstances are well weighed by the police and the courts in dealing with these cases and store keepers do not press complaints rigorously when there is a reasonable prospect of reforming these little amateur shop-lifters by warning and redoubled care. But this thieving practice is a considerable nuisance and source of loss in the aggregate, though the individual thefts are so trivial, and the police are continually striving to stamp it out.

As the shop-lifters grow older, their thefts become larger and more frequent and the watch upon them more strict and sharp. In all the larger stores in the shopping districts of our cities detectives are regularly stationed as guards and the floor walkers and other employees of the establishments are instructed to keep a sharp lookout for these thieves. This system of detection is now so extended and complete that none except the most sly and expert shop-lifters can steal any considerable amount before they are arrested, and the old professional thieves are so well known that they are rarely suffered to enter the stores.

The shame of exposure should be sufficient to deter any amateur or novice in shop-lifting, even if a sentence of fine and imprisonment is not imposed after conviction. The pleadings of conscience may be stubbornly disregarded, but the knave must be a fool as well who attempts to practice shop-lifting for any length of time under the vigilant eyes of the many watchers who guard our stores. The black brand of a thief, the bitter shame of exposure and the hard uphill struggle to regain, in some measure, the esteem and position so inevitably forfeited, are surely a frightful offset to the possible gain of some trifling trinket or bit of clothing.

There is a diseased condition of mind or morals which is termed kleptomania. This disease seems to break out particularly in the form of shop-lifting. We shall not undertake to measure the sanity or responsibility of the genuine kleptomaniac, but we may fairly remark that the cloak of kleptomania has been stretched out very thin, sometimes, in the testimony of compassionate friends and relatives. The college student who "rags" a car-sign or a door plate appears to have fully as clear a title to the plea of insanity as some of our shop-lifters who have posed as candidates for a thieves' hospital. In the case of first offences this plea is not sharply riddled for obvious reasons, but it should be needless to observe that a confirmed kleptomaniac should never be permitted to go shopping. There is too much probability of the aggravation of this disease in the midst of temptation and too much risk of confusing the patient with the commonplace thief.

It would be of undoubted interest to trace the moving springs of this mania where it really exists and examine its apparently astonishing freaks. It is hardly remarkable that

ROSIE VOKAR.

ROSIE COHEN.

JACOB WOLS.

JOSEPH GOLDSTEIN.

a woman like Sophy Lyons, the daughter of a notorious "fence," should have a passion for stealing which her husband tried in vain to subdue, although he was himself a habitual criminal. But it is certainly surprising that the child of parents of excellent character and abundant fortune should be impelled to steal when no real want or taste is unsatisfied. Why should a young lady pilfer piles of meerschaums for her private cabinet or veils enough for a sultan's seraglio? The taste for a collection of rings or precious stones is less inexplicable and kleptomaniacs who show a fine discrimination in the objects of their mania are likely to discredit their plea of insanity. It is our task, however, to deal with the rascal and not with the maniac or the displays of mania.

The regular professional "shop-lifter" is to be distinguished from the amateurs who occasionally yield to temptation as well as from the perplexing kleptomaniac. Both men and women engage in shop-lifting as a business pursuit, travelling from city to city and from state to state in gangs of two, three, four or more.

The early morning, just after the opening of the wholesale stores, is the harvest time for the species known as the "morning hoister." This kind of thief usually goes about in pairs. "Hoisters" are generally young men of fair address who can hope to quiet with some plausible story the suspicion excited by their early calls. One pours this yarn into the ear of the listening clerk or porter while the other snatches an opportunity to steal something which he can put in his pocket or bag or hide under his coat. This offence is accounted a grade worse than ordinary shop-lifting and is punishable by a term in state prison as larceny in the building.

Another set of this order makes a specialty of the plundering of jewelry stores. Two men enter a store together and one engages the attention of a salesman while the other steals anything within reach. These pilferers are distin-

was set on some selected article which was gulped in upon pressing the spring and secured when the bottom was replaced.

Instead of these model hand bags, band boxes or hat boxes, fitted with covers fastened by rubber bands, have been employed. By a slight raising of the cover articles are slipped into the box and the cover instantly snaps back to place. Sometimes a large pasteboard box is made with a movable end which is dropped for the insertion of goods and then put up and securely tied. Ordinarily, however, in stealing from shop counters, the method is much simpler and less mechanical.

One of the commonest ways is to lay a handkerchief down on a chosen bit of booty, with an affectation of thoughtlessness. A few minutes later the handkerchief is hastily caught up with the prize in its folds. A cloak or shawl serves as a cover for a larger article in much the same way and there are known instances where a baby has been carried about by a shop-lifter for the sake of picking up goods under the screen of the child's long dress.

Jewelry stores are among the most difficult to protect from thieves of this class, because of the comparative minuteness of the articles offered for sale and the correspondingly greater chance of concealment. Many thieves can "palm" a ring as expertly as a professional prestidigitateur and, when a tray is placed before one of them, the sharpest watching is needed to prevent a loss. Usually he will have a confederate near by, sometimes a man and sometimes a woman, and he will contrive, if he can, to slip a ring or jewel into the hand of his pal or to open a chance for his companion to steal.

One common and dangerous trick of these thieves is the carrying of false jewels and Brummagem rings to exchange for the real treasures in the tray. This cheat of substitution was refined by one artist to the exchange of a small

KATE FIELDS.

CAROLINE SMITH.

ROSE STADE.

ELLEN McLAUGHLIN.

genuine stone for another slightly larger and so on in succession until a one-carat diamond was replaced by a stone weighing several carats.

This particularly artful diamond thief was a young woman who professed to be deplorably nearsighted. She used to dress elegantly and was so attractive in person and manners that she had little difficulty in obtaining the exhibit of a tray of loose diamonds. Then she would bend over the counter till her eye glasses were nearly touching the jewels and, with a dart of her pretty red tongue, pick up a diamond and cover it with her lips. At the same instant she would drop a lighter stone into the tray so deftly that the exchange was not suspected. In this way she would go from one store to another, apparently trying to match a diamond which she pretended to have at home, and using the alum-coated point of her tongue to such purpose that she finally picked up a gem worth hundreds of dollars. The professional name of this young woman is "Little Scotty" and she was a plague to our Boston jewellers some years ago.

The four shop-lifters who have been taken to fill another representative page are not as attractive as this young woman and others in the profession but there can be no doubt that they are typical as well as notorious. Kate Fields, alias "Annie Upton," is an Englishwoman by birth who favored her country by leaving it. Caroline Smith, alias Myers, is a native of Germany, but has for many years made her living as a shop-lifter in the country of her adoption. Rose Stade, alias "Louise Kauffman," is a product of our own soil which is credited to a Western city particularly, and Ellen McLaughlin was a native of Ireland. Every nationality in America has its representative shop-lifters, as well as its representative men and women of honor.

In the recital and exposure of their tricks there is an evident assistance and warning to our business men who are the sufferers from their depredations. Vigilance and knowledge of their ways of working are very important safeguards against loss. These the police now have, but they should be able to rely on the intelligent and alert coöperation of the men whom they are striving with all their power to protect.

In subsequent chapters we shall show the varied tricks and resorts of all the other distinctive classes of thieves, in the sequence which we shall pursue for the sake of its clear and simple lines of division and course of development. From the petty impositions of the swindling beggar, the succeeding step in the pathway of crime passes the border line of actual theft into the simpler forms of larceny, which we have described. Another step forward reaches the point of felony, when the thief becomes a robber and seizes upon his plunder with violent hands.

FROM JIMMIES TO DYNAMITE.

"LOOK here, upon this picture, and on this!" See that grim, ominous figure, that walking desperado shuffling along heavily with his slouch hat pulled over his eyes, girdled with the tools of his rascally craft, a walking arsenal of burglary. Then turn to that slim, jaunty promenader, a "man-milliner" from top to toe, spotless, clean-shaven, and trim, striding along with easy swing and carrying his neat leather handbag with airy unconcern.

Who could suppose these portraits to be the counterfeit presentment of two brothers in crime, sprouts from the same stalk, charged with the same aims and fears, bent on the same goal, and, in spite of their discrepant masks, as essentially akin as two peas in a pod. The one, everybody will recognize at sight as the traditional bank-burglar—the familiar ruffian whom our fathers and grandfathers knew—the image impressed upon our shuddering fancy in childhood—the consort of bats and owls and all creatures that shun the light of day,—the midnight prowler slinking from cover to cover and

THE OLD-FASHIONED BURGLAR.

fleeing the dawn like a ghost—the sapper and miner tunneling underground noiselessly like a mole,—the scoundrel of such patent mark that the barest glimpse would startle suspicion. That indeed is hardly an exaggeration of the old style stamp of burglar still lingering decrepit in holes and corners or dully counting the slow passing days as a white-haired convict in his prison cell. Years ago, however, the knell was tolled of the passing of the burglar of the ancient order and the modern generation which has taken his place is outwardly a new type, vividly hit off by our artist in his illustration of the burglar of to-day.

THE MODERN BANK BURGLAR.

This is a remarkable transformation but, as we shall show, it is a natural one, an evolution inevitably forced by the change of conditions affecting the craft of burglary.

Tradition fails to hand down to us the name of the first bank burglar, but it is practically certain that he sprung up with some rude tool in his hand within a year or two after the opening of the first bank. For his needs little skill or equipment was required. With a few prods and heaves of a common crow bar, he could tear a bolted door from its hinges or smash a lock or panel with his heavy sledge hammer. Brute strength and the cover of night or the temporary absence of watchers were the only essentials for success in those old days.

But with the easy triumph of the first burglaries, the bankers took warning and began to defend their deposits with redoubled precaution. Armed watchmen were kept on duty both night and day, vaults of stone and iron were built to supplant the insecure chambers, and heavily barred strong-boxes were fashioned as safes to hold money, jewels and papers of value. As the bankers racked their brains more and more in the provision of safeguards, so the robbers, in turn, were forced to devise counter-plots and new weapons of offence to keep pace with the rising blocks in their way. So from earliest history there has been an unending conflict of wits, a neck to neck race of the banker and the burglar, the one, striving by every resort in his power to intrench his treasure and bar out the thief, and the other, straining every nerve to pass the barriers and plunder the strongholds.

For thousands of years the wily burglar might claim to have won the crown in the race. If a vault was constructed with walls so massive that it might seemingly defy a hail storm of cannon balls, bitter experience would prove that even this fortress was not proof against the sly undermining, the persistent sapping and tapping and drilling, the inexhaustible patience and tireless arm of the stubborn burglar. If a lock was fashioned so intricate in mechanism and peculiar in pattern that, it was thought, no thief could master its wards, how vexing to find, after a few fleeting months of fancied security, that the cunning of the rogue had vanquished the craft of the locksmith with a few bits of bent wire or skeleton keys! What cover could be devised for a treasure so complete and perfect at every point that it could baffle the prying eye of the burglar, scanning it inch by inch, or foil his deft hand tapping its weakest spots as surely as the arrows of Locksley rapped at the rivets of the armor of Maurice de Bracy? All too often and too late, it was learned by the mournful banker that one inconsiderable crack had been left in his bulwark of defence, one frail bolt in the plates of his safe, one assailable corner in his impregnable vault, like the undipped heel of the otherwise invulnerable Achilles.

Even when there was seemingly no lack of precaution,— when the bank watchmen were alert and faithful and the walls of the vaults of uniform strength from top to bottom, the craft of the burglar still penetrated the stronghold. When we consider the prodigious feats recorded of Baron von Trenck and other prisoners who have secretly dug through massive walls and cut iron chains and bars with no other tools than a broken fork or a rusty nail, it is not surprising that the expert burglar with his complete kit of drills, wedges, jack-screws and levers, should be able to pierce the hardest walls and wrench away the heaviest bolts and bars if he could contrive to cover his line of assault for a few days or even for a night.

For every new resource of defence he was quick to devise some mastering weapon of attack. When steel began to be substituted for iron in the plates of a safe or vault, the burglar procured a finer and harder grade of steel for his drills and cut his way through the plate of steel as he had through the hardest iron. When progressive invention fashioned a plate that would resist the point of the finest steel drill or make the task of boring insufferably slow, the burglar's drill was tipped with a diamond which no metal forging could long withstand. When the position of locks was artfully hidden and the multiplication of massive doors and walls made attack groping and slow, the determined robber sought the help of explosives and blasted an entrance to the treasure chambers with gunpowder and later with the tremendous rending force of dynamite.

In the provision and device of the common tools of the craft there has been also a display of masterly and progressive ingenuity, however criminally perverted. In the "jimmy," the "jack," the "gripper," the "spreader," the "drag," the "plate cutter," the drill and the wedge there is a really great combination and application of fundamental mechanical forces in exceedingly compact and effective forms.

The "jimmy" is a handy and mighty lever, in the form of a crow bar with a curving wedge shaped point which can be inserted in a crevice or crack between a door and its frame or between bars and plates. For the sake of compactness, convenience and ease of concealment, the latest designs of "jimmies" have been constructed in sections, made with joints that fit into sockets, like the parts of a fishing pole, so that any desired length of leverage can readily be attained. This simple tool is one of the most indispensable in any burglar's outfit and in the hands of a skilled operator it is marvellously efficient in ripping off plates, bars and doors. In the accompanying cut "a sectional jimmy" of the latest pattern is well presented.

The "jack" is a strongly made jack-screw chiefly used for rending off plates and bars and doors by forcing wedges into existing or artificially made cracks. These wedges are nicely graduated from the edge of a knife blade, and are applied, one after another, till the strongest bolts are broken and massy doors split away from their shattered hinges.

In the application of the "gripper" a heavy drill frame is set on the floor in front of a safe, as shown in the illustration on page 63. With a "diamond drill" a hole is bored through the safe door close to the lock. This hole is then enlarged by the use of a heavy bit or other tools and through this opening the clutch, or "gripper" attached to the drill frame, is pushed. The flat side of the gripper is studded with holes for the insertion of pin bolts to hold it fast after clutching the inside of the door of the safe. Then a powerful screw is set at work drilling another hole above the gripper and the resultant pressure and wrench finally tear out a part of the door. For the sake of noiseless operation, when a burglar is not particularly pressed for time, the gripper is still a favorite instrument, but, when he is in a hurry, powder or dynamite is introduced through a drill hole and fired by a short time fuse or electric battery.

SECTIONAL JIMMY.

With the aid of the "spreader" the heaviest bars may be wrenched apart or broken. In its union of simplicity and force this ingenious instrument is on a par with the "jimmy." It is a solid steel screw with two grip nuts of hard steel at one end and another big hub-shaped nut below. This hub nut has a hole or holes for the insertion of a movable arm and when the spreader is set between two bars, as shown in the accompanying illustration, the lever in strong hands turns the hub nut, forcing the bars apart irresistibly. Sometimes, without a lever-bar, the hub nut is turned by a heavy grip wrench with like effect.

THE "SPREADER."

Sometimes a heavy hook is used in place of the "gripper," in combination with a drill frame, for wrenching away part of the door or some other plate of the safe. This device is commonly known as a "drag" or "puller." The tearing away of the door or side of the safe is technically known to the craft as "safe booking."

The burglar's "sledge" of the latest approved design is a mallet of solid copper finely finished. Blows struck with this sledge are comparatively noiseless, falling with a thud instead of the old bang and rattle. In place of the heavy and clumsy old drills small, light and compact tools or machines of various and ingenious patterns are employed. One of these powerful instruments can rapidly drive a tempered steel drill through the side of any iron safe. When the safe plates are of steel, the expert burglar softens spots with his pocket blast blow pipe and makes the hot metal brittle by splashes of water or other devices destroying its temper.

The "plate cutter" is a tool with a keen blade, which can be readily bolted to the face of a wall or door. By revolving the handle of the cutter a round disk can soon be cut through any iron plate and even through ordinary steel. When walls or doors are made by layers of plates, this is an effective tool, unless the plates are of the hardest steel. If alternate layers of boiler plate iron and hard steel plate are used for the sake of the combination of tensile strength and impenetrability, the combination is foiled by cutting the iron plates and shattering the intervening steel disks with picks and hammers. This was alarmingly practicable in the days of the first introduction of cutter proof drill plates, for, in the processes of hardening the steel to resist a cutting tool or drill, the metal was made too brittle to bear repeated blows. But of late years the skill of the steel makers has reached a pitch of perfection that makes the drilling of strong safes a long protracted process.

POCKET BLAST PIPE.

When, after thousands of years of contest and rival advances, it began to appear for the first time, in the course of the present century, that the bankers and safe makers were clearly outstripping the burglars, the latter were incited to extraordinary strains of cunning and labor. The comparatively dull-witted and commonplace robbers were coldly dropped to shift for themselves by the leading craftsmen. It was patent to these experts that in our principal cities, at least, the days were ended where any rational hope of success could be based on mere brute strength and sudden dashes upon exposed or weak bank vaults. So the old gangs fell to pieces and in the leading re-organizations only men of proven skill, address, cunning and perseverance were invited, or permitted, to enlist.

Thereafter no considerable undertaking was ventured upon without the most careful examination and preparation. Years were spent sometimes in surveying a selected bank or "mark" as the burglars termed it, and, after all the plans were perfected, the slightest awakening of suspicion or unforeseen obstacle would cause the deferring of the assault for months or years, if indeed it was not indefinitely postponed or abandoned altogether.

The principals in these gangs, or the men who had charge of all the preliminary arrangements and haunted the neighborhood of the "mark," were almost invariably of good address and appearance,—men who would readily pass muster as prosperous tradesmen or real estate brokers or retired capitalists with a lingering itch for speculation or even for clergymen at a pinch. Even the most ignorant and ill-favored could contrive to mask himself as a lounging "sport" or Brummagem "swell," and drift around as he pleased without attracting particular notice.

When a "mark" was selected, the gang planning the burglary would meet for conference at some distant place or advise one another by mail of the progress of their schemes, shunning with every possible care the sleepless vigilance of the police and the risk of arousing suspicion of the purpose of the plotters. When feasible, however, a building or flat or cellar or room adjoining the "mark" was rented as the base of the actual operations of assault, and these quarters were sometimes occupied for many months by apparently respectable tenants as quiet lodgers or partners in various legitimate lines of business.

It is easy to understand how such tenants could readily become familiar with every outward detail of a neighboring bank and its method of business. If any one of its watchmen, messengers and clerks was dissipated or improvident or from any cause susceptible to corruption, it was the study of the gang to entrap their possible tool and obtain a valuable confederate in their projected robbery.

All this elaborate preparation was tedious and expensive, but from the standpoint of the shrewd burglars it was greatly desirable to advance the chances of success to the farthest practicable notch and to correspondingly reduce the risk of failure. The proper severity of the law in dealing with this formidable class of criminals was duly dreaded, and the certainty of a long term in prison, if convicted, was an ever-dangling sword above the burglar's head. The greatness of the possible booty in view was also a mighty incentive to caution as well as to daring, for a single false step might occasion the fall of all the complex fabric of plot so painfully reared and the loss of a fortune.

So the expert burglar stinted no expenditure of time, brains or money to attain his goal of plunder, and the best cracksmen of the craft were usually able to find unscrupulous backers to advance the funds required for the long siege and final assault, if their own pockets were emptied. The booty from bank-breaking, in the event of success, was so enormous that the immense percentage of profit tempted men of the so-called "sporting" class and other money lenders, with more greed than conscience, to invest in this extra-hazardous line of enterprise.

By the breaking open of the Ocean Bank in New York, in 1869, the burglars got over $1,000,000 in cash and bonds. The Boylston bank burglary in November of the same year robbed a Boston bank of $500,000. In the looting of the bank in Northampton, Mass., in January, 1876, over $1,500,000 in cash and bonds were stolen. The robbery of the Covington bank, two years before, gained a reported booty of $400,000 in cash and $1,500,000 in bonds. And as the culmination of all came the famous robbery of the Manhattan Savings Bank of New York, with its enormous plunder of $2,747,700 in cash and bonds, on the 27th of October, 1878.

Among the foremost craftsmen in these extraordinary gangs were "Jimmy" Hope and his son John, James Dunlap, Robert

Scott, Max Shinburn, Adam Worth, "Dave" Cummings, Charles Bullard, alias "Piano Charley," George Gardner, "Ike" Marsh, George Miles, "Bob" Cochran, "Ned" Lyons and "Sam" Perris, alias "Worcester Sam." Another who is justly entitled to special mention as having been one of the most gifted and accomplished operators in this line of crime in America is Langdon W. Moore. This truly remarkable man, who has reformed and is now leading an exemplary life, has written one of the most faithful autobiographies, detailing a criminal career, which has ever appeared in print.

A wide-ranging repertoire of impersonations was readily filled by these artists in crime. Robert Scott, for one, needed no touch of transformation to stand for the portrait of the jaunty young dandy or broker, which our artist has taken as a fairly typical figure of the new order of burglars. For many years he hoodwinked society with consummate cleverness in his shifting character parts. For some time he was known as a wealthy owner of a racing stable and a patron of art as well as of the turf. From this, by an easy transition, he became a playwright and author apparently enjoying an ample fortune and turning his hand to literary work as a labor of love. Up to the very moment of his arrest as a principal in the Northampton bank robbery, he had deceived his own wife as completely as he had his social acquaintances.

When the illustrated papers were filled with graphic drawings and photographs of the wrecked bank and other features of the robbery, Mrs. Scott, a really accomplished and lovely woman, naïvely showed the pictures to her husband and his mate, the burglar Dunlap, exclaiming indignantly, "I hope that God will lay his hand on the villains and bring them to justice and to the gallows if they deserve it." These men of iron nerve listened without a visible shade of emotion or dissent and examined the pictures with cool curiosity. When Scott was arrested, some months later, and his wife learned first from the lips of the detectives that her husband was one of the villains upon whom she had called the wrath of God, she fell in a swoon, striking her head upon an iron bound trunk, and was out of her mind for several days.

Maximilian Schoenbein, far better known as Max Shinburn, was no less adept than Scott as a character actor and much more of an artist in the conception of and execution of criminal plans. He has been distinguished by those expert critics, the Pinkerton brothers, as the greatest bank, safe and vault burglar of this or any other country. He is a German by birth and first came to this country in or near the year 1860. His school education was excellent, and he soon made himself a mechanic of remarkable proficiency.

To perfect his knowledge of the mechanism of safes, he obtained employment under an assumed name in the works of the Lilly Safe Company which, in the years of the war for the Union, ranked as one of the best manufacturers in this country. In this employment, he gained a knowledge so intricate and exact of the construction of safe locks that he could readily duplicate any then in the market. Moreover, his ear was so acute and sensitive that by the turning of the dial he could determine at what numbers the tumblers dropped into place. In those days the combinations were far more simple than the complex ones since perfected, and it can readily be perceived that a rogue so expert was greatly to be dreaded by the banks and other holders of money and bonds.

He soon heaped up a fortune by his successful burglaries and, although an inveterate gambler, he was so shrewd a speculator that he actually made another fortune by lucky turns of the market. He spent his income at first with an extravagant hand in dissipation and luxurious living, and was a typical "high-roller" until he was arrested at Saratoga Springs for the robbery of the Walpole (New Hampshire) Savings Bank in April, 1865.

Shinburn, at the time of his arrest, was masquerading as a New York banker, but a complete workshop for making all kinds of burglars' tools was found in his house, and the evidence against him was so conclusive that he was convicted and sentenced to ten years of imprisonment. He broke out of the jail in Keene, N. H., on the night following his conviction and contrived to elude capture for many months but was finally arrested after an unsuccessful attempt to rob a bank at St. Albans, Vt. He was sent to the state's prison in Concord, but again this crafty and daring burglar was an over match for his guards. His escape from the Concord jail after an incarceration for nine months was one of the most dashing and skilfully planned in criminal history.

His confederate in this escape was his partner in the robbery of the Walpole bank, George Miles, alias George White. A masked hole in the gate of the prison was cut one night by the contrivance of White and Shinburn, and the next day Shinburn broke away from a marching line of convicts in the yard of the jail, jumped through the hole in the gate, sprang into a light wagon in waiting outside, and, in a minute, was flying away with his confederate White as fast as a fleet horse could carry them over the state line into Massachusetts.

Three times in succession, in 1867, he entered and robbed the vault of the Lehigh and Wilkesbarre coal company at Whitehaven, Pa., by successfully manipulating the combination lock on the vault. His marvellous coolness and calculation were strikingly illustrated in this series of raids for, in his first two robberies, he took away only insignificant sums, just covering the expenses of his trip to Whitehaven, as the deposits in the vault were not enough, in his judgment, to offset his prospective loss from the revelation of a burglary. The thefts were so trifling that suspicion was naturally directed, as Shinburn presumed, against clerks in the office of the coal company and two were discharged in succession upon suspicion of pilfering.

MAXIMILIAN SCHOENBEIN.

GEORGE MILES.

CHARLES BULLARD.

ADAM WORTH.

The third raid of the burglar was timed exactly upon the deposit of the money for the monthly pay roll, and he then succeeded in carrying off $40,000 in cash and some bonds and other securities, the entire contents of the vault, at one swoop. He reached New York City in safety with his booty but some weeks later was cleverly shadowed and seized by detectives while slipping out of a saloon on Broadway. He was taken under close guard to Whitehaven upon a requisition from the governor of Pennsylvania.

Shortly after his arrest he made a bogus confession implicating a number of innocent men in Whitehaven and during the investigation of the case he was held in custody in a hotel of the town. Every night Shinburn was handcuffed to a detective and both slept in the same bed in a room directly adjoining the chamber occupied by the General Superintendent of the detective agency. To ensure the utmost practicable security, the clothes of Shinburn and his bed fellow were taken from them nightly and locked in a closet of the room in which the superintendent slept. The handcuffs used were of the ratchet pattern, a design at that time esteemed the safest.

Yet in spite of all this precaution, Shinburn succeeded one night in dropping a steel pen into the ratchet of the handcuff which held him, a second before the bolt snapped into place. This bit of steel blocked the locking of the bolt, though the handcuff appeared to be fastened securely. It was then an easy matter for the sly burglar to slip his hand out of the cuff at midnight when his bed-fellow was fast asleep, and steal into a neighboring chamber. There he dressed himself completely in the clothes of a sleeping guest, and succeeded in escaping from the hotel and town before the alarm was given.

After this extraordinary escape he became the leader of the gang of burglars which successfully broke into the vaults of the Ocean Bank in New York City in 1869 and bore off plunder to the amount of a million dollars. This was the first of the series of gigantic burglaries which culminated in the looting of the Manhattan Savings Bank, and for the devices which made these crimes practicable Max Shinburn probably deserves the lion's share of credit or infamy. It is credibly reported that he was the first to design and make the fine, small but marvellously effective burglar tools which have largely supplanted the old fashioned and cumbersome instruments of former generations of burglars. His complete working kit could often be packed in a small handbag like the one shown in our picture of the modern burglar, and Shinburn himself was accustomed to carry such a valise. An excellent illustration of a set of modern tools of this style for safe cracking is given in the accompanying cut of an actual outfit in the possession of the Boston Police Department.

After the robbery of the Ocean Bank, Shinburn next applied his talents to the promotion of the robbery of the Boylston Bank, and, a little later, robbed the West Maryland Bank of money and securities to the extent of $25,000. This was Shinburn's last achievement of the kind for many years, for he was so hotly pursued by the police and the organized detective agencies that he was soon forced to fly from the country and find shelter in Belgium, where he could live undisturbed through the lack of any treaty of extradition.

For a few years he remained in Brussels, quietly enjoying the proceeds of his years of plunder, but he later purchased an estate and an interest in a large silk mill, winning a place in aristocratic society and taking the title of "Count," which, it seems, nobody cared to dispute. He cut off completely every thread of association with his former confederates, and none of them knew what had become of him except his single confidant, a young Englishman who had long been his agent in disposing of stolen securities.

He might have lived in his fine feathers to the end of his life but he could not restrain his passion for gambling and, after some thirteen years of fickle fortune, he failed in business and came to the end of his pile of plunder. Then he cast about to fill his empty pockets and either by chance or design came into touch with one of his old associates, "Charley" Bullard, otherwise known as "Piano Charley," who had also fled from this country, after escaping from the Massachusetts state prison. "Piano Charley" had been one of the prime movers in the famous Boylston bank burglary and was entirely qualified to act as a second to Shinburn or any other rascal of high degree.

The two old companions then plotted the robbery of the Provincial Bank of Viveres, Belgium, and attempted to execute it in 1883. They readily gained an entrance into the bank through a rear door, by unscrewing an old-fashioned lock. Shinburn set the lock carefully aside in order to replace it and put the screws in his waistcoat pocket. The burglars then entered the bank and made a careful study of the vault and safes. After completing their study at their ease, they returned to the back yard and replaced the lock on the door. Unfortunately for the rogues, however, one of the screws stuck in a piece of wax in Shinburn's pocket and the burglars hunted about for it in vain.

While they were looking for the screw, a patrolling watchman came upon a pair of shoes which "Piano Charley" had carefully taken off, just before entering the bank, and carelessly left in the alley outside the bank yard. These tell-tale boots made him suspicious and he called for help, searched the bank yard and arrested both of the burglars. Still the resourceful Shinburn was not at the end of his wits. He actually succeeded in accounting satisfactorily for his presence in the yard, and would have been discharged if the search of his pockets had not brought to light the missing screw imbedded in a lump of wax. The door lock was then examined and it was seen that a screw was lacking, precisely like the one in Shinburn's pocket.

Upon this circumstantial evidence both burglars were tried

and convicted. Shinburn, oddly enough, got off with a sentence of five years' imprisonment while his comrade, "Piano Charley" whose shoes had betrayed him, was sent to prison for ten years. On such apparently slight slips of precaution or luck does the fate of burglars often turn.

"Piano Charley" died in prison, but the craftier Shinburn served out his sentence, plotting meanwhile to throw the police off the track and blot out his identity by the industrious circulation of a tale of his own death in Belgium. This convenient fiction was widely published in the papers of this country, at Shinburn's instigation, but the police were too wary to be victimized by any such yarn.

About four years ago there was a singular revival of country bank burglaries here after the marked cessation of such offences since the day of the great Manhattan Bank robbery. Keen inquiry of the police and detective agencies ascertained that in nearly every instance one of the persons implicated or gravely suspected was an old man who spoke at times with a marked German accent. Some witnesses thought that he had a scar on his chin and others described the mark as a deep dimple. Finally a banker, who had been robbed, identified this old man with the long lost Max Shinburn by the aid of a picture taken at the time of Shinburn's arrest in Belgium.

It was found by a tracing process that Shinburn had gone to England after his release from the Belgian prison and, it was supposed, had come to this country a year or two later. The marked ability with which the present bank robberies had been conducted showed plainly a master's hand in design and execution. The remarkably adroit use of nitro-glycerine was a pronounced feature of the principal burglaries, and all expert detectives throughout the country were well convinced that the phenomenal brain and hand that had reconstructed the burglar tools of America and successfully perpetrated some of the greatest robberies ever known, were alone adequate to this expert adaptation of dynamite to burglary.

So the police and detectives followed up every possible thread of connection between Shinburn and the bank burglaries and he was finally arrested by the Pinkerton agency in New York, on June 28, 1895, on the charge of robbing the First National Bank of Middleburg, N. Y., in the previous April. He was tried upon this charge and convicted in January, 1896. His sentence was one of four years and eight months, and he is now serving out his term in Dannemora prison.

He is a figure so preëminently remarkable and so representative of the highest order of the criminals of his class that we have no hesitation in giving his story with a minuteness of detail that would otherwise be out of proportion to the plan of our work. Personally, Shinburn is a man of refined manners and marked cultivation. He has travelled through Europe from end to end and speaks and writes several modern languages fluently and well. He would pass in any society as a foreign gentleman of means and fine tastes. At the time of his latest conviction, he was about 62 years of age.

He is a trifle over five feet eight inches in height and his weight is approximately 160 pounds. He is broad-shouldered, rather thick-set, and his muscles are still supple and strong in spite of his years. Before he was sent to prison, his hair and beard had a soldierly cut, and his grizzled head was fast turning white. He wore a thick moustache and slight chin tuft or imperial, perhaps to veil the deep and distinguishing dimple in his chin. His forehead is broad, full and shapely, and all the lines of his face are strong and fine. No one who sees him can fail to be struck also by the exceedingly keen glances of his blue eyes. A photograph which fairly depicts him is reproduced in the collection of representative portraits which illustrate these pages.

Shinburn's confederate and comrade, George Miles or

George White, as he has sometimes been called, has also a fair title to a representative place in our set of portraits. His part in the escape of his comrade from the prison at Concord has already been told. He was a participant in the epoch marking robbery of the Ocean National Bank of New York in 1869, and took a leading part in other notable burglaries. The conduct of one of these was so dramatic and typical that it deserves special notice.

In the dead of the night of the sixth of July, 1875, Miles and three other burglars, wearing white masks, entered the house of the cashier of the bank of Barre, Vt. Every movement of the gang was apparently mapped out beforehand, with complete forethought, and was executed with military precision. The cashier and his family were suddenly seized in their bed-chambers. Strong screw-hooks were driven into the floor of one of the chambers, and the cashier's wife and daughter gagged and bound to the floor. Then the cashier was dragged to his bank, a quarter of a mile away, and forced to open the door by the pressure of two loaded revolvers against his head. He unlocked the outer door of the safe under the same pressure, but the inner door was fitted with a time lock and could not be opened. As the burglars were not prepared to blow open the safe, they were perforce content with what they found in the outer safe, $10 in cash and $1,300 in unsigned bank bills.

When they were satisfied that no more could be got from the bank, they marched the cashier back to his house and tied him fast like his wife and daughter. Then the gang fled from the town before the alarm was given, but by keen pursuit one was captured by the breaking of his leg when jumping from a train. He turned state's evidence and his information caused the arrest of Miles, in New York, in the following September. Miles was part owner of a fashionable livery stable and so influential a man that the officers from Vermont thought it prudent to carry him away to Barre secretly. At his trial extraordinary efforts were made by his friends to secure his acquittal, but he was finally convicted and sent to Windsor prison for fourteen years. He made two desperate attempts to escape before the expiration of his term, but failed both times. Soon after his discharge from prison, he joined a gang which blew open and robbed the safe of a jeweller in Gloversville, New York, and, a few months later, attempted to open a safe in Utica. He was caught in the act by the Utica police, in company with two other notorious burglars, Daniel Leary, alias "Black Dan," and James Brady, known as "Big Jim" Brady. Miles drew a revolver instantly when the police tried to seize him and fired upon the advancing officers, holding them at bay until he reached the street. Then he was surrounded and overpowered, but fought on like a wild cat until knocked senseless. In February, 1891, he was tried and convicted for this attempted burglary and sentenced to a term of five years in state prison.

How "Piano Charley" joined Max Shinburn in the robbery of a Belgian bank and how his shoes betrayed him has been told in the story of the life of "The Count." Charles Bullard, alias "Piano Charley," was a rascal of peculiar ability and characteristics. He was the son of a respectable Massachusetts business man and had a good common school education. Dissipation and a restless craving for morbid excitement made him a "fly crook" and later an uncommonly daring and wily burglar. His sobriquet of Piano was given to him by his comrades as a testimonial to his skill as a player, for his delicacy of touch was illustrated on piano as well as on skeleton keys. He was so artful in covering his tracks that it was difficult to procure evidence against him sufficient to convict and he went up the ladder of crime round after round until he planned and executed the great Boylston bank burglary in 1869 in conjunction with Adam Worth, "Ike" Marsh, "Bob" Cochran and other lesser stars of burglary.

After this crowning feat he fled to Europe with Worth and Marsh but his ill-gotten gains soon melted in his hands and he came back to this country with his chum, "Ike" Marsh, and robbed an express messenger who had more than $100,000 in charge for delivery. For this crime Bullard and Marsh were arrested in Canada and taken to the jail in White Plains, N. Y., but they soon contrived to escape with the help of confederates outside the prison walls. After his escape, "Piano Charley" next turned up in Paris, where he opened the famous "American Cafe" at No. 2 Rue Scribe. In the gay French capital he soon became a man of mark as a gambler and roue; but, after a few years of dissipation, he had the nerve to return to America, coolly facing arrest and frankly confessing his guilt when brought to trial. He was sentenced to a term of twenty years in the Massachusetts state prison.

His conduct as a prisoner was uniformly docile and good for many months, until one day he surprised his keepers by a seemingly inexplicable outbreak of insolence and riotous disturbance. For this offence against discipline he was confined over night with five other rioters in the cells for refractory prisoners. The next morning it was discovered that the birds had flown. Bullard had somehow fitted keys to the locks of the cells, released his confederates and found a way of escape. Again he fled the country and, after some tarrying in England, joined Shinburn and engaged in the robbery of the bank at Viveres, as before related.

Adam Worth, "Little Adam," was a fitting fourth in this quartette of accomplished rogues, and appropriately fills a place in our page of portraits side by side with his comrade, Bullard. He was a remarkably cunning plotter and performer of robberies and a master hand in fashioning false keys and other implements of his craft. After the robbery of the Boylston bank, in which he took a leading part, he fled to London and for many years had the criminal distinc-

JAMES HOPE.

JOHN HOPE.

DAVID CUMMINGS.

EDWARD LYONS.

tion of being the chief counsellor, broker and fence in Great Britain for American burglars and thieves. In October, 1892, this artful dodger was arrested in an attempt to steal a lot of valuable bonds at a railway station in Liege. He was convicted for this attempted robbery and shut up in a Belgian prison for seven years. While in prison he made a sensational revelation of his possession of the famous picture of the "Duchess of Gainsborough," which was sold at auction at Christie's, in 1876, for £10,100 and, eighteen days later, cut from its frame in the exhibition gallery of its purchaser, a leading picture dealer of London.

Our second page of representative portraits depicts four burglars of equally unenviable distinction. "Jimmy" Hope was perhaps the most notorious of his class in America, beginning his known career of crime in the year 1870 by the attempted robbery of Smith's bank at Perry, New York, and running up the scale to an alleged culmination in the famous burglary which robbed the Manhattan Savings Bank of nearly three millions in cash and securities. Six years later Hope was captured by the police in the attempt to rob a private bank in San Francisco, and for this crime was convicted and sentenced to a term of seven years and a half in San Quentin prison. He was brought to New York, on requisition papers from the governor, for complicity in the robbery of the Manhattan bank, but for lack of convicting evidence he was discharged and is now living by honest industry in a neighboring state.

His son "Johnny," whose portrait appears side by side with his father, was a hopeful slip from the parent stock but his career was cut short by his arrest and conviction for complicity in the Manhattan Bank robbery. For this crime he received a sentence of twenty years in Sing Sing. His conduct in prison was so excellent that he was pardoned by Governor Flower in 1891, after a confinement of a little more than nine years. He, too, like his father, should be credited with a genuine reformation since his discharge, and he is now earning a living as a good citizen.

David Cummings, commonly known as "Little Dave," was one of the principal consorts of Dunlap, Scott and Hope as well as an organizer and leader of his own gangs of burglars. He began his professional career with robberies on the Mississippi River, in 1865, in the convenient mask of a waiter on a steamboat.

In March, 1873, Cummings, "Red" Leary and two other burglars robbed the Falls City Tobacco Bank of Louisville, Kentucky, of nearly $400,000 in money, stocks and bonds. The gang chose Saturday night for the beginning of the assault, in order to have two nights and a day for their work before the opening of the bank on the Monday following. They broke into the Masonic Temple immediately over the bank and, after digging under the altar, cut a hole through the floor. Through this hole they dropped one after another to the roof of the bank vault about three feet below. The steel lining of the vault dome was covered with a thick layer of firmly cemented brick, but the determined burglars broke through the cover with picks and sledges and reached the metal lining. This they bored with drills and finally weakened a spot so that a section of the lining yielded to the blows of a heavy sledge. Then they dropped through the hole in the ceiling to the floor of the vault, blew out the door of the safe, and dragged out their booty.

Before leaving the vault, they artfully wedged the outer door, so that the discovery of the burglary would be delayed for some hours after the opening of the bank. To mask the raid further, they carefully replaced the plank over the hole which they had sawed in the floor of the temple above the vault, nailed down the carpet which had been neatly taken up, and piled a stack of books above the patch in the floor. Then all contrived to escape with such dexterity that it was years before any one of the gang was caught.

In the fall of the same year Cummings joined Dunlap, Scott and others in an attempt to tunnel through the vault of the First National Bank of Quincy, Ill. This design was very shrewdly planned and executed, and the gang succeeded in carrying off $89,000 in cash, $100,000 in government bonds and $350,000 in other securities.

This successful burglary was further remarkable in marking the first introduction of the air-pump for the purpose of blowing powder into a safe. The fine lines of junction between the safe door and its frame were carefully covered with putty to exclude the air completely except through a narrow interval at the top of the door. In this break in the cover of putty a fine pointed tube was inserted, and the air in the safe drawn out through the tube by an air pump. After exhausting the air, the removal of a bit of putty from the crack between the door and the frame caused a pressure of air which forced in through the crack sufficient gunpowder to blow open the safe, when fired by a fuse. This very effective and dangerous device was unfortunately made known to the burglars by a travelling salesman for one of the safe companies, who was tempted to become the accomplice of the men who were fighting the safe makers.

Since his notable success in 1873, Cummings has taken part in a long series of burglaries in this country and Great Britain, in spite of repeated arrests and imprisonments.

THE AIR PUMP.

When he came before Judge Cowing of New York in 1891, for his latest offence, the judge remarked in addressing him: "Your record shows that you have spent about all of the last eighteen years in prison. By actual

individual threads in the tangled skeins of crime spun by these rascals and there is no interest attaching to a bare enumeration of burglaries or to the myriad variations of device by which they were effected. In the half dozen burglaries which we have particularly noted as especially startling and prolific of booty, the really distinguishing methods are practically comprehended.

In the robbery of the Ocean Bank of New York, the basement below was hired ostensibly as an exchange. A partition was put up in the rear behind which the burglars worked, as they could seize opportunity, in cutting through the stone floor of the bank. At length the work had progressed so far that an entrance into the bank was effected on Saturday night and before Monday morning the vault was torn to pieces and the bank robbed of more than a million dollars. The Boylston Bank of Boston was robbed a few months later in the same year, 1869, in nearly the same way. In this case a room adjoining the bank was hired on the pretence of using it as an office for the sale of patent medicines. An old-fashioned bureau served as a screen to hide the progress of the work of cutting through the brick walls to the bank vault. In this instance only one night was required to break into the vault, but the inner vault was left unbroken for lack of time to complete the job. The Northampton Bank was robbed by seizing upon the cashier in his own house at midnight and compelling him to give the combination of the bank safe by the pressure of a loaded revolver on his ear. The looting of the Manhattan Bank was the outcome of an elaborately plotted scheme, in which the corruption of one of the watchmen of the bank was an essential feature. How the gang that robbed this bank seized and bound the janitor, opened the vault and got away with millions of booty has been told with graphic detail by Byrnes and Hawthorne, the authors of the dramatic tale of "The Great Bank Robbery."

It must be confessed that the extraordinary feats undertaken and executed by the new generation of burglars were startling and humiliating to law-abiding society and, particularly, to its appointed defenders, the police, and the bankers and safe makers who saw their guard lines penetrated and their redoubts taken by storm or undermined. But the alarms and the losses were fruitful in profit as well as in shock and disaster.

One immediate result was the resolute bracing and exercise of every arm of defence throughout the country. Bankers generally took better precautions in selecting their employees and scrutinizing their conduct. There was a more frequent and sharper examination, also, of the condition of bank vaults and the character of the occupants of adjoining premises. Old-fashioned iron vaults and old style safes, which had been tolerated before through carelessness or a misjudged economy, were reconstructed or replaced with those of the latest design. Doors and windows and entire walls even were fitted with an elaborate net work of burglar alarm wires. The vault and safe makers, too, had their needed warning and impulse, and have since made wonderful strides toward the perfection of safes to resist burglar tools of every kind and the application and shock of explosives.

Last, but not least, we may note the advances in the organization and efficiency of the police and detective forces throughout the country. In every large city the police departments were overhauled, toned up and rightly amended. Special patrols were instituted for the protection of the banks and the business heart of our cities. Lines of mutual help were multiplied and extended to all parts of this country and Europe, uniting the police and detectives of every state in our Union and of foreign nations as well, in cordial coöperation.

It is, of course, beyond question that this arousal of self protection and of coöperating defenders has been greatly serviceable to our country, and for this incitement the new generation of bank burglars deserves full credit, if not special thanks. It is further to be noted with satisfaction that this rallying of antagonists has gone far to foil and discourage the schemes of the once formidable bank burglar. There has really been no great city bank robbery since the warning shock of the assault on the Manhattan Bank, and minor robberies are growing year by year more infrequent and difficult of execution. Our banks are now, with rare exceptions, excellently protected and guarded.

It is true that no device of man is impregnable to man's assault, but in the case of the bank and the burglar there is fortunately the saving element of the time indispensable for the demolition of vault walls or safes. Undoubtedly a burglar of our day could cut or blast his way into the best of strongholds, if he had all the time he needed for the completion of his job. But, unfortunately for him, he can't command the sun to stand still or make forty-eight hours out of twenty-four.

There is, however, reason to apprehend that the development of electrical science may require a reformation of modern safeguards for money and other valuables. The use of an electric current of high power for penetrating the plates of a safe by melting the metal has lately been demonstrated in a series of experiments conducted by a West Point graduate, Samuel Rodman, Jr., in behalf of an United States government commission and a number of banks in this country. The same expert has shown also how swift and irresistible the application of high explosives may be in the hands of cracksmen of the first rank.

It is true that few burglars of our day can approach such an expert in the utilization of explosives for safe cracking, and serviceable electric currents may be difficult to reach and command. But Mr. Rodman's experiments unquestionably urge the expediency or necessity of the furthest feasible stretch of precautions. He lays particular stress upon the desirability of extending and perfecting a burglar alarm system in the form of an envelope of wires about safes and vaults. Such a barricade as he calls for could not be penetrated without giving an alarm that would bring a police force, in a few moments, to the point of attack. His recommendation strongly supports the suggestions that have been made to the same end by other expert authorities.

In view of the heavy responsibility necessarily attaching to the guardianship of deposits in banks and the appalling losses that may follow from a successful burglary, it is certain that the expense of the best attainable precautions and safeguards is comparatively inconsiderable.

We should urge, therefore, that nothing should be left undone by a bank to secure the best possible safeguards.

Its watchmen should be bright, wide-awake, faithful, honest.

Its vaults and safes should be of the best of steel, of the latest improved designs, and of uniform strength.

All suspicious characters entering or loitering about the bank should be keenly watched and questioned.

The slightest indication of any tampering with the locks of safes or vaults, or with any of the external defences of the bank, should be daily sought for and instantly reported to the police.

USING THE GRIPPER.

the case a generation ago. The construction of bank vaults and safes of all descriptions has been very greatly improved, also, in the last thirty years, as we have before noted, and the extension of burglar alarm circuits and other precautions has been widespread.

So the class of skilled bank burglars, who would rarely deign to stoop to lesser prey, has been greatly thinned and humbled. When these princes of the craft have not been cast into prison or driven from the country, they have been forced to look for booty among the small country banks of the West and South, usually, and even to drop to the meaner level of ordinary "safe blowers" and store breakers. The veterans that have escaped death, prison or exile are but an insignificant, dejected and demoralized remnant of the formidable gangs that once were a terror to the country, and the broken ranks have not been filled with new recruits.

In like manner, though to a much less marked extent, the line between the safe breaker or the robber of offices and the ordinary robber of stores has been blurred or overrun. The men who made a special study of the construction and demolition of the safes in offices and large stores were accustomed to work in gangs distinct from those engaged in breaking and entering for the purpose of stealing costly goods which they carried away in light wagons or, by hand, with the help of many confederates. These safe breakers were of a grade below the bank burglar, though many of the rank and file in the gangs of bank burglars did not turn up their noses at the sight of an easily cracked office safe. But as the bank burglars at large have been pressed down of late years into the ranks of the ordinary safe breakers, so the latter in turn have been driven by the perfection of safes and police protection to more indiscriminate robbery.

With the introduction and extension of the use of explosives for safe breaking in place of the slower operation of tools, the safe breakers of the country have come to be styled "safe blowers" by the police and themselves, because almost every safe breaker now carries a can of powder or dynamite cartridges to use, if necessary, and, with the improvement of safes, explosives have usually become necessary or desirable in order to break open a safe in the few hours available.

If, however, the safe to be opened is an old-fashioned one, or a cheap, so-called fireproof safe,—and too many of these safes are still lingering or are even now sold in this country,—the burglar of to-day with his modern kit of tools will smash the lock or break in or cut through the door or side as if it were pasteboard. These cheap or old safes are merely a laughing stock to burglars. Their only possible service is for the protection of papers from fire, for a common band-box would be cheaper and just about as strong a safeguard, if assailed by a robber.

FILLING SAFE WITH GUNPOWDER.

A practical object lesson to this effect was given some years ago in a New York court. A notorious burglar, one Patrick Cody, designed a little boring machine for his own private use in opening "fire-proof" safes. When he was captured by the police, his machine was taken also, and, in the course of his trial, a common safe was brought into the court room for the sake of an instructive illustration. Cody obligingly consented to serve as the operating lecturer and bored a hole through the door with his unpatented drill in just forty-five seconds, without using a drop of oil. In actual practice he had entered a room, opened a safe, taken out its contents and got off clear in less than six minutes, without disturbing a sleeper in the adjoining chamber.

"Johnny" Dobbs, another of the leading artists in safe-breaking, was even more expert and successful than Cody, and there are scores of others who can open an ordinary safe much more handily than the ordinary servant girl will open a refrigerator. The notorious "Red" Leary used to keep one of this kind of chest, as a standing joke, in his saloon in Brooklyn. Once "Big Frank" McCoy, a safe breaker of some reputation, and one of Leary's friends, was using it as a seat, when Leary came in and ran up to him with mock alarm, crying: "For God's sake, get off that safe, you'll crush it!"

This significant little story shows what the representative burglar thinks of such a little block in his way as the cheap "fire-proof" safe. Many hundreds of property owners have come by bitter experience to the same opinion as the burglar, and many hundreds more will help to make public opinion unanimous if they do not take warning in advance of a costly lesson in burglary.

A Southern railroad, some time ago, was greatly annoyed by the blowing open of a number of safes in the offices of its local agents. Finally it printed a card reading "Don't blow me open! Turn the knob and you will save time!" The card was posted on all its weak safes, to which only books and papers were thenceforth trusted. When the burglars found on investigation that this notice was put up in good faith, they did not plague the road by breaking the paper holders. Some such device may save those who note its suggestion from a similar plague of burglars, but it is not warranted as a specific.

The safe breakers infesting this country to-day are commonly young men ranging in age from twenty-five to thirty-five years. Their customary field of plunder covers the country towns and villages, but rarely extends to the larger cities on account of the greater blocks and risks in their way.

Before striking a "mark" in a country town they usually select it in advance and ascertain every condition favoring or opposing their plan of robbery, which is modified accordingly to ensure the best prospect of success. This preliminary survey is made in the guise of tramps or it may be as pretended drummers or ordinary travellers. Next in importance to locating and planning the robbery is the provision for escape, and no professional safe breaker or burglar will make any attack until he has clearly defined and secured his line and means of retreat in the event of success or failure. This provision is justly esteemed of such consequence that assaults on stores or safes are often postponed for weeks, or even abandoned, if the available means of escape with the possible booty are insufficient or unsatisfactory.

In the execution of burglaries the robbers usually travel in gangs of two or three, to evade the suspicion likely to attach to a larger gang and also because two or three men are usually an ample force for the work required. A gang is always provided with an excellent county or district map covering the proposed point of assault and its environs. The latest railroad time tables, noting the arrival and departure of trains at all points in the district, are also procured and carefully studied.

On the eve of the attack on a chosen mark, the gang

usually drops down upon an adjoining town and hires the best team procurable at a livery stable. With a fast horse and buggy or other light wagon the robbers drive during the evening, under cover of the darkness, to their mark, either directly or by a roundabout course if greater wariness of approach is thought requisite. A dark lantern is always a part of their outfit, but the rest of their kit varies in pro-

BREAKING OFF KNOB.

portion to the known requirements of the job in hand. In many cases a heavy sledge hammer, a bit-stock, a sharp steel drill and a steel punch are the only tools needed to crack the safe in their eye. If the lock of the safe is directly behind the knob, it is only the work of a few moments to break off the knob with the sledge and drive the spindle through the lock with a few hard blows on the punch. Or, if the safe is of a more modern and stronger design, a hole is drilled with the bit-stock through the door or side and powder enough blown in, with a light pair of bellows or blow pipe, to open the safe, when exploded. When dynamite is

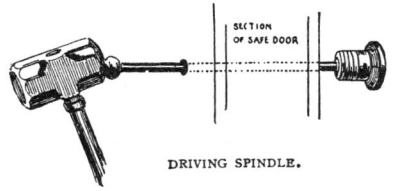
DRIVING SPINDLE.

employed, the cartridge is so placed within or without the safe that the firing of a charge of powder by means of a wire and electric battery will cause the concussion necessary to explode the nitro-glycerine which is relied upon to shatter the safe. If powder or a dynamite cartridge is used, the safe is commonly covered with a carpet or rugs to deaden the report of the explosion, or, in case of a grocery or produce store, sacks of grain or bales of hay are piled up about and on top of the safe as a bulwark and sound breaker.

When experienced burglars are executing the job, the amount of powder or dynamite used is so nicely calculated and the swathing of the safe is so perfect that the explosion only produces a dull rumbling sound which may readily be mistaken for a roll of thunder by untrained ears. Before the mistake is discovered or any alarm is spread, the alert burglars have hastily ransacked the safe and are off with their booty, driving so fast that their escape is often unnoticed and pursuit is only a chase at random. At some previously determined station on the line of a railroad in the district, the robbers leave their horse and wagon and take a night or early morning train to some distant place of refuge and concealment. Sometimes, two or three "gophers" or "peters," as the burglars call the safes, are cracked in succession in a single night, and, by a neatly planned division of time, a "get away," or departing train, is reached and boarded just at the moment of its flight from the station.

Entrance into a store, shop or office containing the marked safe is commonly effected by bursting in a rear door, or snapping off a window catch by prying up the bottom sash. If there is any risk from the noise of such an entry, the door lock will be picked by skeleton keys, or a pane cut out of a window by the use of a diamond while the glass is held by a bit of strong paper, glued to the outside of the pane, or by a rubber stamp. After a pane is cut and removed, it is, of course, easy to thrust in a hand and unfasten the catch.

The special tools made for this class of burglaries are lighter than those required for the entrance into massive bank vaults, and less varied and complex. The drills in common use are so small that they may readily be carried about in a coat, or even a waistcoat, pocket. In jobs in which a sledge hammer, punch, bit-stock and bellows are nearly all the implements needed, it is quite common to procure some or all of these, only an hour or two before the robbery, by breaking into a neighboring blacksmith, wheelwright or carpenter's shop. After the robbery these stolen tools are sometimes designedly left on the ground or in places where they will be likely to direct suspicion to their innocent owners, who are often seriously annoyed or blackened by their apparent implication in the burglaries. At other times, the tools are hidden in places from which they may be later recovered and even used again, perhaps, in subsequent robberies in the same district.

It is rare that the actual cash obtained by these raids amounts to more than a few hundred dollars, but securities and other papers of value are sometimes taken away and held for redemption through the agency of "fences" or the professional dealers in stolen goods. Postage stamps are a common and highly prized booty, as it is impossible to detect this stolen property from the lack of any distinguishing mark. These stamps are sometimes obtained in large quantities and are readily sold for nearly their face value to the dealers in stamps in every city and large town of the country. This description of plunder is so easily marketed that the United States government has been seriously annoyed by the frequent robberies of the post-offices in small towns, and has fixed a standing reward for the arrest and conviction of post-office burglars.

BURGLAR'S JIMMIES.

To facilitate escape it is not uncommon for the burglars to break into a clothing store, in the course of their drive to or from their "mark," and make a complete exchange of their former dress, which is often a ragged, filthy, old tramp suit, for new and neatly fitting apparel. The ragged old clothes are usually left in a heap on the floor of the clothing store as a disgusting memorial of the visit, but, if the cast off suits have any manufacturer's mark or any peculiarity which may be recalled or used for tracing purposes, these marks are carefully removed or the peculiar clothing is burned, buried, sunk in ponds, or otherwise concealed or destroyed.

These safe breakers are a particularly dangerous and desperate class of criminals, less adroit and accomplished than the better class of bank burglars and less inclined to shun a deadly fight or a brutal assault on the way to their booty. If surprised, they are likely to stickle at nothing in their dash to escape or even to carry through their plan of robbery. They almost uniformly carry loaded revolvers and, at times, other weapons, and will shoot to disable or kill with ugly recklessness. The certainty of long terms in prison, if caught in the act of burglary, is an ever present dread that drives them to murder, at a pinch, to escape the jail. To prevent the loss of good lives, the force that attempts the capture of a gang should be plainly of overwhelming strength, if possible.

After a burglary has been effected, the gang seeks hiding places, sometimes scattering as tramps through the country, sometimes taking the trains to distant states, or even flying abroad, but usually resorting to the larger cities where they rely on sinking out of sight in obscure lodgings or in the swarms of visitors. They kill time by every kind of dissipation while loafing between their works of burglary.

One of the most expert, notorious and really representative safe blowers in this country to-day is Edward, or "Eddy," Kelly, now serving out a term of five years in the Massachusetts state prison.

It is of interest to trace his method of correspondence in arranging for a descent upon a selected mark and his actual procedure in the case that ended in his arrest and conviction just as he was on the point of breaking into the office of a large manufacturing establishment in the outskirts of Boston. His planning and course of execution are unquestionably typical of the devices of the advanced order of safe breakers, and the foiling of his schemes is likewise fairly representative of the countering methods of the police, now generally pursuing the good prescription which the sarcastic Balzac has put in the mouth of a chief of the detectives of Paris, "Prevention of crime—that's the function of the police!"

When Eddy Kelly was arrested by the Boston police, early in February, 1896, the following letters, were found in his pockets.

Jan. 29/96.

Friend Jim:—

What I wrote you about is very desirable, I have been there three times and think it A good investment, would not write you if I was not sure, I am waiting for an opening and will get A decition this week. I have been obliged to keep rather quiet since my business failure in N. Y. You will find everything as I represent, have all your friends gone out of business there, I value the property I write of at $5,000 that is the lowest estimate, but I am sure you will be pleased at one other investment I have you cannot imagine a more desirable location with every advantage, everything is very antique but it will be A place where if successful one can retire, I could be very enthusiastic over this last matter, but you know we Real Estate men prefer to have Customers on the ground where they can see things for themselves. I cannot say anything more to-day I expect to sell A piece of land before this letter reaches you and will communicate with you the latter part of the week if I succeed, in any event I will write you as early as possible and arrange matters in my next letter, Have plenty news for you. My address is 95 Tyler St. not Taylor St.

Yr's Truly
Ed.

P. S. I send you a piece of map marking first location. I wrote of Madison County.

This precious missive is here reproduced without the change of a letter or punctuation mark. The dear "Jim," who was addressed, was defined on the envelope as J. B. Dunlap, Esq., then residing, as the direction noted, at a fashionable hotel in Chicago, Illinois. "J. B." was supposed to be the well-known "Jim" Dunlap, who was a star of the first magnitude as a bank burglar, in his shining days, and had been released from the Massachusetts state prison, a few months before, after serving a long term as a principal in the great Northampton bank robbery. It is hardly necessary to explain that, under the thin veil of an investment in real estate, Kelly was writing in regard to two tempting "marks." His "business failure" in New York was the collapse of an attempted burglary. The anticipated sale of "a piece of land" was the projected cracking of a safe in Boston.

In the postscript Kelly informed Dunlap that he was sending to him a map in which the location of the first "mark" was defined by an oval figure drawn with a pen or pencil around a town in "Madison County." The wariness of the experienced burglar is shown by his enclosure of this map in a separate envelope addressed to Dunlap, so that the miscarriage of one of the letters, for any reason, would not block or give away the scheme of robbery.

Kelly's letter was in response to one from Dunlap, written in Chicago a few days before.

Chicago, Jan 25, 1896

Friend Ed;

I received your letter and was very glad to hear from you I was a little afraid you was in trouble. I saw in the papers about your Friends. I am glad you got away from them I havent been doing any good for my self and have spent what little money I did have I shall be glad to go into buisness with you if thair is a chance to make a little money but only you let me hear from you as soon as you can

Nobody in Chicago and buisness as dull as a grave yard.

I will tell you a lot as soon as I see you that pop is go out of buisness in a Short time he is going west.

with best wishes

Yours

D—

P. S Send letter to Hotel ——

Dunlap's lament of the dullness of "buisness" spoke well for the efficiency of the Chicago police. It would appear that this crafty correspondent was willing to go into "buisness" again with his friend Kelly, if assured that the partnership would not be further extended. The "pop," referred to as on the point of retiring from "buisness," was supposed to be a noted receiver of stolen goods.

While thus laying his plans with noteworthy forethought for future operations, Kelly was meanwhile busily engaged upon a job in hand, the disposal of "a piece of land," as he wrote, in Boston. In order to effect this sale as rapidly as practicable, he made appointments with George Perry and two others of his own stripe to meet him in Boston, and this curious confederation of "real estate men" hired rooms together in a respectable lodging house in the South End of the city.

The Boston detective bureau soon learned of the arrival of this gang and detectives were detailed to "shadow" them or, more explicitly, to watch and follow them night and day while they remained in the city. One detective took lodging in a neighboring house and with the coöperation of his associates was able to mark and report every movement of the gang outside of their quarters. So day after day the chief inspector was promptly informed of every step of the suspected burglars, whom they met, with whom they talked, and what they were apparently planning. It was soon ascertained that the probable "mark" in view was the safe of a large manufacturing establishment near the city, in which the money for the month's pay roll was usually deposited on the day preceding the pay day.

About eleven o'clock on the evening of the night presumably fixed for the burglary, Kelly left his lodging house and stealthily proceeded to a harness shop in the West End. Close upon midnight he reached the shop door and paused for a minute, warily glancing up and down the street to see if any one was watching. Apparently his reconnoissance was re-assuring for he stepped quickly to the door, drew a key out of his pocket, opened the door and darted in. After a few minutes, he came out with two bundles under his arm, but popped back instantly at the sight of two men passing by on the other side of the street.

Again, after a few moments of wary waiting, he slipped out of the door with its bundles but, to his profound disgust, he was instantly nabbed by watchful detectives guarding the doorway. He tried to draw his revolver, but, after a moment's scuffle, he was mastered and handcuffed. Upon searching the shop, a valise was found on the floor, close to the door, partially filled with burglar tools. Other tools were found in both bundles, wrapped in paper, comprising a complete kit of the latest patterns of jimmies and drills together with a blow pipe, fuse and dynamite cartridges. One

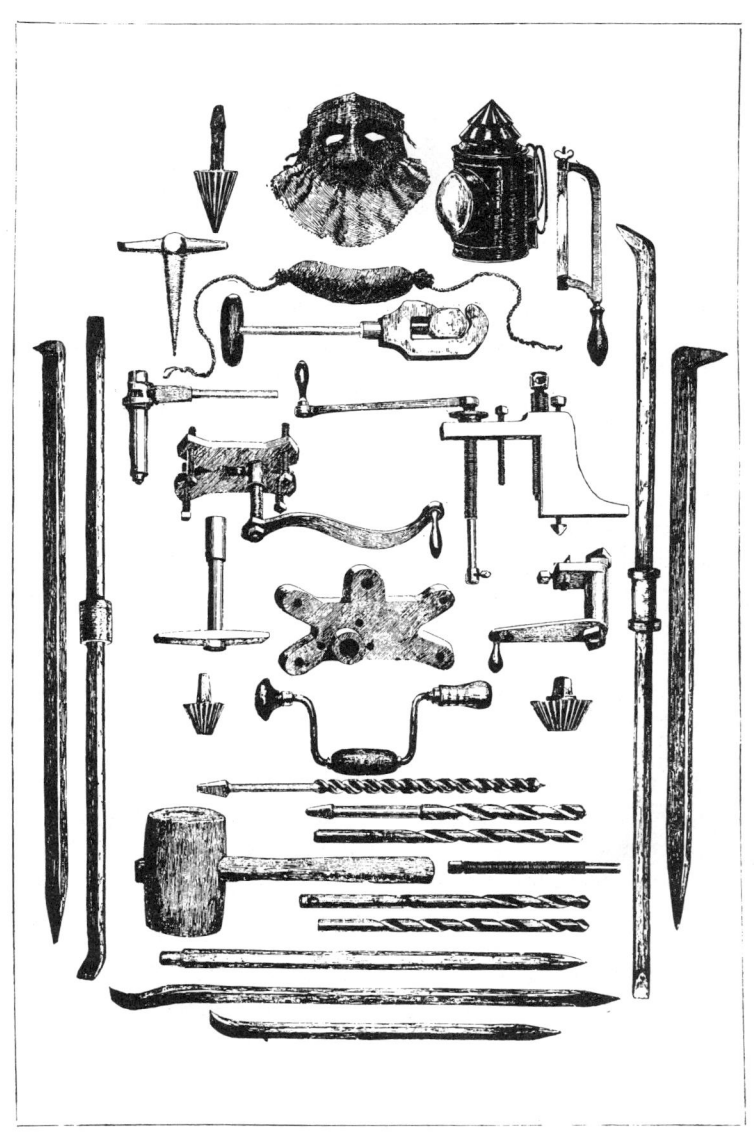

BOYLSTON BANK BURGLARS' KIT.

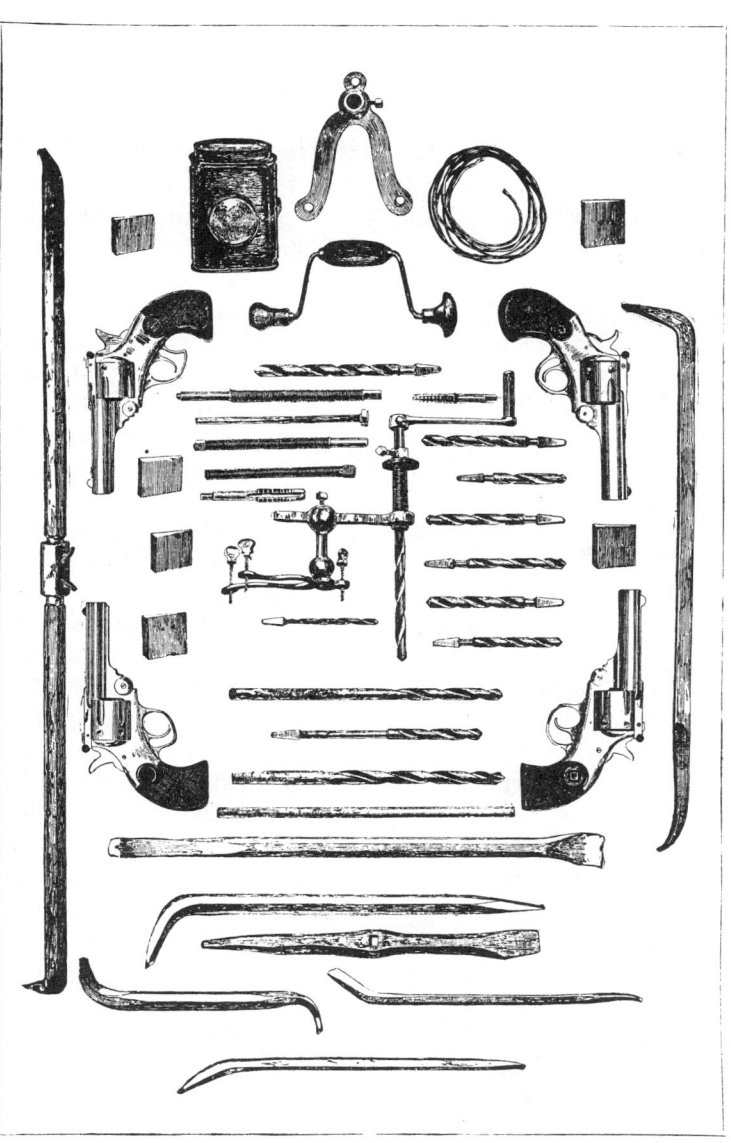

"EDDY" KELLY'S KIT.

of the tools was particularly notable, a specially designed instrument for safe boring, made in parts which could be compactly packed and easily fitted together for use. In the accompanying drawings this kit is reproduced for the purpose of comparison with the corresponding outfit of the old-fashioned burglar. The reader should remember, in contrasting these two illustrations, that the old-fashioned kit is necessarily reproduced on a more reduced scale than the modern tools. When this is understood, the lightness and compactness of the modern tools will be clearly seen, especially in comparing the various cumbersome parts of the old-fashioned drills made with solid brass plates, as shown in the centre of one page, with the slender but effective apparatus on the other page.

Immediately after the arrest of Kelly the police made a descent on his lodging house where his confederates were found lying on beds, completely dressed, although it was then one o'clock in the morning. They sprang up instantly upon the entrance of the detectives and showed fight, but were soon overpowered. Every one of the men had a loaded revolver on his person when arrested. The whole gang was then taken to police headquarters as suspicious characters. As the evidence was not sufficient to convict them of an actual attempt at burglary, the men taken in the lodging house were discharged with the warning to leave Boston on the first train running out of the state. All were happy to get off so easily and the first train was none too early for them. Kelly was sent to prison for five years for having burglar's tools in his possession, and his gang has since been completely broken up. Perry was soon after arrested in New York for robbing a jeweller in Troy and sentenced to the state prison for nine years. Two others of these queer "real estate men" are in jail awaiting trial on the charges of robbery and burglary.

The portraits of Kelly and Perry appear on the page, entitled representative safe breakers, and their title is clear to this distinction. The other two, whose photographs complete this representative page, are John Talbot and John, or "Jack," Walsh.

John Talbot has built up a reputation as one of the most adroit and dangerous cracksmen in this country. In 1879 he gained a special black mark in his class by breaking into a store on West Fourteenth street in New York and shooting at the proprietor who was trying to catch him. For this offence Talbot served a term of two years in Sing Sing.

Within a year after his release he cut through the floor of the parlors of a theatrical costumer in New York, and, with the help of his pal, "Patsy" Carroll, carried off goods valued at $10,000. For this robbery the pair were sent to Sing Sing for four years, and, as soon as they got out of jail, planned another burglary, this time cutting a hole through the ceiling of a Brooklyn dry goods store, dropping a rope ladder through the hole, and descending by the ladder to the floor of the store. Talbot then cut through and blew open the safe, in twenty minutes, and the gang carried off its contents of cash and valuable papers.

A few days later both Talbot and Carroll were caught in New York and taken to Brooklyn for trial. They were placed in the court pen of the examining police justice, an apartment twelve feet square, lighted only through a glass cover in the middle of the ceiling. There was only one door to the room, which was carefully locked, but when the court officer in charge opened the door and looked into the pen, a few moments after the entry of the prisoners, Talbot was missing.

He had first torn the register from the ventilating shaft and climbed up the shaft to the end, but had been unable to squeeze through the top. So he dropped back and set a bench on end upon which he climbed while Carroll held it upright. Standing on top of the bench, he noiselessly broke the glass in the skylight, carefully collecting the broken pieces in his handkerchief. Then he squeezed himself through the opening, passed over the snow covered roof of the court-house and an adjoining building, and dropped down safely into a yard from which he escaped to the street.

After this feat, he fled to Montreal and robbed a jeweller there of diamonds worth $8,000, carrying off the booty while his confederate held a pistol at the head of the proprietor. His next remarkable venture was the breaking of the safe of a wealthy produce and commission merchant, in Philadelphia, and carrying off four hundred dollars in cash and securities valued at $315,000. With this plunder he went to New York and, soon after his arrival, took part in the robbery of a manufacturing jeweller of Burling Slip.

When the gang to which he belonged was arrested, a remarkable arsenal of burglar tools was found in their rooms, together with descriptions of all the principal safes in the market and a list of the New York stores that were provided with burglar alarm wires. In a trunk in Talbot's bedroom all the securities stolen from the Philadelphia merchant were found as well as a number of diamonds, which were supposed to be relics of the robbery of the Montreal jeweller. Talbot was indicted for the Brooklyn burglary, pleaded guilty and was sentenced to a term of ten years at Sing Sing.

He served out his term only to drift back into his old haunts and plan new crimes. He was arrested a few months ago by the Boston detective bureau, for persistently hanging about a leading jeweller's store in the city, and sentenced to a year's term in the House of Correction as a vagabond. Such a sentence is even more disgusting than the state prison to the old professional burglar, who fears with reason that his old chums will turn up their noses at a safe blower who has fallen to the level of a tramp. "Don't 'vag' me," is often the rueful plea of these robbers to the police, "for 'twill spoil my reputation!"

On Saturday night, the fourth of February, 1888, a large jewelry store in Norfolk, Virginia, was broken into and robbed of watches and jewelry to the amount of thirty thousand dollars. The burglars escaped with their plunder but, when the alarm was given, there was a hue and cry through the country for miles around. A day or two later, two suspicious looking men were hailed by the Petersburg police. When ordered to stand for examination, the strangers fled to a swamp in the woods pursued by the police and armed citizens. Bloodhounds were also put on their trail and the swamp was surrounded, yet the fugitives succeeded in stealing through the circle of the police, unobserved, and escaping.

But descriptions of the men had been wired to all parts of the state, and, the next day, both were arrested on a street car entering Richmond. Their clothes were torn to tatters by the briars of the swamp, and their faces, hands and legs were sorely scratched and bleeding. They gave their names as Joseph Murray and John Ward, but were soon identified as "Joe" Dollard and "Jack" Walsh, two notorious New York safe breakers, who had just returned to this country, after serving a sentence for burglary in an English prison.

The evidence against them was not sufficient to convict them of the Norfolk burglary and Walsh was discharged, but his companion Dollard was held to answer a charge of complicity in a recent burglary at Bridgeport, Conn. All the valuables stolen from the Norfolk jeweller were recovered by the police, before the end of February, from their hiding place in a hole dug in a country road, seven miles from Norfolk.

"Jack" Walsh continued to be a moving figure in a succession of burglaries, winding up with the cracking of the safe of the Pawling (New York) Bank in March, 1893, and

In this case, they are accustomed to rob fruit, provision, cigar and grocery stores, and feast in secret upon their stolen dainties.

The second and main class is made up of the professional store breakers, men ranging in age from the young novice to the old, experienced burglar. Their descents upon stores are usually in gangs of three or more, according to the need of hands for the particular job in view, and the burglaries are planned systematically like the cracking of safes, sometimes for weeks or months in advance of the actual raid. They effect an entrance into their chosen mark by unscrewing the locks from doors or by the use of skeleton or counterfeit keys, or by the ever handy jimmy, or through a window by breaking a pane or turning the catch with a tool inserted between the sashes.

When an entrance has been gained, the selected goods are rapidly made up into bundles or cases and carried away by light wagons in waiting, in charge of confederates, or by cab-men or expressmen engaged for the purpose and hoodwinked by some plausible pretence. The stolen goods are generally shipped to some distant point in barrels, crates or boxes adroitly marked to shun suspicion, or, it may be, delivered in secret to receivers of stolen goods in the city where the robbery has been committed. Only a fraction of the actual value of the goods can usually be obtained by the robbers, but the receivers do not realize the full margin of profit, for they, in turn, are obliged to dispose of the goods at a discount and hold the plunder sometimes for many months before they can prudently venture to market it.

The expert bank burglar, Adam Worth, was also a master hand in the execution of robberies of stores. Once, after robbing a jewelry store in Boston, this daring burglar slipped out of the front door, only to meet a policeman face to face. Without an instant of tremor this man of iron nerve politely saluted the officer and stepped back to re-open the door coolly and call to his confederate within: "William, be sure and fasten the door securely when you leave! I have got to catch the next car." So indeed he did, after bidding the officer a pleasant good night, but he hopped off the car, a few blocks beyond the store, slipped back stealthily, signalled to his confederate and both escaped with their booty.

Michael Kurtz, alias "Sheeny Mike," is a flaming meteor still in this line of burglary, and has been uncommonly sly and lucky in escaping conviction. He began his criminal career as a member of the notorious Howard gang engaged in a number of successful burglaries in Philadelphia, in 1876. Early in the next year he was arrested for the robbery of a cloak house on Broadway, New York, but was discharged from the lack of complete identification. A few weeks later he was re-arrested in Baltimore for the robbery of a Boston silk store and sentenced upon conviction to a term of twelve years in the Massachusetts state prison.

By his exceedingly clever counterfeit of dangerous illness, brought about by swallowing pills of hard soap, he contrived to secure a pardon, after a confinement of four years, as a man on the verge of the grave. After his release he recovered his health so quickly that he was arrested, three months later, on the charge of robbing a dry goods store in Washington, D. C. Again he was discharged for lack of evidence only to "fall" again the next year on the charge of the possession of burglar tools. He was suffered to go free after a short detention and, two months afterwards, was arrested in company with a notorious burglar, John Love, for the robbery of the Italian American bank of New York City. Once more the lack of evidence saved him, but he could not escape arrest, the next year, for the robbery of a jewelry store in Washington. He was taken to that city, admitted to bail and skipped.

In the following February the store of a jeweller and diamond dealer in Troy, New York, was entered at night by a remarkably expert gang of burglars. This gang forced open a window in an adjoining building and made an entry into the cellar. From this base of assault the burglars tore a hole through a twelve inch brick wall into the basement of the jeweller's store, climbed through the hole, forced up a trap-door and reached the floor above. Then they broke open the door of the safe with heavy sledges and took away diamonds, jewelry, watches, and money to the amount of over $50,000.

Immediately after this big robbery "Sheeny Mike" and "Billy" Porter, a burglar of high degree, sailed for Europe on a White Star steamer. "Mike" was known to his fellow passengers as Henry C. Appleton, a retired Californian mine owner, and Porter masked himself as Leslie L. Langdon, the owner of a great cattle ranch at San Luis. These polite capitalists visited Paris and London together, stopping at the best hotels and dropping golden showers wherever they went.

During their stay abroad a number of daring robberies was committed in the heart of London, evidently by most accomplished hands. Safes were blown open so noiselessly that people in adjoining dwellings were not alarmed, and the burglars escaped with their booty in every instance. Oddly enough, suspicion fell, at length, upon the wealthy American tourists, Messrs. Appleton and Langdon, and they were so shocked that they determined to cut short their projected stay abroad and go home.

"Billy" Porter was arrested, a day or two after landing in New York, for the burglary in Troy, but "Sheeny" Mike reached Jacksonville, Florida, and calmly proceeded to establish a large wholesale tobacco house there under the firm name of Kurtz Brothers. He was arrested in the midst of the orange grove which he had purchased as a suitable residence, and, after a long legal fight, was taken to New York to stand trial for the same offence with which Porter was charged. He was convicted upon his own confession to the prosecuting attorney and sentenced, March 30, 1886, to a term of eighteen years and six months in the state prison at Dannemora. His case, however, went to the court of appeals on a legal technicality and he was discharged after a few months of imprisonment. His confessions have been so reckless of the alleged honor proverbial among thieves, that he has been blacklisted by his old associates, in all parts of the country, as a professional "squealer." His portrait is given on our representative page of typical store breakers, for his sentence to the state prison was for robbing a store, although his talents were not cramped by confinement to this single line of burglary.

John Hamilton, alias "Brooklyn Johnny"; John Mahoney, alias "Jack Sheppard"; and Henry Hoffman, complete the page of portraits with the faces of three rogues representing their class, the store breaker, as well as any that could be selected. All three are especially noted, too, for their impudent craft in capturing trucks, loaded with goods, which chanced to be standing, for the moment, in front of stores in our principal cities.

"Brooklyn Johnny" was arrested in the fall of 1883 by the New York police detective bureau, in company with another notorious thief, James Quigley, for coolly mounting and driving away a truck load of goods, valued at $6,000, from the front of the store of a leading clothing house on Broadway. He was convicted and sentenced for this offence to the New York penitentiary for two years and a half. Within a year after his release, he was caught in the act of robbing a tea store on Eighth avenue, in the same city, and arrested while breaking open the safe. For this crime he was given a term of nine years in the state prison, and since his discharge he has been consorting with his old confederate, James Quigley, and the notorious burglars Carroll, Talbot and Kurtz.

"Jack Sheppard" won his sobriquet from his remarkable nimbleness and ingenuity in dodging the police and effecting escapes, like his namesake, the famous English robber. No ordinary jail was tight enough to hold him for a week, if his hands were free, and old-fashioned hand-cuffs were no more binding than mittens upon his slippery wrists.

He is even credited once with a successful break out of the police headquarters in one of the largest cities. He had been arrested for handling a jimmy, and the vigilance of the officers was a little relaxed after he was within the doors of the police station. Watching his opportunity, he made a dash for the door, a flying jump over the steps, and sprinted round the corner and down the street. There was a great hue and cry on his heels, but this Mercury of burglars ran like a hare or a scared coyote and soon distanced the hunters.

Burglary seemed to be too deliberate a method of robbery to suit his ripened and more fastidious taste and, in the later years of his career, he has been especially distinguished as a persistent eloper with goods in wagons. In 1866 he was arrested in Boston for stealing a truck loaded with broadcloth and served out a sentence of five years in the Massachusetts state prison. After a brief vacation, diversified by burglary, arrest and escape, he was shut up for four years in the prison at Joliet, Illinois. A few months after his discharge from Joliet, he was arrested in New York for stealing another truck load of goods, but a disagreement of the trial jury set him free until he was arrested again in Boston for the same offence, in 1879, and again passed a term of five years in the Massachusetts state prison. It was only a few months after his release when he was again arrested and convicted of larceny in Philadelphia, for which he paid a penalty of three years in the Eastern Penitentiary.

One of his favorite tricks has been to put on an ink-stained duster and step out, apparently from some busy merchant's office, as one of the clerks. Bareheaded and with a pen thrust behind his ear, he has made so good a counterfeit of a regular clerk that he has imposed upon draymen and expressmen over and over again, and they have delivered their loads to his confederates, in various places, without any suspicious questionings.

When he has been caught and convicted, his plaintive and plausible pleas for clemency have unquestionably shortened his sentences, for this habitual criminal can put on the face of a well-meaning man, driven to crime by want or pitiless persecution, and only begging one more chance for repentance and reform. He is the Artful Dodger of American thieves, but he has not been able to escape eight convictions with aggregate sentences of thirty-two years in different prisons of this country. His latest conviction was in February, 1890, for the larceny of a lot of shawls in New York City. He secured a sentence of five years in Sing Sing and, since his discharge, he has been repeatedly arrested in company with well-known thieves, although he has never ceased to protest his determination to reform.

The fourth in line of our representative store breakers is Henry Hoffman, alias Tannis, alias "Mug." He is a notorious store breaker with a penchant for running away with wagons loaded with goods. In the past twenty-five years he has served out three sentences for burglary, and is now confined in the state prison in New York. He is accounted one of the most desperate men of his class, ready to shoot, at any time, if threatened with arrest.

The police and the organized detective forces of the country are constantly on the look-out for these dangerous criminals, and endeavor to keep in touch with all their movements from place to place through the country and with their conduct at all times. This oversight is clearly a concern of proper precaution and is not carried to any extreme of offensive espionage.

MICHAEL KURTZ.

JOHN HAMILTON.

JOHN MAHONEY.

HENRY HOFFMAN.

The complaints of police persecution, often made in the courts by arrested burglars, or confided to the ears of gullible sentimentalists, are wholly unfounded in the great majority of cases, at least. Nobody has more reason to promote the sincere reform and the well doing of these offenders than the police to whom the active, plotting or working criminal is an object of anxiety and dread, night and day. It is, of course, inevitably difficult, under present conditions, for the discharged convict to secure the employment or the pay open to workingmen of unquestioned steadiness and character. This difficulty is a part of the penalty which the man, who has preferred the life of a rascal to that of an honest man, must expect to face and overcome. But the experienced police authorities of the country are not inhuman. On the contrary, it is safe to say that they lend a helping hand to men in need, who are honestly seeking to live by honest work, with a good will and discretion that will bear comparison with the services of the perennial petitioners for the shortening of the sentences of professedly penitent criminals.

It is the purpose of the police, however, to distinguish as sharply and justly as possible, between the discharged convicts, who are sincerely trying to live an honest life; and the hardened criminals who are merely trying to hoodwink the charitable public and the eyes of the defenders of society. The instances are unfortunately legion of feigned repentances and the thankless deceit of confiding employers. So the vigilance of the police must advance and extend with the growth of our country, in order to be faithful to its trust of guardianship.

We would urge upon the business men of the country, also, the need of their alert coöperation to perfect their defence. The cheap, "pasteboard" safe should be everywhere discarded as a supposed strong-box for the keeping of money, and safes of the best modern designs substituted. Against the burglars of our day, the ordinary "fire-proof" safe is only a mockery of protection. As far as practicable, iron shutters or bars should be used as a guard for the windows of the lower stories of stores, factories and office buildings. This protection is now frequently confined to the basement floor, but it should certainly be extended to the second story, as the entrances of burglars are largely effected through the windows of this floor.

In the cities where there is a nightly patrol of police, a light should be kept burning on the street floor of all business establishments, and the safes, on this floor, so placed that a clear view can be obtained of them by the passing watchmen, on the street, through the uncovered glass of a front window. No curtain or other obstacle should be allowed to obstruct this view. When the contents of a store or safe are especially valuable, the additional protection of burglar alarm wires is strongly advised.

The night police patrols of Boston and our larger cities are instructed to watch the condition of the safes with particular scrutiny, try the locks of the doors frequently, note that the lights are burning, and warn away or, if justified, arrest any suspicious persons loitering near a store or office block. With the uniform observance of such vigilance and the general co-operation of the public, it is safe to say that the annual losses through burglars might be materially diminished.

UNDER COVER OF NIGHT.

NO other class of robbers is so universally dreaded as the house-breaker. He is the "bogey-man" of our childish fancy, the burly ruffian who is expected to pop up like a jack-in-the-box, in the dead of the night, from some secret lurking place, and turn us into shuddering, gasping little wretches by his murderous menace. His horrid black mask is the cover of a face so inhuman that we dare not let our fancy run riot in conjuring its image, but bury our heads under the bed-clothes as hunted ostriches plunge theirs in the sands of fiction, if not of the desert. Still, through the thickest screen of sheets, bed-spreads and blankets we can feel the scorch of those basilisk eyes glaring through the slits in the mask and making us squirm like bugs under a burning glass.

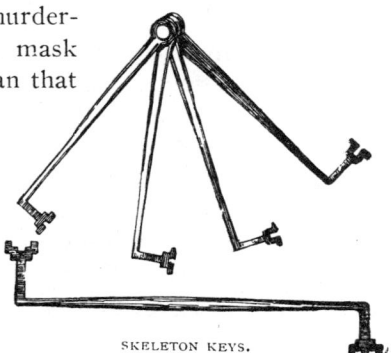

SKELETON KEYS.

This is that Methuselah of burglars who from time immemorial has crouched under beds or stowed himself away in the corners of closets, to rise up and murder the sleep of the good, easy man of the house and his slumbering family. His resurrection is always as startling as an earthquake, even to the traditional old maid who has let no night pass without a peep under the bed, as if a burglar was a visitor who was likely to drop in any day in the year.

It is not to be denied that this nerve-shattering image has a solid skeleton of reality which is justly an object of dread. One need only recall a bare tithe of the instances of brutal night raids that have been made upon unprotected households in the last twenty years to justify in great measure the common fear of burglars, and there is, of course, a black record of deadly assaults in the annals of house-breaking stretching back to the earliest dawn of history. The peculiar heinousness of the violation of the sanctities and safeguards of the home and the imminent threat of bloodshed that attaches to such an outrage are justly recognized in the extraordinary penalties imposed by the laws of all countries upon this description of burglary.

The house-breakers and the sneak thieves who commonly make their inroads in the day time or in the early hours of the evening are usually to be distinguished from the professional burglar. Often the rascals who steal in this way are boys or youths, still in their teens, who particularly infest the cities and larger towns and slyly watch for opportunities to enter houses closed for the summer or temporarily untenanted. They may use a simple jimmy or skeleton keys or perhaps only a chisel and screw driver with which they unfasten window catches or take off common locks. Unless they know positively by careful spying that the "mark" in view is unoccupied for the time being, it is a common practice for this class of house-breakers to ring the bell in the disguise of a pedler of knick-knacks or an inquirer in search of some fictitious person and thus ascertain definitely whether any guardian is still in the house, before attempting to force an entrance. They rarely attempt more elaborate robberies than the ransacking of trunks, drawers and closets, and the carrrying off of jewelry, silverware, money or articles of clothing which they can readily pawn. If they dispose of this plunder to pawnbrokers, it is commonly kept in good condition; but any plate or jewelry, which is sold to dealers in old gold or silver, is broken up or beaten into lumps in a way to destroy the possibility of identification with the stolen articles. These petty robbers are particularly reckless and annoying in the

UNDER COVER OF NIGHT. 95

damages which they inflict on fine furniture, bureaus and dressing cases, in their hasty search for the valuables which they chiefly prize.

The most common and dangerous classes of these housebreakers are known as the "second story" and the "flat workers." The first are agile young men who can mount on top of a veranda almost as quickly as a monkey, sometimes bare handed or with the help of some chance prop, and sometimes with the aid of a spiral wire or chain ladder, that can be compactly rolled up or folded. A hook at the end of this ladder is fixed on a window sill or water pipe or gutter, and the robber then runs up and quickly passes in through a window to the second floor of the house. His first act is to lock the door of the chamber by its bolt or key, and then he rummages about for booty without fearing the sudden entrance of any one of the family or of a servant of the house. He usually wears rubber shoes or "sneakers," as shoes with rubber soles are termed, and he can skip over a roof or floor as noiselessly as a cat. With a jimmy or chisel he soon bursts open any closet door, trunk or bureau drawers, and he can ransack a chamber with astonishing rapidity and noiselessly, leaving a trail of wreck behind him when he finally slips out of the window and slides down to the ground. Even if he is startled by any one who tries to enter the chamber, he has commonly time to slip away and escape before the alarm is spread and his retreat cut off. There are instances, however, where one of these robbers has been forced to a desperate jump by the heat of pursuit and has broken his leg or even his skull by a fall on stone-steps.

He is, as a class, a keen as well as a daring robber, who makes his preliminary surveys carefully before undertaking a raid. He picks out the best class of houses commonly as well as the particular ones most easy of assault. The hours of meals and the habits of the occupants and especially the posting of the servants are exactly noted. He makes the sharpest possible inspection of the dress of all persons entering or leaving the house, observing what jewelry is worn and what is probably left in the chambers.

Ordinarily this "second-story worker" or "climber" is accompanied by a confederate pal, who helps in the work of spying and location and stands by as a watcher to warn his comrade of any signs of discovery or danger. These robbers find their favorite "marks" in fashionable watering places among the hotels and lodging houses and in the fine residences in the suburbs of cities. Sometimes they select a chain of "marks" near together and make what they call a "circuit" at one swoop, carrying away their booty and delivering it by previous arrangement to some confederate "fence" or receiver of stolen goods. If they are seized or in danger of arrest, these robbers will usually show fight and are to be feared, for they commonly go armed and will shoot if cornered. But when the chance is open, they prefer running to facing any encounter.

They are expert judges of the solidity of plate and settings and the value of jewels. Usually they break precious stones out of their settings in robbing a chamber, or as soon as possible after escaping, in order to reduce the risk of detection. It is almost impossible to identify loose stones, and the robbers can dispose of them to dealers to better advantage than they can obtain from pawnbrokers by the pledges of jewelry. Whenever practicable, their stolen goods are marketed through a fence or dealer "who stands for stuff" in the lingo of the craft.

One of the most noted of this class of robbers was David Mooney, (Little Dave) who, under this familiar title and various false names, was a marked man in the principal cities of the country twenty years ago. He was uncommonly adroit and daring in his attempts and generally lucky in his escapes, although he was caught and sent to Sing Sing for a term of two years in 1874, upon conviction for burglary. In

February, 1880, in company with his pal, Edmond Lavoiye, alias Charles E. Marshall, he broke into the house of a Boston banker by climbing up the veranda and carried off bonds, stocks and jewelry to the amount of $14,000.

On the very next night he killed his pal in a Florence Street lodging house and fled from the city. It was reported, with probable truth, that the murder was the outcome of a quarrel between the partners on the score of a valuable pair of diamond earrings, the fruit of a joint raid, which Marshall, or "Frenchy" Lavoiye, had presented to his mistress, a well known woman of the town.

When the dead body of Lavoiye was found, a scrap of paper was lying beside it carrying this rudely scrawled message, "Dear John, I am sick of Life. Please forgive me. I remain yours, Marshall." It was supposed by the murderer that this scrawl would be accepted as a certificate of suicide, but he was mistaken. When arrested, Mooney denied, at first, all knowledge of the murder, but later confessed that he had shot Lavoiye in self defense, as he claimed, as his pal was on the point of shooting at him. Unfortunately for the credibility of this story, it appeared that one arm of Lavoiye had been paralyzed for years; and the pistol which so terrified "Little Dave" was found in his paralyzed hand where it had clearly been placed to justify the pretence of suicide—the first invention of his murderer. Upon this evidence and the further proof that Lavoiye could not possibly have shot himself in the places in which he was wounded, the jury found Mooney guilty of murder in the second degree and sentenced him to the Massachusetts State Prison for life in September, 1881. His portrait, as a representative "second story" man, is given on our illustrative page.

Another of these nimble robbers was James Gleason whose portrait fitly accompanies that of "Little Dave." Gleason made his first notable mark about fifteen years ago in a series of robberies in the suburbs of Boston, in company with his "pal," familiarly known as "Dutch Charley." These two rascals made a circuit of entries into the residences of well-to-do people, without any other instruments than a ladder and a chisel. One house in the Highlands was entered, while the family was at church, by prying up a small rear window with a narrow mortising chisel. After a hasty search of the house the thieves went out through the front door with a bundle of silverware and jewelry valued at three hundred dollars. Unfortunately for the rogues, they were reckless in pawning their plunder, and both were arrested by the Boston detectives. In the house of one, the blade of a chisel was found that exactly fitted the marks in the windows of the residences that had been robbed, and the handle of this cheap working tool was afterwards found in the house of the other thief. Dutch Charley was wearing a gold watch and chain when arrested, as well as a handsome overcoat that belonged to another man; but Gleason was more cautious and had none of the stolen property on his person or in his room, though he kept the chisel handle which proved to be weighty evidence against him. Valuable deposits made by these thieves were later unearthed and both were sent to the State Prison for long terms. Gleason was arrested in New Jersey, soon after his discharge, for a like offence, and is now serving out another sentence of five years in prison.

To guard against the raids of these "climbers," the windows of second floor rooms should always be fastened securely during the early evening hours, in the absence of the occupants, for the robbers rarely risk an entrance by breaking the glass or window catch. Like attention should be paid to the fastening of the front door, for the thieves frequently steal up stairs or down through this door. During the dinner hour a servant should always be kept as a watcher on the second floor, for this hour in the evening, in the fall of the year, is the time commonly chosen for making these raids in the dark. Valuable jewelry should always be locked up at this time in

DAVID MOONEY.

JAMES GLEASON.

EDWARD WILLIAMS.

WALTER EVANS.

some secret place of deposit and preferably in a small, strong safe. Attention to these precautions will certainly prevent many heavy losses that will otherwise be suffered.

The "flat worker" is a cunning thief who usually makes his own skeleton keys to fit any ordinary lock. He watches sharply the habits of the occupants of a flat and lies in wait to rob when no one is at home. Having gained an entrance by a skeleton key or jimmy, he locks the front door and opens a line of escape through a back door or window. His favorite selection for a raid is in the topmost flat of a house; as from this place of vantage he can overlook approach or attack, and run off, if hard pressed, over the roof to an adjoining building and down through the scuttle, air well, or fire escape.

He is constantly on the lookout for a vacant building in a row of houses of the better class, that will serve as a lurking place from which he can pass out through a scuttle over the roofs of the neighboring houses until he finds an unfastened skylight or one that can be easily opened. Perched on the roof, he watches for a chance to slip down unobserved into an attic or the upper hall of an apartment house, where he may find unlocked rooms or gain an entry with skeleton keys. His descent is commonly made when the inmates of a house are at dinner on the street or basement floor, or when they are temporarily absent. This method of theft is as crafty as it is common, for, if the thief is discovered, he has a way of escape open through the skylight over the roofs to the place from which he set out. These sly descents of the "flat worker" may usually be prevented, if uniform care is taken to provide strong fastenings for skylights or scuttles and to see that they are well secured when the upper floors of a house are temporarily vacated.

The ordinary thief of this class seeks chiefly for money, silver forks and spoons, watches and jewelry, and rarely cumbers himself with the theft of clothing or articles that he cannot slip into his pockets. In his ransacking he is even more destructive than the "climber," ripping open bureau drawers one after another with his chisel or jimmy, and flinging their contents in heaps on the beds or floor. As his marks are commonly the residences of people of moderate incomes, his prizes are correspondingly less than those of the "climber." His booty may be pledged piecemeal to pawnbrokers or, for greater safety, melted and sold to jewellers and others using gold and silver bullion.

Robbers of this class are usually young men between eighteen and thirty years of age, of fair appearance and address. They are generally recruited from the ranks of the wayward and unruly boys whose parents are careless, intemperate or pinched by poverty. These boys bitterly feel the lack of clothes and money to gratify their appetites for tobacco and liquor or amusements, and are inclined to take the shortest cut to these prizes, which is open to them. They spend their plunder, as the "climbers" do, in all kinds of dissipation and are especially fond of frequenting opium joints. Many of the wrecks known as opium fiends are thieves of this description.

A fairly typical portrait of one of this class is given in our picture of Edward Williams, alias "Ellicott," alias "Morris," who persisted in naming himself "John Doe" when he was arrested by the Boston police three years ago. He was a graduate from the Baltimore House of Refuge and the Maryland Penitentiary, and distinguished as an exceedingly adroit plunderer in his special line. Stolen goods were traced to his hands, and, when arrested, a quantity of broken jewelry and bric-a-brac of various kinds was found in his room at a fashionable Boston hotel. He was convicted of breaking and entering hotel flats in Boston and the larceny of a large amount of jewelry. For these offences he was sentenced to a term of five years in the state prison.

For safeguards against these "flat workers" there is first the evident need of employing watchful and trustworthy janitors. Doors should be fitted with Yale locks or others which will defy the skeleton key instead of ordinary mortise locks which can be readily picked. It is no less essential to make a back door secure than it is to fasten the front, but, strangely enough, this provision is too often overlooked. If jewels or money are left in a flat, they should be locked in safes or put in hiding places that will be likely to escape the search of the thieves, which is almost always hasty and superficial. Sometimes an apparent carelessness or oddity of choice is really a shrewd one, as in the case of the woman who put her jewels in a common cream jug on a top shelf of her china closet, where they escaped a raid that sacked every bureau drawer and trunk in her flat.

The "house sneak" is the nimble rogue who slips into hall ways and carries off coats, cloaks, hats, canes and umbrellas, that chance to be within reach on stands and racks. Sometimes he works systematically as the "boarding-house sneak" who hires a room of some imprudent landlady and watches his opportunity to rob in the chambers of the house, or to carry off spoons, forks, clothes and any other light articles that fall in his way. These thieves are often of insinuating manners and neatly dressed, and it is necessary to enjoin the invariable demand of satisfactory references before letting rooms to plausible strangers. If coat racks are placed in the halls, there should always be a servant in waiting to watch persons entering at meal hours and especially at dinner in the early evening. This is the favorite time of the day for the depredations of these sneak thieves, and the stationing of a servant on the hall floor is an almost indispensable precaution, as many a worried boarding-house keeper will bear witness, after her costly experience in buying new coats and hats for her boarders. The hotels, also, should warn their waiters and servants to keep a sharp lookout for these thieves who make a practice of stealing coats from the racks in the halls and even from dining rooms which they enter as guests. A common trick is the substitution of a cheap old coat for one of the best on the rack, and guests should contribute to strengthen the watch by keeping an eye on their overcoats as well as on the bills of fare.

Far above all these house-breakers and sneak thieves, in his own esteem and in point of offence, is the night raider or professional burglar who makes the dwelling house his mark. These robbers almost always go armed with revolvers and other weapons, and will fire or strike desperately to effect an escape or even, at times, to reach their booty. They travel in pairs usually, sometimes taking a "kid" or young boy with them to crawl through narrow openings and unbolt doors, as Oliver Twist was employed by the ruffian Sikes and his comrade, Crackit. There are instances also where a father has trained his son in this apprenticeship to burglary and the two have worked together for years until both were caught and imprisoned, as was lately the fate of the notorious "Jim" Mains and his boy.

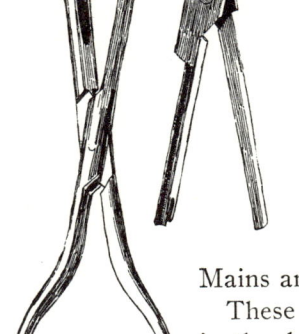

KEY NIPPERS.

These burglars make their approach to a house in the dead of the night, very noiselessly, wearing shoes with rubber or cork soles, and seeking an entrance at some weakly guarded place which is usually marked in advance. With a prod of a jimmy they will pry off a window catch or open the fastening by sliding a thin blade between the sashes. If this is difficult, for any reason, it is an easy thing to cut out a pane with a diamond, while the glass is held by a slip of stiff cloth or paper glued to the outside face. After a pane is cut and taken out dexterously, it is only the work of a moment to insert a hand and open the window. If a key is, by chance, left in the door, it can readily be turned from the outside by the aid of a pair of key nippers, as shown in the drawing here given. When there is no key in the door, the lock can sometimes be opened by the skeleton keys which every experienced burglar carries and knows how to use expertly.

After a door or window is thus stealthily opened, the burglar thrusts his head in cautiously and surveys his line of advance before going further. This first peep tries the nerves more sharply than any other step in the rogue's march of burglary, as old robbers report, and it is a welcome relief to the most reckless burglar when he feels that his head is safe from instant attack. It is a common saying of these raiders that they can enter any place into which they can stick their heads, but they are more wary than rats in their dread of a trap or surprise.

KEY NIPPERS IN OPERATION.

Most burglars are content with ranging over the lower floor and plundering the side-boards, closets and tables, or, in rare cases, taking pictures or other bulky articles of unusual value. Frequently they take their time in this course of inspection, apparently well assured that nobody will disturb their freedom of choice, and they will coolly proceed to make a meal leisurely upon any delicacy in the cupboards and to open bottles of wine with a prodigal hand.

They are expert judges of the character of any silver or gold plate which they find, and turn up their noses at plated goods, no matter how finely made, for they are only looking for "solid stuff." One of the surest, though rather too costly, ways of determining the real bullion value of a basket of plate is to leave it in a place where a burglar will be sure to pass upon it if he calls. Every thing that a burglar prizes enough to steal comes under the head of "swag," which may be carried off in coat pockets or in bundles well wrapped up or even in light wagons when the burglars are traveling about from one country town to another. Sometimes the plunder is hastily buried for the time in the neighborhood of the house, to be recovered later when the scent of the robbery has grown cold, and sometimes it is taken to a confederate or fence who contrives to hide and market it by degrees.

The value of booty carried off in one of these burglaries or in a series of them often mounts up far into the thousands, as was signally revealed in the case of the burglar, Barrett, a year or two ago, where the goods recovered by the police comprised almost every description of fine silverware, china, and bric-a-brac, together with costly furs and other articles worth not less than twenty-five thousand dollars. It took hours to unpack these goods from the trunks and boxes in which they were stored, and yet this extraordinary collection was only a fraction of the amount of the plunder of this one operator; for stocks and bonds representing more than two hundred thousand dollars were also found by the police in the house of Barrett's receiver, Chaffey, and fully half as much more was known to have been burned on the morning of his arrest.

The night raider usually prefers the field of plunder, offered in suburban towns and the suburbs of cities where the police patrols have long routes, and the robber can lie in ambush and watch the passing of the officer. Watering places and other fashionable summer resorts are also favorite marks for him, and he is always discriminating in his selection of residences of the best class for attack. When he is particularly daring or desperate, he will not confine his search for plunder to the lower floor, but will crawl up stairs stealthily or enter through a second floor window and rob the bed rooms.

It is in these ventures, as a rule, that hand to hand grapples and perilous encounters occur, for the robbers who keep to the lower floor have usually an open way of escape when a house is aroused, and are not forced to fight to save themselves from capture. The burglars who take these risks are almost invariably armed, and it should be needless to remark that any one who tries to arrest them should be a brave man, well armed and prepared to shoot at sight.

In the winter of 1887, two of these reckless burglars broke into the house of a well-known insurance man in Chelsea, Mass., at three o'clock in the morning. Some slight noise aroused the master of the house, who thought that one of his children might be sick and needing help. So he opened his chamber door and saw a big man, a few feet away, with a dark lantern in his hand, and another man coming up the hall stairs. Without an instant's hesitation he sprang upon the one nearest him and tried to throw the robber over the banister of the hallway. He was entirely unarmed and in his night dress and physically no match for the burly burglar. While the two men were struggling in this desperate wrestle, the burglar's "pal," on the stairs, fired at the man of the house and the bullet went through his hand, breaking his grip on the man with the lantern. Both of the burglars then ran down stairs and out through the front door, hotly pursued by the wounded man in spite of two more shots that whizzed back past his head. The burglars got off with some silverware and the coat and hat of the master of the house, in spite of his extraordinary demonstration of pluck. In imitating his method of capturing burglars, the prudent householder will not go bare-handed into the arms of two desperadoes.

These robbers were members of the notorious Albany Street or Evans gang, the largest troop of its kind that ever infested the city of Boston. Originally the gang was composed of thirty-seven members, whose accomplishments ranged from petty larceny to highway robbery. They had regular meetings ten years ago in which their garrotings, burglaries, and petty thefts were planned; and their schemes were so artfully laid and executed that it was exceedingly difficult to secure evidence and convictions, when any of the gang were arrested. Still, they were so sharply pursued by the Boston detectives that most of them were lodged in prison for one offence or another, after months of persistent hunting; but it seemed impossible to bring any charge home to the leader. When Boston grew too hot for his comfort, he went into retirement in some out-of-the-way place, but he never failed to keep in touch with every member of his gang, in jail or out. When the prison doors were opened, the discharged convict ran straight to him, like a chicken to a clucking hen, and, within a week, was taking part in some new raid or larceny.

In carrying through the principal burglaries it was common practice for men of this gang to blacken their faces with burnt cork or to use the cover of a black mask, sometimes wrapping towels about their heads in the fashion of turbans. Many of them were escaped or discharged convicts of the worst class, and the terror that their raids excited was amply justified.

Finally, in the winter of 1888, Walter Evans and his chief confederates were captured at one swoop, and the dreaded gang was completely broken up. One of the chief members of this gang was shot in the leg by one of his own pals in a drunken quarrel, and taken to the city hospital, where he was recognized and arrested for a garroting assault. Evans and another notorious housebreaker, Richard Drohan, were arrested, a day or two later, with four of their "pals," all members of the same gang, in their lodging house on Albany Street, where they had rented the upper floor. All these robbers were armed and tried to draw their revolvers, but the dash of the police threw them down before they could fire.

In the lower oven of a stove in their rooms three jimmies were found, and, under the ice chest, a heap of false keys, key nippers, drills and a bit-stock. Between the mattresses of the beds, silverware and bric-a-brac of all kinds were concealed, and a thorough search of the rooms unearthed a French clock, a gold-headed umbrella, and bangles, breastpins, rings, forks and spoons enough to stock a small jeweller's store.

Drohan had already been four times in the Massachusetts House of Correction and twice in state prison, and Evans had served two terms of five years in state prison for housebreaking and larceny. Both were sentenced to a term of twenty years in the Massachusetts State Prison. Four years later, Drohan cut four bars of the window of his cell with a saw fashioned out of a clock spring, and, one morning early in March, climbed out of the window with his room-mate, dropped to the prison yard, scaled the outer wall by the aid of a rope and hook, and escaped. Within a month, however, he was re-arrested in New York with his companion, and disarmed after a sharp struggle before they could use their revolvers. He is now serving out his sentence in prison in company with Evans. Their portraits are given as typical houseburglars and probably the most dangerous of the Albany Street gang.

One of the worst and most formidable gangs of houseburglars that has ever infested this country was known as the "Johnny Dobbs" gang, whose headquarters were in a New York saloon on the corner of Washington and Canal Streets. Some twenty years ago this gang was a terror to every householder in the suburban towns around New York, for their descents were the boldest and most ruffianly ever known in that region. Residence after residence was broken into by this gang, usually masked and always heavily armed. The wealthy country gentlemen and their families were straightway bound and gagged, and the houses were then leisurely plundered. Even an armed watchman was no sufficient safeguard, for these burglars had the nerve to storm a railroad depot, knock down the watchman, blow open the safe and drive off with their booty.

Michael or "Pugsey" Hurley was one of the shooting stars of this notorious gang which was finally broken up by the police of New York in the summer of 1874. Hurley was sent to the state prison for twenty years. In the spring of 1876 and again in the following year, he made desperate efforts to escape, but was stopped by his guards. Then he feigned insanity and was transferred to an asylum attached to another prison. After a few weeks in this asylum he made another dash for liberty, only to be captured by his vigilant watchers. The apparent intelligence which he showed in his scheme of escape made his captors doubt his insanity, and he was reëxamined and sent back to prison as a cured convict.

After several more attempts at escape, his perseverance was rewarded in 1882. By the help of confederates outside of the jail, he cut through the roof of his prison and ran off safely, but was recaptured six months later by the New York police and sent back to serve out his sentence. He was discharged, in 1886, in season to attend the hundredth anniversary of the town of Bennington, Vt., where he was arrested for pocket picking during the unveiling of the centennial monument. Unfortunately the police of the town were not aware of his distinction both as a house and jail breaker, and he was locked up in the county jail with his "pal," another notorious New York thief, masquerading, like him, under a false name. The robbers were confined in separate cells, but they soon contrived to let themselves out with a saw which Hurley made from a common case knife. Then they released another prisoner and broke out of the jail, leaving a wreck behind them.

About a year later "Pugsey" was arrested in Boston while "piping off" one of the leading jewelry stores and identified as one of a gang which had been robbing banks and houses in Springfield, Mass. When his arm was bared for inspection, an eagle and star in India ink were shown, and the prisoner did not further persist in denying that he was the burglar Hurley. He was taken to Bennington by the sheriff of that town and sent to prison for larceny for one year. Since his discharge he has been repeatedly arrested in company with other notorious burglars, and in September, 1895, his gang broke into the postoffice in Duboistown, Pa., and blew open the safe. The noise of the explosion alarmed the neighborhood, and a number of the townspeople gave chase to the burglars. Hurley was shot by his pursuers and captured. He was promptly convicted in the United States court in Philadelphia, and sent to the penitentiary for five years.

Edward C. Smith, alias Charles Daily, a Cuban negro, who can fairly claim a place beside the white men who have been selected as representative house-breakers. He is certainly one of the boldest and most desperate criminals in America, and his face is a speaking image of his character.

At the time of his first arrest, many years ago, for breaking and entering a dwelling house, he effected one of the most impudent and startling escapes ever made from a police court. He had temporarily been left in charge of the clerk of the court who was busily writing, while the judge was questioning the prisoner. Smith begged for the return of enough money to buy tobacco, and the indulgent judge had given him sixty-five cents and was stooping for a piece of memorandum paper when the bold negro made a long reach over the desk, caught up his own loaded revolver, and held it directly in the face of the judge as his honor looked up. "If you stir," he remarked coolly, "I'll shoot the life out of you!" The judge had no weapon. Even his seal and inkstand were buried under the papers of his desk. He could only sit dazed while the negro stepped back toward a window. The court room was on a second floor, but there was a shed roof which could be reached by a bold leap. This was taken by Smith, after driving back the clerk of the court who had started up to follow him, and the prisoner then ran off before an alarm could be given. He was later captured, however, by the police and, upon conviction for breaking and entering, sentenced to the state prison for eight years, in June, 1881.

Immediately upon his discharge from prison he was convicted of larceny and sentenced to the House of Correction for a year. As soon as he was released, he undertook a series of burglaries in the suburbs of Boston, aggravated by a murderous assault upon a coachman who attempted to capture him. He was arrested upon suspicion of these burglaries in June, 1890, by Boston detectives and temporarily shut up in a cell at police headquarters. His cell was secured by a large brass padlock, and the cell room separated from the rest of the basement by a heavy iron door which was always locked when prisoners were in the cells.

Smith's supper was brought to him from a neighboring restaurant, and, while eating this meal, he contrived to secrete a knife and fork, unnoticed by the guard who removed the dishes. Five minutes before midnight, his cell was examined by a patrolman. The padlock was secure and the prisoner apparently asleep in his bunk. Twenty minutes later, the night watchman at the new court-house saw a colored man scale the iron fence beside the entrance to headquarters, run across the square in front, jump into a trench along the new court-house building and run crouching through the trench toward the farther side of the square. He gave the alarm, and the cell room at headquarters was instantly inspected. Smith's cell was empty, the door open, and the padlock lying on the floor.

The burglar had first attempted to pick the padlock with his fork, by bending one of the prongs into a hook. Failing in this, he broke off the blade of the knife and succeeded in starting off the brass face of the lock with the wedge of the knife stub. Then he broke off the iron bale of the bucket in his cell, and with this rude lever forced away the face of the lock. To spring the catch and open the door was the work

RICHARD DROHAN.

MICHAEL HURLEY.

EDWARD C. SMITH.

WILLIAM BARRETT.

of a moment. He was free from his cell but still shut up in the main cell room. He did not try the lock on the room door, but put a table under the narrow window, and, by using his really wonderful strength, forced off the iron grating. It was astonishing that a man of his bulk could squeeze through a passage so small, but he succeeded in crawling through and scaling the iron fence. For nearly a month he enjoyed his liberty, but he was recaptured in July by Boston officers in Portland, Maine, and sentenced to state prison, upon a series of convictions, for an aggregate term of eleven years.

There could be no mistaking of the character of such burglars as Evans, Hurley and Smith. All three bear the stamp of the hardened criminal so plainly on their faces, that any masquerade on their part as respectable citizens would not impose on the most verdant countrymen. Even a child who met one of them in a lonely lane would scamper off with trembling legs, and every householder who saw one of them lurking about his home would fasten every window catch and door bolt with redoubled precaution, and slumber with one eye open if he slept at all. These ill-featured convicts undoubtedly represent the boldest and most reckless class of house-breakers; but a portrait no less typical is given in the picture of William Barrett, now serving out a life sentence in the Massachusetts state prison for the murder of a farmer, after breaking into his house.

There is nothing particularly repulsive or threatening in the face of this burglar, who indeed succeeded in leading a double life for many years, perhaps hoodwinking his wife as completely as he did his common acquaintances. He came of a good English family and learned the trades of a machinist and wood carver, from a natural aptitude for the industrial arts rather than from any pinch of necessity. When he was about twenty-five years old he came to this country and, for a time, went into business as a taxidermist in Detroit. There he met and married an attractive American girl of excellent education and character, who made herself greatly helpful to him when he drifted into the business of a horse dealer after his removal to Chicago. He also set up an electrotyping plant, but was burned out by the great Chicago fire and forced to return to Detroit where he made another start as a taxidermist with remarkable success. He often went as far as California to buy skins, and some of his work was so finely done that he found a ready sale for it abroad as well as in this country.

But he grew weary of this occupation and went to New York with his wife to open a private stable and indulge his taste for the breeding and handling of fine horses. By the death of a rich uncle in England, he came into possession of a large legacy and for several years he lived idly and comfortably in London with his wife. He was not only a fine judge of a horse but a fine rider as well, though in this accomplishment he was excelled by his wife, who was accounted one of the finest equestrians in London and won a medal from the hands of the Princess of Wales for an exhibit of hurdle riding.

This easy kind of living was apparently very congenial to Barrett, but his uncle's bequest ran through his fingers in a few years and he determined to return to America and try his hand again as a horse dealer. He made his residence first in Boston, but, as the east winds were too harsh for his wife's delicate lungs, he removed to Newport and afterwards to New York. Wherever he went, he lived in elegant style and was apparently earning a large yearly income by his business as a horse dealer and breeder. It was a regret to his wife, however, that the demands of his business compelled him to spend so much of his time in Boston, though she claims to have had no suspicion that he was much more deeply engrossed in burglary than horse-breeding. It is fair to him to note that he grudged no pains or expense for the comfort of his wife; and, at least once a week, he would tear himself away from the distraction of house-breaking to ride with her in Central

Park. This companionship and horse-back exercise were an unfailing pleasure to her and usually of marked profit to him, for he could sell at a fancy price the horses which his wife showed off so admirably.

While he was thus posing as a busy horse dealer, the otherwise devoted husband was swinging around in a circle of burglaries through the suburbs of Boston and the neighboring towns. In New York he was living in an expensive and richly furnished uptown flat, but in Boston he rented two small rooms in an unfashionable quarter of the city, where his passing to and fro would attract little notice. As the occupant of these rooms he was known as Mr. Bassett, for he dropped his real name when he first came to Boston, and nobody identified the coarsely dressed horse dealer of Eliot Street with the polite husband of the fashionable Mrs. Barrett of Central Park.

For a number of years Barrett pursued his burglaries with extraordinary craft and fortune. He had no comrade and, for a long time, no confidant. His first undertakings were very cautiously conducted, with long intervals between the acts, but later, when flushed with success, he made raids that plundered a series of "marks" in quick succession. He stole into sleeping chambers, as well as into parlors and dining rooms, and showed a remarkable instinct or information in reaching the secret places for the deposit of jewelry and other valuables. He was an expert judge of plate and nothing but solid ware of the best quality was put in his "swag" bag. His plunder soon mounted high up in the thousands, and the whole circle of suburban residents was plagued and startled.

The police of the towns made every effort to track the burglar and ward off his assaults, but his movements were so sly and his appearance so inoffensive that he slipped through their hands. It was impossible to trace him either by the usual trail of stolen articles from "fences" or from pawnbrokers, for he was too wary to market any of his plunder in a condition that could be recognized. He broke the diamonds and other gems out of their settings, and used to delight his wife with the frequent gifts of unset jewels, which she sent to jewellers to set to her taste. Some of the finest jewelry and bric-a-brac he hid for years in secret places of storage, and invariably melted up the heavy plate before offering it for sale to the purchasers of gold and silver bullion. He was cautious also in suspending his raids, after getting a heap of plunder, and pushing his legitimate business as a horse dealer until the hunt for the burglar had been abandoned as hopeless.

Finally, however, even his extraordinary wiliness failed to cover his tracks. On a night in May, 1894, he set out from his quarters in Boston upon another raid. His selected mark was the house of a well-to-do farmer in Weston, Mass. There were no near neighbors and the approach to the house was not difficult.

Barrett took off his shoes at a spot by the roadside, a few hundred yards from the place, and put on a new pair of "sneakers." Then he crept up to the back of the house, carrying his dark lantern and jimmy. The doors and windows were fastened, but he easily pried up a sash with his jimmy and crawled into the kitchen. From the kitchen he made his way stealthily through the house to the farmer's bedroom without finding anything of value. In moving about in the bedroom he made some little noise which awakened the sleeper, who cried out instantly. At the first alarm Barrett jumped out through a window and was off like a flash. He was chased by the farmer and others of the town's people, but he was too fleet to be overtaken. Still the pursuers did not give up the chase, and, in the early morning, the farmer and his brother came upon a man who was building a fire in the woods near the Cherry Brook station on the line of the Massachusetts Central railroad.

After some questioning of the man, the brothers were convinced that he was the burglar of whom they were in search and called upon him to go back to the town with them. He refused sullenly and when the former sprang forward to seize him, he drew his revolver and fired three shots in quick succession, one of which wounded his captor mortally. Still the plucky farmer clung to him and threw him down to the ground, but, a moment later, fell dying beside him. Before the murderer could escape, the brother pounced upon him and held him in spite of his struggles until help came and the stranger was carried back by a strong escort to Weston. He was identified in the county jail as William Barrett, alias Bassett, and, in the following November, he was tried and convicted of murder in the second degree. For this crime he is now serving out a sentence for life in the Massachusetts state prison.

Upon the search of his rooms, many burglar tools were found together with a crucible in which the stolen plate was melted to bullion. Little of his plunder was recovered until his blundering agent, James Chaffey, was arrested for offering for sale a portion of a very valuable collection of rare postage stamps which had been stolen from a Boston banker nine years before. Oddly enough, the dealer, to whom the stamps were offered, was the same man who had originally mounted the collection and sold it to the banker. Upon Chaffey's arrest with this positive evidence against him, he sought to clear himself by a pretence of ignorance and the delivery to the police of a great quantity of stolen goods of extraordinary value as we have before noted.

The display and identification of these treasures caused a sensation that will long be remembered in Boston, for more than a hundred families of high social distinction recognized and recovered heirlooms and other dearly prized valuables which they had lost all hope of seeing again. These were part of the proceeds of the host of burglaries committed by Barrett, in a criminal career that is almost unique in its length and accomplishments.

William Barrett is surely one of the most remarkable burglars of this or any other country, but even his sensational career is pale in color compared with that of "Gentleman George," which leaps beyond the farthest strain of any hack writer of lurid fiction.

"Gentleman George," or George A. Ellwood, is probably an assumed name of the desperado from Denver, Colorado, who reached the top notch of ill-fame ten years ago as the most impudent and reckless burglar in America.

In 1883, Ellwood and two companions attempted to rob the "Pike" Flats in New York City, but were foiled by a brave woman who was the tenant of a suite on the fourth floor. Just before daybreak she heard the grating of a key in the lock of her bedroom, and made up her mind instantly to face the burglars. So she slipped quietly out of bed, taking a pistol from under her pillow, and crossed the room to the door. Meanwhile she heard the bolt spring back and, after an instant of waiting, she flung open the door and stepped into the doorway. Two men were standing close to her in the hall and another was crouching at the head of the stairs a few yards away. She fired a shot, at sight, at the nearest man and saw him stagger, but his comrades quickly dragged him down stairs and out of the house before the alarm was spread. On the stairs there was a trail of blood and an embroidered handkerchief stained with blood, but no other trace of the burglars could be found.

This was an unpromising start for "Gentleman George," but he soon turned the balance against him in a series of raids that sacked many of the finest residences in St. Paul, St. Louis, Milwaukee, Cleveland, Detroit and Toledo. He and his "pals" wore masks and literally stormed the houses in their burglaries, compelling both men and women to give up their valuables by threats of murder backed with pointed revolvers. Sometimes they drove the terrified householders to set out a feast for them in the dining rooms before they departed. They stripped the rings from the fingers of shrinking women with brutal violence, and made men sign checks as ransoms when the plunder in sight was too little for their greed. One morning in Detroit, "Gentleman George" and his favorite partner, "Joe" Whalen, met a householder coming into his yard as they were passing out of his front door, and actually seized and robbed him on his own porch before he could give an alarm.

In August, 1885, these two burglars broke into a house in Toledo, and fired several shots at the servants who were aroused to defend the family. Then they retreated sullenly and leisurely. A pursuing policeman came up with them and ordered Ellwood to show the contents of a bag in his hand. "Gentleman George" replied gruffly: "Take it and see for yourself!" The officer took the bag to a lamp near by and, while he was opening it, Ellwood shot him in the back and escaped.

For this burglary and assault he was arrested some weeks later in New York, and delivered to the authorities in Toledo, where he was tried and sentenced to a term of ten years in the Ohio state prison. He broke out of jail before the expiration of his sentence and made his escape in a driving snow storm, at the cost of the loss of two of his toes, which were frozen. After some months of hiding he broke into a house in Hartford, Connecticut, in the winter of 1892, and was shot while escaping. He took refuge in the city hospital of Worcester, Mass., where he was identified by Boston detectives and taken to Providence, upon his recovery, to stand trial on a charge of burglary in that city. In this robbery he had engaged single-handed, carrying off money, diamonds and silverware, and terrorizing the family into submission with the threat of his loaded revolver.

At the close of his trial upon this charge, this hardened ruffian, oddly styled "Gentleman George," was asked what he had to say before sentence was passed upon him. In reply he produced a roll of manuscript and read a vilely scurrilous review of his trial, closing with curses for the mother who gave him birth and the hand that fed him as a child. Then he raved insanely cursing God, the court and all the world; declaring that he should be a devil from that day whose sole aim would be "the annihilation of mankind."

He was sentenced to a term of twenty-five years in the state prison, but, six months after his entrance, he was shot dead in a murderous assault upon one of the deputy wardens. "Gentleman George" had planned an escape with another prisoner, who abandoned him when the fight with the guards began. Ellwood battered the warden fearfully with a heavy iron tool handle and hammer, but the plucky guard blocked the way until, in self-defence, he drew his revolver and killed the most desperate burglar whose life story is written in our criminal records. Although he has passed away, members of his old gangs are still infesting our cities, and he is here described as the most striking figure representing this type of burglars.

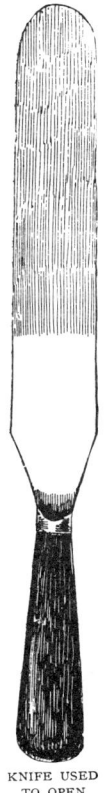

KNIFE USED TO OPEN WINDOW FASTENINGS.

All possible care should be taken by householders to impede and prevent the assaults of these burglars, though fortunately few house-breakers at large to-day are so utterly reckless and fierce as the notorious convicts whose portraits illustrate this chapter. One simple and excellent precaution is to have two locks on a house door, one of which is invisible from the outside. In place of common mortise locks, Yale locks or others of like design should be used, which cannot be picked by ordinary skeleton keys or readily unscrewed from place. Window catches should be of patterns that cannot be turned by the simple insertion of a knife blade between the sashes, and strong shutters should be provided for all windows on the lower floors. If a house is to be closed for the summer or for any length of time, the police should be promptly and invariably notified.

In country residences, especially, a watchdog on the lower floor of a house is an excellent safeguard, and the dog should be so placed that he cannot readily be decoyed away or killed.

It is further of particular importance to keep a sharp watch upon men of suspicious appearance loitering about a house or calling at the door upon various pretexts; and, in any such event, notice should be given to the police and the usual precautions doubled for the next week.

It is, of course, impracticable to note every desirable caution, but householders may readily amplify these suggestions to cover any individual case.

A SLIPPERY AND SUBTLE KNAVE.

IN November, 1888, two men called at a machine shop in Toronto, Canada, to order a cane of a peculiar design. When it was completed, it appeared to be only a fine, straight, stout bamboo stick, nicely polished and fitted with an ivory handle. It was encircled with a heavy band of solid silver, an inch and a half in width, and tipped with a heavy brass ferrule. Nobody who saw it in the hand of a man of fashion would suppose it to be anything more than an elegant walking stick. But, before the cane was ready for delivery, the two men, who left the order for it, were arrested by Toronto detectives for swindling a wealthy Scotch tourist who had accommodated his engaging acquaintances by cashing a worthless check. In tracing the movements of the two swindlers the trail ran into the machine shop where the detectives found the cane and examined it closely.

Upon unscrewing the tip of the ferrule, the secret of the cane was disclosed. There were two narrow pieces of steel, like tweezers, in the hollow centre of the cane. The silver ring near the handle was made to slide down, and its movement pushed out and opened the steel slips. Upon the release of the ring it was pushed back to place by a hidden spring, and its return shut and drew back the tweezers. A little experimenting showed that a parcel of bank notes, or anything that could be nipped by the steel slips, might be picked up with this cane from a point several feet away. This, indeed, was the actual design of the stick, an unpatented improvement on the long wire hook, an instrument which has raked off hundreds of thousands of dollars from the desks of cashiers and paying tellers. It was ascertained that another cane of the same pattern had been

A SLIPPERY AND SUBTLE KNAVE.   121

made by another firm in the same city for the same men, a month before. This was paid for and carried away and it may be still in circulation, for its capture has not been reported. In the hands of such eminent practitioners as the men who were arrested in Toronto, its working value would be thoroughly tested in a year or two.

The urbane customers who ordered these canes were highly indignant when they were arrested, but they failed to convince the Toronto police that they were the victims of a deplorable mistake on the part of the swindled tourist. The elder of the two was a stout man, nearly sixty years of age, of dignified presence and refined manners, who would readily pass for a well-to-do merchant or manufacturer. His companion was still on the sunny side of forty, a well knit, good-looking man, somewhat over five feet eight inches in height and of notably graceful carriage. He wore a full brown beard and mustache, fashionably trimmed in accord with his claim to be a gentleman whose sole labor was the killing of time. Both men were dressed from top to toe in clothes of the finest material and latest cut.

What a shock it was to their numerous acquaintances in the Canadian hotels when it was learned by pushing inquiry that these elegant tourists, Mr. Henry Hunter and Mr. William Alexander, were two of the most dexterous and notorious "bank sneaks" in all America! The younger of the two was Horace Hovan, alias "Little Horace," and his dignified companion with the fine Roman nose, strong, square chin and mutton chop whiskers, was Walter Sheridan, alias Stewart, Ralston, Holcomb, Stanton, Keene and a string of other personages longer than the line of Banquo.

What is a "bank sneak" does any one ask? A "bank sneak" is a thief who fills the gap between a burglar and a forger. He does not seek or dare to break through walls or blow open safes. He lacks the craft of a forger or he does not choose to face the penalty for counterfeiting. So he flits from bank to bank as a shoplifter from store to store, watching for a chance to steal from desks, counters, or open safes, anything in the form of money or valuable securities that he can lay his hands upon. He is to be distinguished from the thief in the store as a rascal of higher degree and accomplishment. The shoplifter is content to purloin any small thing that can be covertly snatched. The "bank sneak" aims to get thousands of dollars by a single, sly scoop and commonly forms and carries out an artful plan of theft with the help of two or three confederates. He is what Michael Cassio was falsely called: "A slippery and subtle knave, a finder out of occasions."

To avert suspicion these thieves imitate, as closely as possible, the dress and general appearance of the ordinary customers of the banks in which they are seeking for plunder. In cities they aim to pass for well-to-do business men or club men, or the clerks of brokers and bankers; and the counterfeit would usually pass current in any city where the thieves were not well known. In country towns they become counterfeit farmers and so put on the character and coloring of every community with which they mingle, with the art of accomplished actors. The prime essential for the success of their schemes is an opportunity for a sly entrance behind the bank counters or for a grab through a window or other opening. This is usually effected by some device, distracting the attention of the bank officials or securing the temporary absence of one or more of them or hoodwinking them in some way.

The two sneaks who were arrested in Toronto for swindling the Scotch tourist were remarkably expert in every trick of their craft and contrived for years to elude conviction for their frauds and larcenies, by using confederates as cat's-paws to execute their schemes and providing every cover for themselves which slyness and money could procure. They were permitted to give bail in Toronto and leave the city, well pleased to escape for the amount of their forfeited bail. Next month, Hovan was caught again in an attempt to rob a bank in Denver, Colorado,

THE BANK SNEAK.

in company with his confederate, Sheridan. Hovan was captured while sneaking out of the vault of the bank, but Sheridan, who was standing outside, slipped away unsuspected, although his face was afterwards recalled and identified. Although Hovan was literally caught in the sneak act, he did not lose his invincible impudence; and his protestations and explanations were so plausible that he would probably have obtained a discharge if he had not been identified. Notwithstanding this identification, he was again permitted to give bail which he was only too willing to forfeit.

It may properly be observed that the requirement of a few hundred dollars in the form of cash bail from bank sneaks of the class of Sheridan and Hovan, is scarcely more than a petty fine, in its practical effect, which these criminals pay nonchalantly as merely an incidental expense attendant upon their career of plunder. Certainly, bail should be fixed at amounts commensurate with the real gravity and danger of larcenies of this description, if the men under arrest are to be suffered to give bail at all. Forfeiting, or "jumping," bail may be said to be the regular practice of these "bank sneaks" whenever this privilege is open to them and they have the money to put up for the opportunity of running away.

Sheridan's schemes and methods of theft and fraud were so varied and far-reaching that the plunder obtained by the gangs which he led, for a score of years, amounted to hundreds of dollars. He took the lion's share of this booty himself, and he was so exceptionally close-fisted and saving for one of his class that his stolen fortune lasted till near the end of his life. He was one of the most versatile of character actors in impersonations and disguises, and his shifts were so artful that he escaped conviction until his arrest in New York in 1876 upon the charge of uttering one hundred and fifty forged bonds of the New York, Buffalo and Erie railroad.

At the time of his arrest he was, as usual, elegantly dressed and wore a long, full, reddish-colored beard. To confuse the witnesses against him, he succeeded in changing his fine clothes in the prison box for the rags of a tramp, and hacked his beard off roughly with a jack-knife. While he was confined in the Tombs, awaiting his trial, he further altered his appearance by eating soap until his portly figure was changed to a thin, sickly shadow of the well-fed broker, Ralston, whom he had impersonated. He dyed his hair with coffee grounds and clipped and twisted it so that he looked, in his rags, like a wretched, half-witted tramp. But all his arts as a masquerader failed to break the effect of his positive identification by William A. Pinkerton, and he was convicted and sentenced to Sing Sing for a term of five years. By maintaining his pretence of illness, he succeeded in shortening his term, and, when he was discharged, he was thought to be tottering on the edge of the grave. As soon as he was out of prison and had no occasion to eat soap, his health came back with such rapidity that he was able to rob jewelry firms in New York and Philadelphia in the course of a few months. He was so well known by this time, however, and so closely watched that he could not conceal his identity and evade conviction as he had been able to do in former years. So, after serving short terms in the Pennsylvania and Missouri penitentiaries for larceny, he concluded to leave this country for a while and try his hand in Europe with a gang of forgers.

In 1886 he was arrested in Portugal for uttering forged Bank of England notes, in company with another criminal of high degree, and both were convicted; but their pretences were so plausible and affecting that the jury specially recommended them to mercy, and the presiding judge let them off with a sentence of eighteen months in the house of correction in Oporto. Upon his discharge from the Portuguese prison he came back to this country stealthily and, under the name of Walter Stuart, invested his stolen money in Colorado lands, and engaged in the business of market gardening on a large scale for the supply of the Denver market. This venture would probably have been profitable, but the comparatively slow returns of legitimate business did not satisfy Sheridan, and he embarked in mining speculations which swallowed up his fortune. Finally, he undertook to "jump" a mine and was driven off by the honest miners of the camp. After this failure of his schemes he drifted back to his old line of swindling and thieving, and joined Hovan and others in a circuit of performances, including those given in Toronto and Denver, as before detailed. His former luck or peculiar adroitness was apparently lacking, for he slid down hill to the point of utter destitution, and he was a sinking wreck when he was arrested in Montreal, in January, 1890, on the charge of vagrancy. When he stood before the judge to hear his sentence, the miserable man sobbed like a child and begged for pity. But the judge knew his record and sent him to jail for six months at hard labor. On the fifth day after his sentence was pronounced, Sheridan died in prison. In talents, education and resources, he was the foremost "bank sneak" of the country, as his remarkable career attests, but, with all his accomplishments, he died a pauper and a felon. Those who are tempted to dabble in crime by glittering seductions may profit by this unvarnished object lesson.

Sheridan's companion in Montreal, at the time of his arrest, was another notable American thief, Alonzo Henn, alias "Henry Morton," and commonly called "Dutch Alonzo." This rogue had been in the habit of attending all the important conventions and other large public meetings in the United States, which he was able to reach, and his face had come to be so familiar to the American detectives that he concluded to change his field of operation. He had won the reputation of having picked more pockets successfully than any other thief in the United States before crossing the Atlantic to try his hand as a "bank sneak." In the fall of 1887 he made a flying trip to Europe in company with two other notorious "bank sneaks," "Billy" Burke and Charles Allen; but this gang came to grief in Geneva, Switzerland, where all three were arrested for the larceny of a bag containing $16,000, which they stole from a bank messenger. The stolen bag was carried off and buried, but it was later unearthed by an honest countryman who turned it over to the police. Burke and Allen were sent to prison for this theft, but "Dutch Alonzo" contrived to escape and made his way back to this country in time to join Sheridan in his visit to Montreal. He was sent to prison with Sheridan as a vagabond, and served out his sentence. After his discharge he went to Europe and has since been haunting foreign banks particularly. He was arrested in Hamburg, in the fall of 1895, in company with another notorious American "bank sneak," George H. Evans, alias "Kid Miller," alias "Lady Hand George," whose portrait is fitly placed with his on a representative page.

Sheridan's former and favorite companion, Horace Hovan, was another apt adjutant of this master of the arts of thieving. He began the noteworthy part of his career by the theft of $20,000 from the vault of a bank in Halifax, Nova Scotia, in 1876, and slipped through every mesh of the law until he was arrested and convicted in 1881 for robbing the safe of a Philadelphia stock broker. After serving part of his term of sentence of three years and a half in the state prison, he was pardoned for the sake of some testimony which he professed to be able to give in regard to two important robberies. His evidence proved to be of no value, and he was free to start again in life as a "bank sneak."

He was almost as shifty in his disguises as his comrade, Sheridan, and he had the advantage, over this accomplished actor, of possessing a brother Robert, who resembled him so closely that it was hard to distinguish one from the other. This duplicate of himself was of peculiar service to Little Horace, for he could use his brother from time to time to establish a perplexing alibi. One of his common practices was to register with his wife at a leading hotel and make the acquaintance of a num-

HORACE HOVAN.

FRANK BUCK.

GEORGE H. EVANS.

ALONZO HENN.

ber of guests. After a few days, Robert would turn up in the hotel, walk up and down the office, nodding familiarly to the guests, and finally order a carriage and drive out to some park with the wife of "Little Horace." Meanwhile that artful dodger would slip away unobserved and try his tricks of thieving in some bank or office. If any suspicion fell upon him from any quarter, he had an alibi already manufactured to order, and sustained by the evidence of the reputable witnesses who really mistook his brother for their polite acquaintance, Mr. Horace Hovan, or whatever his name for the time might be.

Besides his brother and Sheridan he had another favorite companion, Frank Buck, who was his confederate in the robbery of the Philadelphia broker's office, in 1881, and was sentenced with him to the state prison for the same term. After Buck's release, he joined Hovan in Washington and, soon after, the artful pair were arrested, while surveying a Boston bank, by Boston detectives and photographed for the Rogues' Gallery. Their portraits, as accomplished "bank sneaks" of the most dangerous class, appear on a representative page.

Soon after his trip to Denver with Sheridan, Hovan went abroad and has since been a plague to the people of Western Europe. Buck went to Europe a few months before Hovan, and shortly after his arrival, his gang robbed a jewelry store in Munchen, Bavaria, of jewels worth £50,000. He was arrested in London, a few months later, for this burglary, and sent to Bavaria for trial. Ten years in prison and ten years more of police surveillance and loss of civil rights was the sentence in his case.

The devices, commonly resorted to by Hovan, Burke, Henn and other thieves of their class in getting hold of money in banks and offices, may be best comprehended by the aid of illustrative examples.

A few minutes after twelve o'clock on a day early in May, 1895, the cashier of the First National Bank of Plainfield, New Jersey, went home to lunch, leaving the assistant-cashier, the book-keeper and a young assistant book-keeper in charge of the bank. It was the practice of the bank to have not less than three officials on duty during business hours. After the cashier's departure, the assistant book-keeper went into the directors' room to eat his lunch as he was accustomed to do. While he was eating lunch, a stranger, looking like a respectable countryman, entered the bank and went to the window of the paying teller. He made inquiry for the assistant book-keeper by name, and told the bank officials that a lame man, who was outside in a carriage, wanted to see him for a moment on business. The book-keeper courteously called his assistant and the young man went outside to the carriage. There he saw a man sitting in a road wagon, who was apparently crippled and wearing a green patch over one eye. The stranger told him that he wanted to have a job of book-keeping done and would like to talk it over a little. The young book-keeper politely excused himself, saying that he had no time to do any outside work and hastened back to his place behind the bank counter. Meanwhile the seeming countryman was making some natural inquiries which the other bank officers were answering; but, upon the return of the young book-keeper, the inquisitive stranger was apparently satisfied and left the bank, driving away with his lame friend in the wagon.

Nothing more was thought of this little incident until the cashier proceeded to count the money on hand at the closing of the bank for the day. Then he discovered that two packages of bills, amounting to $22,765, were missing and the police of New Jersey and New York were notified at once of the loss. It was only a small consolation to the bank directors to learn that their bank had been the victim of expert "bank sneaks." While the attention of the officers had been engaged by the pretended countryman and his lame friend, a third confederate had slipped in through a back door, opening into a back hallway, snatched up the parcels of money and slipped out again unobserved.

A SLIPPERY AND SUBTLE KNAVE.

Sometimes an unscrupulous woman is engaged as a confederate by "bank sneaks," and she may be the most artful member of the gang, as was notably shown in the case of the notorious Sophia Lyons whose career as a thief and adventuress is a marvel in its way. A few years ago, a circus company was parading through the streets of Mt. Sterling, Kentucky, and when it was passing the doors of the Traders' Deposit Bank, the officers and clerks clustered together at the front windows to see the procession. The cashier stood on the counter, and the paying teller was in the front row at a window. While watching the parade, the teller saw a woman on the sidewalk in front of the bank, giving a signal with her handkerchief. He turned instantly, just in time to see a man's head disappearing behind the cashier's desk, and sprang upon the intruder. The cashier jumped down from the counter, and both seized the sneak who was slipping away with more than four thousand dollars in his hands. The capture of the thief was of such absorbing interest that the teller did not think again of the woman with the handkerchief until she came boldly to the jail where the man was confined and asked to see him. Then she was recognized and held as an accomplice, and both were later identified by a Cincinnati detective as "Billy" Burke and "Sophie" Lyons, two bank sneaks of national reputation. Another member of the gang was arrested on the same day but discharged for lack of evidence sufficient to convict, and a fourth contrived to escape from the city after the arrest of his confederates.

"Sophie" Lyons had been a member of the Burke gang for many months, and had gained wide-spread notoriety by a series of performances of the carriage trick. Burke, or some other member of the gang, would drive up with her in a buggy to a bank in a country town, at dinner time, when only one or two clerks were on duty. Then he would go into the bank and address the clerk in charge, familiarly, as if he were a customer of unquestioned standing. "A lady in the buggy," he would say, "desired information about some stocks, but was, unfortunately, unable to leave her carriage, owing to her lameness." So the obliging clerk would often be persuaded to go out to see the lady and, while he was chatting with her, the gang would steal anything within reach in the bank.

This "invalid" trick has been worn threadbare by repetition but it cannot yet be said to be completely exploded, for thefts by this device still seem to be practicable in country towns. The application of this distracting game is not confined to banks, for the expert "bank sneak" is not above extending his thefts to the offices of express companies and others handling large amounts of money. A gas company of this state was robbed some years ago, in this way, by notorious "bank sneaks," George Carson and "Rufe" Minor, assisted by a young woman of pleasing appearance who was subsequently identified as the versatile "Sophie" Lyons.

One of the two clerks in the office had just gone to dinner when a carriage rolled up to the door, and a woman, elegantly dressed in black, alighted. Her face was hidden by a long black veil, but her bearing was so straightforward and businesslike, when she entered the office, that the clerk in charge had no hesitation in complying with her request that he should step outside for a moment to see an invalid in a carriage at the door, in regard to the gas fittings for his new house. He was detained in conversation for a moment, and when he turned away to reënter the office, the woman in black stood in the doorway. He politely escorted her to the carriage and opened the door. She stepped in with a few soft words of thanks and the driver immediately whipped up his horses and drove away. The obliging clerk returned to his desk, and it was some little time before he discovered that a roll of bills, amounting to over five hundred dollars, had been taken out of the money drawer. The theft and escape were so adroit that the sneak thieves were not captured till a month later, when Carson and Minor were arrested in Chicago by the police of

GEORGE CARSON.

RUFUS MINOR.

WILLIAM BURKE.

SIDNEY MANNING.

that city. Both were admitted to bail and both "jumped" their bail as a matter of course.

When it seems to be improbable that a clerk can be enticed away from his post, it is a common device to seek to engage the attention of all the bank officials on duty by the pretence of business, while one of the gang watches for an opportunity to slip through a door into the bank and steal a parcel of money or bonds from a desk or open safe. Every place that is used for the temporary deposit of money is carefully marked before hand by sharp spies, and the methods of business and habits of the clerks are noted as exactly as possible. Sometimes the face, figure and clothes of a clerk are closely counterfeited by one of the gang, who may in this way gain access to a desk and even to a safe or vault without arousing suspicion. There are known instances where packages of bonds and coupons have been picked up in the vaults of safety deposit companies by the sleight of hand of these sneak thieves, while depositors were examining the contents of their boxes.

Chauncey Johnson, who used to be one of the most expert "bank sneaks" in the world, was a master of arts in tricks of this kind. His businesslike manner and audacious nerve sustained him in a series of remarkable impositions. One of his earliest feats was the theft of bonds worth eighty-five thousand dollars from the hands of their owner, a lady of the best social standing in New York. The artful Johnson saw her taking the bonds from a bank to her carriage. He instantly exchanged his coat and hat for an ink-stained linen duster, thrust a pen behind his ear, and followed her to the street. As she was stepping into her carriage, this sneak, in the mask of a bank clerk, came up to her politely and told her that there was some mistake in recording her bonds. The cashier, as he said, desired to take their numbers once more, and this request was so courteously and naturally worded that the lady gave up her package to him unhesitatingly and promised to wait in her carriage until the bonds were returned. Johnson then went into one door of the bank hurriedly, and came out through another door. The lady waited for him patiently, but it is needless to observe that he never came back.

At another time this same character actor counterfeited the appearance of a cashier of a leading express company so exactly that he was able to slip in behind the desk of this officer, who had gone to lunch, and walk away with several thousand dollars, in the sight of all the clerks in the office. Once when a large city bank vault was open for the deposit of boxes from brokers' offices, Johnson made his way into the bank as a broker's clerk, hung up his cap with consummate coolness, stepped into the vault as if his right to enter was beyond all question, and walked out again bearing a box on his shoulders, containing bonds and other papers worth sixty thousand dollars. When a reward was offered for the return of some of this plunder, he personated an attorney representing the thief, and actually obtained the amount put up for the recovery of the stolen property.

One of his most remarkable thefts was effected by following the President of a national bank of New York, who was carrying a package of bonds amounting to $125,000. When the President entered his bank, he laid the package for a moment on his desk while he stepped to a closet to hang up his overcoat. As soon as his back was turned, Johnson snatched up the package and slipped away before the President discovered the theft.

Johnson can probably claim, with truth, that he has entered more banks than any other sneak thief, living or dead, and stolen a greater amount of money. He drew $37,810 in one lump from the Bank of New York by watching the movements of the bank messenger, who had the money in charge. When this messenger was called away for a moment to another part of the bank, he laid his small canvas bag, containing over thirty-seven thousand dollars, on an unoccupied desk. When he returned a few moments later, the bag was missing and so was

A SLIPPERY AND SUBTLE KNAVE.

Johnson, who had contrived to reach it and carry it off under his coat.

He served two terms of five years each in prison for burglary before entering upon his extraordinary career as a "bank" sneak. This discouragement seems to have led him to turn his hand to a line of theft for which his talents were peculiarly adapted. In the early years of his sly pursuit of plunder, he was comparatively awkward in his operations. He put a wire through the screen in the Bank of North America, thirty-five years ago, and dragged a roll of bills to the window; but he was not quick enough to elude the eyes of the bank clerks. The alarm was given and he was pursued and caught. He gave the name of G. W. Dusenberry and, under this alias, he was convicted and sent to prison for a year.

Upon his release he showed that he had gained experience enough to keep out of jail for more than seven years, although he was continually at work as a sneak thief. It was not until December, 1870, that his life of plundering was cut short by his arrest in the Fifth Avenue Hotel just as he was leaving with several valuable packages which he had stolen from the hotel safe. He was loitering near the cashier's desk when a guest came up to deposit for safe keeping a package which was said to be of great value. Johnson heard this imprudent remark and took the first opportunity to slip behind the counter. He was bareheaded and his movements were so exactly like those of a familiar clerk that he reached the safe unquestioned and took out the deposit, made a few moments before, as well as other packages. There were three clerks in the office, but no one of the three thought of stopping him and he had almost reached the door when he accidentally stumbled over a wastebasket and fell sprawling. This trip was fatal, for the noise alarmed the clerks, and Johnson was chased and captured before he could get away with his booty.

For this impudent theft he was sent to Sing Sing for ten years, and, since his discharge, he has been leading the life of a poor vagabond, hardly knowing where to lay his head from day to day, and turning his feeble hand to a succession of petty larcenies. This "bank sneak" of highest degree—who has made away with hundreds of thousands of dollars and would scarcely deign to stoop for a hundred-dollar bill if it were thrown at his feet—has been picking up an umbrella here and an overcoat there to pawn for a few sups of liquor or rolls of bread. For the past twenty-five years his most comfortable lodging has been in a prison cell, and no words can enforce the deterrent lesson of such a life as impressively as the sight of the wretched old man, friendless, hopeless and homeless. His latest theft was a fumbling effort to pick a pocketbook out of a shopping bag on the counter of a book store in New York City. When he saw that he was detected, he dropped the purse back into the bag, but he could not escape arrest and conviction. He pretended to be an unknown personage named George W. Brown, but his disguise was soon rubbed off, and he was sent for a year to Blackwell's Island, where he is now residing. An excellent likeness of this remarkable old man is given on one of our pages of typical portraits.

In most of our city banks in this country such barricades of heavy wooden counters and metal lattice work protect the paying and receiving tellers that theft by any stretch of arm is almost impracticable, and even the use of the wire hook is barred out. The "bank sneak" is obliged, therefore, to seek an entrance by the way of side or rear doors, if any are temporarily open or unguarded, or through a window under some pretence. So they have taken to the disguise of janitors and workmen employed about the building. No person should be suffered to put up a step ladder or any other perch along the side of a bank for the alleged purpose of washing windows or any other object, unless he is well known and authorized to do so. Every door should be securely fastened or continuously watched, if it is left unlocked for the admission of employees and persons having business to transact with the officers of the bank. No loophole should be left for the antiquated trick of engaging the attention of officers and clerks at the partition windows while a sly confederate slips in through a side or rear door. Special precautions should be taken to secure a constant watch whenever a procession of any kind is passing the doors of a bank, and it should be borne in mind that a circus parade is particularly relied upon to lure clerks away from their places and open chances for sneak thieving. What "Billy" Burke tried to do in the bank at Mt. Sterling has been done many times before and since.

When it seems hopeless to gain an entrance into a bank, the sneak will commonly resort to tricks for robbing the persons who are depositing or drawing money. A favorite trick is known as the "drop game." A few illustrations, furnished by some of the most expert thieves in the country, will show how this game is played.

In October, 1886, two well-dressed men entered the National Metropolitan Bank at Washington, D. C., while one of the depositors was busily engaged in counting over a roll of bills at a desk in the outer office. As the men passed by, one of them touched the depositor lightly on the shoulder—"You have dropped some of your bills!" he said, courteously pointing to a few on the floor at the foot of the desk. "Oh thank you!" said the depositor, stooping to pick up the bills. He found four one-dollar bills on the floor; but when he counted over again his money on the desk, seventy-one dollars were out of sight—and so were the polite strangers.

The next day a well-to-do brickmaker of Baltimore went into the Merchants National Bank of that city to cash a check for two hundred and sixty-eight dollars. He drew the money in bills and went to a desk opposite the window of the paying teller to count over the roll. As soon as he left the window, a man stepped up to ask for change in silver for a twenty-dollar bill. While he was engaging the attention of the teller, another man of fine appearance and suave address approached the brickmaker and courteously informed him that he had dropped several bills on the floor. When the brickmaker turned around and bent over to pick up the money, which was lying on the floor, the polite stranger reached over his head, grabbed a handful of bills from the pile on the desk and ran away.

Fortunately his proposed victim saw the trick in time to start off in hot pursuit, shouting "stop thief!" and caught the sneak in the doorway. After a short struggle he wrenched the handful of bills out of the grip of the thief, but was unable to stop him from escaping. The sneak ran off down the street, but a detective, who was watching the bank, captured him after a sharp run, and another detective collared his confederate at the window of the paying teller. Both of these thieves gave false names when arrested, but they were identified as two of the worst bank sneaks in the country, Joseph (Little Joe) McCluskey and John Burke. George Carson, another member of the same gang, was found in the room which Burke had taken in a fashionable hotel; but he was too drunk to take a hand in this particular "drop game" and was therefore able to escape conviction. The sneaks taken in the act were convicted and sent to the Maryland state penitentiary.

A trick akin to the "drop game" is the distraction of the attention of a messenger or customer just as he is on the point of making a deposit with the receiving teller. This was a favorite trick of the notorious bank sneak, "Billy" Burke, whose unsuccessful attempt to rob the bank in Mt. Sterling, Kentucky, has been before related. Burke ranks in his class with the foremost practitioners, and has repeatedly succeeded in performing this trick; but he failed in his latest recorded attempt, six years ago, when he undertook to rob a bank clerk, who was about to deposit a bag containing £5,000, in checks, notes and gold, in the City Bank of London. Burke's confederate touched the clerk on one arm and asked him a question while Burke slipped his hand into the bag which the clerk

AUGUSTUS RAYMOND.

WALLACE O'CONNOR.

JOSEPH KILLORAN.

CHAUNCEY JOHNSON.

A SLIPPERY AND SUBTLE KNAVE.

was carrying under the other arm. He was slyly extracting a case of money from the bag, when the clerk saw the theft and held the case fast. "Pardon me," said the suave sneak, "I thought it was my bag." This easy explanation failed to satisfy the bank clerk who called for help to catch the two sneaks. Both ran out of the bank, but were caught on the same day by the police with a third member of the gang, and all three were tried, convicted, and sentenced to prison for eighteen months.

Burke has earned the reputation of being one of the slyest and most ingratiating sneaks in America, and the gangs with which he has consorted from time to time have been the most artful and dangerous in this country. Leading figures in these associations of sneak thieves, besides those before noted, are Rufus ("Rufe") Minor, George ("Georgie") Carson. Joseph Killoran, alias "Joe Howard," Augustus ("Gus") Raymond, Sidney Manning, alias "Sid Yennie," William Maher, alias "Billy Marr," William Coleman and Wallace ("Wally") O'Connor. Their portraits are given as a representative exhibit of the thieves of their class.

"Rufe" Minor is a character not less remarkable than Sheridan or Johnson. His early education and associations were such as to give a refinement to his manners and conversation, that has been largely retained through the wreck of his later life. He is so fluent and fascinating in his talk that he has over and over again entertained sharp-witted clerks in our city banks, and allayed all suspicion while his confederates were engaged in taking impressions in wax of the wards of bank door locks and fitting false keys. Then with the help of his pals he has so engrossed the attention of the tellers and clerks that an opportunity was given to a sly sneak to creep into the bank and carry off packages of money or bonds. He is a master hand also in assuming disguises, and with the range of variations in the cut of his beard and the shape of his wigs, he has successfully counterfeited a long line of imaginary characters. He has probably been arrested a score of times in the last twenty years for taking part in a series of thefts and frauds, and his companions have been repeatedly convicted and sent to prison; but, by one shift or another, he has, generally, contrived to escape conviction although his character is so well known that he is constantly watched, or warned to leave, whenever he shows his head in one of our leading cities.

George Carson, who has been one of the most prominent members of the gangs associated with Minor, is also a man of good education and pleasing manners. His ingratiating powers have gained for him the title of "The Diplomat," in his profession and he has usually been employed in carrying on the conversations with the clerks while his confederates did the actual thieving. Like Minor, he has been so adroit in the employment of cat's-paws and in skirting the edge of danger that he contrived for years to escape conviction, although he was a notorious associate of the most crafty and active bank sneaks in this country. He was arrested, however, about nine years ago in Toronto for the robbery of a bank messenger, in company with the dangerous burglar, "Gentleman George," and sent to prison for seven years. Immediately after his discharge, he joined a gang of "bank sneaks" and burglars in a series of raids on postoffices, which will be subsequently described.

There is a certain exclusiveness in the associations of representative "bank sneaks." They do not fraternize with ordinary thieves, and no one who is of distinctly repulsive appearance will be admitted to membership in any prominent gang. There is no scruple on their part, however, against taking a hand in any kind of thieving or frauds, which is sufficiently tempting in its prospect of plunder. When the banks in any city appear to be too well guarded to afford an opening for their tricks, they will divert their attention to business offices or hotels or railway cars or any other places where thefts of money or jewelry are likely to be practicable. So sometimes the same men figure in our criminal records as "layers down" or the companions of forgers, thieves of watches and jewelry, "bunco men" or professional swindlers, and burglars even, as well as "bank sneaks." Augustus, better known as "Gussie" Raymond, is a rascal of this description, who has had a hand, from time to time, in almost every kind of swindling and thieving. One of his most notorious crimes was the robbery of a drummer for a jewelry firm, who was carrying a sample trunk from Boston to Worcester. Raymond followed his victim from a Boston hotel to the railway station, and contrived to replace the check of his trunk with another one, so that he was able to carry off the trunk to New York. After taking out nine thousand dollars' worth of jewelry, he filled the trunk with bricks and sent it to Baltimore. This impudent theft was finally traced to him and cost him a term of five years in state prison.

Favorite recruits for the fraternity of "bank sneaks" are drawn from the ranks of young men who have mingled more or less in fashionable society and have had some training in the offices of bankers and brokers. Some of these youths drift into habits of extravagance and dissipation that involve them in debt, and they may yield to suggestions to take part in schemes of fraud if they are craftily enticed by boon companions. Walter, alias "Wally," O'Connor is a young "bank sneak" of this class who found an expert guide and confederate in Joseph Killoran, alias "Joe Howard," one of the most wily thieves in this country. By the intercession of his friends, charges against him were more than once withdrawn, but he was finally convicted in 1892 of the robbery of a bank in Easton, Penn., and sent to the state prison for a term of three years and nine months.

Sidney Manning, alias "Sid Yennie," is another sneak of the same class and associated, like O'Connor, with Howard and Carson. He had some training in the banking business, first as messenger and afterwards as a clerk for a New York bank.

He slid down hill from gambling at race tracks into cheating at cards, swindling in bunco games, and stealing as a "bank sneak." Finally he ventured to try his hand in burglary, in coöperation with Carson, Killoran and two other notable thieves, Charles Allen and Harry Russell. This gang made a specialty of the robbery of postoffices, until it was broken up by the arrest of Howard, Allen and Russell, on May 1, 1895, and the subsequent capture of Carson and Yennie, in January, 1896. In the following July both Carson and Yennie were convicted of the robbery of the postoffice in Springfield, Illinois, and sent to the penitentiary for terms of five years each.

Joseph Killoran, alias "Joe Howard," Sheldon Hamilton, alias "Shell" Hamilton, William Maher, alias "Billy Marr," and William Coleman represent well the combination of "bank sneak" and burglar. All these have been associated with Shinburn, Cummings and other leading bank burglars in notable raids. Maher was sentenced in 1871 to imprisonment for ten years in the state prison in Trenton for the robbery of the Jamesburg (N. J.) bank, but he escaped, after serving a year, and eluded capture for six years. Then he was sent to prison to serve out his term. Upon his release he went to work again as a burglar and sneak thief, at first with the notorious "Dave" Cummings and later with "Billy" Coleman, another noted cracksman. In July, 1893, Maher and Coleman robbed the postoffice in Rochester, N. H., of several hundred dollars' worth of stamps. Maher engaged the attention of the postmaster by his inquiries while Coleman sneaked into the office and took the stamps from the safe. Fortunately, the postmaster saw Coleman coming out of the office and captured him after a short chase. He was sent to the state prison for three years, but Maher contrived to keep under cover until June, 1895, when he was arrested in New York and taken to New Hampshire for trial. His former companion, Coleman, who was then in prison, gave evidence against him, and Maher

WILLIAM MAHER.

WILLIAM COLEMAN.

PHILIP PHEARSON.

SHELDON HAMILTON.

A SLIPPERY AND SUBTLE KNAVE. 141

concluded to plead guilty in the hope of mitigating his sentence. He is serving out a term of two years and a half in the state prison.

Sheldon, commonly known as "Shell" Hamilton, has been a prominent member of notorious gangs of bank sneaks, burglars, forgers and counterfeiters, for the past thirty years. He was caught twenty years ago, in the act of fitting a key to the lock of a door of a savings bank in New London, Conn., while the clerks were at dinner. He is particularly expert in making and using false keys, but this lock was so hard to pick that he was still at work on it when the clerks came back. He served out a sentence of three years in the state prison for this attempt and since his discharge he has taken part in the operations of the most dangerous gangs infesting this country and Europe.

"Joe Howard," the last of this representative company of "bank sneaks," has been robbing banks and business offices for more than thirty years. In May, 1891, he joined his young friend, "Wallie" O'Connor in grand larceny in the Lewisburg National Bank of Lewisburg, Penn. Shortly afterward he turned his attention particularly to the robbery of postoffices, organizing a gang with Carson, Yennie, and two other professional bank sneaks, Russell and Allen. This gang succeeded in effecting a number of robberies, but was finally broken up as before noted. Killoran, Russell and Allen were confined, in advance of their trial, in Ludlow Street jail, in New York, but escaped on the Fourth of July, 1895, and succeeded in getting away to Europe.

The portraits of these representative criminals show the extent of the range in age and appearance of professional bank sneaks and our collection is well concluded by the photograph of Philip Phearson, one of the oldest and craftiest sneak thieves in this country. He is now a veteran too feeble and slow in his movements to compete with the younger men in his profession; but, in his prime, he was an accomplished "bank sneak" and pickpocket, as well as an expert "till-tapper." This latter distinction marks the sneak thieves who make a specialty of infesting stores and offices, with the design of stealing behind a counter or rail and filching from tills or money drawers while their confederates are distracting the attention of the cashiers and clerks.

We cannot emphasize too strongly the call for constant vigilance in foiling the crafty tricks of these sly rascals. The detectives on duty in the banking districts, known as "the bank squad," in our principal cities, are keeping the keenest possible watch upon these artful thieves, and doing all in their power to shut them out of the business centres. Known "bank sneaks" are arrested, at sight, whenever they are seen to be loitering about a bank or business office, and all persons whose appearance or actions arouse just suspicion are promptly and sharply called to account.

The detectives are instructed to pass through the banks daily and keep a sharp eye upon all strangers or persons who have no apparent business to transact. They are expected to become so well acquainted with the bank officers that they can be readily called upon for any service in the line of their duties. It is a part of their duty to guard bank messengers and other employees carrying money or other valuables from business offices to banks, or from bank to bank; and they are always ready to do any special escort service that may be required. In our larger cities, at the present time, this patrol is so efficient that many of the most dangerous "bank sneaks" have been driven from their field of plunder in this country, and have gone abroad to infest the cities of Europe, where they are not so well known to the police. This migration has unquestionably lessened the losses in this country, but it should not lead to any relaxation of vigilance in the guarding of our business centres.

The establishment of these guards has been of notable service in suppressing the plague of sneak theives, but their watchfulness should be earnestly seconded by proper care and precaution on the part of business men generally. No person depositing or receiving money should exhibit it, in the sight of strangers, except in so far as is inevitable·in the passing between the bank teller and himself. When the messengers of brokers and bankers are carrying any considerable amount of money or securities to and fro from the vaults of banks or trust companies, these valuables should always be conveyed in strong, locked boxes, and it is always preferable to employ two messengers in this service. The doubling of the guard reduces the risk of loss far more than one-half, for "bank sneaks" rarely venture to meddle with such a convoy by trick or assault, and it is not likely that two messengers will be careless at the same moment of time. The like precaution should be taken in conveying jewelry or other tempting valuables, and it may well be observed that the operations of "bank sneaks" have been largely diverted of late to the robbery of jewellers and their travelling agents. When transfers of great sums of money and securities are to be made, as in the case of the moving of a bank from one building to another, special guards of detectives and police can, and should always, be obtained.

THE STROKE OF THE QUILL.

IN one of the most fascinating of the romances of **Walter** Scott the story is told of an extraordinary passage at arms between King Richard of the Lion Heart and the Sultan, Saladin. The two monarchs met as host and guest in the course of a brief truce and Richard willingly gave a display of his surpassing strength at the request of his rival. Heaving

aloft with both hands his mighty sword, he swung it about his head as if it were of feather weight and brought it down with such resistless force that its tempered blade sheared in two the heavy iron handle of his mace and sunk deeply into a block of wood beneath. All the lookers on cried out in wonder and praise of the Titan's stroke of the *Melech Ric*.

Saladin's tribute was ungrudging as any to this demonstration of sheer strength which he could not hope to match. But when the haughty Richard asked him, in turn, for some exhibit of his own powers, the modest Saracen wound a veil lightly over his scimitar, and with a sidelong sweep cut the floating gauze apart.

Such a contrast there is between the smashing onset of the

THE STROKE OF THE QUILL.

burglar, breaking his way with sledge hammer and dynamite into a steel-bound treasure vault, and the insidious craft of the forger, wiling the hidden gold from its strongholds with the flourish of a pen or the scratch of a graving tool. In actual encounter on the field it is probable that the huge sword of the English king was more terrible and deadly than the sultan's potent scimitar, but no ponderous pick or sledge has ever struck such dread into the heart of a banker as the tiny crow quill or slender etching tool in the hand of an expert counterfeiter. Here the pen is indeed mightier than any weapon that ever cut or battered its way into a treasure chamber.

Forgery as a means of obtaining money, credit or other valuable considerations under false pretences is doubtless almost as old as the invention of letters. It is morally certain, in fact, that the claim of the mythical Cadmus, if there ever was a Cadmus, was founded on the counterfeit of another's handiwork. As soon as an honest man learned how to write, in the old days, he found to his sorrow that a rascal was able to use a stylus or some other lettering tool as well as himself. The keeper of his strong box was cheated by a forged draft on a tablet of wax, thousands of years ago, just as the honest man's banker to-day honors a counterfeit check upon his deposit. As civilization advanced and papyrus and parchment succeeded the sheet of wax or the plate of metal, the goose quill served the forger as well as the other scribes who turned their hands to honest work.

Hand in hand with forgery on parchment and paper came on the sister art of the fabrication of counterfeit coins. When a people advanced in civilization beyond the primitive exchange by barter, coins of various denominations were cut by dies or cast in molds and their composition was determined by sovereign authority. The high privilege of producing and issuing these coins was sometimes granted to favored persons or associations by the sovereign, but it was usually jealously guarded as an exclusive prerogative of the crown. Thus, in

England, under the old common law and many statutes, counterfeiting was accounted an act of treason, but, in spite of this sovereign reservation and prohibition, the making of counterfeit coins has been defiantly pursued by the irrepressible rascal.

In strict technical usage counterfeiting may be defined as the crime of making or uttering false or fictitious coins and paper money. The counterfeiting of genuine signatures on a bank note printed from a genuine plate makes what is termed a forged note. If the signatures on such a note are those of fictitious persons, the note is classed as "spurious." In this restricted usage only those notes are "counterfeit" which are printed from false plates. But, in the terms of our statute laws, forging and counterfeiting are alike applied to the manufacture of every description of false coin, paper money, and every obligation or security of the government.

It is not within the plan of our present work to trace in detail the progressive stages in the rise of counterfeiting or to show at length the successive expedients to which nations and individuals have been driven in the provision of safeguards. It is sufficient to note that the plague has been afflicting and portentous since the beginning of history in defiance of every measure of suppression and defence. Even the extreme penalty of death, imposed by ancient laws for this offence, did not deter bold rascals from the execution of their frauds and the modern laws of nations, punishing the counterfeiter by penal servitude for life or for a long term of years, have not been better respected.

In measures of precaution, as well as in the severity of punishment, extraordinary efforts have been put forth to stop the progress of counterfeiting. With the advance of the arts, the device and execution of coins have been carried to a pitch of elaboration and finish that can only be attained by the combination of rare artistic skill and costly machinery. The operation of all government mints is guarded with the most rigid regulations for secrecy and security. The theft of a die or its duplication for any private and criminal use is now almost impracticable. In the design and execution of national paper money and bonds the provision of safeguards is even more complex and complete. Paper of peculiar composition, texture and finish is made to order for government use under conditions that are designed to exclude the possibility of any theft or unauthorized disposal of any part of the product. Only artists of the foremost professional standing are engaged in the preparation of the plates for printing this paper, and the lettering, scroll work, figure drawing and all other embellishments are purposely so elaborate and artful that their exact imitation and reproduction are undertakings of great and constantly increasing difficulty. Scarcely less care is taken by banks, railway companies, and other corporations and business associations to defeat the schemes of the forger by the multiplication and perfection of safeguards. The art of the engraver, the paper maker, the ink manufacturer and the printer has been strained to raise insuperable blocks in the way of a counterfeiter, and all honest and faithful employees are continually vigilant in the detection and prevention of imposition. The regular police forces of the country and the secret service organization of the national government devote special attention to the stealthy workings of the forger and efficient private detective associations are also enlisted in securing protection for the business community.

Against this advancing array of defences the rascal has been striving with a fertility of resource and craft of operation that have found and penetrated every vulnerable point in the barrier. When he has been foiled in any line of imposition by some new invention or safeguard, he has turned his hand to the removal of the block with redoubled energy and determination. If the block proved to be too much for his wits and persistence, he has slipped around it in some way or turned aside to some other avenue still open to him.

Silver coin has been the kind most commonly counterfeited from the earliest times, because of the comparative ease of production of a passable counterfeit and because its circulation was very largely from hand to hand among the classes of people who were least wary and competent in the detection of fraud. By far the greater part of the counterfeit silver coin has been cast in molds because this is the cheapest and easiest method of manufacture. Molded coin lacks the sharp and clear cut appearance of genuine coin struck from fine dies, and the lettering and line marks are usually so inferior that the counterfeit only escapes detection through hasty handling. Coins struck from dies are far more dangerous counterfeits but, fortunately, the cost of making good dies is so large that this mode of counterfeiting has been greatly restricted and chiefly confined to the making of imitation gold coin.

In the earlier and cruder processes of counterfeiting, lead, type metal, zinc and brass—cheap and common metals and alloys—were most frequently used in the manufacture of base coin, but within the present century there has been a great advance in the science of composition and the quality of material. The invention of electroplating gave a notable impetus to the manufacture of counterfeit coins and made their detection far more difficult. One of the most dangerous counterfeit coins now in existence is a compound of antimony and lead very heavily electroplated with silver. The same process is applied to the making of imitation gold coin and some of the best executed counterfeit coins in this country are the gold ten dollar piece or eagle of 1858, and the half eagles of 1847, 1848, 1862 and 1869, which are made of platinum with a heavy plating of gold.

When the plated coin has been worn by use, its base material can readily be detected by the application of strong nitric acid. A drop of this acid will have no effect on a coin of standard gold or silver, but it visibly attacks the baser metals. It should be applied on the edge of the coin as that is the part most worn in handling. The United States mint test for proving gold is strong nitric acid, $6\frac{1}{2}$ drachms; muriatic acid, $\frac{1}{4}$ drachm or 15 drops; water, 5 drachms. For silver the mint test is 24 grains nitrate of silver, 30 drops nitric acid, 1 ounce water.

Perhaps even a more dangerous counterfeit than the electroplated coin has been produced by the use of considerable amounts of the precious metals in the spurious coins. This has been done in particular with marked ingenuity in the case of the counterfeit half eagles of 1844, 1881, and 1882. The gold bullion value in the counterfeit half eagle of 1844 is nearly four and one-half dollars, and there is an additional percentage of silver. The coin is only $1/_{10}$ of a grain lighter than the genuine, and is very closely alike in ring and coloring. It resists acid tests almost as well as genuine gold coin. The counterfeit gold pieces of 1881 and 1882 are almost equally perfect. They were struck from dies by the drop process and closely resemble genuine coins. They are composed of gold, silver, copper and platinum, and their weight does not differ more than three-tenths of a grain from that of the genuine half eagle. The actual bullion value of one of these counterfeit coins has been determined by assay to be four dollars and forty-three cents.

It is obvious that the keenest watchfulness and pursuit are requisite to prevent the imposition and circulation of such counterfeits, although the bulk of the counterfeit coins in existence is far less delusive. Comparatively few coins of this class will bear any close comparison with genuine coin of the same period and coinage. The impress, the size, the weight and the ring will be likely to differ appreciably and it is almost impracticable to produce coins of precisely the same weight, diameter and thickness without using the same exact composition. In examining a suspected coin, therefore, always note by comparison, if practicable, whether it exactly corresponds in these three points with a genuine coin of the same denomination and period.

With the exception of a small amount of the counterfeit gold coin, before noted, the only coins which will bear this test are the very dangerous counterfeit silver coins, lately issued, containing silver of the same weight and fineness as the silver in the genuine coins of the United States. This counterfeit is made practicable and profitable by the large difference now existing between the bullion and the legal tender value of our silver coins. The director of the United States mint has made special note, in his latest report, of the coinage and uttering of these counterfeits, and it is needless to observe that every effort will be made by our national government to detect and convict all persons engaged in issuing these coins.

There are several frauds in tampering with genuine coins, which appear to be foster brothers of counterfeiting. These are known as "sweating," "plugging" and "filling," and gold coins are the chief victims of these devices of abstracting some of the precious metal in circulation. "Sweating" is the removal of metal from the surface of a coin by an acid bath and, when this is done adroitly, a fraction of the weight is taken away without very marked damage to the appearance or ring of the coin. In "plugging" a coin, a fine hole is bored into the edge, preferably, and the gold dust from the hole replaced with some base metal. This filling is covered with a wash or light plating of gold, and the fraud is then difficult to detect in ordinary handling. "Filling" is done by sawing through the edge of a coin and dividing it into two parts which are scraped thin in the centre and lined with platinum or some composition whose weight is nearly equal to that of the gold abstracted. The clipping and filing of coins, as well as these more artful devices, were far more common a century ago than they are to-day, but the frauds are still prosecuted to some extent.

The counterfeiting of paper money has been prosecuted with even more ingenuity than the manufacture of spurious coins. The fine and complex engraving of the modern treasury notes of our own and other countries has been an almost insurmountable obstacle in the way of counterfeiting from the difficulty and expense of duplicating it exactly, but some expert counterfeiters have succeeded in engraving plates which were extraordinarily exact duplicates of the genuine ones. Poorly executed and cheap wood-cut reproductions are still used to a limited extent, as in the case of a recent counterfeit of the United States five dollar silver certificate, but the greater part of the counterfeits in circulation to-day has been produced by the photographic method in combination with pen and ink drawing or retouching. The combination of photography, engraving and pen and ink work has succeeded in fashioning some very deceptive and dangerous counterfeits, although, to an expert eye, the difference may usually be marked between the grayish, brown-black impress from the photographic process and the jet black ink used for genuine notes.

Up to the last thirty years the United States government relied almost wholly on the perfection of the engraving on its treasury notes as a security against imitation, and all such notes issued prior to 1869 were printed on plain bank note paper. Beginning with that year, however, all its issues have been printed on a fibre paper which is manufactured under special patent processes. This fibre paper has proved to be very difficult to imitate, especially as it has been prepared of late years, with two silk threads running lengthwise through the note.

The leading national banks of this country rival our government in the perfection of their issues of paper money, but the notes of many banks have been counterfeited with varying degrees of exactness. Not only paper money but checks, promisory notes, bills of exchange, bonds, certificates of stock, deeds, wills,—in short every written or printed instrument conveying property—have been the prey of the forger. The old common law definition of forgery was the fraudulent making or alteration of a writing to the prejudice of another man's right. Under repeated decisions of the courts it has been held that the fraudulent insertion or alteration, or even the erasure of a single letter, is an act of forgery.

The imperative call for the most stringent legislation and sleepless vigilance in the detection and suppression of forgery is, perhaps, most signally shown in the records and collections of the United States Treasury. It appears that the fifty-cent fractional currency, issued in the years of the War for the Union, was successfully counterfeited to the extent of many millions of dollars. When the distinctive fibre paper was adopted in 1869, it was supposed to be proof against any art of the counterfeiter but, before a year had elapsed, this presumption was fatally shattered by the craft of the remarkable forger, Thomas Ballard, an expert chemist, engraver and paper maker, who contrived to produce counterfeit treasury notes that were almost exact reproductions of the genuine legal tenders.

Ballard and others of his gang were captured in 1871, but he contrived to break out of jail and found a hiding place from which he continued to pour out his dangerous counterfeits. Two years after his escape the $500 treasury note was so artfully counterfeited in his workshop that the issue excited the gravest alarm in all banking circles and caused the treasury department to put forth its utmost exertion to trace out the counterfeiter. Its keen hunt was soon rewarded by the capture of Ballard in his lair in Buffalo, where he was, at the moment, actually engaged in producing a counterfeit, on a steel plate, of the five-dollar bill of the Bank of British North America. This work was designed to be his "chef-d'œuvre" and destined, as he vainly boasted, "to bankrupt all Canada." Fortunately for the Dominion and this country, as well, the career of this extraordinary counterfeiter was finally closed by his conviction and sentence to thirty years' imprisonment in the Albany penitentiary.

Charles Ulrich was only second to Ballard in art and accomplishments. He was a German by birth and, when he was scarcely more than a boy, he won the distinction in infamy of producing the best counterfeit Bank of England note ever made. This feat made Europe too hot for the sole of his foot and, in 1856, he was driven to fly to this country where he began his career in crime by "raising" genuine ten-dollar notes to hundred-dollar bills. This alteration was so artfully executed that a large amount of these forged bills was successfully uttered, and the forger went on to produce a still more elaborate counterfeit. The "raising" of notes was too tedious a process to content him; so he undertook to print hundred-dollar bills from his own counterfeit plates. For a number of years he succeeded in escaping arrest, while counterfeiting and uttering the notes of bank after bank with alarming perfection, but he was finally exposed and captured, in 1868, and sent to the penitentiary at Columbus, Ohio, for a term of twelve years.

The invention of the device of transforming small bills into large by cutting and pasting is credited to an uncommonly well-educated rascal, popularly known as "One Eyed Thompson." There is a series of bank notes in the government collection, which this artist "raised" by laboriously pasting large numbers over the small ones on the genuine bills. The same inventor led the way also in the manufacture of bills produced by cutting ten $10 bills into slips sufficient to make eleven counterfeit bills of the same denomination, when the pieces were pasted together.

Another inventor of the same class, John Peter McCartney, was the first to devise a process of removing the ink from genuine one-dollar bills by a chemical wash, so that he could obtain the government's own fibre paper for the manufacture of counterfeit bills of higher denominations. He made many hundred thousand dollars by this stretch of his criminal ingenuity, but he could not escape conviction, at last, and imprisonment for fifteen years at hard labor, as the outcome of his rascally invention.

Naturally the counterfeiting of a signature on a check or

draft has been one of the most frequent of forgeries because of its comparative simplicity and the extraordinary sum of money which may be obtained by a single successful imposition. Signatures have been imitated so exactly that they have been accepted unhesitatingly by paying tellers, who were experts in handwriting and perfectly familiar with every peculiarity of the genuine lettering. More than this, the counterfeits have been so perfect in some cases that the very men whose signatures were forged would not have doubted their genuineness, if it had not been for their positive knowledge that they had never signed the checks in question.

Sometimes this counterfeiting is done by an overlaying and tracing process which will produce an almost exact fac-simile. This is obviously an imposition which is cunningly calculated to cheat the handler of one of these checks in the ordinary course of business, but it can surely be detected by experts to-day with the aid of modern testing appliances. If the particular signature, which has been copied, can be secured for the purpose of comparison, the fraud may be easily exposed. No person ever writes his signature twice exactly alike; so, if two signatures are so written that one precisely accords with the other when placed upon it, one of the two is a traced counterfeit.

It is, further, well determined that no tracing with pen or pencil will show to an expert eye the same natural movement of the hand which appears in the original writing and this is true of any method of imitation by hand. In the deliberation necessary for exact tracing there is inevitably a cramping of the hand of the forger and a variation in the flow of the pen.

It may be supposed, erroneously, that a slow, awkward and trembling hand can be more readily counterfeited than a fine specimen of penmanship, but this is not the case. Expert forgers are necessarily artists in the use of the pen and really good penmen have an almost insuperable difficulty in feigning to be bad writers. The tendency to produce symmetrical tracing and natural curves is a second nature which cannot be readily overcome, as a leading authority on this subject has keenly observed. "The tremors of a simulating hand," says Persifor Frazer, an expert of the highest authority, "are never so numerous nor so fine as real tremors. Under a microscope the rhythmic lapses from perturbed writing and back remind one of the imitation of a drunken man in amateur theatricals."

Among the most common lapses of forgers is the proper union of the smaller letters which a good writer will unconsciously perform with address. The dash is apt to assume a graceful curve, the dot will usually appear in the place where the counterfeiter is accustomed to write it, and, if all these indications are lacking, there will usually be some betrayal in the crossing of the t, the shading of some of the lettters and the preservation of a straight line for the base line of the writing.

By the application of the microscope the most minute variations in the character of the writing can now be detected and recorded. Even a line half an inch in length may furnish a revelation of strong significance to an expert detector. And throughout the whole of the forgery will be visible what Mr. Frazer terms the tremor of fraud,—"that tremor and uncertainty which result from the slow motion of the pen over the paper, necessary to a hand unaccustomed to writing a signature, when all the minute details visible in that signature must be repeated."

When any writing or lettering has been removed by erasure or washing with chemical reagents, the fact can be determined by the fine microscopic, light and chemical processes now applicable, in spite of every device of concealment. The most minute difference can be distinguished in the ink employed from that used in the original writing and, if a line has been written over another of earlier date, the imposition can be exposed.

In view of the really admirable achievements of modern

science in provisions for the detection of forgery, it seems to be high time for the discontinuance of the ancient custom of calling upon alleged experts to give mere opinions, based on bare eyesight, in trials of forgery cases. Such snap judgments are always offset by a conflicting array of equally indecisive opinions or surmises. For positive determinations of frauds, weeks of laborious examination and a variety of tests may be required, and it is certain that no expert deserving the name will pass with assurance upon any case of supposed forgery without the application of all the tests needed.

Of course these elaborate tests cannot be applied in the ordinary handling of checks in business transactions, but there are simple precautions which can readily be taken.

A lithographic fac-simile can be distinguished from genuine writing by simply passing a finger lightly over the face of the copy which will be smoother than the lines made by a pen. This is easily done in the case of a signature on a check and every such draft should be keenly scanned to note the slightest indication of an erasure or a discoloration of the paper.

Before cashing checks or drafts offered by strangers, or by men whose character and standing are not well known, the drawer of the check should be called upon to certify the correctness of the amount and authorize its payment to the applicant. In these days of the telephone and telegraph, this precaution will involve only a slight delay, if the application is authorized, and the cost of this reference will not be grudged by any honest applicant. If there is any question of the financial standing of the maker of the check, the bank upon which it is drawn should also be called upon to give assurance of its payment, and this should be done invariably when the applicant wants his own check cashed. If this procedure was universally adopted by business men, there would certainly be a great diminution in the losses from forgery and imposition of worthless checks.

It is, however, necessary to add a word of warning in regard to the possible use of the telephone by forgers for the purpose of foiling this precaution of reference. There are known instances in which the presenters of forged checks and notes have previously given telephone messages to bank officers, in the name of the maker or endorser of the note or check. A bank in Albany, N. Y., was imposed upon a few years ago by this device and would have lost several thousand dollars if the cashier had not fortified his supposed assurance by calling upon the professed indorser of the note to certify once more to his signature. The reply was received in time to stop the payment of the check given for the note, and arrest the forger, a notorious "bunco man," John C. Johnson.

A trick even more artful than this has been devised by rogues who arrange to have confederates in the offices of the business men, whose names are forged, when the forged checks are presented at the banks. By some plea or pretence the confederates get the use of the telephones at the prearranged moment for the presentation of the checks, and coolly certify to their correctness when these bank officers make inquiry over the wires. This trick of impersonation and certification is obviously not less dangerous than impudent.

It should, further, be borne in mind that the pretended certification of checks is a common device of the swindlers and forgers who are travelling from city to city, through this country, to-day. Counterfeit certification stamps form part of their outfit, as has been shown in a number of recent arrests. The offer of a check, which appears to be a cashier's or a certified check, is, therefore, no sufficient assurance of payment.

Letters of introduction, or of application for the cashing of checks, are also frequently forged by the swindling adventurers. Sometimes these forgeries are made on an elaborate scale, and a number of letters,—purporting to be written by business firms of known standing or by public men of distinction,—are presented by some plausible impostor. On the strength of these introductions, the swindler will secure goods on credit, or loans, or accommodation in cashing drafts. Frequently these rascals impersonate business men, the agents or members of firms which they pretend to represent; and by this cheat they succeed in procuring the acceptance of checks and drafts through the high commercial rating of these firms. This swindle has victimized so many business men that it is necessary to urge particular caution in verifying these pretences of introduction and business connection.

The same caution applies also to the legion of swindles, in a smaller way, which are effected by ordering small lots of goods to be sent to a well-known address C. O. D. The swindler will meet the messenger, near the door of the house where the goods are to be delivered, and take the parcel out of his hands in exchange for a forged or worthless check. A still more artful device is employed by the swindlers who send forged letters to storekeepers, in the names of well known customers, asking the favor of the cashing of a check. The writers explain this call on the ground that their banks are closed for the day and they happen to need the cash for some special purpose. As the storekeeper desires to oblige a good customer, he is likely to grant the favor and receive a forged check in return. The messenger boy who will carry back the money, will be met by the swindler, who is lying in wait for him, and the storekeeper's money will soon be beyond recall. When such favors are granted, bitter experience has shown that a trustworthy clerk should be sent with the money to ensure its delivery to the proper hands.

A paying teller of long experience in a metropolitan bank has lately discussed the subject of the presentation of checks with apparent candor and point.

"The genuineness of a check," he observes, "is largely determined by the circumstances attending its presentation. By far the greater number come through the clearing house from other banks where they are deposited or cashed. As these banks guarantee their indorsements, the risk here is comparatively small.

"Those presented at the window are carefully scrutinized. Not only the handwriting but the character of the bearer, as well as the peculiarity of the customer's account, are taken into consideration. There is such a disposition with most bank accounts to run into grooves that anything out of the usual run is noted at once, familiarity with a dealer's habits frequently leading to the detection of irregularities.

"A man's bank account is a sort of index to his whole business. It shows with whom he is dealing, what are the sources of his income, and when and how he makes his payments. It reveals the amount of his personal expenditures, and whether he is a borrower or lender, rash or conservative; how much real estate he is holding, and what it costs him to carry it, almost everything, in short, concerning his financial affairs. Needless to add, the knowledge thus obtained is held sacred.

"Perfectly innocent persons are often induced to present bogus checks, and sometimes unconsciously give away the whole scheme. A boy used for this purpose is especially apt to blurt out the truth the very first thing and tell how a nice, pleasant man around the corner has given him a quarter to go and draw the money at the bank. It is hardly worth the while, in such instances, to give the money to the lad and follow him, as before that time the obliging man will generally have vanished.

"Many of the forgeries coming under my notice were committed by the sons of the men whose handwriting they copied. Sons, nephews, trusted clerks, they of a man's own household, are too often those upon whom suspicion rightly falls. Such cases seldom or never come to the knowledge of the public, and sometimes are not even known to the bank, the checks being quietly accepted by their reputed signers as regular charges against their accounts. Pathetic scenes are witnessed behind bank railings when the evidence of crime confronts both author and victim—blanched faces, trembling lips, shame and bitter tears, oftener from the wronged and innocent ones than from the culprit himself."

To these remarks one point of particular importance may properly be added and emphasized. Caution should be more universally taken in the introducing of acquaintances to banks for the purpose of opening accounts, and banks should exercise uniform care in obtaining satisfactory references before accepting deposits and issuing check books to slightly known persons.

It will be found in the great majority of instances that fraud has been successfully perpetrated from the neglect of such simple and easy precautions. It has been shown also that there should be no hasty assumption of invulnerability or of the sufficiency of safeguards against the snare of the forger. Even the greatest bank in the world may suffer by such a conceit as was signally illustrated in the celebrated case of the Bidwell forgeries.

Austin Bidwell, an American of plausible address, succeeded in opening an account with the Bank of England, twenty-five years ago, in the assumed name of Frederic Albert Warren. Bidwell and his associates had obtained nearly eighty thousand dollars by successful forgeries in Europe and they planned to use this booty as capital to establish their credit in London. Bidwell took rooms at one of the most expensive hotels and masqueraded for weeks as an American Monte Cristo. He was introduced to the Bank of England by the head of a firm of fashionable tailors who really knew nothing about him beyond the fact that he was a prodigal customer who asked no credit.

After his first deposit was made with the bank, he contrived to impress the managers with his apparent command of capital and the magnitude of his transactions by a series of open purchases and secret sales of a variety of securities, drawing heavily upon his account one day and replacing the draft on the next day. He was also a considerable dealer in good bills of exchange and acquired in this way an intimate acquaintance with the practice of the bank in discounting these bills.

At that time it was not the custom of this bank to send acceptances, offered for discount, to the acceptors for verification of signatures. Upon the lack of this precaution the gigantic forgery scheme of Austin Bidwell and his confederates was founded. He represented to the manager of the bank that he was about to engage in the manufacture of cars and other railway material on a very large scale and should send on his bills of exchange from Birmingham for discount. By this time, six months after his first introduction, he had so established his credit by his prepossessing bearing and the character of his transactions, that he had no difficulty in putting bills with forged acceptances through the bank to the extent of nearly a million pounds.

Flushed with success, the forgers grew careless if not reckless. Austin Bidwell went away with his young bride on a wedding journey through Spain to the West Indies. His brother George remained in England to forward the forged bills of exchange by mail and dispose of the proceeds. In the course of two months an enormous amount was presented and discounted and it was determined by the forgers to wind up their business and fly with their booty.

The actual work of forging the acceptances on the bills had been done by one of the confederates, George McDonald, in his apartments on St. James's Place, and the confederates met there for a final conference before leaving London. It chanced that a handful of unused bills remained among the papers which the forgers began to burn, and it was hastily agreed to renew the closed scheme of forgery by sending this last batch of bills through the mail for discount. This proved to be a fatal error from the point of view of the criminals, for the date of acceptance had been inadvertently omitted on one of these bills.

The deficient bill was discounted by the bank, but a messenger was sent with the bill to the London firm, whose acceptance was forged, to request the correction of what was supposed to be merely a clerical error. This presentation of the forged bill at once exposed the fraud and, when the alarm was given, the forgers in London had no time to effect an escape. After a few weeks of keen pursuit, two of the principals, George Bidwell and George McDonald, were captured and Austin Bidwell was keenly traced out and arrested shortly afterward by a member of the Pinkerton agency in Havana. Much credit is due to the efficient detective forces of Great Britain for their successful uncovering of the hidden tracks of these extraordinarily artful forgers, and the securing of the evidence which justified their conviction. Their trial in the Old Bailey Criminal Court in August, 1873, was the sensation of the week in London. The two Bidwells, McDonald, and a fourth confederate, Noyes, who was employed to draw out the proceeds of the discounted bills, were convicted of forgery and sentenced to penal servitude for life. These sentences were commuted by pardons, a few years ago, and both the Bidwells have since written and published interesting autobiographies.

Some points of signal importance and representative value are emphasized in this remarkable case. The introduction of "Frederic Albert Warren" by a business man who knew next to nothing about his character was the foundation of the fraud. The neglect to verify references and acceptances made the fraud practicable. The execution of the fraud in spite of all the array of artful preparation shows certain characteristic blundering. "It appears," remarks a keen observer of this class of fraud, "as if the forger's attention is so earnestly directed to overcoming the difficult parts of his task that he is apt to neglect simpler and more obvious parts." The omission of the essential date of acceptance on a bill of exchange caused the exposure of all the forgeries. The failure to destroy a piece of blotting paper bearing a clear imprint of the draft of

"F. A. Warren" for "Ten Thousand Pounds Sterling" furnished one of the most convincing links in the circumstantial evidence that secured the conviction of the forgers. It is by such palpable and characteristic slips that the wiliest rascals expose and convict themselves.

Apart from this propensity to blunder in the execution of their schemes, it is unquestionable that the leaders of the gangs of forgers, which have harassed our own and foreign countries during the present century, have been men of extraordinary ability in devising and executing plans of fraud. Henry Wade Wilkes; alias George Wilkes, alias Willis, was a typical figure of this class and the acknowledged head of a band of forgers and counterfeiters whose operations were on an international scale and, as a whole, more gigantic even than the fraud of the Bidwells. This gang varied in number from time to time in the execution of single schemes but it embraced, in the course of years, all the principal experts in their line in America and a number in Europe. Among these were Gottlieb Engle, Peter Burns, alias "James Joy Julius"; Albert Wilson, alias "Al" Wilson, alias "E. R. Marshall"; Charles Becker, Sheldon, better known as "Shell," Hamilton, Joseph Chapman, and last, not least, William E. Brockway.

The organization of this gang was typical in its enlistment of middlemen and other hands still lower in rank and in brains, who merely obeyed instructions and were never suffered to know the chiefs in command. The expert engraver or penman who executes the forgeries usually remains in strict privacy with a single manager or confidant or middleman who attends to the preparation for carrying out the fraud and engages the tools who do the detail work and are the ones most liable to suspicion and arrest. In the case of a notable imposition on a Lombard Street banker in London, in 1879, there were only three principals who were the real plotters and the subordinates employed never saw the directing head, Henry Wilkes.

Gottlieb Engle made three counterfeit drafts of a leading

New York banker upon his London agents in imitation of blanks and small genuine drafts procured by Wilkes and Burns. Then Wilkes bought a genuine draft for £2,000 upon the same agents, and his employees bought three drafts for a few pounds each at the same time. These small drafts were purchased in order to secure the numbers to put on the backs of the forged drafts which were otherwise complete. Wilkes and Burns took passage for England, as soon as these drafts were procured, and Wilkes transferred the numbers which they bore to the forged drafts. Before reaching London, Wilkes and Burns separated and went to different hotels with their wives. Then, within a day or two, Wilkes presented the genuine draft for £2,000 which was collected without delay. Two days later the three forged drafts amounting to £8,000 were also presented and collected by three persons engaged by Engle in New York, through a middleman, and directed by another middleman in London who received his orders from Wilkes through Burns.

All this complication and secrecy was probably required to reduce the risks of arrest or betrayal which would, otherwise, be incurred by the principals. The cat's-paws fled to the continent and thence to this country as soon as the forged drafts were cashed and their shares paid by the middleman, who turned over the balance for division to Wilkes and Burns. These chief partners remained in London apparently unconcerned for a week longer and then went to Paris where Burns took fine lodgings while Wilkes returned to this country leisurely by way of Havre.

For years the wary principals in the Wilkes gang succeeded in avoiding conviction, if not arrest, and, during their career, swindled bankers, brokers and other business men to an enormous extent, in the aggregate, with their counterfeit bank notes, bonds, income certificates, bills of exchange and forged drafts. Engle, Becker and Brockway were the chief operators in the production of the counterfeits with graving tools

ALBERT WILSON.

RICHARD O. DAVIS.

MAX STEELE.

CHARLES FISHER.

and pens, while Wilkes, Burns, Wilson and the rest were engaged in uttering the forged paper. The organization of this gang became well known to the American police and detective agencies, although its operations were so adroitly conducted that it was exceedingly difficult to secure evidence sufficient to convict the principals. Their movements were so closely watched, however, that any indication of the brewing of a new plot was instantly telegraphed to the police officials at the place or places threatened by the projected fraud. Still Wilkes and his immediate associates were so adroit and plausible that they were commonly able to obtain warning of the suspicion aroused against them in time to change or abandon their plans of imposition. In one notable instance the chief of police in a leading city of Europe was so impressed by the pleasing bearing of Wilkes, in the course of a call, that he imprudently showed to this crafty forger a cabled dispatch from New York warning him of the departure of the gang headed by the man who was, at that moment, admitted to his confidence.

Finally, however, the net for these forgers was drawn so tightly that the leader, Wilkes, and his comrade, Burns, were captured at Florence by the Italian police on Christmas Day, 1880, a few days after the arrest of their confederate, the notorious "Shell" Hamilton at Milan. To secure his release, Wilkes coldly betrayed his accomplices and made a full confession of the workings of his gang. When Burns learned of this treachery, he killed himself in his prison cell, leaving three alleged widows to wrangle over the fortune of $400,000 which he had amassed in his career as a forger.

Wilkes came back to America, after his discharge from his Italian prison, and patched up a reconciliation with one of his old confederates, "Joe" Elliott. With this colleague he made a tour through the United States from Albany to San Francisco, swindling the banks by "raised" drafts to the extent of $83,000. He was arrested on his return to New York but succeeded in escaping conviction and took refuge in Paris, where he spent every dollar of his stolen fortune in dissipation in less than two years.

When his money was gone he was obliged to leave France and made his way back to New York where he lived for four years by begging small loans or gifts from his former companions and acquaintances. He soon fell to the level of a common drunkard and tramp, and roamed through the city streets, dirty and slovenly, getting a dime, when he could, from every chance acquaintance, for rum and food, and finally getting kicked out of resorts where he used to throw money away by the handful. During the last few months of his life he made a bare living by distributing race-cards at saloons, but he was not fit even for this poor service and, one day, in the early spring of 1892, he was knocked down in a drunken brawl and so brutally beaten and kicked that he was found by the police lying senseless on a vacant house lot. He was taken to Bellevue Hospital and well nursed, but he was so badly hurt that he died, seven days afterwards, from the effect of his injuries, aggravated by delirium tremens. So came to an end the career of the man who was once vain of the title of "the king of the forgers."

At the time of the arrest of Wilkes and his confederates in Italy, the gang was particularly engaged in the disposal of forged income bonds and circular notes, and one of the principal agents, Albert Wilson, succeeded in evading the police and returning to this country. But he was arrested in the fall of the same year, in New York, for his share in the forgeries on two Baltimore banks and sentenced to a term of four years in the Maryland state prison. A few months after his release from prison he was arrested in Milwaukee, Wisconsin, upon the charge of attempting to pass counterfeit fifty-pound notes of the Bank of England. He was also charged with the same offence in Chicago and was taken to that city for trial. He contrived to escape from the police station, in which he was temporarily held, and succeeded in reaching England where he rejoined Wilkes, Engle, Becker, Hamilton and others of the old Wilkes gang. Soon a plot was devised to float an enormous amount of forged circular notes in France, Germany and Italy, but this swindle was, fortunately, interrupted by the police at an early stage.

After the collapse of this scheme Wilson went to Canada and undertook to cheat a Montreal bank with a forged letter of credit. In this attempt he failed, thanks to the keenness of the bank manager, who procured his arrest, and he was convicted of this offence and sentenced in June, 1885, to a term of twelve years in St. Vincent de Paul penitentiary. His portrait, as one of the most notorious forgers of this century and a representative member of the famous Wilkes gang, is given on an illustrative page in this chapter.

On the same page appear the photographs of three other representative forgers who were members of one of the most adroit and dangerous gangs which has infested this country during the past ten years. These are Richard O. Davis, Max Steele and Charles Fisher. In the spring of 1895 this gang devised and partially carried through a scheme of forgery in Boston, so characteristic and notable that it is here recounted.

In April, 1895, one of this gang succeeded in opening an account under an assumed name in a leading national bank of New Bedford, Mass., and on the 22d of this month he procured in an ordinary business way a cashier's check for twenty-five dollars, payable to the order of James H. Thorne. A fac-simile of this check is here reproduced for the purpose of illustration. With this check in hand, the forgers made tracings of the signature of the cashier with a fine pencil point on a number of blank checks or lithograph copies of the form used by the New Bedford bank. These pencil tracings were then dexterously overrun with a quill and ink and a delicate brush, so that the forged signatures copied the lines, curves and shading of the genuine name of the cashier with delusive exactness.

CASHIER'S DRAFT.

FORGED DRAFT.

Then Steele went to Roxbury and undertook to negotiate for the purchase of a hotel in order to obtain an introduction to a suburban national bank, under the assumed name of Henry T. Woodruff. Having craftily gained his point, he succeeded in opening an account by the deposit of a few hundred dollars and confirmed his pretence of engaging in business in Boston by hiring an office and employing a young man as a clerk. In the course of a few days the masquerading Steele presented for deposit a check which purported to be the cashier's check of the New Bedford national bank upon its correspondent bank in Boston for the sum of $4,552. This check was made payable to Henry T. Woodruff and, upon Steele's indorsement as Woodruff, it was accepted by the teller of the suburban bank and honored as genuine by the correspondent of the New Bedford bank.

While Steele was thus imposing upon the bank in Roxbury as Henry T. Woodruff, he was proceeding to extend the cheat in the mask of another assumed character, David H. Fielding. Steele, alias Fielding, called upon a furniture supply house and, by wily practice, obtained a letter of introduction to a Boston bank of high standing. With the aid of this letter he succeeded in opening an account and made a deposit like his first in the Roxbury bank. A few days later, he deposited a check of the New Bedford bank for $5,225, payable to his order, and signed apparently by the cashier.

Within a few days after the deposit of these two checks, Steele drew out most of the amount standing to the credit of Woodruff and Fielding, and the success of the fraud was apparently so unquestioned that the gang proceeded to carry it further. When the forged checks reached the New Bedford bank, however, the fraud was detected and the Boston banks notified. So when the office boy of "David H. Fielding" called to make another deposit of a forged check of the New Bedford bank, to the amount of $9,500, the boy was held and the gang which employed him was hotly pursued.

The Boston detectives hastened at once to Steele's office. It was barely furnished with a cheap desk and chairs and a pretence of office books. Nobody was in the office when the detectives reached it, but, in the course of an hour, a man entered who was immediately recognized as the notorious forger, Richard O. Davis. He was arrested and held as a probable accomplice and every effort was made to secure the arrest and identification of the man who had personated Fielding and Woodruff.

Finally information was secured by the chief inspector which pointed to the probability that Steele and Fisher had been operating with Davis in Boston. When Steele's portrait was shown by the Boston detectives to officers of the Roxbury and other Boston banks, it was at once identified as the likeness of the pretended Fielding and Woodruff. As soon as this fact was ascertained, a hunt for Steele was instituted which resulted in his arrest in New York and transmission to Boston. He was informed of the array of evidence against him and, before his trial came on, he made a confession of his connection with the forgeries, with the consent of his counsel, to the Boston police.

This confession is so representative in its way of the procedure of forgers in effecting their frauds that it is given here substantially as it was taken by a stenographer from the lips of Steele. After detailing the circumstances of his meeting with Fisher, and the suggestion of the plot to be carried through in Boston, he told of his coming to this city and of his part in the forgeries.

"I used to meet Fisher," he said, "in two Boston hotels and very often on the Common by the pond. He used to pretend to go away and would arrange an appointment some days ahead. He told me that he would not tell me where he lived; he had reasons for not telling me where he lived, he said. I said that it was very funny that he did not tell me where he was living. He said, 'You are the man; if I want you, I know where you are living and I can send a message there for you.' He would not let me connect with him, at all, only outside.

"One morning Fisher came to me with an 'ad' that he had cut out of the paper, which read that a hotel was for sale and directed callers to a School Street agent. I went to the agent's office and pretended to be willing to buy a hotel, if the location and house were satisfactory. I went up town with the agent and looked over the property from cellar to attic. I told the owner that I would have to wait a little time before buying the hotel as there were other people interested. I was buying it for a relative and not for myself exactly.

"So matters hung until one day when I saw Fisher and he said: 'it is about time for you to find out whether this man has any bank account or not; we must not waste any more time.' I met Fisher again and he gave me the money, $400, to open an account with. He went up with me to the hotel for which I had been bargaining, but stayed outside. I went in and talked with the proprietor and we had some drinks at the bar. Then, as we walked toward the door, I asked him to recommend me to some good reliable bank, where I could open an account. He said, 'there is a bank out here that I have been doing business with for nearly twenty years; it is good enough for me.' He went upstairs and got his hat and overcoat, and we went to the Roxbury bank and he introduced me to the cashier. He said: 'Here is a gentleman that is going to do business and he wants to open an account,' introducing me as Mr. Woodruff.

"I made a deposit, got a pass book and check book, and walked out with the hotel owner, accompanying him back to his hotel. After chatting in the doorway a little while, I walked away. That was the last I saw of him. Fisher was opposite, further down the street. He walked down ahead of the hotel man and myself on the opposite side of the street. He was watching me all the time and when I came out with the book, he knew that it was all right. I met Fisher two blocks down and we took a car. He said: 'Well,

I see that everything is all right.' He took the bank books and went away with them. I met him that afternoon at four o'clock on the Common, by the pond, and he handed me back the books and said: 'You keep those until we need them.' I hired an office on Washington Street and advertised for a boy; got a boy and took him to the bank and introduced him to the cashier as a clerk.

"Two days afterward I met Fisher by appointment on the Common. He said: 'We will be all right to make deposits to-morrow,' and pulled a book out of his pocket and said, 'I have got the things all right.' I met him the following morning and he handed me a check for $4,552 and I went up and made a deposit. About two days after that he told me to send up and draw some money and I did, drawing several small amounts at different times. On the 9th of May, I presented a check for $3,500 which was paid. The boy drew $505 on the same day. On the 10th the boy drew $300, leaving a balance of about $250. Fisher would be outside waiting for me when I went in to get the money and, when the boy drew the money, he would bring it back to the office.

"When the boy went up Fisher would follow him. I would go to the office and take the money from the boy and go out and meet Fisher and he would take the money from me. He never left me with any money, as he said, 'In case you are arrested.' On the 9th of May the boy drew $505, and after Fisher got that money he went away. He sent for me about half an hour later and I drew out $3,500. When I came out Fisher was in sight. We went around the corner and walked over to a little park and we never connected until we sat on a bench. I handed him the money and he said: 'That's all for now.' He took the money and went away.

"A few days after opening an account at the bank in Roxbury, we opened an account in a leading bank in the city of Boston. Fisher told me to go to a well-known furniture store and tell the salesmen that I was about to furnish a house and would like to look at some of their goods. I priced some of the goods and told the clerk I would be back again. Fisher told me to go back and say that I was not ready to take the goods just now, but wanted to have them put on memorandum and I would take them in a few days. In conversing with the clerk I asked him whether he could recommend me to some good bank where I could make a deposit as I had more money on my person than I wished to carry. Through the clerk I obtained a letter of introduction to a bank of high standing and succeeded in opening an account by making a deposit of a good check and some bills.

"May 8th I deposited in this bank a $5,225 check on the New Bedford bank, dated May 7th, 1895, payable to David H. Fielding and signed by the cashier. Different amounts were drawn on that check and on the morning of the 10th I drew $2,000. Fisher was standing outside on the same side of the street up towards Tremont Row, waiting for the money, and I handed it to him. He left me right off. About one o'clock we met, not far from the Quincy House, and he gave me a check for $9,500 and $100 in bills to make a deposit. I gave them to the boy in the office to take to the bank to deposit.

"Fisher followed the boy and I stationed myself at the little steps off Cornhill. Fisher came down there and asked where the boy was. I said I did not know. He asked, 'Has he passed here?' I said, 'No!' He went off and in a few minutes came back again on a very fast walk. He motioned to me to leave my position and said with an oath, as he passed me, 'get away!'

"I asked 'Where?'

"He said, with another oath: 'Oh, anywhere; the boy's pinched.'

"A fellow came out of the bank in a hurry and bare headed, looking up and down the street, and that the game was up. I went off as fast as I could walk to the station and took the first train to New York. There I was waiting to see Fisher when I was arrested, but he never turned up."

It is probable that Steele was disposed to throw the weight of responsibility for the conduct of these forgeries on his alleged confederate, Fisher, and the literal accuracy of his account is not vouched for, but it is, in the main, a graphic description of the actual method of the gang of swindlers in this representative case. It emphasizes, particularly, the care that ought to exercised in giving introductions to banks and in the opening of accounts with strangers. It may further be observed that all possible caution should be taken in the issue of cashiers' checks or drafts, for these are the ones which have been preferred of late years by forgers for their frauds. When the check is not used as a copy, it is commonly raised and passed as genuine. In the Boston case, the loss fell upon the bank which was the correspondent of the New Bedford bank and redeemed the forged checks through the clearing house, but the warning was not confined to the actual sufferer. We may note that an apparently feasible precaution would, almost certainly, have foiled this scheme of forgery. If banks would regularly send, every day, to their correspondents in Boston, lists of all the cashier's checks issued during the day, stating numbers and amounts, these lists would be on hand for ready reference when forged checks are presented. Such a reference would have exposed the forgery in the case which we have narrated and, if this practice were generally adopted, the banks of this country could hardly be swindled by "raised" or forged checks purporting to be drawn by their correspondents.

Steele pleaded guilty to the indictment against him on the score of these forgeries and was sentenced to a term of ten years in the Massachusetts state prison. He has had a hand, during his career, in a wide range of forgeries from checks to railroad bonds and tickets. There was good reason for the presumption that Fisher and Davis were the directing heads in the Boston forgeries, but the evidence against them was not sufficient to ensure their conviction and they were therefore taken to St. Louis for trial on charges pending against them in that city. Here again, unfortunately, for lack of evidence sufficient to convict, both were released.

On the 29th of May following, Fisher presented to the First National Bank of Cincinnati, Ohio, a forged check for $1,500. The forgery was detected but Fisher contrived to escape, for the time, though he was soon afterwards arrested and committed to the Hamilton County jail. In November of the same year (1895) he broke out of this jail with five other prisoners and succeeded in making his escape. He was lately seen in London, England, by Inspector Houghton of the Boston detective service, and it is probable that he will consult his safety by remaining abroad for some time. He has long been known as a dangerous burglar and forger. He was arrested in New York twenty years ago in the act of breaking into a house and fired several shots at the detectives before he was run down and caught. He escaped conviction of this offence through a flaw in his indictment, but was committed to prison shortly afterward through his implication in the preparation of bogus checks. Since his release from prison he has been involved in a succession of forgeries.

Richard O. Davis is also probably sojourning abroad at this time, as he has been repeatedly arrested of late years on the charge of forgery since his discharge from Sing Sing, in 1888, where he had been serving out a sentence of six years for forgery. He is accounted one of the most expert of the forgers now living, and there is not a section of this country which has not suffered, at some time, from the artful frauds of the gang with which he has been associated.

Pickpocket, shoplifter, burglar, bank sneak and forger, Charles J. Everhardt, alias "Mash Market Jake," combines and illustrates in his own person almost every grade and variety in the multiform thief. His education in every branch of his criminal profession has been typically progressive. He began as a street waif by the theft of apples and other petty articles from the fruit stalls and peddlers' trays. From this beginning the transition was easy to the purloining of handkerchiefs and wallets and the sly snatching of gloves and lace from the store counters. Growing bolder with his ascent of the ladder of crime, he joined a gang of burglars and when this description of robbery was judged to be too rude and dangerous, he applied himself to the practice of forgery, beginning as a common tool, or "layer down," as the presenter of forged paper is styled, and rising step by step to the rank of a principal.

He has probably borne more assumed names than any other thief in America, and is one of the slyest hypocrites and beguilers who have ever exhibited their arts in this country. He was first arrested in 1880 on the charge of larceny, in Philadelphia, by the police of that city and sentenced upon conviction to a term of eighteen months in the Eastern penitentiary. His next important conviction was for shoplifting in Toronto and, shortly afterward, for burglary in the same city.

After his release from the Kingston (Canada) penitentiary, in the spring of 1885, he turned his hand to forgery, at first as a sneak thief in stealing blank checks, and later as a "layer down" or presenter of forged checks. He succeeded for a time in evading conviction, although several of his confederates testified to his engaging wiles, but he was finally arrested and convicted, in 1886, for forgeries in New York, as a member of the gang headed by Charles Fisher. For this offence he received a sentence of ten years in the state prison. Within a few months after his release on the expiration of his term he was arrested in New York for the robbery of the New Albany (Indiana) postoffice of over five thousand dollars in money and postage stamps, and he is now serving out his sentence for this offence. His portrait appropriately fills a niche on a representative page.

Charles Becker and his confederate, James Cregan, whose

portraits are given on the same page, are unquestionably two of the most remarkable forgers now living and Becker, in particular, has an international reputation. His first appearance of note was in association with Gottlieb Engel and others in the pursuit of forgery twenty-six years ago. He was a prentice hand then and apparently ready to enlist in any scheme of robbery by force or fraud, for he was one of the gang, headed by Adam Worth, Joseph B. Chapman and "Little Joe" Reilly, which broke into the vaults of the Third National Bank of Baltimore in 1872.

Then he fled to Europe with his confederates and, after their booty had been flung away in varied dissipation, he reorganized the gang for the practice of forgery. Chapman had been trained as a bank clerk in Chicago, and his familiarity with banking customs was of essential service to his confederates. Becker was an exceedingly skillful penman and undertook to prepare the forged drafts, checks and letters of credit which were to be handled by his associates. After all were well drilled in the parts assigned to them, Becker led the gang from London, through the principal cities of France and Germany, leaving a trail of forged paper behind all the way to Smyrna, where it was brought to an end by the capture of the forgers by pursuing detectives and the local police. The captives were tried and convicted in the English consular court at Smyrna and all were sent to prison in Constantinople for a term of three years. A very large amount of money had been obtained by the series of swindles, and the bulk of the booty had been sent to London for safe keeping under the charge of Chapman's wife.

A few months after this committal to prison, Becker, Reilly and a third confederate, Carlo Susicovitch, contrived to escape and made their way secretly to London, expecting to get their shares of the booty in the hands of Mrs. Chapman. They pretended that they had been obliged to leave Chapman lingering in prison because he was too sick to escape with them, but his wife had been informed by her husband that his companions had deserted him and was imperatively instructed not to give up a dollar until he was out of prison. When she refused to part with the plunder, the three escaped convicts resolved to rob her, and, to avoid any outcry, it is reported that they used drugs to put her to sleep, but the dose was apparently so miscalculated that the victim died. Becker and his associates fled in alarm to this country and met in New York by prearrangement.

Here Wilkes and Cregan joined Becker and Reilly in the plotting and execution of one of the most notable frauds ever undertaken in this country, the counterfeiting of the checks of the New York Life Insurance Company. A clerk in the employ of this company was induced to furnish the gang with a canceled check from which Becker made an imitation so exact that it was used to draw $64,000 from the deposit of this company with a New York bank. The forgers were so keenly pursued when this fraud was detected that several were captured including Becker and Reilly. When Becker saw the state prison looming up before him, he did not scruple to betray his confederates by turning state's evidence, and his crony, Reilly, was convicted upon his testimony.

Cregan, who was the financial backer of the gang, contrived to keep out of prison and was soon plotting again with Becker new schemes of fraud. Both were known then, however, as uncommonly dangerous forgers, and all their movements were sharply watched by detectives. Becker was next arrested and convicted for forging script of the Philadelphia and Reading Railroad Company, and, upon his discharge from prison, he undertook to counterfeit Bank of England notes to an enormous extent. This scheme was nipped in the bud in the spring of 1881 by his arrest, but, for lack of convicting evidence, he was discharged. A few years later, in September, 1884, this artful skulker and wire-puller was uncovered in the attempt to counterfeit and pass a thousand-franc note of the Bank of

France. For this offence he was tried, convicted and sentenced to a term of ten years in the penitentiary of Kings County, New York.

Three years later, his partner Cregan was arrested and convicted of a forgery upon the Howard Bank of Baltimore. While serving out his sentence of three years and six months in the penitentiary, he made acquaintances which he used after his discharge in forming a gang with the special object of defrauding the banks of two western states. Becker joined hands with him once more upon his release from prison and these two old foxes in forgery devised an elaborate scheme of fraud which, for the time, was largely successful. Their latest, and, it is to be hoped, their last cheat, was a masterpiece in its way. It illustrates, so clearly, high art in forgery and the methods that are likely to be followed by imitators in the field, that its features may well be presented as an example and warning.

On the 2d of December, 1895, a man of fine appearance and address rented an office in one of the best buildings in San Francisco. "A. H. Dean, Merchandise Broker," was lettered on the glass of the door by his direction. Soon after his occupation of the office, he asked the superintendent of the building for a reference to a bank of the best standing. His manner was so prepossessing that the superintendent unhesitatingly offered to introduce him to the Nevada Bank. When the supposed Mr. Dean was presented to the bank officials, his bearing was so businesslike and engaging that he was cordially welcomed as a customer, and the superintendent who introduced him was privately thanked for the particular favor which he had rendered.

Mr. Dean did not expect to call for any discounting of his own notes, as he said, and presumed that his standing deposit would soon be from twenty to thirty thousand dollars. His first deposit was $2,500 in cash. He drew out a few hundred dollars by check, a few days later, and, in a day or two, drew

JAMES CREGAN.

CHARLES BECKER.

CHARLES J. EVERHARDT.

WILLIAM E. BROCKWAY.

upon his deposit again for seven hundred dollars. On Dec. 13th he deposited seven hundred dollars in cash and a draft on the Anglo-California Bank for ninety-five dollars.

No exception could be taken to these proceedings of the new customer, but the bank was naturally desirous of the expected increase in his deposit. It was gratified on Dec. 17 by the deposit of what purported to be the draft of the cashier of the Bank of Woodland upon the Crocker-Woolworth National Bank of San Francisco for $22,000. This draft was duly paid through the clearing house and it was not until the Woodland Bank received its monthly statement from the Crocker-Woolworth Bank, its San Francisco correspondent, on the 6th of January following that the alarming fact of a forgery was uncovered.

Meanwhile the plausible Mr. Dean had drawn out of the Nevada Bank $2,200 in currency on the day of his deposit of the forged draft and, on the next day, he had reduced his deposit very heavily by taking away four sacks of gold, containing $5,000 each, in return for his check to "self" for $20,000. He was diligently sought for by the San Francisco police when they were notified of the forgery, but it appeared that he had taken his gold to some distant hiding place as soon as he was able to get away with his sacks.

The calculating craft of the directing heads in this forgery was evident in the withdrawal of every dollar of Dean's balance in bank at the time of his deposit of the forged draft, so that, in the event of the possible detection of the fraud by the Crocker-Woolworth Bank, the forgers had none of their own money at stake. It was ascertained that the forgery had been effected by "raising" a genuine draft of the Bank of Woodland from $12 to $22,000. The original draft was made payable to the order of A. H. Dean. It was on safety paper and the amount ($12.00) perforated at each end by a check protector, yet a master hand in forgery had contrived to alter it so deceptively that it passed through the hands of several experienced bank tellers and clerks without detection and it was only by

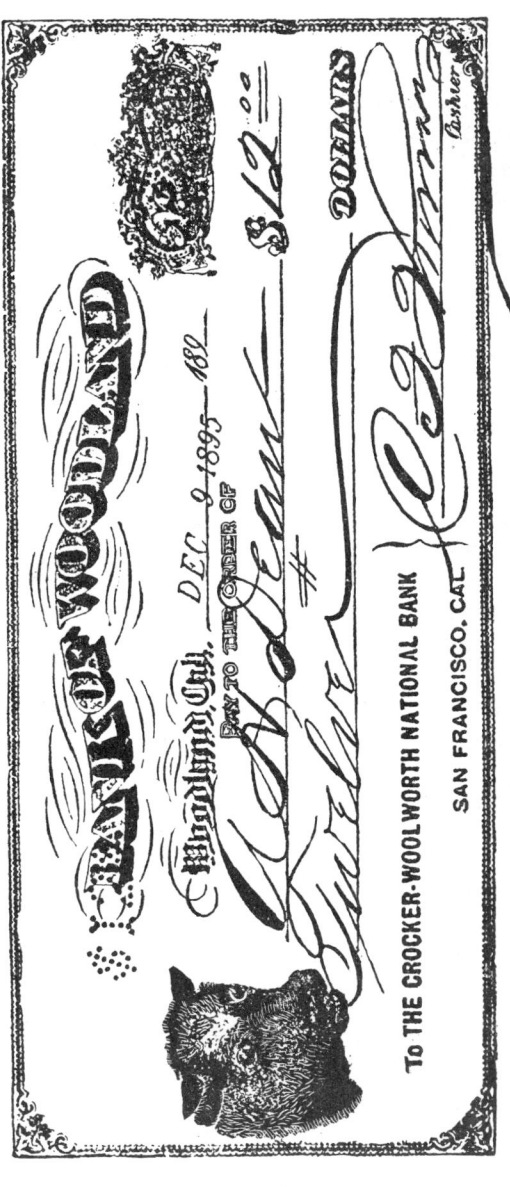

ORIGINAL DRAFT.

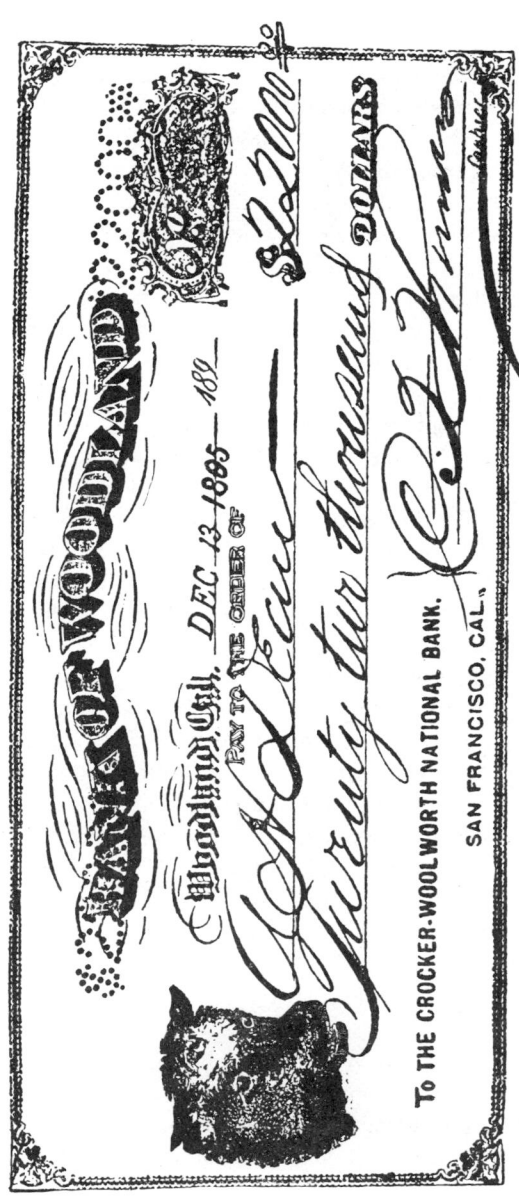

DRAFT AS RAISED.

close microscopic examination that the Bank of Woodland was able to determine positively how the forgery had been effected.

From the extraordinary perfection of its execution it was suspected by the Pinkerton agency, which was coöperating with the San Francisco detective force, that the accomplished Becker was the artist in the forgery and Cregan was naturally presumed to be a leading director in carrying through the fraud. Both men were sharply looked after and every possible clue to the forgery pursued. While this search was in progress, the detectives were informed by the cashier of the St. Paul National Bank that he suspected the design of some fraud by two men calling themselves D. W. Woods and J. M. Shaw, who had opened bank accounts in St. Paul and Minneapolis. Samples of the handwriting of Woods, furnished by the cashier, satisfied the detectives that D. W. Woods of St. Paul and the pleasing Mr. A. H. Dean of San Francisco were the same person. J. M. Shaw was next identified as a noted "bank sneak" and forger, "Joe" McCluskey, and, after some sharp watching, both Woods and Shaw were arrested and taken to San Francisco.

Both men stoutly denied any connection with the Woodland bank forgery and any acquaintance with Becker or Cregan. But, shortly after their arrest, Becker and Cregan attempted to leave the country and take refuge in Guatemala. This precaution on their part was obstructed by their arrest just before taking the steamer for Philadelphia. A complete outfit of forger's implements was found in Becker's baggage, but there was no direct evidence as yet attainable to implicate him in the San Francisco forgery. So both men were simply held under surveillance while every effort was made to extend the links of evidence.

Upon the capture of Woods, his photograph was taken and copies sent to every important city in the country. When one of these photographs reached the Boston detective bureau, it was soon identified with a photograph of Frank L. Seaver, which had been taken in February, 1895. Seaver had rented, in January of that year, an office on State Street under the name of Frederick Stebbins, with the professed intention of engaging in legitimate mercantile business. His cards stated that his cable address was "Stebnett." It is the practice of the Boston detectives to keep a watchful eye upon men of this description whose antecedents are unknown or disreputable, and, upon the first suspicious movement of Stebbins, he was arrested by the "bank squad" and sharply questioned. He claimed at first to be an Englishman, and upon examination it was found that his clothes were made by a London tailor, but he failed to give any evidence or reference in further support of his claim. Finally he was pressed to the point of confessing that his pretences were false. He admitted that he had come to the city under an assumed name and that his pretended business was hardly more than a cloak for some swindling scheme. He professed to be pleased, however, that he had been intercepted by the vigilance of the detectives, before he had gone so far in his scheme as to render him liable to conviction for felony, and coolly complimented his captors upon the keenness of their guard of the banking district. His real name, by his own admission, Frank L. Seaver, was entered upon the records of the police department, with his photograph and other points of identification. In view of the fact that nothing actually criminal could be charged against him, he was then allowed to leave the city, at his own request, with the assurance on his part that he never intended to revisit this part of the country. He was not, in fact, heard of again until his arrest for the forgery on the Bank of Woodland. Then the identification of the pretended "Woods" or "Dean" with Frank L. Seaver was at once communicated to the detectives in charge of the case.

Both Seaver and McCluskey hoped that they would be assisted in their defence by their chief confederates, Becker and Cregan, but, when it was apparent that they had been deserted as so many other "layers down" had been before, McCluskey soon told what he knew of the case, and with his coöperation a full confession was finally extracted from Seaver by the adroitness of Captain Lees of the San Francisco detective force. With the direct testimony thus secured and the further evidence obtained by the labors of the coöperating detectives, two of the most dangerous rascals in America, Becker and Cregan, were convicted after a stubbornly-contested trial in San Francisco, and sentenced to imprisonment for life in August, 1896. Becker was the actual workman in the forgery of the "raised" draft and Cregan, the financial backer and director. Becker made the alterations in his hiding place in Oakland, California, while Cregan, in San Francisco, was the middleman between him and Seaver, the actual "layer down." The banks of this country and the business community at large had signal cause for congratulation that a gang of forgers, so extraordinarily artful and dangerous, had been finally crushed beyond the hope of revival.

If any prize were offered to the oldest forger in America, it is probable that nobody could maintain a better claim to it than William E. Brockway. This noted forger has been known to the men of his craft as "Old Bill Brockway" for the past thirty years. He was educated in one of the foremost colleges of the country, and in natural ability, as well as education, he was fitted to take high rank in other professions than the one to which his perverted talents have been applied. After his college course he went into business as a printer and electrotyper and gained in this employment an expertness which later was evident in the production of counterfeit bonds and notes.

He has been at work as a forger and counterfeiter from 1850 to the present day with the exception of the intervals spent in prison where he was debarred from his favorite practice. In 1880 he was arrested and convicted upon the charge of forging and uttering United States six per cent coupon bonds to the extent of $204,000, as well as a number of United States Treasury notes. Sentence in his case was suspended by the United States court judge upon his undertaking to surrender all the forged plates in his possession or anywhere within his knowledge and upon his further pledge to uncover all schemes of forgery then pending, of which he had information. He was discharged from custody upon the fulfillment of his pledges, with the assurance or understanding that his suspended sentence of thirty years in prison would go into effect if he was ever arrested for forging or counterfeiting any coin, notes, bonds, or other obligation of the United States.

This was an impressive warning to him not to meddle with Uncle Sam's business, but it did not suffice to deter him from other forgeries. Three years later he was arrested for the forgery of a number of bonds of the Morris and Essex railroad and, upon conviction in New York, was sentenced to the State prison for five years. Since his discharge from prison he has been covertly engaged in counterfeiting, but he was so adroit in covering his tracks that he escaped conviction until his arrest in August, 1896, in New York, by United States secret service officers. A counterfeit $500 gold certificate was found on his person and, by searching the headquarters of his gang in Hoboken, a large outfit of apparatus for counterfeiting was brought to light, as well as incomplete counterfeit notes to the extent of six hundred thousand dollars. Upon his conviction he was sentenced to the State prison for a term of years which is equivalent to a life sentence.

Brockway is ranked with the most skillful of living counterfeiters and his art and craft made him one of the most formidable rascals in his line in the country up to the time of his last conviction, in spite of his enfeebling age and known character. He is an inch and a half over six feet in height, with a long, thin knotty neck and face of preternatural solemnity, as well appears in his portrait which completes our pages representative of the American forger.

It is of interest to note in conclusion that the latest report of the chief of the United States secret service shows a gratifying decrease in the counterfeiting of paper money in this country during the past twelve months. This satisfaction is unfortunately offset to some extent by the increase which he notes in the counterfeiting of gold and silver coins, and by the advance in quality of workmanship and material. It is further of particular importance to observe that the practice of "raising" or altering United States notes has been largely extended, and this particular device of forgery seems to be preferred also, as we have before noted, in the case of bank checks.

The national secret service force is specially organized for the detection and arrest of forgers and counterfeiters, and the National Bankers' Association has supplemented this safeguard by the employment of the Pinkerton Detective Agency for the like service. Unremitting efforts are made, also, by the combined police and detective forces of the country, working together to secure the utmost possible vigilance to prevent and suppress this peculiarly dangerous practice, and we may fairly emphasize the call upon the public at large to do all in their power to support the efforts of the police. We may hope, without any vain assumption, that our suggestions of proper precautions will be materially helpful in the reduction of losses from forgery and counterfeiting.

SHARPERS AND DUPES.

ONE may as well try to number the sparks that fly from a fizzing pin-wheel, as to catalogue the shifts and tricks of the swindling hydra. This monster is continually trying to cover his heads with sand and to throw dust in the eyes of spectators; and it is even harder to fight with him than it was with the old water serpent, for none of his heads can be cut off completely and new heads are sprouting yearly from his teeming trunk.

It seems as if every successive generation of men was blindly or stubbornly bent upon burning its fingers in the same old ways in spite of the rows of burnt fingers that stretch back through the centuries into time immemorial. In some form or another the old "shell game" has been played for hundreds of years by sharpers and dupes, yet every year brings forth a fresh set of gulls who are willing to gamble that they can mark the one shell that covers the pea. "Thimble rig" is merely the substitution of three thimbles or little metal caps for the fragile shells, and "three-card monte" is practically the same old game in a mask of cards.

It is said that Sir Walter Raleigh, in his prison in London Tower, had occasion to learn that a man's own eyes can be false witnesses, but it is not recorded that Sir Walter was obliged to pay a "bunco man" in order to have this lesson well rubbed in. Unfortunately for a legion of victims there are many people who are vain of their eyesight and few who get rid of this vanity without some drain on their pocket books. The callow youth, who is surer of everything at eighteen than he will be of anything at eighty, is ready to bet his head that he can put his finger on the shell that covers the pea, for has he not just seen the covering with his own eyes? And there are others, and fairly intelligent men, too, who get crowns of gray and white hairs without getting the wisdom that will prevent them from staking a cent on their eyesight in this antiquated bunco game. In all its variations, the one essential feature is the delusion of the eye by sleight-of-hand, and this is a trifling feat for an expert juggler.

Anyone who has seen the exhibitions of artists like the late Herrmann or Keller can understand how foolish it is to trust to appearances in "bunco games," even when the performers are bunglers compared with really accomplished jugglers. Any artist of the first rank can practically defy detection in the execution of his shuffling and palming tricks, even when he is standing in the midst of a crowd and challenging exposure, as both Herrmann and Keller have frequently done. The professional players of swindling games with cards, dice, peas and other gambling implements are all more or less expert jugglers. Sometimes these swindlers resort to crutches like marked cards or loaded dice; some, like Ah Sin, have taper nails and long sleeves; others are aided by confederate partners or agents,—all are constantly seeking to adopt and employ every form of trick and cheat that will serve their end of plunder.

It should be needless to point out that the honest player is fatally handicapped in any and every game with such swindlers. There are, it is true, current tales and stage plays, in which the honest man confounds and fleeces the rogue, and such a denouement may occur, once in ten thousand times, in actual experience. It is practically certain that the honest man has no chance, worth considering, of winning anything from the swindler. If the greenhorn ever sees anyone apparently winning from the dealer in "three card monte" or in any other bunco game, he may be sure that the winner is a "capper" or confederate. The sole exception to this conclusion is when the amateur gambler is suffered to win small sums once or twice in order to entice him to put up a stake which will empty his pockets. The most dangerous "bunco men" among these gamblers are the rascals of engaging address and pretentious social position,—blacklegs in the persons of men of title or fashion,—human spiders, who weave their nets for flies and drain their victims, if they do not actually take their lives at last, in the manner of Sir Mulberry Hawk and Lord Frederick Verisopht.

The only certain assurance against loss at the hands of these knaves is to keep out of their reach, and, if an honest man is necessarily thrust into contact with them, for a time, by any chance, he can and should refuse to take a hand in any of their gambling games. A common trick of these swindlers is to propose a simple game at cards or billiards, without any stakes, and, after playing indifferently for half an hour or so, they will grumble a little at the dullness of the game and suggest the hazard of a small stake, just to give an edge to the play. The dupes who have been playing with them are apt to consent from their silly dread of seeming disobliging or puritanical or mean, and the practiced swindlers have every device at their finger ends for exciting, deluding and drawing on their victims until their pockets are emptied. "Plucking a pigeon" is a "bunco game" of hoary antiquity and yet it is still played in every city in the world, every day in the year, and it will be played, in spite of all warnings, for generations to come. It was a regular practice of professional "bunco men" to run up and down our American rivers, in the palmy days of the racing steamboat, and there are too many still travelling about on railway trains and ocean steamers. These sharpers play all the games which are commonly termed games of chance, but little is left to chance in their style of play. Unless a player belongs, like them, to the order of hawks, it is rank folly to gamble with chance acquaintances who may be professional gamesters or swindlers.

To describe a peculiar game with dice or cards, which was a swindle with the thinnest of masks, the term "bunco" was probably invented, and it has since spread, in common application, to cover all sorts of swindling "games" and the sharpers who "play" them. The game was apparently a counterfeit of the old English swindling game known as "eight dice cloth." In its original form dice were used with a checkered cloth worked with stars, and numbers covered with a hood called "banco." In the swindle of a victim, he would be induced to throw dice which would be counted to correspond with a losing number under the hood. The term banco, or "the bank," game was probably applied to puff up the swindle by an imposing title. The proprietor of the game was naturally termed the "banco man," or the "banker"; and when the game became a widespread and notorious swindle, "banco," in our free-and-easy American usage, had changed into "bunco," and the "banco man," into the "bunco man."

A curious expert exhibit of the "bunco game" in full bloom was given, a few years ago, in the county court at Albany, New York. The notorious "Tom O'Brien" had been arrested in London on the charge of robbery and taken for trial to this country, where his offence was committed. His partner, George W. Post, another rascal of the same stripe, had been lodged in jail some months before the extradition of O'Brien. As this pretentious "king of the bunco men" had his pockets full of money, he was able to engage the foremost criminal lawyers of New York to defend him. So, when he appeared in the Albany courts, his line of defence was cunningly drawn.

An old farmer was the chief witness for the prosecution, as the victim who had been robbed of ten thousand dollars by O'Brien and Post. He told, on the witness stand, how his money had been snatched out of his pockets by O'Brien, while he was showing to the bunco man a house which he had for sale. When O'Brien took the stand in his own defence, he denied that he had robbed the farmer, as charged in his indictment, but frankly confessed that he had taken his money away in a "bunco game." His partner Post, as he claimed, had lured the old man to his rooms in Albany, where O'Brien showed his visitors how to play "bunco."

Then the leading counsel for the defendant spread out on a table, before the jury, a huge black silk handkerchief or coverlet, checkered with squares marked by gilt letters and figures. "What's that?" asked the lawyer. "Chart of special drawing, or bunco chart," answered O'Brien with a broad grin. "How is it used?" continued the examiner. O'Brien showed to the jury a pack of forty-eight cards in eight sets, each numbered from one to six inclusive. He explained that each player received eight cards from the pack and that the sum total of numbers on the cards in each hand was compared with the numbers on the "bunco chart." If this total corresponded to a number carrying a prize, the lucky holder of the hand won the prize.

After explaining the game, O'Brien proceeded to tell how the farmer had been "roped in" to take a hand with Post, "the bunco steerer," and to suffer the loss of his ten thousand dollars. When the game at O'Brien's rooms had been opened, and the cards gravely counted and compared with the chart, O'Brien said, as he testified: "Gentlemen, you've drawn the grand conditional advertising prize. You're entitled to $10,000 apiece on condition that you prove yourselves worth $50,000 apiece, and promise to advertise our lottery company whether you win or lose. You will have to put up $10,000 apiece against the $10,000 prize. Then you draw once more. If you draw a star number you get only the ten thousand dollar prize and your own money back. If you draw any other number, you get its prize added to your own money and the big prize."

The "bunco steerer" Post, who was masquerading under a false name, claimed that he was worth over fifty thousand dollars, and the old farmer certified that his property was valued at over half a million dollars. Then both the winners went away to get the required stake of ten thousand dollars, and returned with the money which they laid on the chart, as directed. Each drew four cards and the count of each hand was the same, a total of 28. "Why, gentlemen," said the brazen O'Brien, "that's the 'state number,' the total blank. You've lost all." The "bunco steerer" pretended to draw a long face, and the farmer's face fell without any pretence. "It's too bad," said Post. "Yes," sighed the old farmer, "it's so different from what we expected." Then the "bunco steerer" reproached himself for bringing his old friend into the game and stoutly protested that he would refund the lost money. Both went away sorrowing, but, in a few minutes, Post slipped back alone, and the confederates slipped away with the ten thousand dollars. Perhaps O'Brien's story was a lie in this case, but it was, nevertheless, a vivid and good description of the usual course of the "bunco game." O'Brien was convicted of robbery in the third degree, in spite of his plea for himself, and sentenced to a term of ten years in state prison. Within a month after his sentence he contrived to escape from the custody of a careless keeper and fled to Europe, where he remained under cover until early in 1895, when he put a black cap on his infamous life by the brutal murder of one of his old associates, at a railway station in Paris. For this crime he was convicted and sentenced to penal servitude for life.

All the known varieties and possibilities of the "bunco game," with cards and dice and billiard balls and other implements of the professional gamester, are, however, a mere fraction of the resources of the "bunco man." He looks upon the world at large as his oyster and, in some way or other, he proposes to get rid of the sheltering shell. He saw that there was a considerable number of possible gulls who could not be enticed into ordinary gambling games,—thrifty old farmers who had put their savings in banks, and well-to-do store keepers and other business men, who were in the habit of going to church regularly and avoiding cards as a snare of

Satan. For the trapping of these shy birds he invented the "gold brick" swindle and all its variations and varnishes.

This swindle has been worn so threadbare and exposed so often in this country that it should be impossible to find a gudgeon anywhere who will bite at it. But, year after year, we hear of new dupes, who can be deluded into the belief that a man with a real "brick," or ingot, of solid gold is willing to sell it to them at a sacrifice. No doubt, it is hinted, more or less plainly, to the gullible purchasers that there is some cloud on the seller's title to this brick. Yet the most ignorant dupe should have enough scraps of intelligence to know that even a thief would not sell a lump of gold, which could not be identified as stolen property, for less than its actual bullion value. It seems, however, that there are still pigeons waiting to be plucked in almost every state of the Union, who can be induced to swallow the preposterous tale of a gold brick going begging for purchasers, at a fraction of its real value. So these speculators will start off, as they have done, year after year, to meet Lo, the poor Indian, who has carried the brick under his arm from Arizona to Maine; or, it may be, to shave the stupid Mexican miner who cannot speak English, and can only bargain, in dumb show, for the sale of his brick to a keen Yankee countryman.

In the earliest stages of this swindle, many of these bricks had not even a coating of gold, but when the gulls rose above brass bricks, the sharpers put a thin electro-plating of gold over the core of base metal, and challenged the gulls to drop nitric acid on the plated brick, as an infallible test of its character. When the speculators in bricks learned, by bitter experience, that all is not gold that glitters or bears nitric acid without smoking,—the progressive "bunco men" bored holes in their bricks and plugged the holes with pure gold; and some, even, inserted gold wedges or slides. Then the mock test was paraded of boring into the gold plugs, or sawing into the gold slides, and confiding the gold dust, so produced, to the gulls for their acid test or for accurate assaying. This latest device has usually succeeded in closing the sale of the brick, and then the victims wrap up their purchases carefully and store them in strong boxes or the vaults of safety deposit companies to repose until they are wanted for conversion into cash. Then comes the inevitable revelation and the gulls flutter about in dismay, while the "bunco men" are selling new bricks thousands of miles away. The gold plugging trick is a refinement of the art of swindling, which only the masters practice; for it is commonly sufficient to cheat the gull by substituting a little package of gold dust for the dust obtained by boring into a plated brick, if the victim is not willing to confide in the report of a confederate, who is near at hand in the mask of an assayer of high reputation.

Sometimes this moss covered "gold brick" trick has another coat of varnish in its production as the "gold dust" swindle. Then the familiar Mexican or Indian appears as an idiot lugging around bags of gold dust, which he has washed out of the sands of remote placers of prodigious richness, in El Dorado. The mouths of these tempting bags are untied and their loads of glittering dust are dumped on a table. "You can handle the dust yourself," says the spider to the fly, and the dupe revels in the novel sensation of plunging his hands into the heap and clawing over the yellow grains. "Take a spoonful home with you!" says the spider, and the fly goes off with a neat little parcel of good gold dust, which has been slily exchanged for the spoonful which he scooped up and allowed the obliging spider to wrap up for him.

This trick of substitution is nearly as old as the first speculation in gold mining, but it is still current, not only for the sale of portable gold bricks and dust, but for passing off mountains of barren rock as prolific gold and silver mines. Even when examinations are made and samples taken for assay by the agents of the purchasers, it has been shown that the pretentious mine was nothing more than a gigantic "gold

WILLIAM BARRACKS.

LEWIS LUDLOW.

JAMES MINCHEON.

WILLIAM RAYMOND.

brick" with a thin skin of ore. The notion that the "simple Mexican" or the "honest miner" is willing to sell a "gold brick" of any size or description for less than it is worth has been a very costly one to many capitalists who would sneer at the gullibility of their verdant countrymen. A few borings and a collection of pickings from the faces of drifts and cross cuts are of no more value as certificates of a mine than the ordinary tests of a "gold brick." So we may fitly remark that the collection of "bunco men" and gulls, in the "gold brick" game, is not confined to the sellers and buyers of little bricks.

Of late years a frequent substitute for the ordinary "gold brick" game has been played by swindlers who are technically known as "cross-roaders." In this game the "bunco man" appears as a man of property in search of a desirable farm, or else, as an agent empowered to pick out a farm for some wealthy relative. In either case he is invariably well dressed and a fluent, plausible talker. He will drive up in a fine, light carriage to the house of a well-to-do farmer, and ask if any good farms are for sale in the neighborhood. If the farmer knows of any such property—and he usually does—he will be urgently invited to take a seat in the carriage and show the stranger the way to the farm for sale. If he is busy and cannot go at once, the polite caller will consult his convenience and beg the favor of his company with such address and persistence that he usually succeeds in gaining his point. When the farm in question is reached, the sharper will examine the buildings and land with a show of marked satisfaction and close the bargain for it, without much haggling, only stipulating for the proper verification of title. In the course of the drive or the bargaining he will casually extract from his pocket a big wad of banknotes, and impress his companion with his parade of ready cash.

On the way back from the farm, a confederate will appear on the road, who will stop the carriage to make some inquiry. After some bantering the new-comer will propose some game or bet, and the farmer will be led on to take a hand by the certain prospect of winning and by the offer of his companion to put up half of the stake. When the partners have won a large sum, the loser will ask for proof of their ability to make their stake good. The swindler in the carriage will show his money, and the exultant farmer will proceed to prove his claim by drawing out of his bank the amount of his share and carrying the money to the appointed meeting place. This exhibit will leave no loop hole, apparently, for further question, and the stake will be paid over to the winners.

Then the first "bunco man" will ask the farmer to oblige him by taking charge of all the money, including the purchase money for the farm, until he is able to return and close the bargain. This display of confidence naturally tickles the farmer and he is well pleased, also, to put his own money with the deposit of his confiding friend in a tin bank-box, which his friend has fortunately taken along under the seat of his carrige. After a cordial parting, he takes the box under his arm and goes home. When he gets home and, sometimes, on the way home, he is likely to open the box and is confounded to find nothing within more precious than a stone wrapped up in brown paper. He has fallen a victim to the ancient shuffle trick.

If money cannot be extracted from the pockets or hoards of the destined victims by the cajoling and juggling of the sharpers, or if the timid speculators are slow in parting with their cash,— it is a common resort of the rascals to obtain by some device the show of money and then to filch or snatch it away. This is done particularly when the victim is an old or feeble person whom the "bunco men" will entice, if they can, into some lonely place or den of thieves where cries will not be heard and struggles can soon be overcome. Here the old man is sometimes knocked senseless, or gagged and bound so quickly that he cannot raise an alarm, or else he is induced to take a hand in some "fake" lottery or other cheating game and his money is taken away under some knavish pretence. If the victims are men of such standing among their neighbors and friends that they are ashamed to confess any association with "bunco men," or any dabbling in "bunco games," they will frequently suffer their losses in secret in preference to exposing their folly to public contempt. So the rascals, who are robbers as well as swindlers, may escape pursuit and punishment. The aged victims—who are usually selected as marks for the "gold brick" trick and its dependent schemes of robbery—are technically known as "Pappy Guys" in the lingo of bunco.

Some "stars" of the first magnitude in the galaxy of "bunco men" are depicted on our representative portrait pages. William Raymond and James (alias "Doc") Mincheon are a pair of rogues who are commonly working partners in every variation of "bunco." George Post, William Barracks, Lewis Ludlow, Clay Wilson and Samuel Brotzki are notorious knaves of the same stripe, "gold brick men," "cross-roaders" and expert in every "confidence game" from years of practice in almost every state of the Union. Post was a partner of "Tom" O'Brien, the "king of the bunco men," as we have noted. O'Brien is serving out his life sentence, but Post is filling the gap in the ranks to the best of his ability.

Jacob Sondheim, alias "Al" Wise, or Wilson, has a variegated record as a pickpocket, bank sneak and forger, as well as a pestiferous "bunco man," and he has obtained special distinction, of late years, through his successful counterfeits of the "gold sweating" cheat. He is a plausible rascal who contrives to obtain the confidence of men with more money than conscience. He persuades these men that he is the sole controller of a secret process by which genuine gold coins can be "sweated," or reduced in weight, without damage to their appearance.

In several instances he has induced these speculators to construct tanks in the basement of their houses and put in from ten to twenty thousand dollars in gold pieces for treatment in his chemical solution. Then he has filled the tanks with a dark colored mixture, informing his backers that twenty days will be needed to "sweat" the gold perfectly. As the tanks are strong iron vats and their iron covers are securely locked, the speculators are not afraid to leave their gold to soak in their own cellars, for they hold the keys that fit the locks. Unfortunately for them, their agent, Jacob, does not forget to provide himself with duplicate keys and before the allotted time for the "sweating" has passed, he has fitted false keys to the doors of their houses and carried off the gold which has not shrunk a pennyweight, in his mixture. At the end of the twenty days, or before, if the absence of their chemist is alarming, the speculators unlock their vats and usually find a deposit of rocks in exchange for their gold pieces. This trick has given to Mr. Sondheim a European as well as an American reputation.

Other variations of the "gold brick" swindle are offered in the yarns spun over sunken galleons and buried treasures and inheritances awaiting the coming of rightful claimants. In all these cases some money is needed to uncover the treasure or to trace and establish a title, and, in spite of all warnings, this advance is, too often, furnished by the gulls of the "bunco men."

An amusing exhibit of this class was given, not long ago, in the letters of a Spanish swindler to a number of people in this country. The writer sometimes pretended to be a priest who had learned of a buried treasure from the lips of a prisoner dying in a dungeon, and sometimes it was the prisoner himself who told the tale. In the strictest confidence it was revealed that a certain Senor Mateo, a confidant of King Alphonso, had been intrusted with the charge of a million francs in gold and a casket of jewels. Mateo had fled to America and buried the treasure, but he had been obliged to leave his wife behind in Spain. Unfortunately the pining wife fell sick, and the faithful Mateo braved every risk in returning to comfort her. Sad to relate, she died before her chivalrous husband could clasp her in his arms, and he was seized, as he entered his ancestral home, and flung into a dismal dungeon.

There he lingered forlorn till he died, but, on his death-bed, he confided the secret of the grave of his treasure to a compassionate priest. For the sake of the recovery of the jewels the Spanish government was willing to dismiss a suit then pending against the estate of the dead Mateo, if the jewels were returned and the costs of prosecution paid. This concession would leave a balance of nearly a million francs to be divided between the alleged priest and the American agent who would be employed to dig up the treasure. Upon receipt of the sum necessary to satisfy the costs of the suit, the priest would send on complete plans and landmarks defining the burial place of the jewels and the pot of francs.

It is not known how many American gulls responded to this tempting proposition, but it is known that the scheme with varying details was presented to the attention of American capitalists from Maine to California. It may seem transparent "bunco," but it is certain that worse spun yarns have been successful in fleecing American lambs.

A foster-brother, if not a twin, of the gold brick swindle, is known as the "green goods" or "sawdust" game. This is the secret sale of counterfeit money or packages, said to be filled with counterfeit bills, to unscrupulous purchasers. The game is usually opened by the mailing of circulars to addresses obtained from directories or other lists which can be secured for the purpose. These communications are sent out by "green goods" men to the extent of hundreds of thousands annually, and their general style and character are fairly represented in the following typical sample, which lately came into the possession of the Boston Police Department:

Dear Sir:—I am in possession of a *good thing,* and with your confidential and friendly coöperation, I can make you independently rich, and at the same time, better my own condition.

The enclosure herewith gives all the information that could be desired and explains itself.

There's no reason why *you* should be a slave and toil all of your life for nothing. The opportunity is here for you to "switch off" from poverty and benefit yourself in a substantial way. Don't be foolish enough to let conscientious scruples interfere with your aim in life. Few men ever obtain riches honestly. Others have grown rich around you (no one knows how), why not you? A hint to the wise is sufficient. You will see from the sketch that my goods are *not* what the law can class as real counterfeits, inasmuch as they are printed from *genuine* plates, and can easily be passed in your section of the country with impunity.

This is serious and highly important food for thought! Your sober and earnest attention should be given to every word in this letter. A person without the "universal rudder"—the Almighty Dollar—is thought but little of, and is looked upon as of no importance to the world. Isn't this true? I know whereof I speak; in former years I have drank from the "bitter cup" myself.

If you have not the money to buy my goods, I would consent to your taking some confidential friend in with you who has; provided, of course, he is trustworthy and could keep the secret. You could both then come on together and make the deal. However, you would be very foolish to take any one in with you if you could raise enough money yourself.

If my business should suit you, it will be absolutely necessary for you to come on here and see me in person. I only deal face to face with my customers. Experience has taught me that this is the safest and most satisfactory way for both. By your coming on here, you see what you are buying, and I see who I am dealing with. Consequently everything is "on the level," and we both feel better satisfied.

I know it is quite a journey for you to make, but, ye gods, just think of the "gold mine" in store for you—in the way of profits. Furthermore, I always make a liberal allowance in goods to cover the expenses. Make up your mind to come on—I know you will always be thankful for your visit to me. You will find me a *square and honorable* white man in every particular. When you arrive here I will show you my entire stock, from which you can make your own seclections. Then, if my goods are not all that I claim for them, and are not as fine as the enclosure speaks of, I will make you a present of One Thousand Dollars in gold, and also cheerfully pay all expenditures incurred upon your journey. Fair enough—isn't it? My prices are as follows: $300 gets Three Thousand; $400 gets Five Thousand; $650 gets Ten Thousand; $1,000 gets Thirty Thousand; $2,000 gets Seventy-five Thousand. $2,000 is the most I will sell on the first deal. The more you invest the cheaper you get the goods. The sizes run from "One" to "Twenty." $300 worth of my goods is positively the very smallest amount I will sell under any circumstances. If you will invest $650 or more I will agree to give you the exclusive State right. Now, should you wish to do business with me, you must obey the following instructions, and do only as I tell you.

First:—Don't, as long as you live, ever write a letter to me until I give you permission. If you do it will be refused. See? I mean exactly what I say, and, furthermore, all business relations between us will end.

Second:—If you wish to come on here and see me, send the following Telegram (Remember Telegram ONLY will be received), and simply say: "SEND INSTRUCTIONS," then sign your name as per *"password and number"* given you.

Third:—On receipt of your telegram I will send you full instructions how to meet me and where to stop, then no mistakes will be made in finding one another.

In conclusion I wish to say if you cannot come on here, or have not $300 to invest, and you think favorably of my business, send the following telegram: *"What is market prices?"*

I will then make you another proposition. Now kindly allow me to caution you again, *not to write letters!* Be patient, and be guided by my advice. If you do, you will be sure of success. No such thing as fail. Act square! Be true and honorable! Do me no harm, and you will never regret it as long as you live. You can make money faster and easier by dealing in my goods than you ever dreamed of before in your life. Won't you try it?

CAUTION:—No other person is now authorized by me to correspond on this subject. Do not be deceived by shoddy imitations. I am the sole owner and proprietor of this enterprise. Communications from others offering similar goods for sale are absolutely unreliable and positively worthless. Pay no attention to them. "Nuf-ced."

Yours very sincerely,

"YOU KNOW."

Keep this for future reference.

Send your telegrams, (no letters) to

THOMAS HUNT,

Claremont,

New Jersey.

Your Pass-word and Number is "Turnip 573." Do not sign anything else.

CAUTION:—Be sure you have the numbers (plainly written) on all telegrams after you sign the Pass-word "TURNIP" otherwise your telegrams will positively receive no attention whatever. The "figures" are very important. All answers from me will be sent to the same name and address as written on the present envelope—unless otherwise instructed by you.

Above all things do not sign your name, only your Password and number, and send all telegrams over the Western Union Telegraph Company lines, (if possible) to avoid mistakes, also prepay all messages as it is very important. Should

CLAY WILSON.

GEORGE POST.

JACOB SONDHEIM.

SAMUEL BROTZKI.

the telegraph operator ask you for your name or address, refuse to give it, simply say, "My name or address is not necessary."

N. B.—Should there be any official notice stamped on this envelope pay no attention to it whatever, as it is put there by the new administration to find out who has got the plates, as they are missing from the Treasury. Possession of the original plates is the foundation of my success, and as I have the plates, the stamping of this ridiculous notice cannot injure me at all; unless to frighten off some timid agent.

It will be observed that the cheat begins with the false pretence that the counterfeit bills, offered by the "green goods" man, "are not what the law can class as real counterfeits, inasmuch as they were printed from genuine plates." There is a twofold lie in this assurance. Even if the plates were stolen, as the swindler pretends or assumes, bills printed from them by any unauthorized person are no less certainly counterfeit bills, in the eye of the law, than bills printed from the most bungling imitations of genuine plates. The maker or utterer of such bills is liable, therefore, to the full penalties imposed by law for the offence of forging, uttering, or even consciously holding counterfeit money in hand. Secondly, the plates in question were unquestionably made by some process of secret counterfeiting, if they are really in existence at all,—a matter by no means assured by the word of a "green goods" man.

It is calculated, as a matter of course, that only a small percentage of these circulars will reach persons who are willing to comply with the imperative instructions laid down and open communication by telegrams with "Thomas Hunt of Claremont, New Jersey," or other swindlers of the same stripe. But the cost of printing and mailing these circulars is relatively so small, compared with the sums which may be obtained from a few of the geese who are willing to be knaves, that there is likely to be a considerable profit for the "green goods man," if only one of ten thousand of these baits catches a gudgeon.

We will suppose that a bait is swallowed, and the gudgeon

sends a dispatch by wire to "Thomas Hunt" and obtains an appointment to meet the swindler. The financial banker of the gang, who furnishes the money for bait and other expenses, will usually arrange to keep under cover and send one of his partners or hired men to meet the dupe. After this meeting has been arranged with every possible precaution to assure the fact that the correspondent is not a detective in disguise,—the dupe is taken to some private room or unfrequented place in the neighboring country and, by one trick or another, his good money is exchanged for a package of poor counterfeit notes, or a box stuffed with sawdust, or a brick wrapped in paper, or some other worthless parcel.

There is always a great pretence of secrecy and apprehension of arrest in the shuffle of the exchange, and, after the first hasty examination, the victim is hurried away to the cars, or carried off in a wagon to some distant place, with the caution not to expose his purchase to any risk of spies by further inspection before he is beyond the reach of the local police. Frequently the top of a package of counterfeit bills or sawdust is covered by one or two genuine bills, which are shown to the dupe as a sample of the "green goods" which he will be permitted to buy for a small fraction of their face value. Sometimes a roll of genuine bills is actually put in his hands, for a moment, to count and examine; and, after his money is paid over, the roll which he holds will be filched away by some pretence or juggle and a worthless package returned in exchange.

In one of the most artful tricks of the craft, he is allowed to put the roll of good bills in his own tin box and lock it securely before he hands over the purchase money. Then a "green goods man" invites him to take a seat in his buggy and the pair of knaves ride away, after carefully stowing the precious tin box under the seat of the carriage. The bottom of the buggy, under the seat, has a secret slide or panel opening with a spring, and, before the carriage has gone a hundred yards, this slide or panel is opened by the "green goods" man and the box drops on the road, where it is picked up at once by confederates in waiting. Then the panel is put back in place and a similar box, stuffed with paper, is substituted, which the victim will take away when he bids good-bye to his swindling companion. As he has consented to wrap up his box in an envelope of paper or cloth, tightly fastened with string, he is not likely to detect the cheat until he is far away from the "green goods" men.

It is useless to present, in detail, every known variation of this swindling game, for all are founded on the same shuffling device of substitution, unless the resort of pocket-picking or robbery by force is used instead. The ordinary buyer of "green goods" has practically no chance of defeating the schemes of the spiders who catch him in their nets, although there are some instances in which these knaves have been outwitted by rascals of their own stripe. When the swindling exchange has actually been effected, the victims will almost inevitably suffer their loss without open complaint, because they fear to expose themselves to the eye of the law. The only sensible and honest disposal of a "green-goods" circular is to destroy it at sight, and no communication whatever will be held with any rascals of this class by a man of common honesty or sense.

The swindling horse dealer, commonly styled the "horse sharp," is an expert "bunco man" in his line of business. He is the man who picks up worn-out circus horses, or the refuse of breeding stables, or horses of fair outside show but practically valueless on account of their ineradicable viciousness or freaks of bolting, kicking and balking. He is a master of every art of concealing the diseases or faults or tricks of a horse until his sale is concluded and the horse is finally turned over to the swindled customer.

He will sometimes work off his worthless stock at horse fairs and auctions; but his favorite method is to procure an advertisement or to send out circulars, informing possible customers that horses belonging to private families are offered at private sale, for various plausible reasons. Sometimes the head of the family has died, and the mourning widow is reluctantly compelled to dispose of the valuable pair of matched roadsters which her late husband prized as the apple of his eye. Or, again, the family is on the point of departing for Europe for a tour of indefinite length and the stable must be sold at short notice, so that no offer within reason will be refused. Or, may be, it is a physician who is winding up his practice with the design of opening his office in a distant state. So the variations run through the stretch of invention, but one note is invariably sounded. It is the fixed determination of the owners that their horses shall not be sold to professional horse dealers or stable keepers or jockeys or agents, who cannot be trusted to give a fatherly care to these dear animals.

Nobody will be suffered to lead off these pets unless he obtains them for his own personal use or that of his family.

Some lively and vivid illustrations of the conduct of these horse sales and the character of these "family pets" are given in the accompanying sketches.

The first figure shows a gullible customer, known to the sharpers as a "jay," just entering the stable where the pets are lodged and falling into the hands of the first assistant "bunco man" in the person of the faithful groom, "Tom," who has had the care of the horses for years. "Yessah, old mars'r's dead, bless his heart! He was one of de ol' Virginny Persimmons, sah;

SHARPERS AND DUPES.   205

a high-toned S'uthern gen'l'man; nevah gave a cross word to me, sah; an' he was took awful sudden; an' it pretty near done broke ol' missy's heart, sah; and now she's got t' let de po' dear hosses go, dat ol' mars'r yus t' drive, sah; an' lit'l' missy Eva, dat dear chile, has jus' been yere, a cryin' her pretty lit'l' eyes out,—but look yere—yere comes young mars'r Bob, sah, an' he'll tell yer all about it!

Enter "young mars'r Bob," who has the leading part in this "bunco" play. He is masquerading as the eldest son of the family, who has charge of the sale; and he comes in, after faithful "Tom" has reeled off his touching yarn, to take the half-snared "jay" in hand and drop another net over his head. He is rigged up for his part in a suit of solemn black from top to toe, not forgeting a mourning weed that nearly covers his hat, and elegant black gloves that encase his slim and taper fingers without a wrinkle.

After some smooth words with the customer, he calls upon the devoted "Tom" to bring out the choicest one of the family horses; and "Tom" leads this precious animal out of the stall and puts him through a set of paces for the inspection of the visitor. Sometimes the docile pet pricks up his ears, at the start, and tries to jump through a window or jerks faithful "Tom" over the floor of the stable, like the bob of a kite, in his vicious capers; but there is always a flow of smooth talk to cover up any cavorting, and every possible change is rung on the fine spirit and gentle playfulness of this family pet. Our artist has a pen picture of this exhibit, in which "Tom" is dodging the flying hoofs and the showman is filling the ear of the dupe with his oily patter in praise of the lamb-like gambols of the family pet.

In the next scene of this comedy "lit'l' missy Eva" appears on the stage,—coming in, all in tears, through the stable door and running up to her brother or to dear "Tom," whom she clasps around the legs and sobbingly begs not to sell her father's favorite horse. "It will break dear mamma's heart to part with Charley," lisps this little "bunco girl," in a voice broken with sobs,—"Oh, don't let the bad man take Charley away!" Her brother tenderly pats the little one on the head and gently explains to her that mamma is obliged to sell papa's horse now that poor papa cannot drive him any more. But little Eva keeps on sobbing and will not listen to her fond brother. "Oh, come away, come away, come home to mamma," she cries, "and mamma will tell the naughty man that he can't have dear Charley."

Then the scene shifts to the home of dear mamma, depicted in the sketch of our artist. "Brother Bob" brings in the bashful "jay" who nervously fingers his hat and really feels that he is a cruel man to be the cause, even innocently, of so much distress to the little girl and her mother. The "widow" sits weeping in her parlor and the little girl runs up to her, crying: "Oh, mamma, mamma, they are going to take our darling Charley away, and we shall never, n'n'never see him any more."

Mamma sobs, too, hugs the child convulsively to her bosom;

SHARPERS AND DUPES.

and then, with a brave air of fortitude, lifts her head and courteously greets the stranger, while tenderly stilling her weeping child, and wiping her tears away with her fine cambric handkerchief. "Yes, sir," she says, "we must sell dear Charley,—don't cry, dear, mamma must do what is right—we must sell the horse which my dear husband brought up from a colt; but we would not sell him, on any account, to anybody who would not use him kindly and love him as much as we love him. But you look like a good, kind man and, if you will promise faithfully to keep the horse for your own family use, and treat him gently, I am willing that my son should let you have him."

The good-hearted countryman is now melted almost to tears by this piteous play, and he warmly protests that he will treat dear Charley like a brother, if this precious horse is confided to him. "You must arrange the price with my son," says the widow, with an air of overpowering weariness and indifference to such vulgar details.

The visitor takes the hint and goes off with the son, who has usually little difficulty in selling the horse at a price that fills the "widow's" heart with unaffected delight, for she divides the profit with the leading "bunco man" and the faithful "Tom."

Sometimes this parade is varied in another way shown by our artist. The customer meets a spruce young man at the stable, and hears that he is the only son of a gentleman who cannot use his horses—because he is closely confined to his bed-chamber and it may be years before he will be able to go out driving again. This tale may have a rock bottom of fact, as appears in the accompanying picture of the "father" wistfully staring through the bars of his prison cell. But we may be sure that the real style of the bed chamber forms no part of the image conjured up to affect the "jay."

Again, when the caller appears to be more hesitating and wary than usual, there is often a resort to the sly trick of introducing another confederate, in the person of an avowed horse dealer or jockey. He comes in, while the "jay" is still hemming and hawing over a bargain for a horse, and appears to make up his mind in a moment. "That's the sort of horse I want." he says bluntly, "what's his price?" "Who are you?" says the son, who is showing the horse. "Here's my card,"

replies the new comer, producing the card of a horse dealer. "Well, sir, you can't have this horse; no man of your sort can get my father's horse on any terms!" Then the stranger pretends to be moved to hot resentment and starts a squabble which ends with his exit out of the stable door, assisted by the son and the groom, in the manner shown by our sketch.

This display of determination naturally impresses the "jay" and when he goes away half disposed to close his purchase, he meets the pretended horse dealer waiting for him at some little distance from the stable.

"See here, stranger," says the sharper, "that's a mighty good horse those people have for sale up there. What do they ask for him?"

The gull names the price which was stated to him.

"Cheap as dirt," says the "horse sharp." "I'll tell you what I'll do, sir. You don't want that horse particularly, but I do.

They won't sell him to me, because I am a professional dealer; but you can get him easy enough and, if you can buy him at the price named, I'll take him off your hands in a minute, and give you fifty dollars to boot for your trouble. I'll wait here for you, for I mustn't be seen hanging about the stable or they'll suspect there's some deal between us. You get that horse as soon as you can and bring him here, and you find man and money ready."

If the dupe bites at this bait and buys the horse in order to make fifty dollars,—he will spend the rest of the day hunting for the eager purchaser and finally go home with his dear horse and experience.

Another favorite trick to effect a sale is the assurance that the "horse sharp" will send to the purchaser several additional horses to board on liberal terms for the winter, as the customer expects that his profit will largely offset the cost of the single horse which he has agreed to buy. After he has paid for the horse, there will be some pretence for delay in forwarding the other horses, and he will surely grow weary if he waits in hope to receive the promised shipment. He may get, instead, some

trumped up excuse of the "horse sharp" or he may get nothing more consoling than his experience in this "bunco game."

In displaying the horses at these swindling sales, all kinds of expedients are used to disguise the condition and character of the animals; and the certificates or guarantees given to

purchasers are usually queer documents. The form of proper certificates is copied as closely as possible, and there is a wordy parade of catch phrases and legal technicalities to hoodwink hasty readers or greenhorns. But when the supposed guarantees are closely examined, after the fraud is discovered, there is no pledge of redress to the purchaser.

Sometimes it will be certified that the horse in question "feeds well and takes his rest well." Or it is stated that "he is as kind in double as in single harness;" or, again, it will appear that "any lady can drive him as well as a gentleman." It may be averred that "he will stand for hours without hitching and has never been known to run away." The value of this last certificate of docility is well illustrated in the experience of the

young lady depicted by our artist, who is vainly trying to move one of these bunco steeds from his grazing place at the side of a road. A companion picture shows the certified gait of another of these horses who has been formally credited with "a fine easy knee action" and warranted to be "as gentle under the saddle as he is in harness." Another one of these brutes, with a like certificate, is shown tearing away, after upsetting and wrecking a carriage on top of the unfortunate people who trusted in the hollow pretence of a "bunco man." A horse who "will go ten miles as readily as he will one" is illustrated in the last of the series, an instance where the buyer forgot to demand a guarantee that the horse could be moved a foot with less than five men.

Quite frequently the horses put up for sale in this way will go through their exhibit without showing any apparent blemish or fault to the eye of an ordinary purchaser; and many of them may be driven away without displaying their viciousness or peculiar ailments, although there are known instances in which the poor horse has dropped dead before going a thousand yards. But some day—and generally within a few days—the discovery of the bunco game must be made, and the purchasers will try to return their bargains and get their money back.

It need hardly be observed that this restitution is no part of the scheme of the bunco man, and it will never be made if he can evade or escape doing so. If he doesn't hide himself, or leave the city, as soon as he has sold his horses, he will meet complainants with a brazen front and profess to disbelieve any report that is made to him. It is quite common for him to give a guarantee that a horse may be returned at any time within two weeks from the date of the sale, provided the animal is brought back in as good condition as when sold. This apparently reasonable stipulation commonly quiets any anxiety on the part of the purchaser, who fails to observe that the judge of the comparative condition of the horse is a sharper who can never be satisfied that a horse, when returned, is as good as when sold. Moreover, the rogue has inserted in the same guarantee a provision that no verbal embellishments of the written warrant shall be of any binding effect. So the swindled purchaser has often no sufficient legal ground for the establishment of a claim of fraudulent misrepresentation.

There is another noteworthy cheat which is a common practice of "bunco men," because it is difficult to convict the swindler of intentional fraud, even if his trick is detected. A sleek, well-dressed rascal will enter a store or office and ask the cashier to oblige him by changing a fifty dollar bill or some other bank note of a high denomination. If the cashier changes the bill, the applicant will ask for a number of one or two dollar bills or silver, with a suave apology for the trouble of making change. In handing back the bills to be changed, he will slily take out a five or ten dollar bill, and rely on the chance that a busy cashier will not count over carefully the amount returned. If his cheat is detected, he will beg pardon for his "blunder" and give the correct change; but he frequently gets away from the window and out of the store before the trick is discovered. This swindle is known to the craft of bunco men as the "flim-flam game," and the professional players are styled "flim-flammers."

Besides these specially notorious and distinct forms of the "bunco game," which we have described, there are all the variations in play, that are practiced by that legion of knaves who come under the general head of "the confidence man." We scarcely need note that this term has come into familiar usage, because the winning of confidence by some cheating pretence is the bottom of all the wide ranging variations in the swindling practices of these rascals. The "gold brick" man, the "cross-roader," and the "bunco man" of every stripe are

DAVID SWAIN.

HENRY DAVIS.

HARRY GIFFORD.

CHARLES GIFFORD.

"confidence men"; but, for the sake of distinction, the latter term is usually applied to the swindlers who have no peculiar designation fitting their practices. Without attempting to mark every known twist in the shifts of these swindlers, we shall call attention to the representative tricks which have been most successful in defrauding the public.

Undoubtedly an enormous plunder in the aggregate has been heaped up by the knaves who have swindled investors, in this country and Europe, with their "confidence game" of selling worthless town lots and other lands by false representations. The bitter experience of "Martin Chuzzlewit" has a rock bottom of fact which was not the less real because this particular Martin was a creation of fancy. Hundreds of thousands of actual victims would truly attest, if they could be called to bear witness, that they, too, had been caught in the trap of some "General Choke" or agent "Scadder," and dropped their savings into the quagmire of some fabulous "Eden." And, in spite of all warnings, how many thousands more will be gulled like the credulous Martin with showy prospectuses and paper towns in the air!

"Confidence men" of less pretension and celebrity are wandering through the country to-day professedly taking orders for lightning rods and obtaining signatures to notes of hand from ignorant farmers who suppose that they are simply contracting to pay for some wires. Or they are masquerading as "summer boarders" or invalids seeking a fountain of health in "milk fresh from the cow." When they have stretched their line of credit to the snapping point, they will steal away without even bidding good-bye to their hosts; or they will leave paper mementoes in the form of worthless checks which will come back to remind the victims that plausibility is not reliability—that promises or orders to pay are not cash,—and that forged letters of reference are not guarantees of credit.

When the "confidence man" comes to town, he will sometimes rent a house or a suite of rooms and obtain his furniture from trusting sellers on the instalment plan. Then he will get as many loans as he can on this furniture and skip off before his second instalment is due. "Confidence women" are particularly plausible and expert in the execution of this trick, and business men in every city in the country have been victimized by it. Valuable sets of books have been obtained, also, as well as considerable sums of money, by a variation of this fraud. Two "confidence men" carry through this trick,—one, professing to be a physician or some other professional man; and the other masquerading as a book agent. The pretended physician will get rooms on credit in a fashionable quarter of a city and put up his office sign. Then his confederate will get employment as a book agent, and sell a costly set of books to his partner, on the instalment plan. The first instalment will be paid; the agent will collect his commission; and both will disappear with the books and commission money. Sometimes several sets of books and several commissions will be wafted away in this fashion before the cheat is discovered.

Similar swindles on a greater scale are effected by the "confidence men" who open stores and succeed in buying large stocks of goods, wholly on credit or upon small cash payments. Over and over again these stocks have been shipped off to be sold at auction or to be secretly stored with some "fence," or receiver of stolen goods. When the payments, or notes for the goods, fall due, the "confidence men" will "fail" or abscond.

Probably the most frequent and successful frauds of this kind are the operations of swindling commission agents and, especially, those dealing in country produce. These rascals, by means of attractive circulars or advertising, obtain shipments from farmers and dairymen. Then the supplies will be sold to confederates, and worthless notes taken in exchange to make a showing when the swindlers "fail;" or the goods will be quickly marketed at the best price obtainable, and the shippers will wait in vain for any cash returns. To prevent possible identification and recovery of any shipments—the marks are usually scraped from the packages, as soon as received, and every tag cut off. Then the goods are put beyond the reach or recall of their owners.

A common method of obtaining credit and consignments is to counterfeit, with a slight variation, the name of a well known firm in the same line of business in the same city or district. Sometimes an initial in the name will be altered, or the address will be changed to some neighboring town. Thus the firm of "Roe and Doe" of Chelsea has been confounded with the good firm of "Roe and Doe" of Charlestown in a way very vexing to the Charlestown firm and very disastrous to the heedless shippers of produce.

Another device of the "confidence man" is to obtain a good business rating by false representations to the commercial agencies. Then he will make a delusive show of a stable and prosperous business for a few months until his confederates are able to discount his notes without much difficulty. When the notes mature, it will be discovered that the signers and indorsers are "confidence men," but a harvest may be gathered before this frost.

Closely akin to this trick is the one which sets up some bogus business and then offers it for sale in whole or in part. This may be done in the commission business, or in any commercial line which requires only a small investment in stock or plant to make a deceptive show of prosperity. Frequently some patented article, or humbug applying for patent, is the chosen bait for gudgeons, and the victims will be entertained by a lively show of business for a few days before they swallow the bait. Then they learn that parade and bustle and shipping of goods on the shuttlecock plan—out one day and in the next, —are not solid proofs of a real and profitable business.

On a par with these offers of bogus business investments is the solicitation of advertisements from business men for "fake" directories and other swindling publications, whose issue is often limited to the number actually necessary for the collection of the advertising accounts. "Proof of publication" may only mean a single copy carried around and exhibited to the swindled advertisers; but the victims usually agree to pay without any better assurance that they are getting something more than a "bunco game" for their money. This practice has been carried so far of late years that it has become a really serious swindle.

Another common trick of these swindlers is the obtaining of a signature of a business firm to a contract which differs from the agreement which has been made verbally and is supposed to be incorporated in the printed or written form. In this way a fraudulent claim may be set up and the signed contract offered in evidence to sustain it. Sometimes, too, the date of an old contract is altered so that it may be presented again for payment, or the amount stated in the original contract may be erased and a much larger sum inserted.

It is certain, too, that the frauds of alleged insurance or endowment orders are "bunco games" of a most dangerous class; for their range of possible victims is extraordinarily wide, and they have proved to be exceptionally delusive in attracting investors. Their promises of great profit have blinded the speculators to the fact that the rate of profit is apt to correspond to the extent of the risk, and their comparative novelty has given them an advantage over the older forms of swindling.

Everybody has heard of the threadbare trick of the "bunco men" who walk up, smiling, to greet strangers on the street as old acquaintances. If they succeed in learning the real names of their selected "marks," by this trick, their confederates will make a better front, a few minutes later, when they pretend to know the same men. This is a stale and clumsy artifice, however, compared with the wiles of really accomplished "confidence men," who will contrive to gain access to possible victims without exciting any suspicion. These rogues are never at a loss for plausible pretences for scraping an acquaintance, and many adventurers make a practice of roaming from city to city, getting cards of admission to clubs and credit in various ways by false representations. Most of these knaves calculate to get all they can by cheating without actually crossing the penal line into forgery; but they are apt to carry their manufacture of checks and letters so far that they can be indicted for forgery as well as for swindling.

We have before cautioned business men against the acceptance of checks from strangers, who are, too often, "confidence men"; and we have particularly noted that the pretence that a check is certified is no assurance that the certification has not been forged. A swindling scheme that is closely allied to the supposed certification of checks is the use of a single certification to establish a credit which is straightway abused by the presentation of overdrafts or worthless checks. Many business firms in every large city in this country have been cheated, at one time or another, by this specious trick, and there are rascals to-day who are travelling from city to city to carry on this fraud.

The swindler's method is to open an account with a city bank by the deposit of a few hundred dollars and then to make a purchase from some store to an extent not exceeding his bank account. He proposes to pay for his purchase by his check and makes an impressive parade of his willingness to obtain a certification. After his first check is certified, he calculates that his second check will be accepted without the precaution of reference and his calculation is too often well founded. Sometimes, too, the first reference only goes to the point of ascertaining that the plausible customer actually has a bank account, and, in this case, both checks are likely to prove worthless, for the swindler makes haste to draw his money before either check gets through the clearing house. It should be unnecessary to observe, in the way of caution, that one certification does not make subsequent checks good any more than one swallow makes a summer.

Some of the most rascally swindlers in America are the men

who entrap confiding women by pretended marriages or by false promises of marriage, and then desert them, after getting hold of their money. Often these "confidence men" do not stickle at bigamy, if they cannot gain their ends with less risk; and pitiful stories come to us from the poor women who are cheated and robbed and abandoned by these heartless scoundrels.

There are no meaner rascals on the face of the earth than the "confidence men" who make a practice of hanging about steamship wharves and railway stations, and trying to swindle poor immigrants and other travellers. Country people from the eastern provinces of Canada—and especially those who speak English imperfectly—are a favorite prey of these knaves, and their cheating tricks are shifting daily. The leaders of the gangs are usually made up to pass for fatherly old men who gain the confidence and regard of their poor dupes by their sympathetic and kindly ways. Sometimes they take passage on the steamers, or board the trains at stations many miles away from the final stopping place. Before the boats or trains reach their destination, these old rogues have marked their victims and won their confidence so far that swinding is easy, if they are not arrested by watchful detectives.

David Swain, whose portrait is given on a representative page, is one of the worst of these "confidence men." He has fleeced immigrants, countrymen, backwoodsmen and other dupes to the extent of thousands of dollars with the help of his confederates, Henry Davis and a father and son, Harry and Charles Gifford, whose portraits appear in our collection in illustration of one of the most notorious gangs which has ever infested this country.

On another page four other rogues of the same stripe are depicted: John Brady, Charles A. Hicks, John Bernard and James Lewis. The ranks of "confidence men" will be raked in vain to gather another set of meaner rascals.

Sometimes these knaves get their plunder by inducing their

dupes to cash bogus checks or even to intrust their money to them for safe keeping. Another common device is to treat a new acquaintance to several rounds of drinks, and then to persuade him to accompany his liberal friend to his hotel. At the hotel door, a confederate in the mask of a clerk will meet the jolly companions and inform the confidence man that his wife has gone to a railway depot with all his baggage. Of course, she left the hotel bill for her husband to settle, but, unfortunately, the husband has his money in his trunk—could his friend oblige him with a small loan to settle the bill and allow him to pay back the loan as soon as they reach the depot? The dupe finds it hard to refuse this favor to a man who has been so companionable, and the "confidence man" may get fifty or a hundred dollars from him. "Wait a moment for me!" says the sharper, who slips into the hotel and out through a side door. The victim waits with growing impatience until he discovers that his genial friend and his money are both out of sight.

Another common trick is known as the "drop game." The "confidence man," while walking about with his dupe, will pretend to pick up a ring or a watch chain, or some other piece of jewelry from the sidewalk or street. "Hello, what's this!" says the sharper. "Why, it's a ring—solid gold, too! Say, this ring must be worth ten dollars or more. I wonder who lost it!" The dupe will wonder, too, and probably envy the lucky finder. "Now, I tell you what," says the "con" man, "I've got to leave town right off and I can't stop to hunt up the owner of this ring. I suppose that he will advertise for it in the evening papers or to-morrow morning. Perhaps he has got to go off in a hurry, too, and may never try to get his ring back. Anyway, there'll be a good bit paid for returning the ring, or else the finder can keep it. Now, you're going to stay here for a few days. You let me have two dollars for it, and you can have the ring." If his companion bites at this bait—and he often does—the victim will get a bit of pinchbeck metal, worth less than a dime, for two good dollars.

If the "drop game" has been worn too thin in any city, it is likely that the "confidence man" will vary his performance by pulling out of his pocket what is known to his craft as a "fawny" watch, a gift, as he will pretend, from his dear old father or darling mother. He has promised faithfully that he will never part with this precious timepiece, and he could not think of suffering it to pass into the hands of an ordinary pawnbroker, even for a day. But he must have some money to pay his fare home, as he has not received the check which he expected, and he is willing to confide it to a good, trustworthy man, like his companion, as security for the return of the little money that he needs. If this trick succeeds, the dupe will get an oroide watch of the poorest kind, and the confidence man will get away with the money.

Perhaps the most successful snare of all is the trick that is played with freight bills or invoices. The confidence man will be talking with a new acquaintance in a railway station, and a confederate will come up to him and tell him that his goods have arrived and that it will be necessary to pay the freight bill. Unfortunately the sharper does not happen to have the needed amount of money in his pocket at that moment. So his "pal" will ask whether his friend cannot favor him by advancing the money with such ample security. If the "dupe" makes this loan, he will get a counterfeit invoice or a lot of worthless stuff for his money, unless he is willing to accept as security a package of bonds or stock certificates of no value. Confidence men make a practice of carrying about in their pockets parcels of such worthless paper, and the bonds, which they use as traps for gulls, are technically known as "confidence bonds." Sometimes this trick will be slightly varied by the substitution of a bogus check for the bonds or invoice, but the dupe will not be a penny the richer by this exchange.

Naturally the sufferers at the hands of these "confidence men" will make bitter complaints, and it is a black day for one of these rascals when he comes within reach of one of his vic-

JOHN BRADY.

CHARLES HICKS.

JOHN BERNARD.

JAMES LEWIS.

tims. But the knaves waste no time in getting away, after one of their tricks, and the poor people who have been fleeced may never set eyes on their swindlers again. Still, sometimes, they have the satisfaction of seeing that the rogues are caught; and it is particularly gratifying to the police to secure a conviction by bringing a "confidence man" face to face with one of his victims. The rascal, Swain, was once arrested in Boston for swindling a poor wood-chopper out of all of his hard earnings by a long winter's work. When the woodsman came to the police station to identify Swain, that brazen rogue flatly denied that he had ever seen the man before, and actually tried to convince the wood-chopper that he was mistaken in his recognition. "Know ye," cried the big, gaunt woodsman, shaking his gnarly fist at the "bunco man," "I'd know ye, if yer hide was skun off ye and hung on a bush!" Even Swain flinched at this, for it was as plain as a pikestaff that the woodsman was aching for a chance to skin him alive and then identify him.

Every effort is made by the police and detectives of all of our large cities to stop the games of these "confidence men" and catch the rascals. Detectives are specially detailed to guard the railway stations and the steamship landings, and the sharpest possible watch is kept on the movements of any of these knaves. It is a common practice also for a search to be made through the cars and boats arriving at Boston and other cities; and known "confidence men" are arrested or warned away like all known thieves. In spite of all these guards and precautions, the pest of swindlers has been so annoying, at times, from the difficulty of getting evidence enough for conviction, that detectives have been employed as decoys in the disguise of green countrymen, carrying old black "grips" and long leather pocket books well stuffed with bills. When the "confidence men" have gone over the line of the law in trying to cheat these "decoys," they have not been suffered to run away with their booty.

Still, with all the watchfulness and alertness of the police of the country, it is beyond their power to extinguish the "confidence men" completely. It was the observation of a good and keen judge that "there is no law that will entirely protect a fool." The best that can be done is to open the eyes of every possible victim to the wiles and tricks of the swindling hydra.

This we have endeavored to do in the foregoing pages, although we have made no pretence of covering the legion of variations in swindling practices. It has seemed sufficient to present their range and method so fully that the swindles which have passed without special mention may be judged in the light of our representative examples. We shall add only a closing word of caution against the careless habit of confiding too much to chance acquaintances or strangers. It is possible to be as civil and companionable as any occasion may require, without assuming that an agreeable or plausible person may fitly be trusted with money or credit or intimacy.

IN THE CLOAK OF A GUEST.

IN the midst of the gay summer season at a fashionable watering place, the guests of a leading hotel were plagued and puzzled by a series of mysterious disappearances of rings, pins, necklaces, gold and silver toilet sets, watches and laces. Day after day, as they returned to their rooms from breakfast or dinner, the discovery of some new loss would be made, and the landlord and clerks were soon at their wit's end to find any consolation or assurance of protection. At first, there was an effort to keep the news of the losses from spreading to alarm the guests and injure the business of the hotel; though all in the house were specially cautioned never to leave the doors of their rooms unlocked, and a sharp watch was kept upon the servants as well as upon any stranger who came to the house. But the losses ran on in spite of the warnings and watchfulness. It was impossible to keep them a secret, and, within a week, they became an absorbing subject of speculation and discussion.

Strange to say, all the alarm and suspicion and questioning and suggesting did not seem to interfere, in the least, with the flight of the jewels from trunks, boxes and bureaus. Finally the pestered guests almost stifled themselves, in the hot summer nights, by fastening every window and bolting and locking all their chamber doors in order to sleep without fear of thieves. By this scheme of defense they succeeded in making themselves wretchedly uncomfortable; but, sad to say, all this fortification seemed to be of no use as a safeguard. Over and over again, on awaking in the morning, a dismayed guest would discover that his watch or her brooch had flown away in the night, although the chamber doors and the windows were fastened precisely as they had been left when the guests went to bed.

Among the superstitious there began to be a trembling of the nerves, and a relating of ghost stories and of mysterious losses suffered by their sisters or their cousins or their aunts, and never explained. Even the skeptics, who flaunted the idea of any supernatural attachment to the missing rings and pins, had some palpitation of the heart when they became convinced that a thief was creeping into the rooms, at night, in spite of all the bolts and bars, and hovering around their beds in order to steal anything which would serve as "swag." Maybe the rascal would take to his heels if a guest awakened and cried out in alarm, but there was a hanging dread that he might prefer the chance of assault and even of murder in order to stop pursuit and arrest; so everybody in the hotel had more or less of a shaking fit when they went to bed, and the more timid kept lights burning brightly all night and scarcely ventured to take a wink of sleep for fear of a horrid awakening.

Still the mysterious flight continued, although it was evidently interrupted; for several days would pass without any report of a loss, and the landlord and guests would begin to breathe easily once more and congratulate themselves that the plague was ended. But, as soon as there was any relaxation of the watching and guarding in the hotel, another set of jewelry or other valuables would disappear during the daytime or night. The safes of the hotel were overflowing with precious things which the guests were afraid to leave in their rooms, and the house was on the verge of a panic which would have emptied it completely,—when the mysterious losses were finally accounted for and the long-delayed relief came in the arrest of a guest who had never been under the shadow of suspicion.

He was a tall, slim, spruce-looking young man, whose chief concern seemed to be the care of his finger nails and the fitting of his necktie. He pretended to be a foreigner travelling for pleasure; but he spoke English so well that his foreign accent was only a sauce piquant to his conversation. He was a fluent and engaging talker, and so courteous in his manners that he became a general favorite and was fairly showered with invitations to join in boating and driving parties. He was an uncommonly graceful dancer, too; and many a pretty girl was pleased to guide over the waxed floor with a partner so skillful in avoiding the bumps of the whirling crowd.

It was therefore really distressing to a good many people beside himself when this nice young man was caught, one night, by a wide-awake servant just as he was slipping out of the room of a sleeping guest. When he saw that he had no chance of escape, he pretended to be full of wine and vowed that he had mistaken his room in his wandering. He was so dripping with mortification and plausible patter that he might have succeeded in deceiving his captor, if the guest in the chamber had not awaked and discovered that his watch was missing. Unfortunately for the yarn of the blundering drunkard, the watch was fished out of the coat-tail pocket of the thief; and when his clothes were thoroughly searched, several articles, that are not usually kept in the pockets of tourists, were brought to light. These were a ring full of skeleton keys, a pair of small nippers, and a piece of wire bent at one end and carrying a loop or noose of silk thread.

The guest, whose lucky awakening probably saved his watch, recollected, perfectly, locking his chamber door and also fastening it with the iron sliding bolt, which was put on for additional security above the lock. So far, so good; but it did not occur to him to take the key out of the door after locking it; so the sly thief had little difficulty in catching the end of the key in his nippers and turning it until he unlocked the door. After doing this, he pushed the key in until it fell on the carpeted floor of the chamber so noiselessly that the sleeper within was not disturbed. Next he slipped his bit of bent wire through the keyhole, and succeeded, after a few attempts, in casting the loop of silk thread over the pin of the bolt and pulling it down to the open slide-way. Then he slid the bolt out by simply drawing the thread with the wire; and, in a moment, opened the door gently and slipped into the chamber. By groping around, he soon found the watch and he was starting away with his prize when he was detected. If he had not been interrupted so unexpectedly, he would doubtless have locked the door carefully behind him as he had been accustomed to do in his former calls.

Upon searching the room of this elegant thief, a large collection of valuables that had been stolen from the guests of the hotel was recovered and returned to the owners; but the greater part of the lost goods was beyond reach and identification. The industrious "tourist" had been working by night and day for several weeks, and had taken most of his plunder to a "fence" in a neighboring city, when he went to town professedly to visit his banker or his manicurist. Either in his room at the hotel or in the workshops of the receiver of stolen goods, the diamonds and other jewels had been taken out of their settings, and the gold broken up for the melting pot.

The experience of this hotel is only one in ten thousand of similar instances, although in this case the length of the series of thefts was phenomenal. There is scarcely a hotel of any distinction in this country or any part of the world, which has not been plagued, more or less, by the rascals distinctively known as "hotel thieves." These knaves are among the most artful and sly of all thieves; and it is especially difficult to prevent their depredations, because they can usually contrive to enter the houses which they propose to plunder, as ordinary guests. Unless an applicant for a room in a hotel is a known thief or a man of notoriously bad character, he will necessarily be admitted on the same terms as other guests, and he is thus enabled to gain access to the rooms on every floor of the house.

With rare exceptions the professional hotel thief is a well-dressed and ingratiating rascal, who knows well every trick of the "confidence man" and will spare no pains to make a pleasing impression on the clerks and servants as well as the guests with whom he mingles. Often he will be in a house for days, and even weeks at a time, before he ventures to steal anything; and he will employ his time in making the acquaintance of the guests and studying their habits and marking the rooms that can be most easily entered and plundered. Within a week after his entrance, he will be likely to know the people who have valuable watches or jewelry, and he may even learn precisely where the valuables are kept during the day and night, and what instruments he will need to open or force the locks that protect them. If anybody is in the habit of carelessly leaving his chamber door unlocked at any time in the day, or if any jewelry is left in a room which is temporarily unoccupied, the thief will almost certainly mark the room for a raid.

Sometimes he will watch for an opportunity to slip in stealthily while the occupant is at breakfast or dinner; and during all meal hours there is especial need of keeping a sharp eye on every floor of the house to stop the prying and plundering of these thieves. If the house is well guarded in the daytime, the thief will wait till nightfall before making a raid; but he will usually find an opportunity in advance to examine the locks and bolts of a number of doors and to put his private mark, in the form of a slight scratch or gimlet hole, on the outside of a door, indicating the exact position of a bolt pin or any other fastening which he must remove.

It is also a common practice of these thieves to visit a hotel several times in close succession, changing the rooms assigned to them as often as possible, and using this opportunity to tamper with the locks and bolts. When the outside and inside keys have different key holes, the thief will bore through the inside key hole until the door is pierced or only a film of wood remains to cover the hole. Then he will carefully hide any mark of his drill under cover of paint and putty, and note the exact position of the key hole so that he can use his nippers outside the door. Another common device is to extract the screws of the nosing or catch of a lock bolt and to replace them with smaller screws; or, else, to enlarge the holes so that little pressure is needed to pry off the catch, although the screws are replaced and there is no external evidence of any tampering with the fastening.

It may be, too, that a thief will pick up clothes containing watches and other valuables by using a flexible pole with a hook at the end, or a long, bent wire inserted through a window or transom. Sometimes, instead of fishing in this way for articles within reach, a bold rascal will crawl through a window or ventilator, and clamber back through the same opening after he has ransacked the room. This mode of entry is so frequently adopted, if a room can be approached by the way of the fire escape, that it is advisable for guests to look to the fastening of the windows of their rooms as sharply as to the locking of their chamber doors.

It is remarkable how quickly an expert thief can make his way into a chamber with the aid of the few little implements which compose his "kit." With a pair of nippers, a piece of bent wire and a bit of thread,—thousands of doors have been opened in the manner before described; and a gimlet and screw-driver, with perhaps a little wax or putty, are the only other articles that one of these thieves is likely to use in effecting an entrance into a room. Usually the door will be opened so noiselessly that no ordinary sleeper would be awakened, if any one is in the chamber; and the thief will glide in and lay his hands on any valuables that he can reach and carry away. Watches have been taken in this way from under the pillows of a bed without disturbing its sleeping occupant; and clothes, hung up in closets, or laid on chairs, have been thoroughly overhauled. The thief will rarely venture to pry open any drawer or box, if any person is sleeping in the room, but he may use skeleton keys to unlock them. If a room is unoccupied for the time, he may tear open bureau drawers with a stout chisel, like a "second-story" or "flat worker"; but he commonly prefers to carrry no heavy tools. In fact, his entire outfit or kit can be hidden in one pocket without any outward show to excite suspicion.

It will readily be perceived that a rogue of this class has extraordinary opportunities for his thefts and is one of the most elusive and annoying rascals on the face of the earth. His operations are not confined to hotels; for many thieves of this class seek lodgings in boarding houses and even with private families, for the sake of opportunities to steal in chambers and dining rooms. It should always be borne in mind by persons who let rooms, that other recommendations are necessary than the bare fact that an applicant is well dressed and willing to pay in advance for his room. One of the most frequent of complaints to the police comes from the keepers of lodging houses who have imprudently admitted these rascals. Before the end of a week, a rogue of this class may make himself popular with all his fellow boarders and a particular favorite of his landlady. Then it will happen that articles of value will begin to disappear from the rooms; and nobody will be more interested and indignant, apparently, than the newcomer in discussing the losses. Finally the most valuable watch or ring or bracelet in the house will be missing; and the thief will go off with his booty in response to a letter or telegram which he will produce to explain his hasty departure, unless he runs off without saying good-bye.

Sometimes these "hotel thieves" engage in schemes of deception far more flagrant than the temporary hoodwinking of landladies and lodgers. Some of them have houses where they pass for respectable members of society, and their wives and children have no idea of the character of the occupation which they are pursuing. There are known instances, also, in which a particularly artful rascal of this class has figured as a man of fashion and fortune and entrapped a wealthy and beautiful young girl into a marriage—doomed to end in misery sooner or later when the wife discovers that her husband is a thief.

When any of these thieves are arrested, they are likely to "jump" their bail as a matter of course, if it is fixed at any amount which they can procure, and a large proportion of the hotel thieves at large to-day have indictments hanging over their heads. Many years may elapse before they are finally brought to trial; and, in one memorable instance, a young thief had become a gray-haired man before receiving his sentence for a crime which he had committed. This case is so remarkable and so illustrative of the resorts by which wily rascals evade the law, that it deserves special notice.

In 1868 the notorious gang, headed by "The" Allen, was one of the worst that infested the country. Its headquarters were at a New York hotel; and sallies were made from this rendezvous to any point where an opening for plunder was reported. Among the recruits of this gang was James E. Lyons, a young man of a good family, who had found employment in the hotel but had been persuaded to enlist in this company of thieves.

In some way the gang learned that a man was going to take the train from New York to New Haven, who would carry with him a bag containing thirty thousand dollars in United States government bonds. So Jesse Allen, one of the brothers of "The" Allen, and the young recruit, "Jimmy" Lyons, took the same train which carried away the man with the bag of bonds, with the design of stealing the bag before reaching New Haven. They did pick up a valise on the way; but, through a mistake on their part, it was not the bag of bonds but a similar bag filled with underclothing of little value. This was so disgusting that they went to the town of Granby, Conn., at once, and broke into a store, in the night, in order to get some plunder which they could show without a blush to their gang in New York. They succeeded in

JAMES E. LYONS.

JACK CANNON.

ROXIE McKENNA.

JOSEPH PRIOR.

IN THE CLOAK OF A GUEST. 231

carrying off considerable booty to Hartford, where they took lodgings in one of the best hotels.

Here they were arrested by the Hartford police for the burglary at Granby; and when their room at the hotel was searched, the valise, which was taken by mistake, was recovered. They were held for trial in the Granby case under bonds of $450 each, which they promptly furnished; and, before the day set for the trial, the police succeeded in tracing out the owner of the stolen valise. The thieves had little dread of conviction for burglary; but they knew that they could not escape conviction for stealing the valise, if the owner appeared as a witness against them. So he was warned by members of the Allen gang that his life would be in danger if he took the witness' stand, and threats were made to his wife, also, that a brutal revenge would be taken if her husband should testify to the theft.

These threats were made known to the prosecuting attorney for the State, and he instantly applied for a bench warrant charging the thieves with intimidation of witnesses. The application was granted and the two thieves were arrested by an officer, holding the warrant, when they came to Hartford, exulting in the belief that they had succeeded in breaking down the prosecution in the case of the stolen valise. They were put under bonds of $1,000 each to appear for trial, in this case, and, at the moment, were unable to put up the money. So they were taken to jail; but the gang at New York headquarters was at once notified by a telegram, and the "fall money" was sent on to Hartford immediately.

On the morning after their arrest, their counsel asked the court to accept the money for the bonds while the trial of the burglary case was in progress. Allen was permitted to give his bond and then walked off as fast as his legs would carry him. Fortunately the prosecuting attorney was fully as sharp witted as the thief, for he had stationed officers at all the doors of the court room with instructions not to let either of the rogues pass out. So when Allen tried to push by the guard, the officers seized him, and there was, for a moment, one of the liveliest wrestling matches that has ever taken place outside of a ring.

Meanwhile the State Attorney had requested the clerk to call the thief case for trial, and applied to the court for an order to take Allen into custody. In view of the wrestling officer and thief, the judge had no hesitation in giving the order, and the thief was dragged back to stand his trial. Then his indignant counsel sprang up to deny the right of the court to order a freeman into custody; and, after a hot and heavy debate, the motion of the State Attorney was altered to one for the increase of the bonds, as it was visible to the court that a bond of $1,000 was not sufficient to hold the rascals for trial. The judge admitted his own eyesight as a witness to this fact and added five thousand dollars more to each bond. This "raise" was too much for the Allen gang; so the two thieves were surrendered into custody and all the bonds were released. Then the two prisoners were tried for the theft of the valise, and convicted by the testimony of the owner who pluckily appeared notwithstanding the threats against him.

When the verdict of guilty was rendered, the court adjourned, with the expectation that sentence would be passed, next morning, and the trial of the burglary case resumed. But the resourceful "The" Allen bribed a prisoner in the jail, who was employed to clean the halls; and, during the night, jimmies and fine saws were used to such purpose that both thieves escaped in company with the hall-tender and another prisoner. So the curtain fell on the first act in this case, on the morning of the 22d of February, 1869.

More than twenty years afterwards, in the closing week of April, 1890, a man was arrested by two Boston detectives, shortly before midnight, as he was leisurely strolling along Washington Street. He might readily have been mistaken by a stranger for a worthy business man, who had grown prematurely old under the weight of his anxieties as a trustee for widows and orphans. Only a few thin hairs were left on the top of his head, and his closely trimmed beard was a mixture of bristling white and gray. His forehead was deeply furrowed, and his eyes were dim and sunken. His voice and manners were notably gentle and his dress in every detail was neat and tasteful.

There was no doubt, however, that this apparently inoffensive member of society was the same "Jimmy" Lyons who had broken out of the jail in Hartford, twenty-one years before, and had since made a record as a notorious hotel thief. So there was no hesitation in searching his clothes, and no surprise when a curious little package was extracted from his hip pocket. When this package was opened, it was shown to contain about one hundred and fifty small diamonds, more than forty rubies, two sapphires, and two stones known as California cat's eyes. In addition to these loose stones there was also a fine and costly pair of diamond earrings. When Lyons was asked to account for this collection of gems and its place of deposit, he preferred to leave his question open for investigation; but his friends later stated that he had recently purchased the collection at an auction sale and was fully entitled to put the gems in any pocket, which suited him better than a burglar-proof safe.

This may have been a fact; but Lyons was, nevertheless, held in custody, as it was known that the Connecticut authorities had never abandoned their efforts to arrest him since his escape from the jail in Hartford, in 1869. The Hartford police were promptly notified of his arrest; but while the officers from Connecticut were on their way to Boston with the necessary requisition from the governor, Lyons was admitted to bail, giving a bond for three thousand dollars, and immediately afterwards running away.

For several months he was able to keep under cover, but

he finally became weary of trying to evade the keen pursuit and surrendered himself on the second of December, 1890, to the superior court then sitting at Hartford,—to receive his long deferred sentence. "An indictment," said the Hartford Courant, "on paper so old that it had faded yellow, folded and unfolded so often that it had split and been pasted and split again, and scored all over with endorsements—an indictment, that the officers of justice had persistently kept alive for nearly twenty-two years, finally found its victim and secured his sentence to state prison." The judge said that he considered it his duty to impose, as nearly as possible, the same sentence upon Lyons which he would have received in 1869, if he had not broken out of jail. This, in his judgment, would have been two years in state prison, and he would therefore pass that sentence. So the case, which had been called in vain at every term of the court in Hartford for more than twenty years, was finally brought to an end.

In the long interval between his trial and his sentence, Lyons had been married and divorced, and had acquired an international reputation as one of the most expert hotel thieves in the world. It was his custom to register at the hotel which he proposed to plunder, and spend money, for a week or more, with so lavish a hand that he would become a favorite guest with every employee from the manager to the smallest bell boy. After gaining this secure position, he would inform himself thoroughly in regard to the habits and means of all the other guests of the house; and then would begin a series of visits to selected rooms. It is reported that he was usually considerate in his plundering, picking out one or two choice articles from a collection of valuables, and leaving the rest for the contentment of the owner. But it is suspected that his discrimination was due less to any lingering scruples than to his desire that suspicion might fall upon the chamber maids and bell boys.

After this country became too warm for his comfort, he

went abroad and plagued the principal cities of Europe, until he was finally caught in Edinburgh and sent to prison for seven years. His sentence expired in May, 1889, and he returned home only to fall into the waiting hands of the Boston police. The portrait of this remarkable rogue appears on a representative page.

This prolonged contest between the law and the law-breaker had its own peculiar features; but it is a fair representation, in the main, of the range of devices employed by gangs of thieves to shield their members from punishment. The requirement of light bail in any case, as we have before noted, is commonly regarded by a thief in the light of a new tax or special license fee, which is merely a disagreeable imposition to be paid for the sake of having his hands free to plunder. If bonds cannot be "jumped," and keepers cannot be bribed, and prison bars cannot be sawed,—there is still the resource of hushing complaints by cajolery or threats, or of suborning witnesses to perjure themselves on the stand for the defence of any rascals who may be brought to trial. If there is any way of evading conviction and sentence, by hook or crook, these thieves are likely to search it out; for they are usually well supplied with money or able to reach friends and backers who have money. So it is even more difficult to convict them than it is to arrest them unless they are actually captured in the act of stealing.

Few of these thieves have the nerve to make any resistance, if detected, trusting, as they do, to their shyness and nimbleness in making an entry and running away. So there is rarely, if ever, any personal danger to the occupants of rooms in hotels from the raids of these rogues. But there are occasionally gangs of these thieves who are burglars as well, and will make an entrance into lodging houses whose occupants are known to possess large amounts of jewelry. Diamond earrings have been taken out of the ears of helpless women by these marauders and bracelets and rings stripped from their hands, but raids of this character are now practically restricted to remote mining camps and frontier settlements. Gangs of this character usually carry loaded revolvers and will fire, at a pinch, at anybody who is trying to arrest them. John H. Cannon, commonly known as "Jack Cannon," is a criminal of this dangerous class, who has repeatedly fired on officers who were attempting to capture him. His portrait is given on the page with Lyons and the likenesses of two other notorious hotel thieves, Joseph Prior, alias "Walking Joe," and Roxie McKenna.

During the past thirty years Cannon has had a hand in a wide range of robberies, from the picking of a pocket to the opening of a safe. His favorite field of plunder was, at first, the Gulf States, but he is to-day as well known in the North as he is in the South. He was repeatedly arrested as a known leader in many robberies, but his remarkable craftiness in finding cover made loopholes of escape for him until his arrest in Springfield, Massachusetts, in 1889. He had engaged a room at a leading hotel in that city for two days and left his kit in the room. Then he took a room at another hotel, under a different name, and it was observed by the hotel men that he showed a kindly interest in the care of a guest who was considerably under the influence of liquor and making a reckless display of diamond jewelry. During the night he was seen prowling about in the halls and sneaking back hastily to his room when the watchman approached him. So his door was opened unceremoniously and he was found in bed in his underclothing with a handkerchief wrapped about his delicate throat, and a pair of skeleton keys and key nippers hidden in his sleeve. Upon further search a self-cocking revolver was taken from under his pillow. This performance gave him a sentence of five years in the state prison at hard labor. In the spring of the year after his discharge in 1893, he was again arrested in Jacksonville, Fla., while trying to enter a room in a hotel and sent to the state prison for a year. Within a month

GEORGE MASON.

CHAS. McLAUGHLIN.

JACK STRAUSS.

CHARLES HALLERT.

or two after his discharge he came to Boston to attend a Christian Endeavor Convention in his professional capacity of pickpocket and hotel thief. Here he was arrested at sight and ordered to leave the city. In July of the next year he was caught in a hotel in Detroit, with a complete kit of tools in his pockets, and promptly knocked down before he had time to fire his drawn revolver. His record was so well known to the judge at his trial that he was sent to the state prison in Michigan for ten years.

"Walking Joe" Prior is another veteran of the same stamp as Cannon and with a record equally varied and infamous. He has twice been sent to prison at Sing Sing, N. Y., besides serving out sentences in other states. His face is now so well known to the detectives in all the principal cities in this country, that he is commonly warned away whenever he is seen on the streets.

Roxie McKenna should be able to give some interesting notes on prison life and administration, for he has been confined in four different penitentiaries in the past ten years. Immediately after his release from prison in Ohio, in 1891, he undertook to rob a hotel in Memphis, Tennessee, and shot the porter who tried to capture him. For this robbery he was sent to the Tennessee penitentiary for eight years; but he was pardoned, after serving two years of his term, and returned to work again as a hotel thief until he was arrested in the Astor House in New York, in April, 1895, and sent to the penitentiary on Blackwell's Island for nine months. This experience did not prevent him from trying his hand again in the same line of operation, as soon as his term expired; but after a few months of practice, he was caught in a room in the hotel Marlborough and he is now serving out his sentence of four years in state prison in New York.

On another illustrative page the portraits of four other notorious and representative hotel thieves are given. George Mason has probably visited every state of this country in pursuing his varied range of occupation as a pickpocket and hotel thief. Some years ago he went through three Washington hotels in succession. In the first one he registered under the name of G. A. Wilson. During the night he slipped into the room of a guest who caught him while he was searching for plunder. He had a watch and some jewelry in his hand, which belonged to the wife of the guest, but he told such a plausible story of his blundering entry into the wrong chamber that his captor was persuaded to let him go. The next night he registered at another hotel as "J. A. Johnson," of Virginia. Here he stole a watch and twenty-one dollars in money out of one of the rooms and got away with his plunder. Two nights later, he appeared in a third hotel and engaged a room in the name of G. A. Walker. Before daybreak he succeeded in getting into two other rooms and carried off a gold ring and six dollars in money from one room and a watch and revolver from the other.

He was apparently bent on making a round through the hotels, one after another, but two detectives got on his track and traced the man whom they suspected to a boarding house of excellent character. On inquiry they learned that the man with many names had been living at this house for two weeks. He was a "Mr. Williams," the landlady said, and he had shown himself to be a truly good boarder, of marked piety. He had expressed a strong desire to meet her pastor and was anxious to join her church as soon as possible. She knew for a fact, too, that "Mr. Williams" could not possibly have had a hand in any wrong doing, because he stayed in his room all day long and was such an invalid that he passed most of the day in bed. Unfortunately for "Mr. Williams," this testimony did not deter the detectives from disturbing his sleep. When he saw the officers he pretended to be violently sick at the stomach; but the detectives ruthlessly searched him and found the stolen property in his pockets together with key nippers and a pair of heavy woolen stockings which he wore over his shoes in his raids. He had been accustomed to call at the hotels at about one o'clock in the morning, and the practice of registering after midnight, robbing rooms, and departing before sunrise had made him so sleepy in the daytime that he was a quiet boarder in his regular lodging house.

The portrait of Charles McLaughlin, alias McLain, alias Lambert, alias Seaman, alias Johnson, etc., shows the face of one of the most artful hotel thieves in the country. He was the son of a Southern planter who was ruined by losses during the war for the Union, so that young McLaughlin was obliged to earn his living as a book-keeper. Closely confining work was not to his taste, so he soon began to roam about from city to city as a hotel thief. In 1875 he was arrested in a New York City hotel for the theft of a watch and diamonds, and sent to Sing Sing for a term of three years. After his discharge he returned to his thievish practice and was arrested and convicted in Quebec, in 1881, for robbing a hotel. Three years later he was again arrested in a New York hotel and a full set of the tools of a hotel thief were found on his person. He had stolen two watches and four hundred dollars in this hotel, and was convicted of burglary and sent to the Blackwell's Island penitentiary for two years.

Another exceptionally impudent and artful thief is depicted in the portrait of "Jack" Strauss, alias Charles H. Dorris. This rascal is commonly called "Jack Straws" by his mates and is known, like Mason, from one end of this country to the other. In 1878, he was arrested for shooting one of his companions, "Sam" Perry, familiarly known as "Bottle Sam," and sentenced to state prison for five years; but he was set free by some legal flaw in the conduct of his trial and suffered again to roam over the country. Four years later, he made himself familiar with the office hours and habits of a wealthy physician of New York, and called one day at his house, at an hour when he knew that the physician would not be at home. He asked permission to leave a line for his old friend and medical adviser, and was politely ushered into the parlor where he spent a quarter of an hour in a close examination of the costly fittings and portable ornaments. During the following night he called again stealthily with his corps of expert burglars, and sacked the parlor and dining room very rapidly with the aid of the inventory which he had made in his former call. Then the gang made its escape with such a stock of plunder that it was able to gratify its taste for dissipation for a number of months.

In July, 1887, he led another gang in the robbing of a large jewelry store in Bridgeport, Connecticut, and carried off about fifteen thousand dollars' worth of diamonds and other precious articles. When he was arrested in the following month for his share in this burglary, three of the most valuable of the stolen diamonds were taken from his person. He has served three terms in state prisons for burglary, as well as several shorter terms for minor offences. When he was not engaged in schemes of breaking and entering, he has taken a hand in stealing by way of the "panel" game. This device is the decoying of victims into rooms where a secret sliding panel in one of the walls admits a thief during the night or gives an opportunity for the sly filching of money in a bunco game. Of late years he has particularly applied himself to the practices of the hotel thief.

He is a man of robust and portly figure and invariably dressed in the best clothes that money can buy. He has been accustomed to live in the finest hotels and has remarkable address in making the acquaintance of the guests whom he is seeking to rob. He has been repeatedly arrested and is now so notorious that he is warned away from all our larger cities whenever he is seen on the streets.

"Red Hyle," or "Cincinnati Red," has earned the reputation of being one of the most expert hotel thieves in this or any other country. His nickname was given to him on account of his florid face and red hair. He has robbed hotels in every

IN THE CLOAK OF A GUEST.   241

part of this country and has been a master hand in disguising himself to avoid recognition. There is no style of cutting a beard which he has not tried on his own face, and he has filled a score of character parts, at least, in a way that might have won for him an honorable reputation on the stage.

This class of thieves is so annoying to hotel men and their guests and it is of such importance to the public that a full exhibit should be given of the range of typical representatives that we present a third page of portraits, including two more notorious hotel thieves who have been particularly notable also for their thefts in sleeping cars, William Fale, and Henry Curtis. The page is completed by the addition of the faces of Henry Hoffman, alias Carl Schultz, and Edward Farebrother, a pair of rogues who have been plaguing hotels for years. Farebrother is a particularly dangerous thief, although he is now so old that the burden of years has seriously handicapped him. He was educated as a physician and has frequently assumed the title of doctor, making the names of Dr. Edward S. West and Dr. St. Clair particularly obnoxious to the people with whom he scraped acquaintance. He was a graduate of a leading English university and had a profitable practice as a regular physician in New York until he was convicted of malpractice in 1863 and sent to state prison for five years. After his discharge he became a professional thief and was convicted of grand larceny in 1873 and sent again to the state prison for two years. Six years later he distinguished himself by committing twenty-two robberies in New York City within seven months, and carrying off in one instance six thousand dollars' worth of diamonds and jewelry from a private house on Fifth Avenue. He pawned this jewelry for four hundred and fifty dollars and had only twenty dollars left in his pockets when he was arrested by the police in January, 1880. In the course of his identification, he was recognized by a poor man from whom he had stolen a coat unintentionally; and Farebrother took thirteen dollars out of his pocket and gave it to the witness. Then a servant girl gave evidence to a theft of some small article belonging to her, which had been taken in the same way. This story moved Farebrother to empty his pockets of his last seven dollars to give to her, but she refused to take more than five. He is a rascal but he is not one of the meanest class.

There is always a mustering and swarming of hotel thieves particularly, whenever there is any great anniversary meeting or celebration in any city, that is certain to fill the hotels with visitors. A crowd is the favorite cover for a thief to-day as it has been for years beyond reckoning. "Out upon him! prig, for my life, prig; he haunts wakes, fairs and bear-baitings," cries the clown to Autolycus; and we have the expert evidence of that famous pick-pocket himself: "Every lane's end, every shop, church session and hanging, yields a careful man work."

Just before any of these gatherings, streams of hotel thieves will pour into the place of meeting from every part of the country, unless their entrance is blocked by guards of detectives on all the railroads or steamboat lines running to the city, as well as at the terminal stations. This method of safeguarding a great assembly is now a widespread practice, and it has unquestionably prevented losses to the extent of hundreds of thousands of dollars. Still, in spite of all precautions, some thieves are likely to step through these barriers, and it is therefore prudent for guests to use special care in protecting their valuables on such occasions.

Every hotel of importance in the country has an office safe for the deposit of money, jewelry and other precious packages. Notices informing guests of this fact are usually posted up in every sleeping room, with the further warning that the hotel proprietor will not be responsible for the loss of any such package, unless it is put in the safe. This precaution ought to be generally adopted by guests in hotels, and particular care should be taken by the travelling agents for jewelry firms to keep their diamonds secure, for hotel thieves are always watching for opportunities to plunder them.

Another efficient safeguard, which has been largely adopted of late years by the leading hotels in this country, is the employment of skilled detectives as watchmen in the hotel. Experienced detectives are able to recognize and sift out thieves who would not be suspected by hotel proprietors or their clerks. They are familiar also with every trick and device of the sly rascals who plunder hotels, and it is exceedingly difficult for a thief to blind sharp eyes on his track, within the narrow limits of a house. This is so well recognized by professional hotel thieves that few ever venture into a hotel guarded by a good detective, and it is certain that the expense of such a guard is more than offset by the immunity from losses. It is always a grave annoyance and regret to a hotel proprietor when any of his guests suffer from theft; and no one is likely to appreciate so keenly the relief of mind as well as the business advantage obtainable from the assurance that hotel thieves will keep away from his house.

Furthermore, a good detective will be of marked service in the investigation of cases of possible fraud, and in assuring the fidelity and honesty of the servants employed in the hotel. It is, therefore, to be hoped that the value of this safeguard will be universally recognized in this country; and the hotels of Europe may profit by our example.

To supplement the proper precautions of landlords the guests in turn should do their part for their own protection. Valuable articles should not be left carelessly on tables or toilet stands for the temptation and accommodation of prying thieves. Chamber doors should be locked invariably when the occupants are temporarily absent, and the servant who takes care of the room may often be easily notified to keep a watchful eye on the door. We would again emphasize also the importance of attention to the fastening of the windows, and especially to those opening upon air-wells, balconies and fire escapes.

Rascals who are even more numerous and, in their way, as annoying as the "hotel thieves"—are the swindlers known as "hotel beats," and the sharpers practicing every possible device of imposition and fraud. The professional "hotel beat" is ordinarily a well-dressed man who can counterfeit closely the air of a man of fashion or of a well-to-do business man. He may even attempt to get a night's lodging and a few meals, with the intention of slipping away without paying his bill; or he may hold a room for a week or more, and meet the demand for payment with profuse pretences that he has not received an anticipated remittance, but will settle in full in the course of a few days. As these "beats" never have any baggage of any value which can be attached, a landlord will often be unable to obtain any redress, for the proof of actual intent to defraud is difficult to secure. So the "beat" may succeed in getting the best of board for days or weeks before his swindling practice is cut off.

It is also a common practice of the most rascally knaves of this class to give forged or worthless checks and drafts in settlement of their bills, and, also, to secure when they can, the cashing of their checks by the hotel men by various artful pretences. For example, packages of goods are ordered from stores to be sent to the addresses of guests at leading hotels, C. O. D., and when the goods arrive, the hotel men will be requested to pay the messengers in exchange for checks which are usually larger than the amount of the bills; so that the swindlers may get considerable sums in cash as well as the goods in return for their worthless paper.

Swindles on a greater scale are practiced also by sharpers who get a lodging in hotels for the purpose of claiming indemnification for pretended thefts or losses for which a landlord may be held responsible. Often these swindlers will make loud and bitter complaints of the disappearance of valu-

WILLIAM FALE.

HENRY CURTIS.

HENRY HOFFMANN.

EDWARD FAIRBROTHER.

ables from their trunks or from the closets and bureau drawers in their rooms. As the landlord is held liable in many states in this country for losses of this kind, to an extent running as high as a thousand dollars, in some cases, it can easily be perceived that he may often be a victim of barefaced impositions. To avoid a lawsuit, or from the dread that blustering reports of this kind may injure his business, he may be driven to pay these fraudulent claims, even when he strongly suspects that he has been swindled.

Not long ago a noteworthy fraud was attempted in a leading hotel of this state by two rogues who professed to be strangers to each other. One of them came to the hotel with a small trunk which was sent up to his room. The other obtained a room nearly opposite on the same floor, and his trunk, which was unusually large, was put in this chamber. After staying at the hotel for a few days, the man with the large trunk settled his bill and went off, one morning, taking his trunk with him. Late in the afternoon in the same day, his confederate came to the office of the hotel, hotly complaining of the loss of his trunk. His room was searched, as well as the baggage room of the hotel, but no trace of the missing trunk could be found. The complainant claimed that his trunk contained valuables to the amount of nearly a thousand dollars, and the hotel proprietor was actually on the point of settling his claim when it was discovered by a shrewd detective that the little trunk had been stealthily taken across the hall, one night, and put inside the big trunk in the opposite room. Of course, when the large trunk was taken away in the morning, the little trunk was still inside, and the trick was played with such craft that it nearly succeeded in swindling the landlord.

Another device which has been repeatedly tried in our city hotels is the exchange of the checks given as receipts for coats and hand bags, left by guests, temporarily, in going to their meals in the dining rooms or for safe keeping for a few hours. A big and a little man, who are confederate swindlers, will slily swap their coat checks, and one of them will return in an hour or two and make a bitter complaint of the offer of a coat which is plainly a misfit. In such a case, the coat which the swindler pretends to have left for safe keeping is invariably a new and costly one, with articles of value in its pockets; and the landlord is confronted with a claim which is hardly ever less than sixty dollars.

Even when packages have been put in the hotel safe for keeping, there are cases of sly substitution and mysterious disappearances for which the hotels are called to account. A guest, who has taken a cheap room at a dollar a day, may call upon a hotel keeper to bear the responsibility of a deposit of many thousand dollars, and insure him against loss without any consideration of value in return. There was recently an actual case of this kind where a transient guest, who came to a hotel in this state just before midnight, applied for the safe keeping of seventy-five thousand dollars in bank notes. The night clerk was so anxious over this heavy responsibility that he woke up the proprietor of the hotel, and the two hotel men sat up all night watching the safe in which this extraordinary deposit was stored. In the morning, the guest paid a dollar for his room, but the weary landlord would have been glad to have paid ten times as much for a discharge from his task as night watchman.

Frequently, too, a swindler will attempt to obtain credit by requesting a clerk or landlord to deposit in the safe a package which is said to contain several thousand dollars in money or valuable jewelry. If his landlord is hoodwinked by this cheat and gives credit for room and board to the sharper on the strength of his supposed security in the safe, he will have his eyes opened by the disappearance of his guest after his credit has been stretched to the snapping point. Then he will probably examine the package, and find that it is stuffed with sawdust or worthless paper possibly enclosing a brick to give it more weight.

Many of the leading hotels of this country have suffered so much from impositions of all kinds that they have organized associations for mutual protection. The descriptions and records of all known "hotel thieves," "beats," and swindlers of every description, have been procured for the use of every member of this association, and all cases of theft and fraud, within the knowledge of the members of these associations, are promptly reported with the best attainable description of the rogues. There is a special confidential agency also, which undertakes the work of prosecuting these rascals and furnishes the proper information to protect hotel men from impositions.

It has further been the effort of one of these associations to protect its members from losses through incompetent, intemperate and dishonest employees, and records are kept, with more or less care, of the conduct of employees for the information of the association.

By such agencies as this and the increasing employment of competent detectives, the hotel keepers of this country have been able to secure much better assurance of protection for themselves and their guests than was the case twenty years ago. It need only be added that every dollar expended in such proper precautions is certain to be returned, ten times over, in the diminution of losses.

"KNIGHTS OF THE ROAD."

MANY of our readers will recall, no doubt, the wet blanket that was cast over the convivial little party of highwaymen assembled, as Bulwer relates, in the back parlor of "The Jolly Angler" on Finchley Common.

"Long may the Commons flourish," cried punning Georgie, filling his glass. "It is by the Commons we're fed, and may they never know cultiwation!"

"Three times three!" shouted Long Ned; and the toast was drunk as Mr. Pepper proposed.

"A little moderate cultivation of the Commons, to speak frankly," said Augustus Tomlinson, modestly, "might not be amiss; for it would decoy people into the belief that they might travel safely; and, after all, a hedge or a barley field is as good for us as a barren heath, where we have no shelter if once pursued!"

"You talks nonsense, you spooney!" cried a robber of note, called Bagshot, who, being aged, and having been a lawyer's footboy, was some times denominated "Old Bags." "You talks nonsense; these innowating ploughs are the ruin of us. Every blade of corn in a Common is an encroachment on the constitution and rights of the gemmen highwaymen. I'm old, and mayn't live to see these things; but, mark my words, a time will come when a man may go from Lunnun to Johnny Groat's without losing a penny by one of us,—when Hounslow will be safe and Finchley secure. My eyes, what a sad thing for us that'll be!"

The venerable old man became suddenly silent and the tears started to his eyes.

The mouth of the dismal prophet was promptly stopped by the host of "The Jolly Angler," and "Long Ned" was called upon for a song to drive the spectre away; but rollicking songs and flowing bowls could not stop the "innowating ploughs" nor the sprouting blades of corn. The palmy days of the highwayman passed away long ago into yellow-covered romances. The bold Dick Turpins and dashing Jack Sheppards were flattened out by the same irresistible wheel of progress, which had rolled over the bodies of the Robin Hoods and the Kinmont Willies. "Paul Clifford" was too plainly a worn-out puppet show to exert any of the practical influence on prison discipline and the reform of the criminal code, which the author projected. Any lingering glamour attaching to the life of a highwayman was puffed out of sight by the snort of the locomotive, and the "knight of the road" rotted away with the old-fashioned stage coach. Then Hounslow was safe and Finchley secure, and the traveller could ride from Land's End to Dunnet Head without losing a penny.

Naturally enough, the highwayman has been able to keep a foothold in a vast country, still redeeming itself from the aboriginal wilderness, much longer than he could on Finchley Common or Hounslow heath. It is true that the days have passed away when a mining camp was more often entertained by the stopping of a stage coach than by the finding of a nugget. The marvellous outstretching of the arms of our octopian railways have brought the most remote settlements into touch with our bustling cities; and the whizzing trains have confounded the highwayman here as in the old mother country. But there are still districts where the stage coach is running to-day as it did forty years ago, and an express messenger is still sitting in the coach or on the box, with a double-barrelled gun across his knees, as he did in the days of the Argonauts. There are still steep and lonely cañons to climb and long stretches of primeval forest to traverse; and the guardian of the money box is occasionally shot and the reluctant passengers forced to hold up their hands in the same old style.

There has also sprung up here with the spread of the railways an extraordinarily bold and desperate class of robbers, who have gone far beyond any bravado or daring of the old school of highwaymen or of the plunderers of stage coaches. These desperadoes have repeatedly stopped long trains filled with passengers, and held the crowd at bay until they had sacked the express car; and, sometimes, the gang has been of such force that it has robbed the passengers as well as the expressmen. Assaults of this kind have been made in the oldest states of the Union as well as in the newest; but they have been most common, of course, in thinly-settled communities, where assistance could not be readily summoned and escape would be comparatively easy.

Almost all of these men were fugitives from justice, from one cause or another, and many were notorious safe breakers and burglars. The chief, if not actually the first of these bands of outlaws, was the notorious and infamous Reno gang. The ringleaders of this gang were four brothers, John, Frank, Simeon and William Reno. All four had black marks as "bounty jumpers" during the War for the Union, and all had a rooted aversion to any form of honest labor.

When their income from bounty jumping was cut off by the close of the war, they were obliged to get their living in other ways and turned their hands to the pursuit of burglary. The smashing of doors and the cracking of safes did not content their craving for excitement and plunder; and, in 1866, they began a series of novel and startling performances by stopping a train on the Ohio and Mississippi Railroad, and robbing the express car. Their first venture was so successful that they repeated it again and again until "the Reno gang" became a name of terror throughout southern Indiana.

It soon grew to be so numerous and overbearing that it looked upon its selected range of plunder as its own peculiar preserves, and would not suffer anybody to poach in its reservation. So, when two impudent young men stopped a train on the Jeffersonville Railroad and robbed a messenger of the Adams Express Company, the indignant Reno gang suffered the poachers to serve as cat's-paws, but snatched the booty out of their hands as soon as it was secured. Not content with this reprimand, they actually lent their aid to the conviction and sentence of the intruders, who were sent to the penitentiary, while the gang coolly divided the proceeds of the robbery.

After instituting their reign of terror in Indiana by browbeating the country people so that it was almost impossible to induce witnesses of their raids to testify against them, the Reno brothers extended their range into Missouri and began to break safes and rob trains with glaring impudence. Finally the late Allan Pinkerton won the credit of trapping and capturing John Reno, at the railway station of Seymour, Indiana, with the aid of the sheriff of the county and a posse of stalwart detectives. He was seized by a sudden rush of the sheriff and his men, while lounging in the station,—in the midst of his friends and "pals." Then, before the gang could rally from its surprise, he was handcuffed and dragged on board a waiting train, which instantly ran off under full steam. After a stubborn fight in the courts, exhausting every device of delay and technical buffers, this head of the gang was, at length, chopped off and sent to the Missouri penitentiary for a term of twenty-five years at hard labor.

But the three other heads still remained with free hands to plunder, and the arrest of John Reno seemed only a spur to the rest of the gang. Soon they began to rove over a wider range and to rob in Illinois and Iowa as well as in their old preserves. In close succession the safes of the county treasurers at Magnolia and Glenwood, Iowa, were broken into and robbed, and again Allan Pinkerton was first on the track of the robbers.

His clues led him to the conviction that a certain Michael Rogers, one of the most wealthy and highly esteemed citizens of Council Bluffs, was covertly a prime mover in the gang. The local authorities at Council Bluffs gave no credit to this assertion of their eminent fellow citizen; but Mr. Pinkerton, nevertheless, formed a posse of his own men and pounced upon Rogers in his own house in the early morning. Mr. Michael Rogers affected to be highly exasperated by this untimely call and impudent suspicion; but he could not bar the searching of his house and the capture of Frank Reno and two other notorious members of the Reno gang, who were about to sit down to breakfast in the kitchen with their host. A strong smell of smoke was noticed while the detectives were putting irons on the robbers. So Mr. Pinkerton picked up a lid of the stove and saw that it was stuffed with packages of bank notes. The notes were snatched off the burning coals in time to save most of them, and the unburnt notes were later identified as part of the money that had been stolen from the safe in Glenwood. In addition to this damning evidence, two complete sets of burglar tools were brought to light by a thorough search.

The captured robbers were lodged at once in the county jail, and certain conviction was hanging over their heads, when the country round was startled and disgusted by the news that the gang had sawed a hole in the wall of the jail and escaped. In big, scrawling letters, "April Fool" was chalked over the walls and floor, instead of a civil "good-bye."

For a time the fugitives sunk out of sight as completely as if the earth had opened and swallowed them up; but, about two months after their escape, a gang of masked men held up a train on the Ohio and Mississippi railroad at Marshfield, Indiana, and took ninety-eight thousand dollars out of the express car. The express messenger fought like a tiger to guard his trust; but the gang fell upon him in mass and pitched him out of the car into a steep gully, while the train was steaming along at full speed. Another train robbery followed hard after this outrage, and there was no real doubt that both were the work of the same Reno gang. By this time the country about was ablaze with fury. Three notorious members of the gang were arrested at Seymour and put on the train running to Brownstown, the county seat. Before the train reached Brownstown, it was boarded by a band of masked men. The officers guarding the robbers were dashed aside, and the three prisoners were hung on the limbs of a beech tree in the nearest farm yard.

This fierce reprisal marked the forming of a secret organization, which soon spread to cover the range of the Reno gang. It was styled The Secret Vigilance Committee of Southern Indiana. Within a few days after the lynching of the three robbers, three more masked members of the same gang were taken out of the hands of the county officials, in like manner, and hung with instant despatch. The vengeful storm spread from town to town. The gang which had terrorized Indiana was thoroughly cowed and driven to hunt for cover. Frank Reno fled to Canada with Charles Anderson, a member of his gang and a notorious burglar; but William and "Sim" were tracked to their hiding place in Indianapolis. There they were captured and put in the strong jail of a neighboring county, to save their necks more surely from the ropes of lynchers. Finally Frank Reno and his companion were arrested, in their place of refuge, and surrendered, after a stubborn contest, to Allan Pinkerton, representing the United States. He took them to the jail in New Albany, Indiana, where Frank's brothers were still confined. The robbers were put in cells to await their trial, but it never took place.

A few weeks after Reno and Anderson were lodged in the jail, a car was picked up on the railroad near Seymour by a passing train on the way to New Albany. The conductor of the train afterwards claimed that he knew nothing about the attachment of this stray car. It was filled with men wearing Scotch caps and black masks. They were a silent company of fifty and sought to avoid notice. But it was observed by chance that a tall, black-haired man was the recognized leader. When any one spoke to him, he was simply called "Number One."

The train reached New Albany at two o'clock in the morning. "Number One" stood up in the car and took command with the words "Come on." Then he passed quietly out of the car and his company fell into line behind him. He led the way to the jail and called upon the keeper to open the doors. His demand was stoutly refused. Instantly a rush was made to storm the doors. The guards in the jail opened fire and the mob fired back. For some moments the heavy locks and bars bore the battering of the mob; but when the doors were beaten in, the guards were helpless to stop the charging mass. The faithful sheriff was shot through the arm and overpowered. His little force of deputies was soon knocked out of the way, and the lynchers swarmed into the jail. In a few moments, the three Reno brothers and their comrade, Anderson, were taken out of their cells and hung from the beams over a corridor. Then the mob carefully locked the doors of the jail to keep the other prisoners securely, and marched back silently to the car which had been left behind by the train at the station. At half past three o'clock another train came by. The car was coupled on, and the silent company was taken back to Seymour, where the car was dropped and switched off.

That was the end of the Reno gang and the last known act of the Secret Vigilance Committee of Southern Indiana. There was some attempt to lift the curtain and trace out the lynchers; but their escape was too well planned. They had taken the precaution to cut every telegraph wire running from New Albany, and their closing performance was not reported outside the town before the following noon. Meanwhile the silent company had leisure to disband, throw away its masks, and sink out of sight in the ranks of common citizens who had nothing to fear from the testimony of their neighbors.

The example and infamous éclat of this pioneer gang undoubtedly inspired and instructed many bands of less note to pursue the novel line of plunder which it had marked out. The James gang and others of scarcely less mark have since terrorized whole counties and even larger parts of the state, but no subsequent gang of train robbers in this country has defied the law with such brazen impudence and persistence, or intrenched itself so formidably by corruption and intimidation.

Of late years every gang of professional train robbers has had one or more members who were expert "safe blowers" or burglars skilled in the use of dynamite. It is usually of the utmost concern to these robbers to open the safes in the express cars in the shortest possible time. The avoidance of noise in cracking such safes is not so essential as it is to the burglar in banks, stores and offices; so there is no careful muffling of the safes, or restriction of the amount of nitroglycerine to the exact allowance necessary. The shattering of the safes at the first discharge is the prime requisite, and this is done by a liberal use of cartridges.

Besides the "safe blower," a modern gang will commonly include, also, some man who is able to handle a locomotive well enough to run it for a few miles, at least; as it is sometimes of service to the robbers to use the engine in effecting their escape. The leading gangs are made up, as a rule, by some leader who picks his men for the varied service that may be needed, and considerable skill is required, as well as desperate recklessness, to make a successful assault on a train which is carrying a large amount of money.

No robber bands within the past ten years have been more formidable than the notorious Hedspeth and Morgan gangs. Hedspeth's gang had its range in the Central Western, and Morgan's in the Southern Atlantic States. By a sketch of their methods of operation the general character and devices of professional train robbers may be clearly set forth.

Marion C. Hedspeth, the leader of the first-named gang, became notorious as a robber in Missouri and Kansas, twenty years ago, in company with two other well-known "store breakers" and "safe blowers." After some years of this work Hedspeth and Cody, his partner, were surprised in the act of blowing open a safe in a small town in Kansas. Cody was shot dead on the spot, but Hedspeth broke through the line that hemmed him in and escaped. After a keen hunt he was finally caught in November, 1883, and sent to the penitentiary in Jefferson City, Missouri, for seven years. While in prison he tried to break out and nearly killed a deputy sheriff who blocked his escape. Soon after his discharge he formed a gang of three other ex-convicts and desperadoes like himself for the practice of safe blowing and train robbery. One of the gang was his brother-in-law, Adelbert Sly, who had just served out a term of seven years in the Missouri state prison for the robbery of the American Express Company in 1883. Under the leadership of Hedspeth and Sly this gang soon became a pest in Missouri, Nebraska and Kansas. In the early part of 1891 the outlaws impudently raided the office of a street car company in Kansas City. With a show of their loaded revolvers they forced all the clerks in the office to face the wall and hold up their hands while they blew open and robbed the safe. A few weeks later the same gang made another raid of the same kind in Omaha. Then, after making a round for diversion through a number of post-offices in Missouri, they entered upon a series of train robberies.

Their first venture was on the line of the Missouri Pacific road. They coolly boarded a train at West Omaha, blew open the locked door of the express car with a dynamite cartridge, rushed into the car, knocked down the messenger and robbed the safe. After this exploit, the surrounding country became too hot for them; so the gang scattered, found cover and came together in Wisconsin, at Western Union Junction, on the line of the Chicago, Milwaukee and St. Paul Railroad. Here they made another raid on a train, overpowering the train hands and blowing open the door of the express car. Again the messenger was unable to stop their rush, and the robbers carried off about five thousand dollars in money and a considerable amount of jewelry.

Once more the gang dropped out of sight to reappear in Missouri, on the night of November 30th, in the same year (1891). Their chosen "mark," this time, was in Glendale, a suburb of St. Louis, on the line of the St. Louis and San Francisco road. Here they raided another train, as they had done twice before in the same year, mastering the unarmed railroad men by force and threats, and blowing open the door of the express car. The passengers on the train made some show of resistance, and the robbers fired some shots in return into a passenger car; but no one was hit. In this raid the robbers took a booty of forty thousand dollars, which they promptly divided and then fled in different directions.

The plain repetition of method and other points of identification in these robberies left little doubt that all were committed by the same gang; although, in every case, the robbers wore masks in their attacks, and covered their movements from point to point with remarkable craft and success. The men composing the Hedspeth gang were well known; and after the Glendale robbery, every possible effort was made by the Pinkerton Agency and the combined detective forces of the Western States to track the fugitives. Sly was arrested by the Pinkertons in Los Angeles, California, after a chase of four weeks; and, in the following February (1892), Hedspeth was captured in the hall of the San Francisco post-office by Captain Lees of the city police and a squad of his men.

The robber had shaved off his heavy mustache to change his usual appearance, and had the dress and air of a thriving young broker. He was off his guard at the time, for he supposed that the detectives had been completely thrown off his track. While he was calling at the delivery window for letters addressed to H. V. Swanson, one of the watching detectives cautiously brushed past him in order to learn whether he had pistols in his overcoat pockets. The touch was a slight one, but Hedspeth felt it and instantly thrust his hands into his coat pockets. He was quick to turn, but the detectives were quicker in seizing him and pinioning his arms. Two loaded revolvers were taken from his coat pockets and he was then led to the city police headquarters. Over a thousand dollars in money and valuable jewelry were found on his person, but nothing particularly incriminating. There was no question of his identification, however, and he was held in custody until he was delivered to the Missouri authorities for trial in St. Louis.

While he was confined in the city jail, awaiting his trial, he laid a crafty plan of escape. A young rascal, charged with forgery, was lodged in the same cell. He was a youth of nice appearance and good education, and succeeded in getting an appointment for service in the jail, by which he was enabled to get a view, one day, of the key to his cell. He was a good draughtsman and sketched the key rapidly on a piece of paper. That night he passed the sketch to Hedspeth, who succeeded in passing it on to confederates outside the jail.

In a few days his wife came to the jail with some fruit for her husband, and the exultant robber and forger found a key within an orange in the fruit basket. They tried it, at night, in the lock of the cell; but to their disgust it did not fit. So the young forger melted a tallow candle and made an impression of the lock. Then the prisoners filed the key to fit the mold, and found that they could unlock the cell door. But, before Hedspeth could plan their escape further, his young companion was taken to trial and sent to the workhouse for a year.

Some time afterwards, Hedspeth used the key to unlock his cell door and succeeded in reaching a window in the jail.

MARION C. HEDSPETH.

ADELBERT D. SLY.

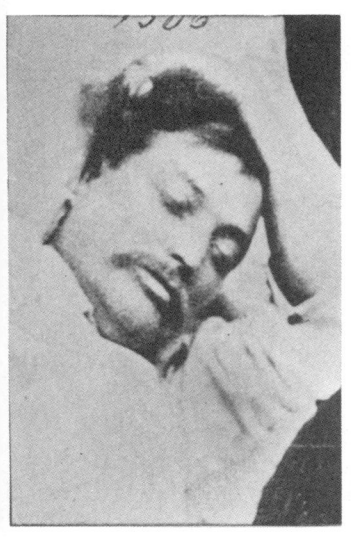
CHARLES MORGAN.

OLIVER CURTIS PERRY.

He had arranged with confederates to crawl under the gate of the jail yard and open the bars of one of the windows with "a spreader," and it is reported that this was done; but Hedspeth went astray in the darkness, and, when he found the right window, the jail guards were upon him before he could squeeze through. So he sullenly gave himself up and was taken back to his cell, where he was strictly guarded until he was tried and convicted of the robbery at Glendale, and sent to the state prison for twenty-five years. His brother-in-law, Sly, received a like sentence. A third member of the gang was killed at Pleasanton, Kansas, shortly after the Glendale robbery, in the attempt to rob a train with only a single assistant; so the Hedspeth gang is no longer to be dreaded.

In the spring of 1893, a train on the M. & O. railroad was held up by two train robbers at the first water tank north of Cairo, Illinois. This was the first performance credited to the "Morgan gang," although the leader, Charles Morgan, was no novice in crime, and had already earned a bad reputation. His true name was probably D. M. Speer, but his latest alias was Morgan, and this name may be used as the one best known. His companion in the robbery near Cairo was C. J. Searcy, a carpenter by trade, who was persuaded by Morgan to try his hand as a train robber. A third confederate was expected at Cairo; but, when he failed to arrive, Morgan and Searcy undertook the job without delay. Searcy kept the engineer and fireman quiet with his gun, while Morgan went through the express car and took all the money obtainable, which was a little over twelve hundred dollars. After dividing this booty the robbers fled and soon separated; but, early in the next year, they met in Florida.

Here they enlisted a new recruit,—one "Sam" Martin, who had been trained as a locomotive driver. One night in June (1893), this party of three boarded a train near Homerville, Georgia. Searcy took charge of the engineer and fireman as before, and Martin held the passengers in check while Morgan hung a dynamite cartridge on the door of the express car and blew it open. After robbing the car, the gang uncoupled the engine and rode off on it, leaving the cars behind. They ran along the track for a few miles and jumped off at a convenient point and let the engine go wild. After dividing their plunder, the robbers parted, but, in September of the following year (1894), the three met again at Harper's Ferry in Virginia. While they were planning a robbery in Maryland, Martin was arrested and locked up on the charge of carrying concealed weapons and dangerous explosives; but Morgan and Searcy contrived to escape to Washington and from that city into Virginia.

On the night of the 12th of October in the same year, 1894, they boarded a train on the R. F. & P. R. R., near Brooke Station. After passing Acquia Creek bridge, the two robbers climbed over the tender, and with their leveled revolvers compelled the engineer and fireman to stop the engine and get off. Then Searcy kept the two trainmen under the threat of his pistol while Morgan blew open the door of the express car with dynamite. The messenger and his assistant were apparently helpless, and Morgan took out of the car nearly three thousand dollars in cash and some valuable papers. It was next in order to get some free instruction from the engineer in the practice of stopping and starting a locomotive; and after the lesson was over, the instructors were put off the engine again and the pupils, Morgan and Searcy, took the engine about a hundred yards to a cross road, where they turned it loose. The wild engine ran into a couple of coal cars on a side track, and fortunately toppled over just in time to avoid a collision with an express train on the main track.

Morgan and Searcy divided their booty and tramped over the country to a station on another line of road. Here they took the cars, but the pursuit on their track was so keen that Morgan was arrested a few days later in a suburb of Cincinnati, and his companion was captured shortly afterward.

Morgan was convicted in the spring of the following year and sent to the Virginia Penitentiary for eighteen years. Searcy received a lighter sentence of eight years in the penitentiary, chiefly for the reason that his evidence was used to convict his partner. Morgan's portrait, as the convicted principal of this gang, is given on a representative page.

When train robberies are committed by bands which are not professional gangs, it is generally easy to mark the distinction. As in the case of burglaries, something in the planning, the execution and the escape will show to experienced detectives whether the robbery was a professional job or the work of green hands. This is none the less sure even if there has been a labored effort to counterfeit the proceedings of experts, so far as their methods can be learned from yellow-covered "flash" novels or current report. The amateurs in this line will not forget to parade in black masks and to brandish revolvers recklessly; but their counterfeit will almost certainly fall flat through some awkward bungling or neglect of the precautions which expert robbers are careful to take.

This distinction was signally shown a few years ago, in the case of a robbery on the Mineral Range railroad, a little narrow gauge line running from Houghton, Michigan, to the mines of the Calumet and Hecla Company. One morning in September, 1893, the train running to Calumet over this line was held up by a band of robbers at a little woodside station called Boston. A stop was made at this place to allow two passengers to alight, and as the train slacked up, a masked man, wearing a long linen duster, jumped upon the engine and forced the engineer and fireman to throw up their hands, in face of his heavy, loaded revolver. Then the robber started the train and ran along slowly, away from the station. Meanwhile, two men, similarly dressed and masked, boarded the forward end of the express and baggage car, and burst open the door with a single heavy blow of a sledge. Through the open door they covered the express messenger and baggage man with their revolvers and called upon them sharply to throw up their hands. Both obeyed, although the express messenger was well armed with revolvers like the robbers. Then they took the loaded pistols out of the pockets of the messenger and ordered him to open the safe in the car. He obeyed submissively, and the masked men took out several packages of money which they put in a grain bag. There were seventy-five thousand dollars in the packages which the messenger was carrying to the Calumet and Hecla mine for the monthly pay roll. After filling their bag the robbers told the engineer to keep the train moving or he would be shot, and then all three jumped off and were soon lost to sight in the thick woods bordering the railroad track. The train ran on to Osceola, where the robbery was reported and the telephone actively enlisted in rousing the country for the capture of the robbers.

It may seem at the first glance that there was no apparent slip in the conduct of this robbery; but the blunders were soon shown in a bright light by the expert detectives on the track of the robbers. This first obvious blunder was in the behavior of the express messenger, Dominick Hogan. Instead of the stout resistance which a faithful man would make, his contemptible submission without firing a shot branded him, at once, as a probable accomplice of the robbers. Now, a trained gang of robbers would have arranged an imposing parade of devotion on his part, if he had been one of their confederates; so that it was almost certain, at this starting point, that the robbers were amateurs and it was almost equally sure that recent meetings between this clumsy actor and his associates could be traced out.

This was done by the Pinkerton detectives and the police of the district with extraordinary despatch, and the pursuit of the fugitives was equally swift and acute. The robbery had been committed in the heart of a dense wood, many miles in extent, where men could lie in hiding for weeks and probably defy detection. Nearly all the people living on the woodland clearings were of foreign birth and few could speak English. It was certainly a difficult ground for the prosecution of the chase and there was, apparently, little prospect of a speedy capture of the robbers and recovery of their plunder.

But again the stupid errors of the gang soon put clues into the hands of their hunters. It was learned by close questioning of the neighboring people that a horse had been tethered in the woods near the station, on the morning of the robbery and the day preceding. The detectives found the place where the horse had been standing, and took an imprint of his hoof marks on paper, as they had no plaster to make a mold. The print showed that the horse was shod with plates instead of shoes. This was a clue of great value, as it showed that the animal was probably a race horse, which could be readily identified in a district of this character. Then the detectives tracked the horse to a road and measured his stride. This measurement narrowed the search still further, for it was shown that the race horse was a fast pacer.

By pressing inquiry it was soon learned that a fast pacing horse, named "Champ K," was owned by a man in a neighboring town. Detectives were then sent out over every road leading from Boston, with instructions to get all possible information touching this horse or any other fast pacer which had been seen on the road, immediately before or since the robbery. Their inquiries brought to light the fact that "Champ K" had been driven slowly over the road from Houghton to Boston, just before the robbery, by two well-known "sporting men," "Jack" King and "Jack" Butler; and that the same horse passed through Hancock, steaming and sweating, forty minutes after the robbery. This gave the detectives sufficient assurance to warrant the arrest of Butler and King. Thus the use of a horse, which could be easily identified and was certain to attract attention, led straight to the detection of part of the gang; and another fatal blunder soon brought about the arrest of another principal, and drew the net tighter about the other prisoners.

Michigan is not a warm country in the latter part of September, as a rule, and in that particular month almost everybody was wearing overcoats. But the amateur robbers had apparently been impressed with the conviction that long linen "dusters" were part of the regulation costume of men who "held up" trains. So two of them bought new linen dusters at a store in a neighboring town, and a third stole a duster for his outfit from a saloon. This fact was soon found out by the searching detectives, and the three dusters were traced to Butler and King and a discharged fireman of the Duluth, South Shore and Atlantic railroad, George La Liberté.

So the ex-fireman was arrested, and as he was not a hardened "crook," but a poor, ignorant French Canadian, a confession was soon extracted from him which completely exposed the robbery. It appeared that the scheme had been put up by a former express messenger, who was the brother of Dominick Hogan. He induced his brother to become an accomplice, and informed Butler, King and La Liberté that they could capture the money in the car without any risk of being shot in the operation. So, within three days after the robbery, all the robbers were traced out and held for trial and a large part of the stolen money was recovered. Other confederates were arrested at the same time and all the principals were, soon after, tried, convicted and sentenced to the Michigan penitentiary.

This was a notably brilliant and creditable piece of detective work, although the detectives were aided, as we have shown, by palpable blunders on the part of the robbers. It is much more difficult, as experienced detectives will testify, to follow the track of expert professional robbers, who often lay their plans as artfully as bank burglars and are masters of every trick of disguise and concealment. Sometimes, too, the track of the robbers is intentionally covered by accomplices on the trains; although this is fortunately of rare occurrence, for the regular messengers and train hands are usually men of sterling faithfulness, as the sacrifice of their lives in the discharge of their duty has so often and so nobly shown.

It has happened, also, that a robbery of an express car has been planned and executed entirely by train hands, as in the remarkable case of the Rock Island express car robbery, ten years ago, where the messenger was brutally shot and beaten to death by a brakeman and a baggageman. This is an instance so exceptional that we should scarcely refer to it, except for the sake of a word of just tribute to the really superb detective work in coping with uncommon craftiness in knavery and finally securing the conviction of the criminals.

Outside of the rare cases where a robbery has been effected by train hands, the robbers have usually got their plunder by stopping a train at some little signal station, in the midst of woods or in a thinly settled country; or, else, by boarding a train, like ordinary passengers, and waiting for the best opportunity to make a raid on the express car. In view of the evident blocks in the way of one of these robberies—the resistance of the train hands, the possible rallying of the passengers in force, and the entrenchment of one or more express messengers in the stronghold of a car with bolted doors,— it is very rare that any assault is attempted by less than two men, and three or more men usually band together in making such raids. There are, however, isolated instances in which a single man has "held up" a train or boarded and robbed an express car, and the most remarkable of these was, unquestionably, the performance of Oliver Curtis Perry on the line of the New York Central railroad, about four years ago.

At that time Perry was only about twenty-six years old, but he was far in advance of his age as a criminal. He was the son of a poor farmer in Fulton county, New York, and grew up, as he himself has said, "without schooling." Probably his lack of the ordinary primary school education was largely his own fault, for he was a self-willed, wayward and roving boy from his earliest childhood. He was set at work on his father's farm as a chore boy; but this plodding labor was so little to his liking that he took a hand in burglary, in the town of Amsterdam, N. Y., when he was only fourteen years old, and was sent to the state reformatory and subsequently to prison. When he was discharged, an opportunity was given to him for a fresh start in life, with a good opening in a store owned by his uncle in Minnesota. He took advantage of this chance to rob his uncle's store, but he was caught, shortly afterward, and sent to a Minnesota penitentiary for three years.

After graduating from the penitentiary, he went to Montana to enlist as a cowboy. In his new employment he was shot in the breast and sent to the almshouse in Mills City for treatment. While he was recovering from his wound, he had some wrangle with one of the other inmates of the almshouse and finally threw a heavy spittoon at him which crushed his skull. The man died, but Perry in some way contrived to escape conviction for murder.

After leaving the almshouse, he got employment as a brakeman and worked on several roads with an apparent resolution to live honestly. But plain, hard work with the pay of a train hand made Oliver Curtis Perry very weary. He was continually repining because he could not make money faster. As he did not see any honest way of improving his income, he concluded to try, as he said, "a bold stroke with big chances." This was nothing less than the single-handed robbery of a fast express train passing through the heart of the greatest state in the Union.

The young man, who was proposing to undertake this job, was altogether unlike a common ideal of a desperado. He was only five feet five and a half inches in height and slightly built. His weight was not more than 130 pounds. His complexion was dark sallow, and what is known as "pasty." The wrinkles between his eyes gave to his face a somewhat troubled and careworn expression, and he was nervous and uneasy except when actually at work; but there was nothing ugly or brutal in his appearance and manners. On the contrary, he would be likely to impress a stranger favorably. His forehead was square and high and there was evidently no lack of brains in his head. His voice was soft and delicate in tone, and he could use it with touching effect, as he had frequently shown in church meetings when he was pleased to play the impostor. He was scrupulously neat in person and his clothes were well chosen and well cut. Although he had little or no school education, he had learned to read and write well, and had picked up a considerable miscellaneous stock of information. So he was far from an unpleasant acquaintance or companion, although he was secretly puffed up in his own conceit and had a string of petty vanities, one of which was the wearing of gloves to keep his hands white, even when he was handling a brake. An excellent likeness of Perry, as he appeared at this time, is given on our page of representative portraits.

It was this young fellow with pensive brown eyes, effeminate voice, almost invisible mustache and general air of weakness, who was going to distinguish himself by robbing a train single-handed.

Train No. 31, on the New York Central railroad, left the Grand Central Depot on the evening of the 29th of September at half past eight o'clock. It was made up of eight cars, and the last in line was the express car, carrying money and valuables. Young Perry had been laying his plans for two weeks and had marked this particular train for robbery. He had a thin, sharp-pointed saw made especially for use in this job. This was the only tool that he had except a gimlet and common jack-knife, but he carried one or more revolvers.

When the train reached Albany, it was shortly after midnight; and, at that time or within the next two hours, Perry contrived to board the train and reach the front platform of the "money car." This car was divided into three compartments with heavy sliding doors. The express messenger was in the middle section, and the conductor and other train men were in the last compartment.

Perry first bored a "peep-hole" with his gimlet in the forward end of the car. Through this hole he could see that no one was in the front compartment. Then he quietly inserted the sharp tip of his saw, sawed out a square panel, and crawled through the opening into the car. In a moment he reached the middle compartment, stealthily, and put his revolver close to the messenger's head. The messenger was busily examining way bills, in front of an open safe, and was taken utterly by surprise. Perry fired a shot over his head to startle him, and told him to hold up his hands. He could not do otherwise, for Perry had slily picked up his revolver, and he had no other firearms. Then the young robber took what money he could lay his hands on, and crawled out backward through the same opening by which he had entered the car. To make his escape the more readily, he cut the air pipe controlling the brakes and brought the train to a standstill just before reaching Utica.

While the people on the train were trying to find out what was the cause of the stop, Perry slipped down and away before the alarm was given. He ran back along the track until he came to a ravine where he hid during the day. When an eastbound freight train came along, at night, he found a hiding place on it; and from that point all trace of him was lost until the middle of the following December. Then the secretary of the Troy Railroad Y. M. C. A. received a letter, mailed near Toronto, in which Perry confessed that he had robbed the express and professed to be very penitent. This communication would have been more affecting, if he had proposed to make any return of the plunder which he had carried off, amounting to several thousand dollars; but restitution was no part of his scheme of atonement.

After easing his conscience by his confession, he took a trip through Arizona and Mexico, and found sight seeing very pleasant until he had spent nearly all of his booty in junketing and gambling. Then, when he had only a few hundred dollars left in his pockets, he concluded that he ought to make some further provision for his wants; so he went back to New York for this purpose, as it occurred to him that it would be a master stroke to rob the same express train No. 31, once more, in the same state.

In place of the sharp-pointed saw and gimlet, which he used in the first robbery, he provided a short rope ladder with clutching hooks. By making a roll of the ladder he easily stowed it in a small leather hand bag. During the night of the 20th of February, 1892, he made his way stealthily to the New York Central railroad station at Syracuse, carrying his hand bag containing the coiled ladder. When the express train, No. 31, reached this city, in the darkness of the early morning, Perry climbed up the rear end of the "money car" to the roof. In a moment the train was off and soon sped over the track at the rate of forty miles an hour with Perry clinging to the icy roof of the swaying car.

In spite of the jerks and swings that threatened, momentarily, to fling him headlong from his slippery perch, the robber crawled to the edge of the car and clamped the hooks of his ladder over the jutting cornice. Then he stretched the ladder over the roof, and let it dangle down over a sliding door on the other side of the car. The upper half of this door was of glass, but the night was so dark that McInerney, the express messenger within the car, could not see the ladder nor the form of the dare-devil stealthily dropping down to the level of the door sill.

When Perry had crept down so far that he could look through the grimy glass top of the door, he hung for a little while with his toes barely touching the door sill, and peered into the car. McInerney was standing near him, at the moment, but soon moved away to the other side of the car and sat down with his back to the door, to check over a list of packages. Then Perry smashed the glass in the door with his elbow, thrust his hand in, and fired a shot just over the head of the messenger, crying out, at the same time, with an oath: "Hold up your hands."

Startled by the sound of the breaking glass, McInerney started up from his chair, and turned to face the grim, masked head of the robber and the smoking revolver. Then his hand went up, but not in surrender. He had snatched up his revolver and fired at Perry, who shot back at the same instant. McInerney missed, but Perry's shot shattered his hand and his pistol fell to the floor. Before he could stoop for it, the robber unbolted the door and sprang in at him, yelling, "Hands up." The plucky messenger closed with him, in spite of his shattered hand, and the two men strained and heaved in a fierce wrestle, while the car went whizzing along.

The high wind through the open door blew out the lights; and, in the darkness, McInerney broke away for a moment, and pulled the bell rope twice while Perry was groping about. As soon as the robber touched him and learned where to shoot, he fired twice in quick succession. One ball went through the messenger's thigh, and the other cut the skin over his eye. Then the two men clinched again, dragging each other over the floor.

Perry's muscles had been hardened by his work as a brakeman, and he was a tough, wiry fellow, notwithstanding his sickly look. McInerney was a small, weak man, and crippled by his wounds; but he fought with a heart so strong that for some little time the desperate struggle hung in the balance. But Perry, at length, threw the messenger on his back, and got a knee on his chest. "I'll kill you, if you don't give up," he hissed; and the fainting McInerney stopped his vain struggling. Then Perry struck a light, picked up the keys of the safe, and was searching for money when the train came to a stop. The engineer had heard the signal of the messenger.

CHARLES SPENCER.

FRANK VAN HORN.

THEOPHILUS GEORGE.

WILLIAM E. STEWART.

Perry sprang out of the car, without even a handful of plunder, and ran along the track to the engine, firing his revolver and crying out to the engineer to go ahead. In the darkness, it was impossible for the engineer to see that he only had one man to deal with; so he prudently started his engine and ran on.

Perry had the coolness and cunning to choose, deliberately, a line of escape so impudently bold that it was likely to be the safest; for who would suppose that a train robber would ride straight into the hands of the people who were trying to catch him. He climbed back on the express car, as it ran by him, and rode on to the next station, Lyons. On the way he took off his mask and disguise, and put on a pair of gold-bowed spectacles. As the train slacked up to make a stop at the station, he jumped off and circled about in order to approach the station like a man hurrying down to catch an early train.

His manner was so easy and unconcerned, as he mingled with the crowd that was standing about the train, that no suspicion fell on him until he was recognized by one of the train hands, who had seen him in the station at Syracuse. He stoutly denied that he had been in that city; but the train men said, "We'll hold you, anyhow."

"No, you won't!" cried the demure young man with the spectacles, whipping out his revolver. "You just keep easy, boys,—keep off or you'll get hurt!"

This threat stayed the rush upon him for a moment; and Perry seized his chance to run under the train and jump upon an old freight engine which was standing in the yard at the head of a line of coal cars. He drove off the engineer and fireman of the engine with his revolver, uncoupled the locomotive, pulled the throttle wide open and started down the road as fast as the lumbering old engine would carry him.

For a moment, the crowd stood gaping after him; but, in a trice, the fast engine of the express train was uncoupled, and the engineer and fireman with two other volunteers went off in hot pursuit. They had only one gun, a double-barrelled, smooth-bore shotgun, while the robber had two revolvers; so the superiority in numbers scarcely balanced the advantage in arms.

The speedy engine of the chase gained rapidly on the old freight engine; and Perry, seeing that he would soon be overtaken, desperately reversed his engine and ran back to meet his pursuers. As the two engines rushed past each other, the robber leaned out of his cab window, with a revolver in each hand, and fired at his hunters as fast as he could pull the triggers. The four men in the other engine crouched on the floor under cover, and the broadside did them no harm beyond a sprinkle of broken ·glass. But when Perry's engine had passed by, a following shot was fired at him from the gun, in exchange for his fusillade.

The shot did not hit him, but the plucky men on the fast engine had still another charge in their gun. So they reversed their engine and ran back in pursuit of the flying robber. Again Perry met this pursuit with a challenge, and ran down the track to renew this strange duel. He had reloaded his revolvers and sent another volley into the other engine, as he went plunging by. The second barrel of the shotgun returned his fire, but this shot exhausted the ammunition of the hunters and they were forced to relinquish the chase for the time.

Nevertheless, their pursuit had forced Perry to use up almost all the steam supply for his engine in racing and fighting, and he had no time to fire up. So he took his engine a little further down the track until he reached a strip of woodland, and then jumped down and ran into the woods. Twice he succeeded in getting horses from farm houses by the threat of his revolvers, but the whole country around was aroused and he was readily tracked through the snow that covered the roads. Just before noon he made a last stand behind a stone wall, hoping to keep his hunters at bay till nightfall; but when he heard them calling for rifles, he knew that he could not hold out, and gave himself up to the deputy sheriff who had driven him to the wall.

He was put, for the time, in the little stone jail of the town of Lyons. Within forty-eight hours he had planned an escape and contrived to slip into his father's hand, through the bars of his cell, two working drawings of a key to fit the door lock. On the slip with the sketches was written: "Make of very hard wood; be sure and not get it brittle, for it must be very tough and strong. Make it about the size of this drawing. Hole in key, three-eighths of an inch. Make the key blade as thick as it is drawn above."

Fortunately the passing of the slip was seen by a keen-eyed detective, who arrested the old man and threatened to search him, unless he gave up the paper. So the father reluctantly produced a folded leaf from an old book, with a picture on one side and a blank page on the other, covered with pencil sketches and writing. This attempt put riveted shackles on the ankles of the prisoner, connected by a heavy log chain. The jailor in Lyons was determined not to lose such a robber by the lack of any precaution. When Perry was finally called to trial, three months later, he pleaded guilty to five indictments and was sentenced to the state prison at Auburn for a term of forty-nine years and three months.

Shortly after his committal to Auburn he threatened his keepers with a drawn knife, and was put under the strictest guard in a cell in the basement of the north wing of the prison. These basement cells had thick walls of brick, and were considered so secure that they were not regularly inspected like the cells on the floors above. Perry was closely confined to his cell and not permitted to go to work in the shops. At first he was sullen and rebellious; but he suddenly became submissive and cheerful. His good behavior was so long continued that he seemed to be well on the way to permanent reform.

This fond hope was suddenly blasted by the discovery that

the docile prisoner had cut his way out of his cell, through a brick partition, a foot thick. He had left a straw dummy to represent him, but that was not a satisfactory substitute. The cell on the other side of the partition was temporarily vacant while its occupant was at work in the shops, and Perry was able to steal unseen from this cell, out of the north wing, across the prison yard into the basement of the broom shop. Here he lay hid until night, when he tried to enter the shop above. This shop was so closely guarded that he slipped along toward the marble shop, and tried to enter it, but he was seen and pursued by the guards. He ran toward the collar shop and was seeking for a knife when he was knocked down by a guard and taken back to his cell.

After this escapade he was comparatively quiet for a year, and then he secured his transfer to Matteawan Asylum by counterfeiting insanity with extraordinary craft; unless he was, in fact, half crazed at the time. His transfer to the asylum was in December, 1893, and in April, 1895, he had recovered his wits so far that he planned and executed a remarkable escape from the asylum in company with four other inmates. They knocked down the night watchman at midnight, and bound and gagged him. Then they took his keys, unlocked the chapel door, passed through to a main building, mounted to the roof, and dropped down, thirty feet, to the ground outside the walls. For some days Perry succeeded in evading pursuit; but he was finally recognized by a detective, in the midst of a gang of tramps, sitting about a bonfire in Weehawken, New Jersey. After a sharp run he was captured and taken back to the asylum.

On the 1st of July, in the same year, he was sent back to Auburn to serve out his sentence, by the judgment of a commission which declared him to be sane. In the following November, however, he was returned to the asylum, because of his unruly and demented conduct. He made an attempt to blind himself by thrusting needles into his eyes; hoping, as

"KNIGHTS OF THE ROAD." 275

he said, to gain the pity of the governor and possibly a pardon. Whatever may be the final conclusion touching his sanity, there can be no doubt that he is one of the most dangerous men who has ever run at large in this country.

Fortunately, such desperate and wily robbers as Perry are rarely known, and the penalties for the robbery of trains are so heavy that comparatively few rascals venture to face the risk of lifelong imprisonment coupled with the probability that they will be shot in the act of robbery. On all the principal railroad lines in this country such watchfulness and safeguards are used that a successful robbery is almost impracticable today, and the robbers are certain to be pursued with all the resources of the united police and detective agencies of the country. The best that any such robber can reasonably expect is a few months' hiding in constant fear and harassment, followed by many years of close imprisonment at hard labor.

A dwarfed and petty offshoot from the professional "train robber" is known as the "sleeping car worker." Thieves of this class make a practice of riding over the country in sleeping cars and trying to steal the watches, money and hand bags of their fellow passengers. They will mark, whenever they can, people carrying gold watches and those that are likely to have the most money in their pockets. If there is a vacant berth next to the sections occupied by such passengers, the "sleeping car worker" will try to secure it by an exchange under some pretence. Then, when the curtains are drawn for the night, the thief will slip a groping hand around the partition and try to filch a watch or pocketbook from under a pillow or from clothes on the coverlet of a berth or hanging from a hook. If it is possible to unfasten and draw out a sliding partition for a few inches, the "worker" will then thrust his hand through the gap thus made between the slide and the wall of the car. If the berths are too sharply watched by the porter to give any chance for such sly groping, the thief will wait for an opportunity to steal while the passengers are dressing or using the toilet rooms of the car.

One of the most notable thieves of this class in the country is Charles Spencer, alias Spence, alias Bronson, who has been robbing passengers on the trains by his sly thefts during the past ten years. He learned to be expert in every trick of vaulting, tumbling and swinging as a member of a circus company; and then found a new opening for his nimbleness in the exercises of a pickpocket, hotel thief and bank sneak. About twelve years ago he applied himself particularly to the occupation of a "sleeping car worker." Here he soon earned a reputation as "the fastest worker in this country in his line."

He has been known to pass through a whole train in the course of a single night and rob more than a dozen people in the ordinary cars as well as in the "sleepers." When he has been put off a train as a known thief, he has sometimes jumped on board again while the train was leaving the station, and swung himself up on the roof of a car with the celerity of a monkey. Then he has ridden on top of the car to the place where he wished to stop, and jumped off as nimbly as he mounted. He has dodged arrest and conviction with uncommon dexterity, but he has served out one sentence of imprisonment for seven years at Ogden, Utah, for the robbery of passengers on the Southern Pacific Railroad. There is probably no more dangerous thief of this class in this country.

Frank Van Horn is another thief of equal mark, who has been roaming over the country from Maine to California for many years. He was long associated with a partner of the same stripe, John Dennis, who is now dead; and no pair of thieves were more crafty and annoying. At one time Van Horn was credited with the ownership of a large estate in Mississippi, but he has wasted all the property, that he has inherited or stolen, in gambling and other dissipations. He has always been fashionably dressed like all noted hotel thieves and sleeping car workers, and his appearance would hardly prejudice a stranger against him, though his face is so pitted by the small pox that he has the nickname of "Pock-marked Frank."

Theophilus George and his partner, William E. Stewart, alias "Billy Jackson," fitly supply the portraits to fill up a representative page with Van Horn and Spencer. Both are notorious sleeping car workers and hotel thieves. Stewart is a fluent talker and dangerously ingratiating. He has served time in the prisons of New Jersey, Pennsylvania, Illinois and Wisconsin, and has probably been in the jails of every large city in this country. His occasional trips to Europe for the sake of diversion and plunder have made him of note in the old world as well as the new.

All employees of railroad and sleeping car companies are particularly instructed to keep a sharp watch to protect passengers from the hands of these thieves and it is needless to remark that no known thief is permitted by the detectives at railroad stations to enter any train of sleeping cars. Passengers should not neglect, however, to take reasonable precautions for their own protection. Large amounts of money should not be carried on the person when travelling except in the rare cases where this method of conveying money is the only practicable one. There should be as little parade as possible of the possession of money or jewelry. If valuables are not put in the keeping of the porter, they should be so placed in the berths that they cannot be reached by a groping hand without disturbing the sleepers. It is worth noting that thieves take much greater care not to be robbed by other thieves than is shown by ordinary travellers, and few of them have ever had occasion to lament the loss of a dollar unless it was taken away by violence. Very little ingenuity is needed to provide places of deposit as secure as the undershirt sleeve, which usually holds the money of a sleeping thief.

It is a far descent from the pinnacle of crime reached by

such robbers as Perry, Morgan and Hedspeth, to the level of the thieves who watch for chances to break into freight cars temporarily sidetracked or unavoidably left for the night at some distance from the freight depots. Thieves of this class have light carts in waiting to carry off their plunder in the same manner as goods from stores are taken away, and the stolen property is then repacked and concealed or put in the hands of receivers.

It is the practice also of these thieves to seek every opportunity of stealing packages from loaded express wagons on the way to and from the railroad stations or when stopping for the delivery or receipt of goods. Unless a sharp watch is kept on the wagons also, the most impudent of these thieves will jump upon the driver's seat and carry off the entire wagon load to a place from which the goods can be rapidly shipped to distant points in boxes or barrels consigned to a confederate. In the winter holiday season, especially, thefts of this kind are frequent as the wagons are then most heavily loaded and the expressmen or drivers are often obliged to wait for many minutes in the throngs of people and teams about the railway stations. At such times, wagons should never be left standing along the sidewalk or at freight depots without some watchful attendant. If a driver is obliged to leave his team, temporarily, for any reason, he should have an assistant to take his place. Any boy with sense enough to keep a sharp eye on the contents of a wagon will be a sufficient guard, for thieves of this class are usually too wary to meddle with any goods that are constantly watched.

In the portraits of Harry Kelly, Walter Borsch, Frederick Lawrence, and Ernest V. Schneider—the "express thief," so called, is well represented; for all have been repeatedly sent to houses of correction and other reformatory prisons for terms of varying length, and Borsch, in particular, has been convicted and sentenced eight times for larceny in the past twenty years, and spent three-quarters of his life, since 1877, in all the

ERNEST V. SCHNEIDER.

FREDERICK LAWRENCE.

HARRY KELLY.

WALTER BORSCH.

grades of penitentiaries from a reformatory for boys to the state prison.

Frequently these rogues vary their pilfering from wagons by calling at houses to deliver bogus parcels, said to contain goods of value and sent C. O. D. They will personate express messengers and the employees of city stores, and may present a close counterfeit in dress and manner. Another trick of theirs is to lie in waiting for messengers carrying packages and obtain them by false pretences. Some of the bolder rascals have decoyed express messengers into a room hired by a gang, by sending to some fictitious person a parcel which is registered as a package of money or other valuables. When the messenger has called to deliver this parcel, he has been caught, bound and gagged by the gang, and then robbed of his money bag. It is common also for these thieves to call at stores where signs are displayed requesting expressmen to stop for packages, and carry off the bundles by the impudent pretence that they are expressmen. It would be well to caution clerks not to deliver packages to any unknown person unless he can clearly show that he is duly authorized to receipt for the goods in the name of a reputable express company.

THE ROVING FOOTPAD.

FOR the gratification of the "gentlemen highwaymen" or "knights of the road," there has been considerable straining to draw a gilded line of distinction between robbers on horseback and robbers on foot. The Macheaths and Duvals reckoned themselves a superior order of beings in comparison with the vulgar footpad. Their clothes were as fine and their linen as dainty as any fop of the court, and they were as fastidious as any popinjay in their particular care that no ragged rascal should come betwixt the wind and their nobility. The belated "Paul Clifford" was constrained to tolerate the companionship of the swaggering "Ned Pepper," but he did not affect to conceal his disgust at this pinch-beck counterfeit of a man of fashion.

In the light of our matter of fact civilization which jumbles all robbers together in the same pit of infamy, and has the same convict dress and the same prison cell for the defaulting cashier and the common pickpocket,—the highwayman's distinction seems a farcical vanity. But it was undoubtedly recognized to a considerable extent by popular sentiment in the palmy days of the "knights of the road," if not by the cold eye of the law. This was natural enough in an age when the evergreen custom of living by rapine was still stubbornly maintained in the turbulent Highlands, and bands of moss-troopers and caterans were making their forays and restocking their pastures as their forefathers had done for generations unnumbered. When a notorious freebooter like William Armstrong, alias "Kinmont Willie," was so unlucky as to fall into the hands of an English warden, he could count with confidence on the intercession of his kinsmen of high degree; and he might even be plucked out of his prison cell, like Kinmont Willie, by the dash of a "bauld Buccleuch." And the still more famous "Johnny Armstrong" would have turned purple in the face, if any impertinent moralist had presumed to put him in the same class as a thief in Whitefriars.

Some of the keener-witted robbers, too, were in the habit of making very odious comparisons between their occupation and that of the great princes of their day and former sovereigns of glorious memory. It was recalled on the authority of an old historian that even the magnificent Alexander, who wept because there were no more worlds to conquer, was impudently informed by the robber Dionidës, that he was only a bigger robber than himself. Frederic the Great is said to have suffered a like affront, and the king who appropriated Silesia promptly broke on the wheel, no doubt, the saucy little rascal who annexed a purse in Berlin.

It was observed also that even a robber of low degree was on a par with the average citizen in some large provinces that were not entirely barbaric, and that such robbers had been known to climb the steps of a throne. The illustrious Nadir Shah was the son of a poor shepherd of Khorassan, and began his career as an ordinary robber; but was nevertheless able to mount to the throne of Persia. Nadir Sing was an East Indian robber, who attained scarcely less distinction as a leader of the Bheels, and struck terror to the heart of Hindostan. And there were ten thousand chiefs of the Pindarries and Mewatties and Baugries and Moghies who were not without honor in their own country before the advent of the famous robber Cheetoo, whose daring foray so astounded the extenders of the British empire by the strong arm. It was by the brazen assertion of the likeness between the extenders of empires and the appropriators of smaller plunder that the ordinary robber of to-day is frequently and familiarly styled by his "pals," a "strong arm man."

But in spite of all this parade of distinction and logical contention for the recognition of the rank of robbers in society, the highwayman has sunk so low in the popular estimation that it makes scarcely a whit of difference to-day in the eye of society whether a robber is mounted on a horse or a dromedary or a palace car, and wears the clothes of a prince—or whether he lurks in a slum or roves over the country as a footpad in the filthy rags of a tramp. With the possible exception of the gilded pretences of sovereigns, barbarism is barbarism and robbery is robbery, in our own day, regardless of their masks.

There is little essential variation in the method of robbery by the footpad in all the thousands of years since the first robber "held up" or knocked down his victim. The cover of darkness, or the loneliness of the place of attack, the ambush, the surprise, the helplessness of the victim, or the overpowering force of the robbers—have been constantly recurring features of this form of robbery from the beginning. The footpad has struck his foul blow alone, and he has had comrades in crime, ranging from a single partner to gangs that have terrorized whole provinces in organized bands of brigands, which might swell into such a legion as followed the Wild Boar of Ardennes. Sometimes, too, the footpad has had the craft to magnify himself by the aid of dummies, like the Sicilian bandit who levied tribute for years from a score of villages with the aid of some masks and hats and ten men of straw.

When a gang reached the size of a band of a score or more, the leader was usually distinguished by the title of chief, and, in this event, he was raised in his own conceit far above the level of the common footpad. It might be, also, that he would wear the title of count or some other lord of high degree, which would give him the privilege of being beheaded, instead of being hanged like a robber who was not one of the gentry. It was possible, however, for a footpad of humble origin and no particular distinction of title to obtain a widespread reputation, of the infamous kind, even in the beginning of the present cen-

JOHN H. MEYER.

JOSEPH STACK.

LINDSAY C. BOYD.

JOHN J. MARTIN.

tury. This was signally shown in the case of John Buckler, who was a "bogey man" to the country people of Western Germany, even more dreadful than the great Napoleon. The name of Schinder Hannes, or "Jack, the Flayer," which was given to this footpad in commemoration of one of his diversions, is still in use to conjure up a spectre that will raise the hair of disobedient children. In view of the legions of footpads that have lived and died on the banks of the famous river, it was no slight distinction to pass into history as "The Robber of the Rhine"; but it did not compensate John Buckler for the penalty of death on the wheel which overtook him.

In the ruder weapons of the robbers in our city slums and mining camps there is often no mask at all on the perpetuation of the barbarism of the stone age. A bludgeon or rough stick, broken or cut from a tree, is still used to-day as it was in the days of Cain. The use of iron instead of wood for a club is a step down from simple barbarism to viler brutality. The footpad, who uses a wooden stick to strike down his victim, might shrink from wilful murder, but the ruffian who strikes with an iron bar either strikes to kill or is utterly reckless.

With the spread of civilization, however, there has necessarily been a falling off in the use of the old savage weapons. The professional robber could not stalk down Broadway or even through the rudest mining camp with the war club of a Fiji islander over his shoulder or bulging out under the back of his coat. So the footpads were obliged to make their weapons smaller and more easy to conceal. Some armed themselves with heavy riding whips with loaded butts; or carried canes with handles of solid horn or of plated metal. It was difficult, if not impracticable, to draw a line of toleration and proscription, defining the style and weight of whips and canes which people must not carry,—and such instruments of robbery could not be classed as concealed weapons. It was hardly practicable, either, to prohibit a man from carrying in his coat pocket a piece of lead water pipe or iron gas pipe.

Hence the robbers who were debarred from using the clubs of ordinary savages, provided themselves with makeshifts of their own, no less brutal and deadly.

There was, however, a general unwillingness to add murder to robbery, if their plunder could be secured by threats or any violence that was not punishable by death on the gallows. The pirate, declaring war to the knife against all civilization, might be seeking for blood as well as booty; but the ordinary footpad or highwayman was not a rover whose swift ship might defy pursuit over a trackless ocean. Unless he had some personal and deadly spite to gratify, he had no wish to take his victim's life as well as his purse, and arouse such a passion of indignation that he would be hunted like a wolf from cover to cover by the people at large as well as the police. Rascals, too, who would steal or rob without any scruple would often shrink from cold-blooded murder and would aim to stun or stupefy or entrap their victims rather than to kill them. So from the dread of the gallows, or some lingering compunction, or simply to avoid the spattering of blood, bars and spikes were covered with leather and slung shot encased in thick, close woven, nets. Cord and leather cases served to deaden the thud of a blow and make it less mutilating and fatal without detracting from its stunning effect. The handle of these clubs were usually fitted with loops of leather or cord intended to slip over the wrist so that they could be readily grasped again if they dropped or were knocked from the hands of the robbers.

By the device of the sand bag, the purpose of the covered or padded club was carried out still more effectively. This invention is credited to the rascally art of French footpads. It is a roll of canvas tightly packed with sand or emery and closed at the ends so that it can be handled as a club. A hard blow from this dangerous weapon will almost certainly stun and knock down a man, and the skull may even be fractured without any external mark of injury beyond a slight bruise. Within a few years after its introduction the sand bag was known and feared all over the world and it is still a favorite weapon of footpads in this country and Europe.

Sailor men who take to robbery use occasionally the slung shot which was their device in the old days when almost all merchant ships carried guns, and little cannon balls could be readily picked up and put in slings. Sometimes, also, small brass or iron plates with four holes for the insertion of the fingers are worn as a cover for the clinched hand to make the blow of the fist more stunning. This dwarfed substitute for the cestus of the old Greek and Roman boxers, is known as "brass knuckles." It is a product of the slums and foully used in the fights of ruffians more often than in robberies.

Instead of a blow that will knock down and stun, a noose may be cast over the head of a victim and tightly drawn about his neck while his cries are stifled with a gag, or by muffling his head in a heavy coat or shawl. This imitation of the East Indian thug was too often given twenty years ago on the outskirts of new mining camps and in the slums of our cities as well. It is termed garroting and the practice has not yet been discontinued, although it has been greatly abated.

A remarkable variation of this method of preventing any outcry has been described in detail by M. de Calvi, who wrote, two hundred years ago, a curious and minute account of the robbers and thieves of France under the title "Histoire Generale Des Larrons." He credited to a certain Palioly, a French robber in the days of Henry of Navarre, the invention of the so-called "poire d'angoisse," or "choke-pear." This instrument appears to have fully deserved its name, "the pear of anguish," as it was originally fashioned; if the account of M. de Calvi is to be credited.

A Parisian locksmith of considerable perverted ingenuity made the first "choke pear" to the order of Palioly, and it was first tried in practice in the mouth of a wealthy merchant named Eridas. Palioly and three other members of his gang succeeded in taking the merchant by surprise in his house, and thrusting into his mouth the new invention. This was in the form of a little bottle which was charged with an artful core of springs that expanded as soon as the bottle was in the mouth of the merchant. The more widely the victim gaped in his effort to cry out, the more the "choke-pear" swelled and suffocated.

In this state of helplessness and torment, Eridas was bound to a chair, and saw the robbery of his strong box and store of jewels by Palioly and his "pals," who coolly packed up their plunder under the bulging eyes of the merchant and leisurely departed, leaving him still gagged with their pear.

It was a further peculiarity of this truly "diabolical" device, as M. de Calvi remarks, that the pear could only be dislodged by the use of a key made especially for it by the wicked locksmith. So when the servants of Eridas finally came to his help after some hours had passed, they were powerless to extract the pear and relieve their master. The more their clutching fingers strained to pluck it out, the more firmly it stuck in the mouth of the merchant. As the victim could scarcely breathe and was entirely cut off from eating and drinking, he was in great terror of dying, but he was happily relieved by the compassion of one of the gang who begged the key of the pear from Palioly, and sent it secretly to the suffering Eridas.

M. de Calvi reports that the multiplication of this "choke-pear" worked great evil in Paris and throughout France. Fortunately for us this "diabolical invention" appears to be one of the lost arts, if, indeed, it ever existed outside of de Calvi's head. There is no doubt, however, of the fashioning of a pear-shaped gag which has been largely used in former days by robbers in Europe, and may still be employed to some extent. This is also known as the "choke-pear," though it is far less marvellous and dangerous than the pear of Palioly.

When robbers are desperate ruffians whose greed for booty is utterly reckless of bloodshed, they will shoot or stab ruthlessly in seeking plunder or in resisting capture. We shall not call up any ghastly series of blood-boltered pictures by the selection of any of these horrid crimes for the sake of profitless and needless illustration. They are only too familiar already to every reader of the newspapers that aim to reproduce with the vividness of a mirror all the horrors of the day as a principal part of its news and reckon that murderers are of far more news value than missionaries. A reader must, indeed, be insatiate who is not yet glutted with every nauseating variety of savage assaults in lonely lanes and congested slums, in luxurious mansions and dens reeking with opium fumes, in the cabins of ships at sea and in snowbound camps on mountain perches.

There is, however, an exceedingly dangerous and dastardly mode of robbing which has been practiced for centuries but is more common and threatening to-day than ever before. Opium and other potent drugs have been used to stupefy victims ever since this possible application was perceived by rascals of every degree. Jewelled hands have daintily poured out a few drops from a phial into golden cups of rare wine, and dirty fists have flung doses into pots of muddy ale. Men of all kinds and conditions have been decoyed into vile dens and drugged and robbed, and often the doses have been given so slily that the victims could remember nothing of the place or manner of the robbery. The discovery of chloroform gave to the robber a chance to use a wet cloth or a saturated sponge to paralyze his victim; and the same advance of medicinal art, that has done so much to heal the sick and to banish pain, has been shamefully perverted to the use of the footpad.

Of all known drugs and powerful anæsthetics no other is so menacing and so widely employed to-day as chloral hydrate. This is the common base and often the only ingredient in the doses that bear the ugly, but expressive name of "knockout drops." The foul use of this drug has rapidly extended of late years and is now gravely alarming. A prominent newspaper recently published a list of over twenty deaths which were reckoned to be from the use of "knockout drops," and subsequent violence. In addition to this forty robberies were enumerated in some of our principal cities, in which the same drug was used. The victims ranged from a "bonanza king" to an organ grinder, and a few dollars of plunder was apparently sought as greedily and brutally as the spoil of a millionaire. A wealthy mine owner was found dead, on a street corner, in November, 1896. He had been robbed of his gold watch and chain, a diamond ring, diamond shirt studs, two hundred dollars in money, and an overcoat. From many others, watches, jewelry and considerable sums of money were taken; but the rascals would drug a man to rob him of a dollar, if he had no more, and strip all the clothes off his back in addition.

It is true that evidence of the use of these drops was lacking in a number of the cases cited, but it is probable that there was no material exaggeration in the list given; and it is certain that the experience of the police in every large city will attest the alarming spread of the use of knockout drops and the need of special legislation to assist in checking this danger.

It is difficult to carry about a slung shot or a sand bag or a club of any kind without attracting suspicion and arrest; but what external sign will there be of the presence of a deadly little phial in a waistcoat pocket? Then, too, if an ordinary policeman had as many eyes as Argus,—he could scarcely observe every glass of beer or wine or liquor that is drawn on the line of his route, and insure them from the mixture of a few drops out of a tiny bottle. So the rascals have watched for chances to use their drops when their victims were looking away from their glasses, and it has been peculiarly difficult to stop this practice. The solution of chloral used is a nearly colorless fluid, with slight odor or taste; and a man who has been dosed will rarely suspect the use of the drug, which acts subtly and gradually, in bringing on drowsiness without any sickening or disagreeable sensation. As he grows sleepy, he

ARTHUR FLYNN.

WALTER SEARS.

JOHN W. MURRAY.

WILLIAM E. SMALING.

will be lured or led to some dark room or alley or nook where he is speedily robbed and left to sleep off the effects of the drug, if the robbers are not afraid that he may suspect them and cause their arrest. If so, he may be knocked in the head or thrown into the water, if opportunity serves.

The rogue's name for the professional users of "knockout drops" is Peter-men or Peter-players, and there are women who are as expert as any man in this use of chloral. Sometimes a dose is given as an introduction to the "panel game," and other deliberate robberies; but the victim is usually robbed as soon as he is stupefied by the drug. Beyond the crime of robbery grave peril to life is entailed by this reckless use of chloral. The same dose will affect different persons to a varying extent, and what will barely stupefy one may kill another. There is little or no precaution taken in pouring a dose from a phial, and a number of deaths have unquestionably followed the administering of "knockout drops" when no other murderous agent was enlisted. To a man suffering from heart disease or any pronounced weakness of the heart, "knockout drops" are very likely to be deadly.

On representative pages are ranged the portraits of eight "Peter-men," perhaps the most dangerous rascals now infesting our cities. Joseph Stack, alias "Spanish Joe," is a noted blackmailer and thief, who was sent to Sing Sing in 1885 for ten years. On the occasion of the conclave of Knights Templar in Boston, in 1895, Stack was arrested and a bottle of "knockout drops" taken from his pocket. He was sent to the House of Correction for six months upon conviction as a vagabond, but there is no doubt that he deserves to be classed with habitual criminals, for his term in Sing Sing was not his first term in prison. John H. Meyer is no less notorious in the same line of robbery. John J. Martin was sentenced in August, 1895, to the Massachusetts House of Correction for four years. In the same month of the same year Lindsay C. Boyd was sent to the Massachusetts state prison for six years.

John W. Murray was sentenced to the House of Correction in September, 1896, for five years; and, two months later, William E. Smaling received a sentence to a term in the state prison, which will range from three to five years. Arthur Flynn and Walter Sears are also serving out sentences in Massachusetts. All these offenders were convicted of larceny from the person with the use of "knockout drops."

The Massachusetts district attorneys fully appreciate the gravity and dastardly character of this offence, and have spared no effort to secure the conviction of the criminals. The trial judges have taken the same view of the cases and imposed sentences corresponding to the offence. Thanks to this cordial coöperation with the efforts of the police, Peter-men and women have been driven to stop or suspend their practice in Massachusetts of late and this is satisfactory so far as it goes. But the danger of a revival and the constant effort that is required to hold this vile practice in check are cogent reasons for the enactment of the most stringent legislation to suppress this latest resort of the footpad.

Strict regulations in all cities should govern the sale of dangerous drugs and the carrying of such drugs on the person with felonious intent should be made a felony. The judgment of the prosecuting officers in our larger cities is fully in accord with that of the police authorities, we believe, in the call for stringent treatment of this abominable practice for the extension and aggravation of robbery.

THE RECEIVER.

THE receiver is as bad as the thief. That is a moss-grown adage which has long been a current truism. It might be added with equal truth that the receiver is often worse than the petty thief whom he incites or employs. There is some hope of reform for a feather-brained young rogue like "Charley," or even for a prematurely old rascal like the "Artful Dodger"; but what can be done with a Fagin except to put him in a prison cell for life, if he is not brought to the gallows in spite of his wiliness and a cowardly vileness that would plot murder without daring to strike the deadly blow. Such a scoundrel is even more to be dreaded than a mere ruffian like "Bill Sikes," for he has the cunning to keep under cover as well as the craft to find the tools for the execution of his schemes of plunder.

An "Artful Dodger" picks up a few dozen of handkerchiefs and a watch or two, and then an officer puts his hand on the collar of the young pick-pocket and he is escorted to a house of correction. A brutal Sikes and a "flash Toby Crackit" may break into a few stores or houses and get a few thousand dollars' worth of booty; but before many months they are caught in the act or tracked to their hiding places, and lodged in prison for years at hard labor. But a Fagin lurks in his den year after year, gloating over the spoils which his pupil, the pickpocket, or his cat's-paw, the burglar, brings to his storehouse; chuckling when one of his tools dies without "squealing"; destroying every mark that might identify his plunder; slipping through the net of the law like an eel; enlisting new recruits as fast as the prison doors swing behind the heels of old apprentices; and growing white-haired, perhaps, before he comes to the end of his shifts in the convict's cell.

It is true that all "fences" or receivers of stolen goods are not Fagins in craft or villainy. Dickens was an artist who never spared paint in intensifying an effect. His marvellous "fence" is a living picture but the caricature of a type. A creature so diabolic could not be permitted to slink off the stage or drop through a trap into a dust-heap like "the Artful Dodger." It was necessary to throw him on the rack in the midst of blue fire, with the gallows creaking over his head. So the great melodramatist got a jury to convict him as an accessory to the murder of "Nancy" on evidence that would not have hung a cat, and thus wrung the neck of his leading character actor in a way to satisfy the gallery if not the critics.

A real Fagin would perhaps have slunk out of the country as soon as he had put the wolf, Sikes, on the track of the doomed "Nancy"; but more probably he would have defied the officers of the law to prove that he was anything worse than a decayed "fence." It is not the custom of real Fagins, either, to keep a stock of stolen watches, rings, brooches and bracelets on hand to gloat over, or any other articles that may be readily identified. The receivers of stolen goods are well provided with melting pots for the swift conversion of gold and silverware of any kind into lumps of bullion. It is the custom of thieves, too, as we have before noted, to destroy, at the earliest opportunity, the possibility of identifying any of their "swag." They will tear precious stones out of their settings, and beat the metal into an indistinguishable mass. When they present their booty to the "fences," it is usually in a condition which gives to the receivers the possible pretext of claiming that they did not know that it was stolen.

It is not common for thieves to deal direct with the receivers. Some intermediary is employed to offer the stolen property, and this agent is frequently the wife of the thief or some other near relative whom he can trust with his booty. The "fence" may be morally certain that the offered goods are stolen, and he is likely to know the character of any person from whom he makes repeated purchases; but, if he is unscrupulous, he will not be disagreeably inquisitive if the goods can be bought for a small fraction of their real value and are not of a sort that can be easily traced and identified.

A large per cent of professional "fences" are women. Many years ago, a considerable number of the lower class of pawnbrokers were covertly acting as receivers of stolen property; but of late years this class has been nearly weeded out by the vigilance of the detectives and police, and to-day the regular pawnbroker is one of the most serviceable coadjutors of the police in the detection and recovery of stolen property. Reputable pawnbrokers will not only refuse to make loans on goods which they suspect to be stolen but they will contrive, if they can, to detain the persons applying for loans on such property until they can communicate with the police and secure their arrest.

Some receivers still lurk in the slums like Fagin and considerable plunder is hidden temporarily in the rooms of persons who are connected with the thieves by blood or marriage; but most of the professional "fences" are men and women who are ostensibly engaged in respectable business on a small scale as dealers in cheap clothing or haberdashers or milliners.

It is obvious that a "fence" must have some plausible pretext to account for the receipt of goods, and accommodation for the storage and concealment of stolen property. So he puts on the convenient mask of a small storekeeper and if any stolen goods are traced to his store and discovered, he will plead his ignorance of the theft and pretend that he has bought the goods in the ordinary course of business. As all marks of identification are destroyed, if possible, by the thieves before they attempt to dispose of their plunder and as the "fence" is careful to inspect his purchases at once and efface any compromising marks which he can discover,—it is often very difficult to convict the receiver as an accomplice in a robbery.

Probably the most remarkable rascal of this class, who has

ever been known in this country, was the notorious woman familiarly called "Old Mother Mandelbaum." Frederica Mandelbaum came to this country from Germany, forty years ago, and, a few years after her arrival, she opened a small dry goods store, with the help of her husband, in New York City. The conduct of the business was a joint concern, but the husband soon fell into the background behind his scheming, wily wife. The business thrived from the start, but the grasping woman was not content with the narrow margin of legitimate profit; so she opened lines of secret communication with the most notorious "store breakers" and "shoplifters" in New York, and gradually extended her net to all parts of the country. Her little dry goods shop soon expanded into three connected buildings, and she had outlying storerooms in various parts of the city, and in adjacent cities. She was willing to pay spot cash for her purchases, but she practically made her own price in the bargaining, buying often for a petty fraction of the cost of the stolen goods. She could sometimes get a camel's-hair shawl worth two thousand dollars for a hundred dollars and silks worth three dollars a yard for half a dollar a yard.

By such speculations her selling profits were immense, and she rapidly piled up a fortune which enabled her to buy in a lump the booty of the largest robberies. Here her range of profit was even greater than in her petty bargains, for burglars were often hard pressed to hide their plunder and anxious to get it off their hands at any price. By being able to pay in full for any bargain on the spot, "Old Mother Mandelbaum" towered above the "fences" of her class, and almost all the big bargains fell into her lap, especially if the stolen property was costly silks and other dry goods which she could dispose of in her regular business as a storekeeper. She had no losses in the delivery of her bargains, for she would pay no money for any bird in the bush. She asked no credit and gave none. Her cash was paid over on the instant when the stolen goods were put in her hands and not a moment before.

Although so strict in her bargains, she was more speculative or partial, at times, in other dealings. She would frequently furnish the "fall money" when one of her pet burglars or shoplifters called on her for bail, but she did not forget to deduct any advances of this kind when her favored agents brought in their next batches of booty. Her husband died, but this bereavement was apparently no loss to the Mandelbaum business It is reported that she was so determined to provide a regular supply of stolen goods for her market, that she organized gangs of shoplifters, both men and women, whom she trained and employed. She made a specialty of dealing in silks, satins and fine dry goods; but she would buy anything that she could sell on her own scale of profit. She was so crafty and keen that her ill-gotten gains reached close to a million dollars, in 1884, when evidence was finally obtained against her that secured a warrant for her arrest.

In order to bring the possession of stolen property home to her, an adroit detective succeeded finally in gaining her confidence and buying a number of pieces of silk for shipment out of the country, as he pretended. On some of this silk the private marks of leading dry goods houses in New York were found. So "Old Mother Mandelbaum" was arrested and all her tenements were searched. In the piles of silks in her store several pieces were found with private marks that had not been obliterated, and a glittering mass of jewelry of every description was brought to light on opening her old safe. On a table in her magnificently furnished bedroom, there was a curious array of melting pots, pennyweight scales of various sizes, and scales for weighing diamonds. The trunk of her confidential clerk was stuffed full of watches, chains, scarf pins, shirt studs and collar buttons, and in a big "Saratoga" trunk in a closet, India and white lace shawls of extraordinary value were stowed away.

On the 4th of December following her arrest, her case came up for trial in the New York court, but she had departed meanwhile to Canada; for she had been permitted to give bonds to the extent of $21,000 for the appearance of her son, her clerk and herself, and preferred to "jump" her bail rather than to stand trial. A few days afterwards, the old woman and her two companion bail-jumpers were arrested in Hamilton, where they had registered at a hotel under assumed names. As they were not subject to extradition, it was impossible to prosecute them successfully. So Madam Mandelbaum and part of her family resided for several years in their place of refuge. She lived in a style suited to her income, but for the sake of occupation she put the following advertisement into a Hamilton newspaper in 1886:

OPENING,
Tuesday, Aug. 10.
F. MANDELBAUM,
Ladies' and Children's Furnishing Wear,
Fancy Goods, Novelties, etc.,
72 King St., East.

In the closing years of her mercantile career she was twice arrested for smuggling costly laces and jewelry into her adopted country, but escaped conviction in both instances, and continued to live in apparent affluence until her death in 1893. It is doubtful if any "fence" has ever matched her in craft, and it is certain that few have been able to make such gains or to hold them even in exile.

The portraits which we give on an accompanying page represent four notorious and typical receivers. James H. Chaffee, who had in keeping the goods stolen by the burglar, Barrett, and fully described in a preceding chapter, represents that class of receivers who try to make money at both ends by imposing on honest purchasers and cheating the rogues who use them as agents. This practice might be lucrative if it was feasible, but it is apt to result, as in Chaffee's case, in the exposure of these knaves by the thieves as well as by the honest men. When Barrett became convinced that Chaffee was trying to pocket

JAMES H. CHAFFEE.

GADALIA BERKOWITZ.

AMELIA LEVY.

LENA KLEINSCHMIDT.

all the proceeds of the stolen property, he was more than willing that his agent should be put in a prison cell. On the other hand when Chaffee undertook to dispose of the stolen property, in order to get the highest price, he went to a dealer of the best standing and offered sets of stamps which the dealer had mounted for a customer, and knew to be stolen. It is practically certain that Barrett would never have blundered so grossly, but the receiver was obviously a combination of fool and knave.

The portraits of two sisters are ranged side by side on the same page. Lena Kleinschmidt, alias "Black Lena," and Amelia Levy, alias "Black Amelia," are two of the most notorious shoplifters and receivers in this country. Under various assumed names, and in association with other women of like character they have visited nearly every prominent city east of the Missouri and attempted to plunder the leading dry goods stores. They have been repeatedly arrested and convicted, but both are incorrigible, habitual criminals, and as soon as they are discharged from prison, they return to their old occupation.

Two months after the release of "Black Lena" from prison in New York, in 1883, she was arrested in Chicago in company with a third sister, Mary Anderson, better known as "Mother Weir," the head of one of the largest organized gangs of shoplifters that ever infested an American city. Both women, when arrested, had just passed out of a wholesale millinery house, carrying large bunches of valuable ostrich feathers under their long black circular cloaks. A search of the room which served as the headquarters of the gang uncovered two large "Saratoga" trunks filled to the brim with miscellaneous goods from various stores. The method of this gang was to hire a showy carriage in which the women would drive about and go shopping as ladies of fashion. One of the sons of "Mother Weir" commonly acted as coachman, and his mother and aunt, assisted by another elegantly dressed shoplifter, would fill the carriage with plunder in a few hours. The arrest broke up this dangerous gang and "Black Lena" was sent to Joliet prison for a term of eight years.

A few weeks after her discharge in July, 1889, she went back to Chicago again and rented a room in one of the cheap hotels. Within a month after her return, she was caught while on the point of leaving a large dry goods store, and three full bolts of silk were extracted from the bag which she wore beneath the folds of her skirt. In her room at the hotel she had a trunk filled with stolen silks, laces and dress goods. Again she was convicted and sent to prison and, as soon as she was discharged, she went into business again as a shoplifter and receiver. She was sent to the workhouse in St. Louis, in 1894, for petty larceny, for a term of nine months, and has served three terms in New York City prisons.

Her sister, "Black Amelia," has a record no less black. She has been arrested in nearly every large city in the northern states and sent several times to penitentiaries. Her favorite companion has been the notorious "Lizzie Myers," whose portrait has been given on a page illustrating the "shoplifter," and the two women have stolen almost every kind of portable article from a diamond bracelet to a roll of silk. A bolt of eighty-five yards of silk has been easily slipped into the skirt pocket which serves as a bag, and once, when Lizzie Myers was arrested in Boston, seven jerseys, a silk cap and two light shawls were stowed away under her dress skirt.

The fourth on the page of portraits is Gadalia Berkowitz, the notorious "fence" who was in confederacy with the Wols-Vokar gang of shoplifters described in a previous chapter. In June, 1894, he was sent to the House of Correction in Boston, for two years, as a receiver of stolen goods. Shortly after his discharge from this prison, he was convicted of an assault with intent to kill and sentenced to the Massachusetts state prison for four years. He is now serving out his sentence.

THE INCENDIARY.

EVEN among rascals the "fire-bug" is a monstrosity. He is not merely a man of an abnormal type, not merely greedy, brutal and cruel, but a creature essentially inhuman. No other distinct class of rascals exhibits such callous indifference or utter recklessness in the sacrifice of life and property. For the sake of a possible handful of plunder, or a few hundred dollars of insurance money, these scoundrels are daily kindling flames that threaten our towns and cities with destruction, and may subject hundreds of helpless men, women and children to the intolerable agonies of death in a fiery furnace. If lesser losses and horrors follow the touch of the incendiary's torch, the preservation of our cities and citizens is not to the credit of the rascal who has risked all to put a few vile dollars in his pocket.

The malicious incendiary, whose motive is revenge or wantonness, probably traces a long lineage back into the dawn of history, although the laws of England did not recognize this crime sufficiently to provide for official inquiry into the circumstances and origin of such a fire until the year 1297. The swindling incendiary, or the incendiary for gain is of more recent origin, following the birth of fire insurance which dates from 1681. This class, it is needless to say, forms by far the greater part of the wilful incendiaries of to-day.

The gravity of the offence has ever been recognized by the law. Blackstone says of arson,—which the common law defines as the "wilful and malicious burning of the house or outhouse of another man," but which has to-day been extended by statutes to cover the burning of any building,—"This is an offence of very great malignity and much more pernicious to the public than simple theft: because, first, it is an offence against that right of habitation, which is acquired by the laws of nature as well as by the laws of society; next, because of the terror and confusion that necessarily attends it; and, lastly, because in simple theft the thing stolen only changes its master, but still remains *in esse* for the benefit of the public, whereas by burning, the very substance is absolutely destroyed. It is also frequently more destructive than murder itself, of which it is too often the cause; since murder, atrocious as it is, seldom extends beyond the felonious act designed; whereas, fire too frequently involves, in the common calamity, persons unknown to the incendiary, and friends as well as enemies."

The punishment of arson was death by the ancient Anglo-Saxon law of England, and in early times this sentence was executed by a kind of *lex talionis*, for the incendiary was burnt to death; and until quite recent times, in England, the malicious burning of houses in towns and contiguous to others was the capital offence.

The first law on this subject in Massachusetts was passed in 1652, and provided that whoever "wittingly and willingly set on fire any Barn, Stable, Mill, outhouse, stack of wood, corne or hay . . . shall . . . pay double damages to the partie damnified, and be severely whipt" and that whoever "shall after the publication hereof, wittingly & willingly & feloniously set on fire any dwelling house, meetinghouse, or store house . . . shall be putt to death." Under the present Massachusetts law the severest punishment for arson is imprisonment for life, but in recent years the sentence of the court has been the minimum penalty of from five to ten years imprisonment, with occasionally a longer term in peculiarly aggravated cases.

From the beginning of fire insurance, as above stated, by far the greater percentage of incendiary fires has been for the purpose of swindling insurance companies. In Boston, during the past seven years, it appears that seventy-five per cent of the criminal fires were cases of incendiarism for gain; and that more than sixty per cent of all the fires set for the purpose of defrauding insurance companies were the work of insurance swindlers who had a record—who had previously collected, or attempted to collect, insurance from one to five times, and, in one case, twenty-two times, on fires which were believed to be incendiary. The chief incentive in such cases comes obviously from over-insurance and the attention of insurance companies may well be called to the need of careful examination into the real value of the property insured. The risk is often taken on property by a broker whose commission is proportionate to the amount of insurance which he can place. If he be not scrupulously honest and thoroughly wide-awake, he may be persuaded into writing a policy largely in excess of the value of the goods or premises insured.

Such cases as the following will illustrate what might almost be called criminal over-insurance. A young man in one of our large cities, without previous knowledge of the business, opened a grocery store which he stocked with about three hundred dollars' worth of goods. By representing to an insurance agent that he was going to increase his stock to the amount of one thousand dollars, he secured a policy for that amount, and the agent allowed the insurance to remain in force, although he saw the stock from time to time and knew that it was not increasing. Soon after, an incendiary fire occurred and the investigation which followed resulted in the arrest and conviction of the proprietor who was sentenced to three years in the house of correction. This store was in the central part of the city, attached to a dwelling, and surrounded by wooden buildings. The fire occurred in the night time and only the prompt and efficient efforts of the fire department prevented great damage to the surrounding property and probable loss of life.

On another occasion a Russian herdic driver, without experience, leased a store for a month and started in the jewelry business. He put in a stock of goods which inventoried less than $500 and which he himself did not claim to be worth over $1,000. Through a small broker he procured an insurance of $5,000 on the representation that he expected to increase the value of his stock within a short time. Two weeks after taking out his insurance the place was burned, all the gas-jets being found unlighted and turned on at the time of the fire. This man was convicted and sentenced to four years in State Prison.

When it is realized how great is the danger that threatens the lives and property of the public, from such cases, not to speak of the financial loss to the insurance companies,—it will be seen that great caution should be exercised both on the part of the insurance company in appointing its agents and in the placing of insurance by the brokers; no pains of investigation should be spared to guard against the insuring of the property of any person who has a previous record for swindling insurance companies, as such persons may frequently be found engaged in business under a different firm or company name.

Another class of criminal fires comprises those set wantonly by boys. In Massachusetts, during the year 1895, seventy-one fires, causing a loss of over $88,000, were set by boys. It is apparent that the match of a small boy is liable to destroy as much property and imperil as many lives as the brand of the professional firebug; and in prosecuting this class of offenders, the danger to society should be considered more than the lack of actual malice or the tender years of the young criminal.

It seems quite evident that, as the kleptomaniac merges into the thief in such a way that it is difficult to draw exactly the line between moral responsibility and insanity, so the incendiary includes various degrees of accountability,—varying from those who set a fire from mere general malice or "pure cussedness," as the homely New England phrase would describe it, to those whose motive is to cause excitement or see the engines come out; and so on to the true pyromaniac who seems to be impelled to his act by an irresistible impulse which he cannot control. "Pyromania" is the apparent result of certain abnormal physical conditions, and most of the persons suffering from this alienation of mind are women. Patients in this state are sent to an asylum for treatment and usually recover; the mania passes away with the disappearance of the physical irregularities.

Every one will recognize the need of a thorough system of investigation into the causes of fires, but while legislation to this end has been enacted in many states, it has not been as effective as could be desired. The experience of Massachusetts in this line and the present system of fire inquests in this state probably mark the farthest advance yet made in dealing with incendiarism.

In 1867, provision was made for the holding of fire inquests, by a specially appointed jury upon a complaint subscribed and sworn to by any person before a police court, alleging that reasonable grounds existed for believing that the fire was caused by design; and accompanied by a certificate in writing from a majority of the mayor and aldermen of a city or the selectmen of a town, attesting that the case was a proper subject, in their opinion, for investigation. This law, which was similar to laws passed in many other states, became in all of them practically a dead letter. Citizens hesitated to take an oath that a neighbor's property had been wilfully burned, and perhaps to run the risk of having their own property destroyed in revenge by the same incendiary. It was seen, therefore, that a general law must be made for the investigation of every fire. This, the state tried to do, by a law passed in 1889; but the inquest was provided for when the preliminary examination furnished reasonable grounds for believing the fire to be of incendiary origin. Since the examination was to be made by the fire engineers, in cities having a fire department, and by the selectmen in towns,—in the greater number of cases these officials neglected to order inquests after the preliminary examination, fearing the displeasure of owners of property or the revenge of the incendiary. It then became apparent that the investigating power should be lodged in the hands of officials entirely removed from local prejudice, fear, or favoritism.

In 1886, at the solicitation of prominent insurance men of Boston, the Massachusetts legislature created the office of a Fire Marshal for the thorough investigation of fires in the city of Boston and Mr. Charles W. Whitcomb was appointed to fill the office. The duties of this position were partly those of a prosecuting attorney and also quasi-judicial. Every fire must be investigated; the marshal could subpœna witnesses, administer and verify oaths and, if he deemed it advisable, could prepare the case for submission to the district attorney. In five years after the creation of the office, incendiary fires materially decreased and convictions for incendiarism increased over four hundred per cent. By the thorough system of examination instituted by the new marshal, the annual percentage of incendiary and unknown fires in Boston was reduced from 33 per cent to 5 per cent.

In view of the very favorable results obtained by this system the legislature, in 1894, enacted a new law and Mr. Whitcomb was appointed State Fire Marshal. To this officer is entrusted the duty of thoroughly investigating all fires in the state and arresting and prosecuting incendiaries in the lower court. If an accused person is held in this court, the case is prepared by the marshal for presentation to the district attorney and to the grand jury and then to the superior court, if an indictment is found. In addition to these duties, the marshal is required to prepare and file full indexed records and reports upon all fires, for the inspection of house owners, insurance companies, and the public generally. This important trust has been ably and faithfully discharged by the present fire marshal, and it is undoubtedly a fact that the moral effect of the existence of the office has accomplished much in deterring incendiaries and preventing crime. While the principal advantage may accrue to insurance companies, the indirect benefit to the public is very great, not only on account of the interest of the public in having the insurance loss reduced as much as possible; but, also, because of the decrease in danger to life and property from the assaults of incendiaries.

A recent writer of authorities has said: "It is as much the duty of the state to hunt down and punish the man, who for personal gain puts the match to his own property, at the peril of the lives and property of his neighbors, as it is to hunt down and punish the footpad, who, also for personal gain, puts the pistol to the head of the traveler upon the highway." Massachusetts is obviously trying to do her duty.

ARREST AND IDENTIFICATION.

IN sketching, chapter by chapter, the distinctive classes and types of criminals and their representative methods of reaching their ends, we have incidentally described to some extent the planning and working of the defenders of society to foil their scheming and arrest the law-breakers. But it seems to be fitting that the organization and operation of the police and detective forces in the discharge of their great trust of guardianship of the lives and property of law-abiding citizens should be presented no less distinctly than the criminal arts of the rascal.

Probably no one of our ever ready and caustic critics regrets more sincerely than the police themselves the imperfections in their service of guardianship, or the occasional delays in the detection and capture of fugitives from justice. But perhaps even our critics might find that they, too, were human and liable to err, if they were entrusted with the charge of guarding society instead of the congenial task of scoring its defenders for their short-comings. And if we, the police, should become in turn critics by such a miracle of transformation, we may humbly trust that our former experience would dispose us to be more patient than acrid if a rascal should occasionally elude the new police officers.

Meanwhile we may venture to note for the encouragement of the public and our own satisfaction that the discipline and service of the police have progressed notably during this present century and even this present generation, like the condition and efficiency of every other arm of society. This progress is none the less certain and incontestable in face of the fact of the multiplication of criminals with the multiplication of population. It is true that rascals are far more numerous to-day than they were fifty or a hundred years ago. It is true that the temptations are greater and the slums are larger than in the days of our fathers and grandfathers. But it is equally true that civilization has, on the whole, gone forward greatly and there has been a corresponding advance in the security of life and property throughout the length and breadth of our American union.

Broadly speaking, it is no longer possible for gangs of thieves and ruffians to maintain a foot-hold for any length of time in any one of our cities or in the country at large, and their possible places of hiding or refuge have been yearly diminishing. The penetration of the wilds of America by the resistless march of the pioneer, the opening of clearings, the foundation of settlements, the expansion of paths into highways, followed fast by the outstretching of railways and the network of the telegraph and its ally the telephone—have driven the rascal to hunt vainly for cover. He can no longer count safely on the enjoyment of plunder in some far off city or remote country district, where the story of his crime is utterly unknown or disregarded. With the spread of swift and certain communication, our cities and towns have been linked together in one vast organism, sentient and responsive to any affliction of the smallest part. If a crime is committed in farthest Oregon or rock-ribbed Montana, electric couriers bear the news with lightning swiftness to every city and town throughout the length and breadth of our union, and the flying criminals can find no rest for the soles of their feet, no weakening in the strain of pursuit on their track, no hamlet so obscure and no thicket so dense that it will hide their shrinking heads.

Even if they take to water, and hope that the ocean may cover their tracks, the submarine cables will tell the tale of their crimes throughout all Europe and even to the uttermost parts of the earth before the sea-greyhounds that carry them have covered one-half of their course from port to port. 'Tis true there are still spots on the globe to-day where the guilty can hide themselves and say "we are safe"; there are still countries so insignificant or so rude and barbaric that they are not allied to the civilized world for the repression of crime by treaties of extradition;—but these lands are far off and can rarely be reached except by roundabout routes with intervening delays that are likely to be fatal to any hope of escape from keen pursuit, where the fugitives are only a few hours ahead of their hunters. It is a grand coöperation that binds together to-day not only every town in our union in zealous alliance for the detection and arrest of our rival the rascal; but embraces, as well, practically the whole of the civilized world in its league for the common defence and mutual helpfulness.

In order to clearly present the practical workings of this vast confederation, we shall begin with a sketch of the organization and local method of one of its members, which will fairly represent and illustrate the composition and operation of the police force in all large American cities. American towns still hold, as a body, to the old English and colonial institution of the constable, and in the smaller towns a single officer usually composes the entire constabulary. When a town becomes a city, it organizes a police force of varying size under the direction of an officer ordinarily called the Chief of Police. As a city expands, its police organization is correspondingly enlarged and becomes more complex. In our larger American cities police boards or commissions are sometimes instituted by the city or state, and entrusted with powers of direction and control, as is the case in Boston. In all these cities, however, there is an executive head of the force, styled the Superintendent or the Chief of Police. The force under him is made up of the regular city police and a special body of detectives which has a distinctive organization. In Boston this organization is styled the Bureau of Criminal Investigation and its official head has the title of Chief Inspector.

The entire control of the police department of Boston is

vested in a Board of Police, composed of three members appointed by the governor of Massachusetts. The present members of this board are General A. P. Martin (chairman), Robert F. Clark and Charles P. Curtis. It makes all appointments to the police department of the city, subject to civil service rules, and has the power of discharge also, in accordance with established regulations. Transfers and all general regulations of the department are made by its authority.

The Superintendent of Police, appointed by this board, is the designated executive head of the department. His office is at the department headquarters together with the offices of the board, and the Bureau of Criminal Investigation. The city is set off into sixteen police divisions, one of which is termed the harbor station. Each of these divisions is in the immediate personal charge of a captain of police, with the exception of the harbor station, which is under the charge of a deputy superintendent. The other fifteen divisions compose two districts, in charge of two deputy superintendents under the direction of the Board of Police and Superintendent. A squad of special officers, known as the "liquor squad," is also stationed at headquarters under the charge of a captain. Two other officers at headquarters with the rank of captain are intrusted with the purchase and sale of all department property and the investigation of all claims against the city, arising from accidents.

The captains are held responsible for the maintenance of the peace and good order of their respective districts and the conduct and discipline of their divisions of the police. Two lieutenants and three sergeants are the subordinate officers of a division. Each division has its separate police station. All these stations as well as headquarters are kept open day and night throughout the year, and the superintendent, chief inspector and captains, or their representatives, are always present to respond to any proper call and to discharge their unceasing trust of guardianship.

Each district is laid out like a prodigious checker board into sections which are continually traversed by patrolmen in their respective "routes" or rounds. A patrolman's "route" is always confined to the same limited district, but his course is varied from time to time to prevent any accurate calculation by burglars or thieves, that he will not pass a certain block until a certain time has elapsed.

All the district stations have telephone connections with headquarters for the instant interchange of communications, and signal boxes are placed at short distances throughout every police district, which serve to connect the patrolmen with officers in charge. Once, and often twice in every hour, every patrolman on duty is required to open the nearest signal box and communicate with the district station, by pulling a hook, which registers the box number on a tape in the station, and also the time of his call. There is also in the box an electric bell and telephone; and should the officer in charge at the station desire to communicate with a patrolman for any purpose, a switch is set on a signal machine in the station, which will cause the bell to ring in the box when the patrolman pulls the hook. This is a notification to him to open communication by telephone.

These switches on the signal machines at the stations are repeatedly set during the day and night to notify officers that they are expected to watch for criminals that have escaped arrest and are charged with various offences. A call can also be sent from the signal boxes throughout the city for the police wagon for the conveyance of prisoners. Besides the regular cómmunications, termed "duty calls," the patrolmen are required to use a box at any time when they have occasion to give any alarm or special notice.

In the course of his rounds every patrolman is expected to attend sharply to the keeping of order and the law in the section which he covers, and he is further required to look to the proper securing of doors and windows during the night, and mark any sign of tampering with any fastening or of attempted burglary. He must also watch for the possible outbreak of fires in order to give the alarm notice, and attend to a variety of other important matters. It is his duty to remain on guard until he is regularly relieved by his successor at the designated relief post.

The day patrolman's service begins at 7.45 o'clock in the morning, when he is expected to be present at roll call in his district station. He will then go out under the charge of the sergeant of the day and relieve the night officer at his post. He will remain on patrol duty until relieved shortly before 6 o'clock P. M., with the allowance of an hour for dinner during which his route is covered by officers on adjoining routes, who are subsequently relieved themselves for the same purpose.

His successor, the night officer, will report at the district station house for roll call at 5.45 P. M., and then proceed, under charge of a sergeant, to relieve the patrolman on duty. His term of duty lasts till his relief by a patrolman, who comes on duty at the roll call at 12.45 A. M., and serves till relieved by the day officer. After their relief all patrolmen are required to report immediately for roll call at the district stations, unless unavoidably detained; and they must account satisfactorily for any detention. Their service is an arduous and often dangerous one; for, in addition to the constant vigilance required, they must be ready at any moment to suppress any turbulence and arrest armed criminals who do not hesitate to use their weapons to effect their escape. In recognition of exceptional service medals of honor have rightly been given, and all members of the force are fully aware that their promotion depends upon their proven fearlessness and fidelity in the discharge of their duties.

During the day each district station is under the immediate personal charge of the captain, who is relieved for dinner by the day sergeant. In the night time the station house is under the immediate personal charge of one of the two lieutenants, alternately; or under a sergeant, if the lieutenant is unavoidably absent. The sergeants are expected to inspect the patrolmen on duty in their platoon, and to report any neglect of duty to their superior officer. At some of the principal stations, in addition to the regular force, officers in citizens' clothes are detailed for special service under direction of the superintendent and captains.

The Bureau of Criminal Investigation has, at present, a force of thirty experienced detectives in constant service, in charge of the chief inspector or his assistant, who has the rank of captain. This force keeps watch, day and night, over the entire city to detect and report the appearance and workings of criminals of every class; and special oversight is given to the banks and the business heart of the city, during business hours, and to all railway stations, steamboat landings and probable resorts of criminals. All known thieves, professional swindlers and other dangerous persons are arrested at sight when they fail to give a satisfactory account of their presence in the city, and held for trial or warned away if evidence sufficient to convict cannot be obtained.

The office of the bureau is open at every hour of the day and night throughout the year, like police headquarters and the district stations. During the day the chief inspector or captain is in immediate personal charge, and, at night, they are relieved by two subordinate officers. The detectives of the force are regularly on duty at all hours of the day and evening, and are frequently employed till after midnight, and even all night, in their watch to intercept and arrest criminals. Details are made to protect churches, halls and theatres from thieves, and the like oversight is given to out-going and incoming trains at the railway stations. Detectives also watch the street railway cars and all crowded thoroughfares, and are frequently detailed to attend large weddings and other ceremonies. Every morning this force reports for roll call at the office of the bureau, and assignments are made for all cases under investigation. This systematic and comprehensive patrolling of the city has proved to be of invaluable service in the prevention of crimes of all kinds, and in securing prompt arrest of all law breakers.

As a matter of course, if any crime is committed within the sight of any one of the members of this department, the offender will be arrested if any officer can lay his hands upon him and hold him. A detective has practically entire freedom of movement, and a patrolman may leave his route, if it is necessary, to pursue a criminal who is trying to escape arrest, but he must account for his absence to his superior officer. Many of the arrests made by the force are of men intercepted in the commission of crimes or caught in the act. But in spite of all the vigilance which is exercised, there are criminals who elude the watch of the police and run away before they can be reached and arrested.

To illustrate the way in which the pursuit of such criminals is organized and carried on, we shall suppose that a burglary has been committed in the heart of Boston, at midnight, and that the burglars have contrived to get away unobserved with their booty. In less than an hour afterward, the raid is discovered by a patrolman, in the course of his examination of the doors of the building which has been entered by the burglars; for he finds that the bolt of a basement door has been broken. He enters and searches the building at once, and finds that a safe has been broken open and ransacked, and that glass cases containing valuable goods have also been plundered. A jimmy and dark lantern have been left on the floor near the safe, and, by looking around, the patrolman comes upon a sledge hammer which had apparently been used in breaking off the handle of the lock of the safe, for it was of an old pattern, and dynamite was not needed to force the door.

As soon as he has made his investigation and satisfied himself that none of the burglars are still in the building, he proceeds at once to the nearest signal box, stopping, for a moment, on the way, to question a private watchman employed in the same block. This watchman has not been startled by any unusual sound, and knows nothing of the burglary; but he is able to recall the passing of two strangers, shortly after midnight, apparently on their way to a hotel from a late train; for both were carrying handbags. He noticed their appearance sufficiently to give some important details in regard to their height, figure and dress. One of the men had a full dark beard, and the face of the other was closely shaven. The watchman was standing in the recess of a doorway at the time, so that the men did not see him until they were nearly opposite; and he remarked that they quickened their walk perceptibly after passing him, and soon crossed to the other side of the street. He did not feel warranted in stopping them, on such slight ground for suspicion, but their movements impressed the other details on his mind.

After getting this clue to the persons possibly engaged in the burglary, the patrolman hastens to the signal box and rings up his district station. Then he telephones to the officer in charge the fact of the burglary and all the details that he has learned in regard to it and the men who may have had a hand in it. This information is fully noted by the officer at the station, and reported at once by telephone to police headquarters. At the same time the officer sets the switches on the signal machine in the station, to ring the bells in the signal boxes throughout the district as soon as the patrolmen on duty pull the hooks in making their hourly or half-hourly reports.

As soon as the report is received by the officer in charge at headquarters, he notifies every district station in the city by telephone, and the officers at these stations set the switches on their signal machines to open communication with their patrolmen all over the city. As fast as the men report they are informed of the burglary, and ordered to look out for two men answering to the description given by the watchman. The officer in charge of the Bureau of Criminal Investigation is also notified at once, and details of detectives and of police are sent out to get the fullest possible details of the burglary, and trace, if possible, the track of the burglars.

The superintendent and chief inspector are reached by telephone calls within a few moments, and they send instructions for the further extension of the pursuit of the burglars. The owner of the property which has been stolen is promptly informed of the burglary, and called upon for any facts or suggestions which he may be able to give touching the extent of the robbery, and any possible participants whom he may suspect. It is soon ascertained that the burglary is one of extraordinary importance in view of the estimated amount of the loss, and extraordinary measures are taken to uncover the fugitive burglars.

By direction of the superintendent and chief inspector telegrams are sent out from headquarters to the police and detective forces of all the neighboring cities in the state, and to the cities in the surrounding states on the lines of the railways radiating from Boston, informing them of the burglary and requesting their coöperation in the capture of the suspected men, who are described as fully as possible. All possible information is sought also from the heads of these police and detective departments which may lead to the identification of the burglars and any of their accomplices. Every railway and steamboat station in Boston and all vessels on the point of clearing from the port are watched at once by the city detectives and police, and every probable resort of the robbers within the city and the surrounding district is sharply searched.

All this coöperating force is aroused and at work within a few hours after the discovery of the burglary. Then the morning newspapers of the city and the associated press agencies spread abroad through the country all the news that they can obtain from the police record book and other sources in regard to the burglary. So the police of every city and town in New England—and probably of every large city and town in the country—are soon apprised of the crime and incited to the capture of the burglars, if they slip through the net of the Boston police.

Before noon of the same day, too, official details of the burglary are sent from police headquarters on hundreds of sheets of manifold paper to every station in the city of Boston for the information of all the members of the police force, with accompanying descriptions of all the persons suspected of complicity in the burglary. Inquiries are addressed by the chief inspector and captains to all members of the force, to identify the burglars if possible, and the officers are instructed to obtain every possible clue to the persons implicated and their hiding places. The Rogues' Gallery and the records of the department are also searched for the same object. The manner in which the robbery was committed, will usually indicate whether the burglary was the work of experienced hands and the effort is made to trace the maker or seller of any tool left behind by the fugitives, which might lead to their identification. If the police officials of any city or the leading detective agencies have any information to communicate touching the persons probably engaged in the burglary, they will usually send it at once to the Boston police without waiting for any special appeal; but, during the day, circular letters are sent out by the superintendent and chief inspector, giving the details of the burglary and the descriptions of the persons suspected, and requesting the coöperation of the officials addressed in the identification and capture of the criminals. These letters are mailed to the chiefs of police and the heads of detective bureaus and agencies in every city and large town in Massachusetts, and to the like officials in all the principal cities and towns of the country at large. As soon as fuller and more exact descriptions of the burglars are obtained by the search of the Boston police and detective forces

ARREST AND IDENTIFICATION.

and the coöperation of other police and detective departments, these details are sent out in another set of circulars addressed like the former one.

In response to these telegrams, letters and circulars, descriptions and photographs are sent to the Boston police department by the like departments in other cities of all persons arrested, whose appearance corresponds with that of the fugitive burglars. There is further a cordial and active coöperation with the Boston department in tracking and uncovering the hiding place of the fugitives; and, if any department or detective agency is able to identify the persons described in the circulars or has reasonable ground for suspecting any known criminals at large,—this identification or probable ground of suspicion is at once communicated to the Boston police. This coöperation would be rendered in turn by the Boston department, if the like appeal was made for its assistance, and the procedure in this case is simply given as a representative instance of the practice of the police departments of all our leading American cities in similar cases. No special credit is claimed for the organization and method of the Boston department which is only a fractional part of the great national confederation of police departments, but it is our design to give a fair comprehension of the manner in which all are enlisted in mutual support for the protection of the people.

If there is ground for supposing that the fugitives have found means of flight to Europe or some other part of the world by a steamer or sailing vessel, cable messages are sent by the superintendent of police to the police authorities of the port to which the vessel is bound, and to the police of any other port which may be entered on the way, requesting a search of the vessel before any passengers are allowed to land, and the arrest of the persons described and accused of burglary. These messages are followed by letters containing a fuller description of the burglars and the official application of the superintendent of police for their arrest and detention in custody, until the necessary requisition papers can be forwarded and extradition proceedings taken.

It will be seen that a keen and comprehensive pursuit of these supposed burglars, or of anybody committing any serious crime at any hour of the day or night, would be promptly organized and set moving. Even in the possible event of the lapse of several hours before the discovery of such a crime, the burglars have only a scant allowance of time in which to fly or find cover; and their movements are likely to attract notice, and even suspicion and arrest, in advance of the actual discovery of their crime. Burglars can hardly carry about heavy bags or bundles of booty without giving cause for suspicion to patrolmen, or to good citizens whom they may meet in their flight, and city policemen and detectives have no hesitation in stopping and questioning persons whose actions arouse just suspicion. If they fail to give a satisfactory account of themselves, the police will promptly arrest them and take them to the district station or to headquarters where they will be thoroughly investigated.

It is a recognized duty of all policemen, and particularly expected of all detectives, that they shall familiarize themselves with the appearance and names of persons known to have criminal records, or to be of bad character, whom they may be called upon to arrest, at any moment, for the commission of crimes. The larger his range of acquaintance, the more efficient an officer will he be in the detection, arrest and identification of criminals. It is presumed and required, of course, that a patrolman shall first learn to know the persons of bad character residing on his route and in the neighboring district, or frequenting this quarter by night or day. The field of the regular service of a detective is wider than that of a patrolman, and it is often his principal duty to single out and arrest, or warn off, the thieves and swindlers who are seeking plunder in the crowded streets, stations, banks, stores, and business offices of our cities. So it is obvious that he should have a considerable collection of faces in his mind's eye in order to render efficient service.

This is invariably an acquisition of the experienced detectives in our principal cities. All of them know hundreds of criminals by sight; and some with remarkably retentive memories could recognize and name over a thousand rascals. To aid the detective and police forces in the recognition and remembrance of criminals, every one of our large American cities has a collection of photographs commonly styled, "The Rogues' Gallery." These collections are made by photographing noted criminals brought to police headquarters, and adding by exchange and purchase similar photographs taken in other cities. Sometimes these portraits run far up into the thousands, and even the smallest gallery is of marked service in promoting the arrest and identification of criminals.

It is certain, too, that the study of these collections, and direct personal inspection of criminals are of very material service in increasing arrests beyond the range of immediate recognition or recollection. Detectives who have studied the range of faces, manners, and habits of criminals for years acquire such a comprehensive familiarity with the professional rascals of the country, that they hardly ever make a mistake in picking out thieves and other criminals, at sight, in a crowd. This detective faculty has more than memory behind it. Keen observers have over and over again marked and arrested apparently inoffensive rogues, whom they had never seen before in person or in pictures. Long experience and sharp eyesight have made them sensitive to the slightest mannerisms and tricks of the various species of rascal. There is also an almost instantaneous mental process of grouping and comparison. Without any conscious effort of will, the general features and traits of a criminal class come to the mind's eye as a composite photograph, and the members of any group actually in sight are assimilated or differentiated at a glance. This swift judgment is analogous to that of an expert handler of money in the detection of counterfeits, or of an expert in handwriting in the determination of forgeries. Often some impression made by the appearance of rogues, which is beyond exact definition and explanation, will assure the trained detective that he is warranted in making arrests.

When a suspected person is arrested, he will be taken to the nearest police station, or directly to police headquarters. If the person is unknown, or if he is not recognized at once by the officers at headquarters, it becomes of manifest importance to obtain his true name and record. In January, 1890, the Massachusetts Board of Prison Commissioners formally recommended the adoption of the French method, commonly known as the Bertillon system, for the identification of criminals, after a prolonged investigation into its merits by Mr. F. G. Pettigrove, the general superintendent of prisons for the state. Its adoption in the state prison soon followed with very satisfactory results. This system, concisely stated, is the classification of the measurements of those parts of the human body that do not change in size after a person has reached the age of about twenty-one years.

The inventor, M. Bertillon, is the son of a French physician who was a man of eminence in his profession. After completing the prescribed military service of a young Frenchman, M. Bertillon was appointed to a position in the prefecture of police in Paris. Soon after his appointment, he was so strongly impressed by the difficulties in the way of the identification of the large number of criminals passing daily through his office, that he began to devise the system that now bears his name.

His design was based on the fact that certain measurements of the body do not change after the period of full growth has been reached. These are, for example, the length and width of the head; the length of the middle finger, the foot, the forearm and the outstretched arm; the height of the figure standing and seated; and the dimensions of the ear. As no two persons are exactly alike, it is practically impossible that

LEFT FOOT.

LEFT MIDDLE FINGER.

HEIGHT.

OUTSTRETCHED ARMS.

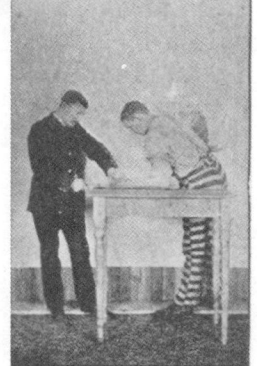

LEFT FORE-ARM.

APPLICATION OF BERTILLON SYSTEM.

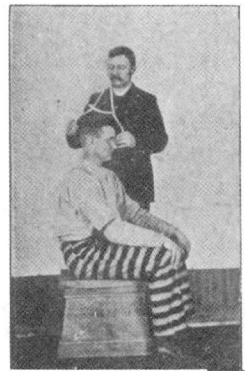
LENGTH OF HEAD.

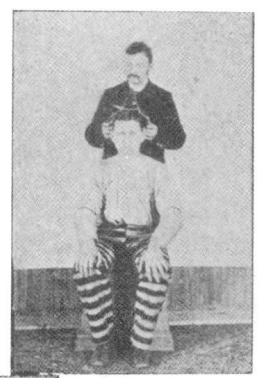
WIDTH OF HEAD.

COLOR OF EYE.

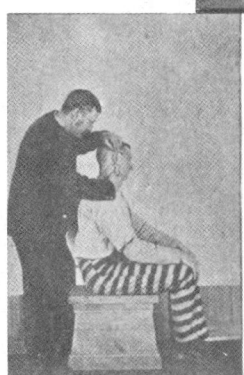
LENGTH OF RIGHT EAR.

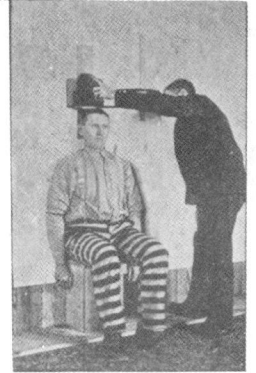
LENGTH OF TRUNK.

APPLICATION OF BERTILLON SYSTEM.

any two complete sets of measurements of different persons should agree in every particular. Should it be found therefore, after measuring an unknown prisoner, that the record of measurements agrees precisely in every detail with any record on file, it is practically certain that both sets are measurements of the same person. If, then, the earlier record is one of a known criminal, the unknown prisoner will be inevitably identified with that criminal. This comparative process may be styled a mathematical demonstration of identification.

To facilitate the comparison and identification, every set of measurements that is taken is recorded on a card, and this card is filed in a cabinet divided into compartments, each of which is subdivided. These separate compartments are used for the classification of cards in a way approximately resembling the filing of book cards in a public library. In searching to identify any person who has been arrested, the examiner—who has measured him and ascertained that the length of his head is within a certain range—can turn at once to a compartment in the cabinet containing all the cards of persons whose heads come within this range. This compartment is divided into smaller compartments, each of which contains its special range of measurements of other parts of the body, or marks distinctions in the color of the eyes and hair. So if there is any card of measurements corresponding exactly to the set taken by the examiner, he will soon put his hand upon it.

The measurements under the Bertillon system are taken with fine caliper and sliding compasses, accurately marking very minute variations. In the illustrations which are given in this chapter, the process of measurement is so clearly presented that no further description is needed.

Besides introducing this use of certain measurements of the body, M. Bertillon perfected a method of notation of the color of the eyes, which is very exact; and this forms a part of his regular system to-day. He lays particular stress, also, on the desirability of obtaining photographs in profile as well as front views; on the ground that the outline or profile of the face changes less in the course of years than the full face, and that it can be less readily contorted or disguised. His system further includes what has been generally recognized as very important and trustworthy for the purpose of identification,—the more ineffaceable scars or marks, noting their exact position and size.

In 1862 M. Bertillon had the satisfaction of seeing the adoption of his system by the police of Paris, and within a few years afterward it became the recognized official system throughout France. Its use has since been largely extended through Europe. In this country its introduction has not progressed so far, but it has been regularly adopted for making records of criminals in the Massachusetts state prison; and in Illinois it has been in use for some years not only in the state penitentiaries but in the police department. Several other states are also employing this system to a considerable extent.

There can be no question that admirable results have been obtained by the development of this system in France. In the year following its adoption, it is reported that forty-nine criminals were recognized by this method when all other means of identification had failed. In 1884, when its use had become more general, 241 criminals were identified; and, in 1885, more than 500 persons, whose characters would have been unknown but for this method, were recognized as habitual criminals.

A remarkable example of the possible application of this system was furnished in November, 1891. Early in this month one of the workmen employed in a box factory on the Rue de Charonne, in Paris, went down into the cellar to get some boards. A few moments later he came flying back into the workroom, with his face as white as a sheet. He was trembling like a man with the palsy, but he managed to stammer out the cause of his terror. The lighted candle which he had in his hand went out before he reached the foot of the cellar stairs; but he did not take the trouble of relighting it, as

ARREST AND IDENTIFICATION.

he was familiar with the storage room and was able to grope along in the dark to the corner where the boards were piled. While he was picking out the boards which he wanted, he touched something cold and clammy. This strange thing so startled him that he lit his candle to see what he had touched, and was horror struck to find that it was the headless and decomposed body of a man.

As soon as his story was told, the police were notified. The body was sent to the Morgue and, in the hope of possible identification, it was measured by M. Bertillon. The record was then proved to be identical with one taken of an old criminal named Boutry.

Keen inquiry brought to light the fact that Boutry was last seen in company with one of his friends, a workman whose name was Vancourt. When Vancourt was called to account, he was caught tripping so often that he finally refused to answer another question. Then he was bluntly informed that the body of Boutry had been found and positively identified. He was so shaken with this apparent revelation of the supernatural knowledge of the police that he broke down and confessed that he was the murderer.

He had brutally killed Boutry, who had shared his bed for a night, because the sleeping man had accidentally struck him in a fit of unconscious restlessness. Then he hid the body at night in the cellar of the factory, cut off the head, mutilated it beyond recognition, wrapped it up in a bundle of linen and threw it on the roof of a shed by the river side. It is practically certain that this horrible crime would never have been disclosed, and the murderer convicted, if the Bertillon system had not given a positive identification of the corpse in the cellar.

Almost simultaneously with this signal revelation in Paris, the extraordinary service of the same system was notably marked in Chicago by the identification of a burglar who was killed by a druggist in self-defence. The robber persistently claimed that his name was Charles Holmes; but measurements of his body, taken after death, fully identified him with a notorious "safe blower," whose true name was Charles Kinney.

Undoubtedly the extension of this system would have been more rapid in this country, if it had been possible to secure its general adoption by the concurrent action of every state in the union. It is obvious that the practical working value of any such system depends largely upon the completeness of its records and the certain assurance of coöperation and accuracy in their preparation. This coöperation and uniformity of record have naturally been secured in France more readily than is possible when more than forty different states must be brought to an agreement upon the adoption of a single system. So the common dependence throughout this country for the identification of criminals still rests on the simpler records which are taken with a close approach to uniformity by the police and prison officials. There has been, however, of late years, a marked improvement in the extent and precision of the descriptions and records prepared for local use and general circulation. Photographs of all known criminals and persons charged with crimes are now almost invariably taken by the police in American cities; and particular care is exercised in noting as precisely as possible all scars and indelible marks of any kind.

The customary character of the descriptions prepared and used for tracing out and identifying criminals may be best comprehended by the use of a few representative examples.

HEADQUARTERS OF POLICE DEPARTMENT,
BOSTON, MASS.
Superintendent's Office, 7 Pemberton Square.

Wanted for Murder of Josephine Brown,
ON DECEMBER 24th, 1891.

ROGER T. SCANNEL al. R. O'CONNELL,

Twenty-six (26) years of age; five (5) feet eight (8) inches in height; one hundred and forty (140) to one hundred and forty-five (145) pounds weight; complexion medium but inclined to light; small light-colored mustache; high cheek bones; face narrowing sharply from cheek bones to chin; consumptive look; pretty square shoulders viewed from behind; small waist and hips; one shoulder a little lower than the other; first joint of forefinger on left hand a little stiff and turned in on account of an accident.

Wore at that time a flat-topped Scotch Cap with two or three buttons in front; blue and white Gingham Shirt; black cutaway Coat and Vest; blue and black stripes in Pants, and a Gray Check Ulster, brown stripe, well worn, four pockets on the outside and one in each sleeve.

Speaks with a slight brogue and an affected air; wears a 14 1-2 Collar and No. 8 or No. 9 Shoe. Frequents kitchen bar-rooms and cheap lodging rooms with low women.

FAC-SIMILE OF HANDWRITING:

Send any information to BENJ. P. ELDRIDGE, SUPT. OF POLICE.
Boston, December 26, 1891.

By the Governor of Virginia---A PROCLAMATION.

Information having been received by the Executive that

C. M. FIGGAT,

late Cashier of the Bank of Lexington, Va., stands charged with the crime of embezzlement, and is now a fugitive from justice, and is now going at large, therefore I do hereby offer a reward of

FIVE HUNDRED DOLLARS,

to any person who shall arrest the said **C. M. FIGGAT**, and deliver him to the authorities of Rockbridge County, Virginia, at the place of arrest, said reward to be paid only after such arrest and delivery; and I do moreover require all Officers of this Commonwealth, civil and military, and request the people generally, to use their best exertions to procure his arrest, that he may be brought to justice. The offer of this reward is to continue for six months.

Given under my hand as Governor, and under the Lesser Seal of the Commonwealth, at Richmond, this 19th day of February, 1895.

CHAS. T. O'FERRALL.

By the Governor:
  J. T. LAWLESS, Secretary of the Commonwealth.

DESCRIPTION.

A heavy-set man; weighs 185 pounds; height, 5 feet, 10 inches; legs slightly bowed; short gray beard; full gray mustache; eyes, dark gray, almost brown; walks slightly stooped and very slowly, on account of some inward affection; full stomach; ruddy complexion; face flabby; very affable in manners and speech; talks slowly and nods his head as he talks; his hair has been dark, but is now two-thirds gray; his appearance shows him to be addicted to drink; always wore dark slouch hat, and had on a gray suit when he left Lexington; age, about sixty years; may now be shaved.

$2,250 REWARD.

ARREST TRAIN ROBBER Oliver Curtis Perry, alias James Curtis Perry, alias "Curt" Perry, alias Oliver Moore. Escaped from the State Hospital for Insane Criminals, Matteawan, N. Y., on the night of Wednesday, April 10th, 1895.

As Perry appeared in 1891
BEFORE CONVICTION.

As Perry appeared in 1895
BEFORE ESCAPE.

OLIVER CURTIS PERRY was convicted at Lyons, N. Y., on May 19th, 1892, for train robbery, sentenced to 49 years and 3 months in the State's Prison at Auburn and transferred December 28th, 1893, to the State Hospital for Insane Criminals at Matteawan.

DESCRIPTION.

Perry is described as follows: Age, 27; height, 5 feet 5 1-2 inches; weight, 130 lbs.; hair, brown; eyes, brown; complexion, dark, sallow, (pasty); chin, round; smooth shaven, can raise small dark mustache; large Adam's apple.

Scars: 1 right side of scalp, 2 on back, 1 left side of head. 2 small ones on left thumb, 1 back of index finger (left hand). 1 near wrist inside right hand, 1 large scar left forearm. 1 large scar on throat just below Adam's apple.

Forehead, square and high; wrinkles between eyes gives his face troubled and thoughtful expression.

Perry may use any of the following names: **Oliver, Curtis, Perry, Haswell, Van-Allen, Havens, Hamlin, Allen, Gavens, James, James Curtis, James Perry, James Curtis Perry, Oliver Moore.**

Perry is said to have been at one time a cattle herder (cowboy). Before his conviction for train robbery he was sentenced twice for burglary, and while in prison learned the shoemaker's trade; has also been a freight and passenger brakeman. He professes religion, and will try to impose on ministers and class leaders of churches, particularly Presbyterian.

Please search hotels and keep general lookout around railroad depots, saloons, gambling resorts, etc., and inquire of **Yard or Train Masters** for his having applied for employment, and of **Railroad Trainmen** for his having "beat" his way on freight or passenger trains. Also inquire of ministers, class leaders and at Young Men's Christian Association Rooms for trace of him. He is likely to be travelling as a tramp.

REWARDS.

$1,000 by the State of New York; $1,000 by the American Express Company; $250 by Dr. H. E. Allison, Medical Superintendent Matteawan State Hospital, Fishkill Landing, New York.

Send information (telegraphic or otherwise) to the nearest of our offices.

PINKERTON'S NATIONAL DETECTIVE ACENCY,

66 EXCHANGE PLACE, NEW YORK.

HEADQUARTERS OF THE POLICE DEPARTMENT,
BOSTON, MASS.
SUPERINTENDENT'S OFFICE, 37 PEMBERTON SQUARE.

Wanted on an Indictment Warrant,

For obtaining $6,000 by false pretences, with intent to cheat and defraud by means of the gold dust trick, a Russian Jew, known by the following names, Samuel Brotzski, Solomon Schwartzman, Solomon Tzigainer (means Gypsy), Samuel Schetman, Leitchman and Greenberg. He is from 45 to 50 years old, 5 feet 3 inches tall, 175 pounds weight, dark complexion, dark mustache mixed with gray, beard when worn will be mixed with gray, bluish-gray eyes, small nose, talks slowly and has a slow gait. Is a constant smoker of cigarettes that he makes himself, has small hands with tapering fingers, and full neck. Will be found amongst Jews, and is very fond of women.

If found, arrest, hold and notify me, and I will send for him. Send any information to

BENJAMIN P. ELDRIDGE,

Boston, Nov. 17, 1894.   Superintendent of Police.

$3,000! - - REWARD! - - $3,000!

    The Post Office Department will pay the sum of ONE THOUSAND DOLLARS REWARD, each, for the capture of Joseph Killoran, Harry Russell, and Charles Allen, and their return to the custody of the United States Marshal at New York City.

    Joe Killoran, alias Joe Howard, is an Englishman; age 56 years; height 5 feet 9 1-2 inches; weight, 160 pounds; build medium: complexion, fair; eyes, blue-gray; hair, dark brown; beard, light mixed with gray; letter "P" and round dot on right fore-arm, three dots on left fore-arm, partly burned out; slightly pock-marked; dot between thumb and first finger of right hand.

    Harry Russell, alias Harry Murphy, alias Harry Vosburg, is an American; age, 32 years; married; stout build; height, 5 feet 5 3-4 inches; weight, 160 pounds; hair, blonde; eyes, light blue; features, regular; complexion, florid; light, sandy mustache; two spots of ink on inside of left fore-arm; bald head.

    Charles Allen, alias Charles Robinson, is an American; age 41 years; height 5 feet and 8 inches; complexion, fresh; eyes, blue; hair, light brown; beard, light brown; freckles on shoulders, back and arms; scar on right knee.

    These men were arrested May 31, 1895, and were held for robbing several post offices and for other crimes. They escaped from the Ludlow-Street Jail, New York City, on July 4, 1895.

    The above rewards will be paid upon presentation at this Department of satisfactory documentary proof of the capture and delivery of the persons as above described.

                                         M. D. WHEELER, Chief P. O. Inspector.

POST OFFICE DEPARTMENT.
        Washington, D. C., July 9, 1895.

$500 - - REWARD. - - $500

FOR THE

ARREST AND CONVICTION

OF EACH OF THE

Wisconsin Central Train Robbers.

The sum of **FIVE HUNDRED DOLLARS** will be paid for the **ARREST** and **CONVICTION** of each of the persons who attempted to rob the express car of the Wisconsin Central train, about three miles west of Waupaca, Wisconsin, on the night of September 19th, 1895.

DESCRIPTIONS.

The leader is described as follows: An American, 38 to 40 years old; 5 feet 7 or 8 inches in height; weight 135 to 140 pounds; sparely built, slightly humped, fairly square shoulders; smooth face; dark brown hair; medium sized nose; prominent and fairly broad cheek bones; thin lips; hollow, sunken eyes and haggard look; spare face, with skin tightly drawn; pale, sallow and unhealthy complexion; keen, sharp voice with peculiar nasal twang; wore no mask, and had quick, nervous action. He wore a cheap, dark suit, quite faded; well worn soft slouch hat; cheap shoes, size about No. 8; had trampish appearance. One hand cut during the robbery and bled quite freely. This was the man who used the dynamite on the safe.

A second man who was called "Jack" by the leader, appeared to be about 28 years of age; 5 feet 10 or 10 1-2 inches in height; weight 165 to 175 pounds; apparently full faced, with mustache probably brown in color; wore a wide brimmed light colored slouch hat and hunting coat.

Both men had medium sized revolvers.

Shots fired during the robbery indicated that there were more than two men.

Address all communications to **H. F. Whitcomb** and **Howard Morris**, Receivers Wisconsin Central Railroad Company, Milwaukee, Wisconsin; **J. A. D. Vickers**, Superintendent National Express Company, Rookery Building, Chicago, Illinois, or the nearest of our offices.

PINKERTON'S NATIONAL DETECTIVE AGENCY,

or WILLIAM A. PINKERTON. 201 Fifth Avenue, CHICAGO, ILL.

Chicago, Oct. 9th, 1895.

OFFICE OF
SHERIFF OF HAMILTON COUNTY, O.

R. M. ARCHIBALD, Sheriff.

CINCINNATI, November 12, 1895.

CHIEF OF POLICE:

SIR: — On the 10th inst., at about 7 o'clock P. M., six prisoners made their escape from the County Jail in this city. One of them was recaptured a few hours after the escape. Two of them were charged with forgery, two with burglary and one with picking pockets.

The description of each is as follows:

CHARLES FISHER, alias BOLAND, alias FORD.

Was born in Germany, resides in New York. Age, 39 years; weight, 135 pounds; height, 5 feet 6 1-2 inches; eyes, blue; hair, dark brown; mustache, dark brown; complexion, fair; build, medium; occupation, forger. Arrested June 25, 1895; charge, forgery. Photo. taken September 26, 1895. Scar in palm of left hand and the thumb drawn inwards because of a leader having been cut. He is one of the most accomplished and best known forgers in the country. He was awaiting trial.

[The descriptions of the other escaped prisoners with their portraits, were, in general features, like that of Fisher, and are not reproduced.]

If any of the described persons are found in your city, please make the arrest and we will send an officer for him.

Please send information to the undersigned. The necessary expenses will be paid for the arrest of either one.   Very respectfully,

R. M. ARCHIBALD, Sheriff Hamilton County, O.

The preparation and filing of the descriptions and records of criminals for ready reference is one of the allotted duties of the Bureau of Criminal Investigation. Every person who is brought to police headquarters, under the charge of committing a grave crime, is photographed, unless his photograph and description are already on file in the bureau. His height, weight, figure and any marked peculiarities of person and manner are carefully noted. Close search is made for any scars or indelible marks of any kind on his body, and any such mark is accurately defined and recorded. These photographs and descriptions are kept under lock and key, but are not regularly entered and filed with the other records of the bureau, unless the person is convicted or is known as an habitual criminal. Upon the conviction of the crime charged, the convict's photograph is filed in the Rogues' Gallery and numbered for ready reference. His description is entered in a set of description books alphabetically indexed, and his criminal record is kept in a like set of record books.

In this way a complete record has been made up of all criminals brought to police headquarters, and this collection has been greatly extended by applications made to police departments, detective agencies, and prison officials throughout this country and Europe, for the photographs and descriptions of all criminals of note. The description and record of every person committed to the state prison or house of correction in Massachusetts are promptly secured and recorded. The records show the offence committed in every case, the trial court, the date of conviction, the term of sentence, the date of entry into prison and the date of discharge.

On the first day of every month, a report of the convicts to be discharged during the month in Massachusetts is made to the Superintendent of the Boston Police, by the Bureau of Criminal Investigation. Copies of this report are filed in the Superintendent's office and in the Bureau of Criminal Investigation, and manifold copies sent to every district police station. At the time of discharge, or shortly after, the ex-convicts are sharply scrutinized by detectives to facilitate subsequent recognition if it should ever be necessary. Reports upon these discharged prisoners are sent out also to the leading chiefs of police throughout the country, giving the names, prison record numbers, and a full personal description, and complete criminal record, so far as this can be obtained.

By diligent effort to build up this important department of identification and record, the photographs in the Rogues' Gallery, on the 1st of January, 1897, numbered 3,973. During the year 1896, the records of 697 criminals were added to those already on file, making a total of 20,456. Prison reports of 360 discharged convicts were issued during the year. In addition to the systematic records of this bureau, before noted, a collection has been made for many years past of all information obtained from official inquiry and correspondence, reaching to all parts of the world, and from the press reports of the doings, arrests, and convictions of all criminals of note. This information is regularly indexed and placed in official envelopes, which are numbered and filed away in cabinets for ready reference. In cases where full records are desirable, this collection has proved of great service to the home department, and of value also in answering applications for information from the police officials of other states.

There is a further record in this bureau of all cases assigned to detectives for investigation and report. The name of the officer charged with the duty of investigation is entered in an assignment book; together with the name of the official directing the investigation, the name of the applicant, and important facts pertinent to the inquiry. The investigating officer is invariably required to make a complete report upon the case for use and preservation on file, and all communications bearing upon the case are filed with this report.

A very large number of circulars calling for the arrest of fugitive criminals and descriptive lists of property stolen are yearly received by the department, and, after thorough investigation, carefully put on file for future reference.

Reports of the presence of all known criminals and of their haunts are regularly made by the detectives and police to the police headquarters. The detectives are ordered to arrest at sight and bring to headquarters all known thieves and "bunco men" entering the city. Daily reports are made to headquarters by the Bureau of Criminal Investigation and the police captains, covering all the crimes committed and arrests made in the city. Complete records or abstracts of these reports are daily prepared at headquarters, and hundreds of manifold copies are sent out to the district stations for the information of the captains and their men. When criminals, committing offences in Boston, have not been arrested, full descriptions are prepared and sent out to all the district stations, accompanied by photographs, if obtainable. It is also the practice to send to all stations circulars or other notices sent in by police officials, or other authorities, from all parts of the country, calling for the arrest of fugitive criminals; and such applications are read to all the men on the force.

It is expected that every member of the department will do his duty in the endeavor to arrest all known criminals; but certain classes of rascals, like pickpockets and shoplifters, are commonly arrested by detectives, because they aim to keep well out of the way of policemen in uniform. It is natural, also, that the arrest of thieves and other criminals coming from points outside the city to Boston, should usually be made by the force specially employed to bar them out and capture them. Frequently the services of Boston detectives are given on the occasion of great conventions in other states, and some of them have traveled for this purpose to all the principal cities of this country. Sometimes, too, detectives are sent to attend such gatherings where no formal application for their services has been made, for the sake of the marked advantage to the corps of extending its experience and acquaintance with the range of thieves. In like manner, detectives from other American cities occasionally visit Boston, and their presence and assistance are cordially welcomed.

In view of the plain practical importance of increasing the efficiency of this arm of the service, it seems to us a suggestion worthy of consideration by the police departments of our large cities that a regular system of interchange of detectives should be established by mutual agreement. Such an interchange would inevitably broaden the experience and improve the power of service of the detectives attached to the several police departments, by the institution of what might be termed schools of instruction for the benefit of the guards of our cities. It would also serve to keep thieves continually on the run and discourage them by making it impracticable for them to enter any large city without recognition and arrest.

There is a popular impression, produced by the inventive fancy of the manufacturers of lurid tales of crime and so-called "detective stories," that a detective of any distinction changes his clothes not less than ten times a day and puts on disguises and masks and comical costumes enough to supply the demand for a fancy dress ball. As a matter of fact, detectives rarely wear disguises of any kind, though there is occasionally some service in which a disguise may be of advantage, as in the case of the detection and conviction of "confidence men" in the manner noted in a former chapter.

When some special information is required which the regular detective force cannot procure without the risk of apprising a criminal that his presence or his scheme is known, this information is often obtained by the temporary employment of persons whom the rascal will not distrust. Frequently rogues are exposed by their own confidants or members of their own gangs, for a rascal who relies upon the fidelity of another rascal is apt to be leaning upon a frail reed. The small tools of one or two principal rogues who try to keep under cover, have been scornfully and meanly abandoned over and over again, when they have been in need of assistance; and it is not surprising that they should requite this treatment by doing what they can to throw the burden of guilt and punishment on their principals. Where leaders of such mark and ability as Wilkes, Becker and Cregan betray or desert their confederates, with cold, deliberate meanness, they should expect to be betrayed in turn.

The proverbial honor among thieves is little more than the dread of retaliation, if one rascal exposes the other rascal, and instances of anything approaching self sacrifice for the sake of shielding others from punishment are few indeed. A professional thief or forger does not like to be branded by his old associates as "a squealer," for the reputation will make it more difficult for him to get associates or help in his schemes of plunder. But if he is obliged to choose between turning state's evidence and going to prison for a long term, he is likely to prefer the rating as "a squealer." So, too, if one of the small fry of knaves can get some reward for disclosing the scheme of a gang of burglars or forgers, he may prefer something in hand to his possible share in uncertain plunder. For the prevention of crime and losses, and the reduction of the expense of safeguards and of the arrest and conviction of criminals, it is desirable to shatter, as far as possible, all the bonds of confidence that bind rogues together. It is fortunate, therefore, for society at large that the fear of betrayal is constantly hanging over the head of a rascal who is obliged to confide in another rascal, in order to carry out his scheme of plunder. It is well, also, that among the associates of criminals there are some who can be relied upon to coöperate with the officers of law in the prevention of crime, and their information is always held in strict confidence by police officials.

THE MAKING OF CRIMINALS.

IN the foregoing pages we have sought to distinguish and present as clearly as possible the varied pursuits and characteristics of the criminals comprised under the head of our rival, the rascal. The swindling beggar, the pickpocket, the shoplifter, the burglar, the bank sneak, the forger, the sharper, the "hotel thief," the train robber, the footpad, the receiver of stolen goods and the incendiary—have successively passed in review with other divisions and sections of lesser note, composing the full array. The order of their succession was determined for reasons which need not be entered upon, inasmuch as the precise arrangement within certain limits is obviously a matter of no essential moment.

It is clear, we presume, that the divisions here made represent variations of method in the common pursuit of plunder, the multiform ways and masks of the rascal, and not distinct classes of criminals. The pickpocket may be also a hotel thief; the tramp may be a skulking burglar; the "safe blower" and house breaker may be a train robber, and the sharper may be a forger as well. As a matter of fact many of the criminals depicted in these pages have entered, from time to time, into a number of these pursuits and some of them are versed in almost every description of crime. A rogue's progress is likely to be from round to round on the ladder of crime and not by a single spring from the ground to the top. The wayward, intractable, roving boy tries his hand as a petty thief, and extends with practice his range of plunder. The clerk grows weary of plodding honesty, and drifts into gambling and other dissipations that sap his principles and make him pliant to tempters and temptations that sweep him along into peculation and forgery. The swindler starts off with little frauds that pave the way to viler and greater cheats. The professional criminal is a product of evolution, and it is rarely the case that a novice in crime begins with the commission of some great felony,

We have not undertaken to present crimes or vices which cannot be reckoned as the professional pursuits of rascals threatening the security of property and life. The burglar, the train robber and the footpad maim, wound and kill their victims at times, in their reckless quest of plunder; and in describing their pursuits we have necessarily dealt to some extent with felonious assaults and murders. But we have no intention of exhibiting any chamber of horrors that can serve no useful purpose, and are not the deeds of malefactors who can be classed as professional criminals. Occasionally we meet with abnormal wretches in the heart of civilization, who take a savage delight in barbaric cruelty and the shedding of blood; but these monstrosities are too few to be ranked as a class by themselves, and to make requisite any special description and warning. Nor does our discussion and review of the rascal extend to cover the crimes that are committed on the spur of some uncontrollable passion or frenzy. In such cases murder and other outrages are simply dreadful incidents and not regular pursuits against which society may well be armed and cautioned.

We have so far intentionally confined our review of the rascal to an exhibit of his methods and habits coming within the range of our own personal experience and that of our brother officers, coöperating with us in the discharge of our trust of the repression of crime and the arrest of the lawbreakers. In so far our slight contribution to the great theme of crime will have a certain distinctive value which may merit recognition.

We do not propose now to enter presumptuously into the discussion of the general theme with its far ranging ramifications and perplexing problems. Its initial point, the origin of sin, has probably given rise to more questioning and controversy than any other subject with which the mind of man has sought to grapple. Yet there has thus far been no common agreement even upon this fundamental consideration. Nor has the world advanced much farther in any exact measuring of individual guilt or responsibility. There is still wide variance, too, in the reckoning of the influences that impel men to the sinful acts that are infractions of law as well as of morality.

"Intemperance," says an authority of the foremost reputation, Dr. E. C. Wines, "is a proximate cause of a very large proportion of the crime committed in America." . . . "Orphanage, idleness, misery, and the wretched home life, or lack of home life, in great cities are fruitful sources of crime." . . . "Want of a trade is a permanent and potent occasion of crime."

"The truth is," observes Z. R. Brockway, superintendent of the great reformatory at Elmira, N. Y., "ninety per cent of crimes are against property, and by young men who have neither the application nor the skill to obtain the means of coveted gratifications by their honest work and earnings. But two per cent of the prisoners received into the Elmira Reformatory have had trades, and the trades of these—fifty per cent of them—are of the commoner and under productive kind."

"We all know that idleness is one of the greatest promoters of crime," remarks Chief Justice Hayt of Colorado. "Take the best man in a community and put him in prison and keep him there three years in idleness and I would not give much for his morality when he comes out. If he was able to withstand the temptation, he would be something more than an ordinary man."

The distinguished jurist, M. Louis Proal, author of that notable work, "Le Crime et La Peine," while recognizing other influences, concludes that certain passions are the chief moving springs of crime. "Greed and envy, love of pleasures, debauchery, idleness, hate, vengeance, sudden fury,—behold the principal causes of criminality."

No authority appears to us more justly entitled to respect for his method of research and the precision of his determinations than R. I. Dugdale of the New York Prison Association, the author of that remarkable study in crime, pauperism, disease and heredity, "The Jukes." It is to such collections of facts and acuteness of inference that society must look for the basis of a comprehensive treatment of the criminal problem. His truly scientific conclusion is the cautious statement that "the logical induction seems to be that environment is the ultimate controlling factor in determining careers, placing heredity itself as an organized result of environment."

In his "further studies of criminals" Mr. Dugdale has also made contributions of extraordinary and indisputable weight. His investigations covering the descent, characteristics and environment of large numbers of criminals cannot be too highly commended. The summary of one of his admirable tables will give a sample exhibit of their value and character. By the investigation of forty-eight persons convicted of burglary, he found that thirty-nine were sane and nine either mentally deficient, epileptic or belonging to families affected by some form of nervous disease. Nineteen of the forty-eight were orphans; twenty-eight were neglected children; forty were habitual criminals; eight were first offenders; fifteen were refuge boys; ten belonged to criminal families; sixteen were of pauper stock; sixteen, of intemperate family; sixteen, habitual drunkards; eight had trades, and thirty-nine had no trade.

He has gone far toward demonstrating that heredity depends upon the permanence of the environment and that a change in environment may produce an entire change in the career of persons with criminal tendencies. He has further marked, also, that one of the causes of idle habits and the extraordinarily small percentage of criminals who have learned honest trades is primarily physical and mental disease.

So we might go on to cite authority after authority, differing more or less widely in their estimates of the relative force of the influences impelling to crime, and in their suggestions for its prevention and treatment. Of late years, too, a view of the development of crime has been maintained by a certain group of anthropologists in Europe, which has been urged with such boldness of assertion and definiteness of detail, that it has had the effect of startling novelty, though it is hardly more in principle than the stretching of the theory of evolution beyond any conclusions reached by Darwin. The recognized founder and head of this new school is Cæsare Lombroso, Professor of Legal Medicine at the University of Turin.

According to Lombroso a considerable part of the human race is doomed by inheritance to a life of crime, or born, at least, with such ineradicable taints and characteristics that their development will impel to crime with almost irresistible force. These moving springs of crime are derived through lines of ancestors reaching back to the primeval creatures from whom man and all living animals have been evolved. The primitive man, springing from his animal ancestors, was destitute of any notion of morality and could acquire none because of the limitations of his brain and the necessities of his struggle for life. In the criminals of our modern society the instincts of primitive man are transmitted and revived. So crime, in the eyes of Lombroso, is a distinct return to ancestral barbarism, and the criminal is physiologically distinct from the honest man.

From the analogy of the known transmission of certain diseases of the body and mental ailments, Dr. Lombroso argues with undeniable ability in maintenance of his theory of the transmission of criminal tendencies and brutal instincts. An apparent stumbling block in the way of his sweeping conclusion is the hard matter of fact that the children of criminals and known descendants of convicts often show no apparent trace of any criminal tendency. On the other hand, the children of virtuous parents whose ancestors for successive generations have been unstained by crime, have committed crimes of the worst description.

We are not assuming to enter into a discussion which must necessarily be referred to expert physiologists, and we should not question the assertion that criminal tendencies are sometimes transmitted from parents to children. But we may observe the plain fact that it is a matter of extraordinary difficulty to determine to what precise extent crime is attributable to inheritance, in view of the complications of other predisposing causes—the impress of degrading environment; the impulse of vicious incitements and temptations; the lack of steady, honest and congenial employment; and all the other influences that impel to crime. Some one once asked Dr. Oliver Wendell Holmes when a boy's education should begin, and the witty autocrat replied: "You should begin with his grandmother." But from the point of view of Lombroso, it would be necessary to begin with extinct brutes.

In his assertion of actual physical distinctions between the criminal and the honest man, Dr. Lombroso has undertaken to maintain alleged matters of fact, which may be submitted to exact practical tests. One of the most acute and well-equipped of his challengers is the jurist and author, before quoted, M. Louis Proal. In rebuttal of this contention, M. Proal says pithily and forcibly: "Until now justice did not find the means of recognizing criminals by the features of the face. Honest folk, often deceived by the innocent appearance of the wicked, used to complain because nature had not revealed their criminality by exterior signs. 'O Zeus, why hast thou given unto men a sure method of distinguishing real gold from its counterfeit, while to distinguish good men from bad no sign has been engraved on their countenance!' If we are to believe Dr. Lombroso these revealing signs of criminality exist; he has discovered them. According to him the criminal man differs anatomically from the honest man; he is born a criminal in consequence of a defective organization. The Italian criminalist points out thirty anatomical anomalies on the skulls of malefactors (Acts of the Congress of Rome, p. 58); he also points out a great number of others on the other parts of the body (Ibid., p. 78). All the members, all the organs, all the functions of the born criminal present anomalies; his teeth, eyes, jaws, arms, hand, nose, ears offer peculiar characteristics. According to Dr. Lombroso, the ensemble of the special characters observed in the criminal constitutes a type which effaces the national type: 'Hence the analogy between Italian and German criminals.' The criminal type is the Mongol type. (The Criminal Man, p. 249.) Criminals have a peculiar and almost special physiognomy for each form of criminality. Dr. Lombroso is so convinced of the reality of this type that he advises magistrates to regard it as an indication of criminality in suspected persons. (Preface, p. XIII.) Ferri and Vito-Porto also think that 'the anatomical, physiological and psychological symptomatology of certain types of criminals ought to be useful to the police and to justice.' (Acts of the Congress of Rome.)

"Most assuredly, if nature had engraved on the face and skull of the accused some anatomical and physiological signs of guilt, the task of justice and the investigations of the police would be much simplified. The examining magistrate would not have much difficulty in discovering the guilty if he was able to recognize a criminal by his bad physiognomy, and might address him in some such language as this: 'Independently of the charges which weigh upon you I observe on your face and person signs of criminality; you are dolichocephalous; you have very long teeth, a sinister eye, a strong grip and arm, as long as those of a chimpanzee; clearly you are guilty.' For all that, it would not be a bad thing for the magistrate, before detailing to the prisoner the features in his face that were clear proof of criminality, to assure himself whether on the faces of the record clerk or policemen he would not find the same accusing traits. In fact, the type of the criminal does not differ from that of the honest man. There are no anatomical or physiological signs that enable us to distingush the criminal from the non-criminal.

"If malefactors betrayed themselves by their faces, the police would have less trouble in arresting them. The criminal remains often enough on the very spot where the crime was committed to divert suspicion by the very boldness of his presence; he talks about the crime with the neighbors, with the policemen themselves, who do not perceive on his face any revealing sign. Sometimes the culprit, arrested upon suspicion, is released. In spite of the charges against him, his explanations and his attitude deceive the police authorities so thoroughly that they set him at liberty. When the culprit is arrested and his guilt established, people are naturally inclined to discover that he has a sinister face, but they would never have noticed it before his arrest.

"To strengthen the proofs of the existence of a criminal type, Dr. Lombroso has added to his book an atlas, in which the photographs of criminals are reproduced. These photographs, according to him, reveal the characteristic type of criminality. But it is impossible to see in these physiognomies what Dr. Lombroso claims to see in them. Placed in contact for the last twenty years with a very large number of criminals by my judicial functions, I have never found them different from honest men from an anatomical point of view. My observations do not confirm the existence of a criminal type which effaces the national type; it is not correct to say that criminals of different countries resemble one another; you can distinguish perfectly the Italian criminal from the French criminal, or from the German criminal.

"It is well known that an anthropometric service has been established at the prefecture of police in Paris under the direction of Dr. Bertillon for the verification of the identity of prisoners who give a false name. Now, the observations made and the measurements taken by the director of this service and his employees have not confirmed the existence of a criminal type; the criminals examined present the most varied physical conformations, just as honest men do.

"Of course, we sometimes observe in the case of criminals, faces bearing the brand of debauchery, expressive of dishonesty or brutality. We say, and not without reason, in speaking of some exceptional criminals, that they look like *brutes*. This expression is a very good term to designate the man who, given up entirely to his bad instincts, allows, according to the saying of Aristotle, the body and the brute to reign in the place of a man. There is nothing astonishing in the fact that the brutality of the instincts which are not combated is reflected on the countenance and that the passions leave their impress. 'Yes, by treading underfoot the laws of decency, a man gives to his soul a certain disposition which is shown forth in his exterior.' (Æschines against Timarchos.) But this disposition does not reveal itself by anatomical signs; it can be observed in the case of men who have abandoned themselves to their passions without going as far as crime. It is not then a distinctive sign of criminality. It is by basing their conclusions on the relations between the physical and the moral that the physiognomists have claimed to read the character of all men on their faces. This pretension was not unknown to the ancients; we know that the physiognomist Zopyrus professed to know the temperament and character of men by the mere inspection of the body, eyes, brow. (Cicero on Fate, § 5.)

"Plutarch tells us that a Chaldean physiognomist, after examining the face of Sylla, announced to him that he would be the foremost man in the world (Life of Sylla). In the XVIIIth century, and in our own day, many ingenious works of physiognomy have been written, notably those of the Abbé Pernetty, M. Gratiolet and M. Eugène Mouton. But I can only see the very dangerous illusion for justice in the pretension to search for indications of criminality in the face. It is not even by any means rare to see great criminals whose outward appearance denotes both gentleness and honesty; I have seen very many examples of this. Some years ago, a very important poisoning case was heard at the assize court of the Bouches-du-Rhône; among the prisoners was a young woman with a very pretty countenance expressive of the greatest sweetness, and her mother, whose outward appearance denoted equal sweetness and honesty. However, the acts committed by these two women showed the profoundest perversity. The mother had advised her daughter to poison her husband in order to enjoy freely the fortune which the latter left her in his will. When the young woman, after administering poison to her husband, was weeping at the sight of his sufferings, her mother called her an idiot, encouraged her to renew the potions, complained of the slowness of the husband in dying, and promised that she would dispatch her own much more rapidly.

"The most vicious women have sometimes an air of innocent candor. It is not correct to say that 'ugliness is, on the whole, the most pronounced characteristic of the criminal.' M. Tarde develops with spirit this ingenious paradox in his work on *Comparative Criminality* (p. 16). Still, we cannot yet discard entirely the saying of La Fontaine: 'The good is not always the comrade of the beautiful.' History has preserved for us the names of great criminals whose beauty was remarkable. Tacitus tells us that 'nothing was wanting to Poppéa except an honest soul. Her mother, the most beautiful woman of the age, had given her a beautiful and noble appearance.' (Annales I, viii., § 45.) Atria Galla, a 'woman unworthy of her race, had nothing to commend her but her beauty.' (Annales I, xv., § 59.) Brinvilliers was extremely beautiful. If ugliness was a token of criminality, beauty should accompany virtue. Now Socrates and St. Vincent de Paul have never been considered types of remarkable beauty. Who does not know that in certain countries of the south physical beauty is often united to numerous vices, while, in some northern countries, certain populations, very superior in morality to the Romans and Neapolitans are very inferior to them from an æsthetic point of view? I have often had occasion to judge prisoners of a handsome Italian type, while very honest people have only moral beauty. The costume which the prisoners put on after their condemnation would seem to be the first thing that gives them a repulsive physiognomy. This illusion is provoked by the costume solely, which gives the prisoners an ugly appearance. In reality, their appearance does not at all differ from that of the people in the audience.

"Accordingly, it is rather astonishing that a criminalist so distinguished as M. Tarde should write that 'the accusing features of the countenance should be taken into account,' and affirms that 'when a magistrate hesitates as to which of two individuals he should prosecute, the bad physiognomy of one of them should be enough to decide him.' That justice which is prudent and worthy of the name will never search for proofs of guilt in the physiognomy. Following the very wise advice given by the fabulist and by common sense not to judge people by their appearance, it can draw proofs of the guilt of a prisoner only from hearing the witnesses, questioning the accused and examining into his antecedents. It prefers judging the accused rather from their actions than from their skulls or noses. 'Everything told us by the physiognomist,' wrote Buffon, 'is devoid of all foundation. Nothing is more chimerical than the inductions they have tried to draw from their pretended metoposcopic observations . . . ! A badly formed body can contain a very beautiful soul, and we ought not to judge of the good or evil nature of a man from the traits of his countenance. . . . The form of the nose, mouth and other features have no more connection with the form of the soul and the nature of the person than the largeness or bulk of the members have with the thought. Is a man less wise because he has little eyes and a big mouth?' "

This is a strong rejoinder, on the whole, to an apparently

untenable or extravagant claim, but M. Proal has seemingly gone too far in his unqualified condemnation of any attempt to search out indications of criminality in the face or appearance. It is unquestionably right for him in his judicial capacity to consider the law and the evidence without regard to the countenance of an accused person; but it does not follow from this that all attempts at all times to detect criminality in the appearance of men and women, are prejudicial to justice or necessarily illusory. Over straining of suspicions and hasty jumping at conclusions are no doubt imprudent and objectionable, but within proper restrictions it may be admissible and even very desirable for the guardians of society to judge by appearances.

We have before noted that detectives are often called from distant cities on the occasion of great conventions for the sake of their known acquaintance with the faces of many of the thieves who are likely to flock to their anticipated harvest field. This is the service of exact recognition; but we have also observed that expert detectives at these gatherings will almost unerringly mark and arrest persons whom they have never seen before and who are not at the time actually engaged in picking pockets, or any other overt criminal act.

The grounds of the assurance with which these keen observers venture to make arrests are so complex and in some features so difficult to define that it is doubtful whether many detectives could justify their action in such cases to the apprehension of persons who have not been trained in close personal study and contact with criminals. Movements and manners and general appearance, in which the ordinary eye would see nothing remarkable, are often highly significant and distinctive to the eye of an expert. Moreover, there is, as we have before remarked, a process of comparison and classification performed by the mind in an instant, and usually without any conscious effort.

It is this process which Francis Galton, F. R. S., has termed composite portraiture, the combination or fusing of a number of individual faces, which an observer has seen, into a generic type. This portrait is stamped on the brain, as Mr. Galton says, by the successive impressions made by its component images. It "represents the picture that would rise before the mind's eye of an individual who had the gift of pictorial imagination to an exalted degree."

Then Mr. Galton proceeds to mark the variations and inaccuracies of this image arising from the differences in the minds of individual observers, and the varying force of the component impressions. Hence the composite image is not, in his judgment, accurate or trustworthy. "The human mind is a most imperfect apparatus for the elaboration of general ideas. Compared with those of brutes its powers are marvellous, but for all that they fall vastly short of perfection. The criterion of a truly perfect mind would lie in its capacity of always creating images of a truly generic kind, deduced from the whole range of its past experiences." Inasmuch as no human mind is truly perfect, Mr. Galton draws the sweeping conclusion that "general impressions are never to be trusted."

As a possible substitute for the inaccurate mental image in practical application to the inspection of criminals and the determination of criminal characteristics and types he has suggested the use of the photographic camera. He has undertaken to give in place of the composite mental impression the composite photograph. In this way, as he holds, a portrait may be obtained with absolute assurance of combining individual elements in the same exact proportion. To obtain this composite portrait, he superimposed a number of photographs in such a way that the eyes of each face were as nearly as possible in the same vertical plane. This device brought the other features sufficiently closely in line for his purpose.

The portraits being thus arranged, a photographic camera was directed upon them. His method of preparing his composite photographs may now be described in his own words: "Suppose that there are eight portraits in the pack, and that under existing circumstances, it would require an exposure of eighty seconds to give an exact photographic copy of any one of them. The general principle of proceeding is this, subject in practice to some variation of details, depending on the different brightness of the several portraits. We throw the image of each of the eight portraits in turn upon the same part of the sensitized plate for ten seconds. Thus portrait No. 1 is in the front of the pack; we take the cap off the object glass of the camera for ten seconds and afterwards replace it. We then remove No. 1, and No. 2 appears in the front; we take off the cap a second time for ten seconds, and again replace it. Next we remove No. 2, and No. 3 appears in the front, which we treat as its predecessors, and so we go on to the last of the pack. The sensitized plate will now have its total exposure of eighty seconds; it is then developed, and the print taken from it is the generalized picture of which I speak. It is a composite of eight component portraits. Those of its outlines are sharpest and darkest that are common to the largest number of the components; the purely individual peculiarities have little or no visible trace. The latter being necessarily disposed equally on both sides of the average, the outline of the composite is the average of all the components. It is a band and not a fine line, because the outlines of the components are seldom exactly superimposed. The band will be darkest in the middle whenever the component portraits have the same general type of features, and its breadth, or amount of blur, will measure the tendency of the components to deviate from the common type. This is so for the very same reason that the shot marks on a target are more thickly disposed near the bull's-eye than away from it, and in a greater degree as the marksmen are more skillful. All that has been said of the outlines is equally true of the shadows; the result being that the composite represents an averaged figure, whose lineaments have been softly drawn. The eyes come out with appropriate distinctness, owing to the mechanical conditions under which the components were hung."

We have given this description at length because of the practical application of this process by Mr. Galton to the study of our rival, the rascal.

Sir Edmund Du Cane, the Director General of prisons in Great Britain, furnished him with a large collection of photographs of criminals for the prosecution of his investigation. From these photographs he made an interesting and valuable series of composites by the selection of several sets of criminals convicted of murder, manslaughter, or crimes accompanied by violence. "There is much interest," as he says, "in the fact that two types of features are found much more frequently among criminals of this character than among the population at large. In one, the features are broad and massive, like those of Henry VIII., but with a much smaller brain. The other, of which five composites are exhibited, each deduced from a number of different individuals, varying four to nine, is a face that is weak and certainly not a common English face. Three of these composites, though taken from entirely different sets of individuals, are as alike as brothers, and it is found on optically combining any three out of the five composites, that is, on combining almost any considerable number of the individuals, the result is closely the same." By means of three converging magic lanterns, Mr. Galton effected the combination of the three composites referred to and maintained that the result might be accepted as generic in respect to this particular type of criminals.

In his brief, but acute, comments on the exhibit made by Mr. Galton, Sir Edmund Du Cane observed: "In considering how best to deal with and repress crime, it occurred to me that we ought to try to track it to its source, and see if we cannot check it there, instead of waiting till it has developed and then striking at it. To track crime to its source we must follow up the history of those who practice it, and specially in such lines as are likely to contain the true clue to their criminal career. Among these subjects for observation, the hereditary disposition is one of the most important, and to disentangle the effect of this from the effect of the bringing up. It seems to me to be a correct inference that if criminals are found to have certain special types of features, that certain personal peculiarities distinguish those who commit certain classes of crime—the tendency to crime is born or bred in those persons and either they are incurable or the tendency can only be checked by taking them in hand at the earliest periods of life. Mr. Galton's process would help to establish this point, because if there is any such distinguishing feature, it would come out in his mixed photographs in a clear line, whereas in those features which do not correspond the lines would be more or less blurred. I should anticipate that a great number of those who commit certain classes of crime would be found to show an entirely inferior mental and bodily organization; but, on the other hand, a very large number of criminals are rather superior in intelligence; so much so that I was quite recently informed by Colonel Pasley, the Director of Admiralty Works, that his observation was that convicts picked up a knowledge of a new trade with much greater rapidity than free workmen. In fact, it is often misplaced and unbalanced cleverness that leads to the attempt to commit crime, and this characteristic might very probably be found in the features of criminals of this class."

There can be no question of the interest and possible importance of the extension of the investigation undertaken by Mr. Galton. It is obviously of extraordinary moment to ascertain with certainty, or even with a marked inclination of probability, whether it is practicable by the aid of the camera to distinguish criminal traits, or to differentiate the various classes and types of criminals. Can it be determined and

COMPOSITE OF 5 FORGERS.
COMPOSITE OF 6 BANK SNEAKS.
COMPOSITE OF 4 BURGLARS.
COMPOSITE OF 4 CRIMINALS.
COMPOSITE OF 5 CRIMINALS.
COMPOSITE OF 9 CRIMINALS.
COMPOSITE OF 6 HOTEL THIEVES.
CO-COMPOSITE OF ALL.
COMPOSITE OF 7 PICKPOCKETS.
CO-COMPOSITE OF 28 CRIMINALS.

The six outside portraits are original composite photographs. The four central portraits are reproduced from Galton's work.

maintained on good evidence that criminals have certain distinguishing personal peculiarities?

For the final conclusion, in answer to this question, there must be prolonged and exhaustive investigations with every attainable resource in the supply of photographs of the criminals of all classes. We shall not even hazard an opinion, at this point of the bare opening of this great undertaking, but we have pursued the line indicated by Galton to the extent of a forward step in our preparation of several composite photographs, representing to the extent of their typical character, the forger, the burglar, the "bank-sneak," the "hotel thief" and the pickpocket. These photographs have been carefully produced in substantial accordance with Mr. Galton's method, by the combination of the portraits of five forgers, four burglars, six "bank-sneaks," six "hotel thieves" and seven pickpockets. The selection was made from the representative portraits given on previous pages. We have further obtained a composite by the combination of the twenty-eight portraits selected, which is given on the same representative page together with a reproduction of the composites prepared by Mr. Galton.

We shall leave to expert physiognomists or to professed experts the difficult task of analyzing the results obtained by this process. It may be that Mr. Galton has entered upon a futile inquiry. But this conclusion should not be accepted until it is determined by thorough investigation. Meanwhile we may properly note that his depreciation of the value of the composite conception formed by the mind, is largely unjustifiable. It is true that a general impression is not absolutely trustworthy, but it is equally true that it may well be trusted to some extent in some cases. A general impression will lead a prudent man to keep out of reach of a snarling bull dog or a fellow man who looks to him like a ruffian, unless the encounter is a matter of duty. A general impression may well be suffered to impel a detective to question sharply and even to arrest persons who have the appearance in his eyes of bank sneaks or bunco men or pickpockets.

A general impression is the union, in the apprehension of the mind, of a multitude of details far more comprehensive, minute, subtle and significant than can ever be given by the reflection of a face in a mirror or camera. The photograph only represents a few features which may be wilfully distorted or comparatively insignificant. The eye apprehends at a glance the whole person, with every peculiarity of manner and action, and the mind makes an instant comparison with a mental image comprehending every known trait and habit of a class of criminals, and reaches the conclusion that the individual in sight is or is not one of that class. For the forming of this judgment or impression, a few furtive glances on the part of a criminal may be of more account than any cast of countenance.

It appears to us eminently desirable that every possible line of rational inquiry into the methods, habits, and characteristics of criminals should be pursued indefatigably by competent investigators for the sake of the protection of society, the ends of justice, wiser dealing with the ever-pressing and unavoidable questions of repression, reform and penalty, the increase of the sum of human knowledge, and our common humanity. If the contention of Lombroso should be even in some small measure sustained by the progress of research, it is obvious that the conclusion must lead to greater discrimination in the treatment of criminals. The extent of their individual responsibility will be more fully considered and exactly measured. In so far as criminal manifestations are determined to be the products of disease, of organic conditions, or taints, or defects, they will be made subject to the treatment of skilled physicians, as well as the administrators of the law. This course will be sustained by the common sense of society, not only from considerations of equity and humanity, but from the strictly utilitarian considerations of the checking of the spread of criminality, the better protection of the public, and the reduction of the cost of the present complex array of safeguards against crime and provisions for felons.

Certainly the present exhibit of the development of crime in this country is one that deserves the gravest consideration, and the application of the best practicable checks and remedies. It appears from the statistics of the last national census, in 1890, that there were then 82,329 prisoners in the United States—75,924 of these were males and 6,405 were females.

The tabulation by ages is of evident concern and interest:

	Males.	Females.	Total.
Under 20 years of age	8,822	873	9,695
20 to 24 years of age	18,358	1,347	19,705
25 to 29 years of age	15,354	994	16,348
30 to 34 years of age	10,366	712	11,078
35 to 39 years of age	7,592	737	8,329
40 to 44 years of age	4,953	566	5,519
45 to 49 years of age	3,637	408	4,045
50 to 59 years of age	3,968	456	4,424
60 to 79 years of age	1,761	253	2,014
80 and above	50	12	62
Not stated	1,063	47	1,110
Total	75,924	6,405	82,329

This classification shows that more than eleven per cent of the males and more than thirteen per cent of the females were under twenty years of age. More than forty-four per cent of the males and more than thirty-six per cent of the females were between twenty and twenty-nine years of age.

It is therefore obvious that the process of the development or manufacture of a fresh stock of criminals annually is going on at a rate that is greatly to be deplored, and that imperatively demands the earnest, active coöperation of the intelligent and prudent forces of society for its reduction. It is the duty of the police to prevent the commission of crimes, so far as lies in its power, and it is, we believe, as a body, faithfully trying to do its duty. It remains for society at large to fully recognize and discharge the burden of guardianship which is outside of the special responsibilities and functions of the police.

Doubtless crime is to-day largely repressed by the institution of penalties. A felon's brand and a convict's cell are surely the reverse of alluring. Something, too, has been done, and may be done to make crime abhorrent by impressing the hearts of the young with its sinfulness and its blight. In our foregoing depiction of "Our Rival, the Rascal," we have not failed to point out that the notorious criminals, who have served as illustrative examples, have had cause to regret most bitterly the first fatal step into the quicksand of crime. There has been no evasion in our treatment or process of selection. Our design has simply been to present a comprehensive and faithful picture. But, in so doing, we have necessarily held up a warning that ought to strike home to the heart of the most reckless young man. "How can you hope to fare better on the rough road of crime than those who have gone before you? Have you the brain and hand of a burglar like Schœnbein, or the craft of a forger like Becker, or the wiliness of a 'banksneak' like Johnson, or even the nimble fingers of a pickpocket like Wells? All that extraordinary talent in the commission of crime can do to cover the criminal has been tried and failed. Surely you are even more of a fool than a knave if you think that you can find a safe footing where all others have fallen."

So what we have sought to do in this work, and what thousands of others better qualified than ourselves are doing daily for the repression of crime—is of service as far as it goes. But this is far from enough. In a subsequent chapter, devoted to the general question of the treatment of criminals, as well as the prevention of crime, we shall take occasion to note the suggestions that seem to us most feasible and valuable for the diminution of first steps in crime.

THE CRIMINAL WOMAN.

ANY one examining the prison and criminal records of our own and foreign countries will necessarily observe how few crimes, comparatively, are committed by women. The census record given in the preceding chapter shows that less than ten per cent of the convicts in our prisons are women, although women nearly equal the men in the total population of the United States. A like proportion is noted in other countries where statistics, bearing upon this point, have been prepared. In France, for example, it is reckoned by M. Tarde, a statistician of the highest authority, that only one-fifth or one-sixth of the persons accused of crimes are women; and M. Proal cites yearly records showing that the proportion of female criminals is even less than the estimate of M. Tarde.

In spite of this great discrepancy in the relative contribution of the sexes to the ranks of criminals, it is asserted by Prof. Lombroso that the number of aged female criminals is actually in excess of the number of males of like ages. He attributes this disproportion chiefly to the greater vitality of the women. It is his observation, also, that women bear the close confinement of prisons better than men, and he gives instances of female convicts who have passed more than sixty years consecutively in prison.

He remarks, however, that both senile and precocious grayness of the hair is much more frequent in female than in male criminals, and that certain wrinkles, especially those on the cheek bones and about the eyes and mouth, are more common and deeply marked in criminal women of mature age than in men of the same age. "In this connection," he says, "we may recall the proverbial wrinkles of witches, and the instance of the vile old woman, the so-called Vecchia dell' Aceto, of Palermo, who poisoned so many persons simply for the love of lucre. When already of mature age, the idea of these murders occurred to her. The bust which we possess of this criminal, so full of virile angularities, and above all so deeply wrinkled, with its satanic leer, suffices of itself to prove that the woman in question was born to do evil, and that, if one occasion to commit it had failed, she would have found others."

Baldness is also more common, he states, among criminal women than among those of reputable life. The stature, stretch of arms, and length of limbs are less in all female criminals than in normals, but in proportion to the stature, the weight of murderesses is greater than in moral women. Female thieves are inferior to moral women in cranial capacity and circumference, and their cranial diameters are less, but their facial diameters are larger, especially in the jaw. Homicides, poisoners and incendiaries have more prominent cheekbones than the average normal type.

Beyond these alleged physical anomalies, or peculiarities, Dr. Lombroso professes to distinguish in female criminals a certain refined, diabolical cruelty exceeding the brutality of men. He explains this abnormal condition on the ground that woman is less sensitive to pain than man, and that "compassion is the offspring of sensitiveness." Women, in his eyes, "have many traits in common with children: their moral sense is deficient, and they are revengeful, jealous, and inclined to vengeances of a refined cruelty."

"In ordinary cases these defects are neutralized by piety, maternity, want of passion, weakness and an undeveloped intelligence. But when a morbid activity of the psychical centres intensifies the bad qualities of women, and induces them to seek relief in evil deeds; when piety and maternal sentiments are wanting, and in their place are strong passions and intensely erotic tendencies, much muscular strength and a superior intelligence for the conception and execution of evil, it is clear that the innocuous semi-criminal present in the normal woman must be transformed into a born criminal more terrible than any man."

"What terrific criminals would children be if they had strong passions, muscular strength and sufficient intelligence; and if, moreover, their evil tendencies were exasperated by a morbid psychical activity. And women are big children; their evil tendencies are much more numerous and more varied than men's, but generally latent."

Almost all of the alleged criminal peculiarities distinguished by Lombroso are held to be uncharacteristic or merely fanciful by other European anatomists and physiologists, although his conclusions are largely sustained by the members of his new school. One apparent weakness in his contention is particularly remarked—the fact that his examination of criminals has been chiefly confined to Italian convicts, in place of the comprehensive investigation essential for the determination of any conclusions affecting criminals at large. It is also observed even by those who admire him greatly, like Dr. Pauline Tarnowsky, that he is too apt to rear air castles of assumption on a few stepping stones of fact.

M. Proal is particularly cutting in his remarks. "Some writers belonging to the school of criminal anthropology have claimed that the criminal woman revealed her character by exterior signs. 'That which distinguishes,' says Dr. Lombroso, 'female criminals from normal women and especially from mad women, is the extreme abundance of the hair; in 39 out of 122 I have not found a single one bald, and out of 122 3 murderers only had their hair prematurely whitened.' [The criminal man, p. 238.] Let women who have abundant hair remain reassured, and let those who are bald not be in any hurry to attribute to themselves a monopoly of virtue. The verifications of Dr. Lombroso are explained quite simply by the fact that female prisoners in general are almost always young. Dr. Lombroso notes, also, as an indication of criminality, the black color of the hair. Black hair is, according to him, more common than fair hair among criminal women. What is there astonishing in this, since the criminal women who were the subject of his observations were Italians? If Dr. Lombroso had examined the women of the North, would he not have observed, in the case of criminal women, more with fair hair than with black hair? This pretended type of criminal woman drawn from the abundance and color of the hair is really drawn by the hair and from pure fancy.

"After affirming the existence of the criminal type, Dr. Lombroso acknowledges that the characters that constitute this type are only met with forty times out of the hundred. If, by his own confession, there is a deficit of sixty per cent, what sort of a criminal type can that be which does not exist among the large number of criminals? The characters Dr. Lombroso claims to have observed in criminals cannot constitute a special type, since they are lacking in sixty per cent of these same criminals. Dr. Lombroso has tried to answer this objection. 'Besides, that forty per cent is not to be disdained, the insensible passage from one character to another is manifested in all organic beings; the passage even from one species to another is manifested, *a fortiori;* it is so in the anthropological field, where individual variability, growing in proportion to its capacity for perfection and civilization, seems to efface the complete type. Out of 100 Italians, for example, it is hard to find five who present the type of race.' [Preface, p. xiii.] This reply is anything but satisfactory. An authority on anthropology, M. Topinard, declares that it contains almost as many errors as words." (Revue d'Anthropologie, 15 Nov., 1887.)

Besides the alleged deviations from the normal types of women which are noted by Dr. Lombroso, it is remarked by him and other distinguished criminalists that certain habits are characteristic of the criminal woman, "The born criminal," says Lombroso, "constantly endeavors to prepare a preventive alibi or proof of innocence; but her ideas, however ingenious, are often ill-adapted for their purpose." "The female delinquent," observes Rykère, "is more sophistical and argumentative than her male prototype. She finds pretexts and excuses which astonish one by their fantasticality and strangeness." Pasteur Arboux remarks, "not only do women, when they fall into crime, fall deeper than men, but they lie with greater coherence and audacity. They are bolder in the stories which they tell and more hypocritical."

These observations appear to be, on the whole, well sustained by facts. A frank admission of guilt will often be made by male thieves, when they are caught in the act of stealing or when they know that the evidence against them is overwhelming. But it is exceedingly rare for a criminal woman to admit that she has consciously committed any offence against the law. When silk, laces or any other valuables are extracted from a female shoplifter's bag, by arresting officers, she will volubly protest that she has bought the goods, and defy the police to prove that they have been stolen. As experienced shoplifters try to destroy as quickly as possible any mark of identification, it is sometimes a matter of great difficulty to convict such thieves, although it may be morally certain that their pretences are lies.

Even when the stolen goods can be readily traced and identified, the professional woman shoplifter or pickpocket will stubbornly maintain her innocence with every resource of counterfeit indignation or plaintive appeal, or mock bewilderment. She cannot account for the presence of the "swag" in her pocket or bag. Somebody must have slipped the pocketbook or handkerchief or gloves or lace into her bag, to escape the detection of the police or for the wicked purpose of bringing her to shame. Some enemy, some persecutor, is secretly following her and trying to send her to prison maliciously. This pretence of persecution is a staple resource, even when it is clearly preposterous, and it will be supplemented by a dogged protest that she didn't know that any stolen article was on her person. She never took anything that didn't belong to her; but if she had picked a pocket or pilfered from a counter, she was absolutely unconscious or irresponsible. The plea of kleptomania will be made by the most hardened professional thief, as a last resource, with the utmost glibness and brazen assurance. If tears, shrieks and hysterics are thought to be of any service in bolstering up this pretence, they will be furnished with even more facility than is shown in cases of probable mania.

So even the most notorious and hardened offenders will insist, before conviction and after, that they are really persecuted and innocent women. Some of the keener-witted will perhaps admit that their lives have not always been correct in past years, but they will unflinchingly maintain that they have reformed; or, at least, that they have not committed the particular offence with which they are charged. The characteristics and methods of the criminal woman,—the adventuress, the blackmailer, the swindler, the shoplifter, the pickpocket,—will be most distinctly shown in typical instances.

As a study for criminalists and in the general interest attaching to her character and life "Sophie" Lyons is unquestionably in the forefront of living women. She is the offspring of generations of criminals. Her line of descent has been traced into the last century, and it may be possible to follow it farther with certainty. Her grandfather was a noted English burglar named Elkins. She used to boast that he was "a cracksman to whom Scotland Yard took off its cap." Her father and mother came to this country from England before she was born. Both were professional thieves and blackmailers. They made their home in New York where their daughter Sophie was born. It is credibly reported that she was trained to steal as soon as she was able to toddle about alone. She was arrested for shoplifting when she was only twelve years old. Her father and brother were then in the same prison in New Jersey for blackmailing. Her mother was in a New York penitentiary for shoplifting. Her elder sister was in prison on Blackwell's Island as the keeper of a disorderly house.

When she was sixteen years old, she married Maury Harris, a professional pickpocket. Before her short honeymoon was over, her husband was caught in the act of picking a pocket and sent to the state prison for two years. It is presumed that she obtained a divorce, though she was not likely to stickle at the commission of bigamy, for within two years she took a second husband. This privileged partner was Edward Lyons, at that time on the lower rounds of the ladder of ill fame which he afterwards mounted as "Ned" Lyons, the notorious burglar whose portrait has been given on a representative page, Lyons was then an uncommonly good looking rascal, not yet thirty years old, and his bride, Sophie, is described by those who knew her well as an exceedingly beautiful girl, with brilliant dark eyes and auburn hair that flowed to her feet when shaken from its coils.

The young couple came to Boston in 1866 and made their home for a year or two at a lodging house in the North End. They probably would have prolonged their stay if the young wife had not been caught picking pockets at a cattle fair in Portsmouth, N. H., on one of her pleasure trips from the city. She was then only nineteen years old, but her phenomenal talent as an actress was already far developed. She could mould her face to every shade of emotion. She could make her eyes, at will, a fountain of tears. She treated her captors to a moving display of her art. She was by turns horror-struck, proudly indignant, heart-broken and convulsed with hysterics. Who could press a charge against such a blushing, trembling, sobbing, young beauty, piteously claiming that it was a dreadful mistake, painting the agony of her dear husband and parents at the bare suspicion of her spotless innocence, and subtly hinting at the grave censure that would surely fall on her maligners? It was her shrewd calculation that the authorities in charge of her case would prefer to let it drop quietly, and so they did. Either conclusive evidence was lacking, or it was judged to be an unusually clear case of kleptomania, for the artful "Sophie" was suffered to disappear.

It is well known that her diversions of pocket-picking and shop lifting were for years directly contrary to the desires and commands of her husband. He was himself a burglar, it is true, but he was passionately in love with his beautiful wife and would have been glad to keep her beyond any possible risk of arrest. His own plunder was sufficient to support her luxuriously, and he was ready to gratify her slightest whim, but he could not control her apparent passion for stealing. Day after day she would dangle before his eyes the fruits of her ramble through the streets and shops,—handkerchiefs, gloves, laces, pins and bracelets. She would pick up anything that caught her fancy for the moment, without any apparent discrimination in the measure of value, or any consideration of the stock of trinkets which she had at home.

In 1869, about a year after her performance at Portsmouth, her husband took a leading part in the great robbery of the Ocean Bank in New York, in company with Max Shinburn and other burglars of note. Lyons had a large share of the booty, but it melted away like snow in the mist. He bought a villa on Long Island and begged his wife to live on his stolen fortune without dabbling in petty thefts. A son was born to them, and he hoped that the tiny hands of the baby might hold his mother at home. But when her baby was only six months old, "Sophie" Lyons was caught stealing in a New York jewelry store. By her artful pretences she escaped with a light sentence of six months on Blackwell's Island, but her home was broken up and her child was put in the care of friends.

In 1870, while she was in the penitentiary on the island, her

 "SOPHIE" LYONS.

 BERTHA HEYMAN.

 "MOLLIE" HOEY.

 LOUISA JOURDAN.

husband with three other notorious burglars robbed a bank in Waterford, New York, and was soon after arrested, convicted, and sent to Sing Sing for seven years. Before a year of his sentence had expired, his wife was under the same prison roof. After her discharge from the Blackwell's Island penitentiary, she made an alliance with "Old Mother Mandelbaum," and was caught while shoplifting in New York city. Goods from two of the largest stores were extracted from her clothing; and, as the stolen property was valued at more than a thousand dollars, she was convicted of grand larceny and sent to Sing Sing for five years. But even in the state prison she was not at the end of her wily resources.

In December, 1871, a suit of citizen's clothes was smuggled into Sing Sing by confederates of Lyons, and the burglar contrived to slip on this suit in place of his convict's dress. Then he found a way to escape by hiding himself in a wagon which carried him away from the prison to liberty. As soon as he was at large he began to plot for the escape of his wife. After some months he succeeded in opening communication with her and devised a plan to take her out of prison.

It is reported that she was employed in housework by the warden, and it is evident that she was not confined to a cell. For, one winter night, she was standing close to the outer door in the warden's house, when her husband drove up to the prison in a sleigh with a companion equally daring. Lyons rang the bell at the warden's door sharply, and his wife answered the call. He threw a blanket over her head, caught her up in his arms and carried her to his sleigh. His companion whipped up the horses and the fugitives sped away. Their escape was made in a driving snow storm which hid them flying and covered their tracks. There is some variance in its reported details of this escape. According to one account she slipped out of the female prison when the guard opened the door to receive a basket of fruit for a sick convict. But there is no question of the main matter of fact. The fugitives escaped to Canada and from there to Europe. They came back stealthily and Lyons went into business as a diamond broker in Montreal. This was probably a cover for his regular occupation, and when he had only a little money left of his plunder, he undertook to fill his pockets with the help of his wife by picking pockets at a country fair in northern New York. Here they were caught by Brooklyn detectives and Lyons was sent back to Sing Sing; but his wife escaped on the plea that she had been kidnapped at the prison and that the time of her sentence had expired. There is little doubt that the melodramatic show of forcible abduction from Sing Sing had been planned cunningly to clear her of the charge of attempting to escape, in case the bold venture had failed.

Soon after her release she became an adventuress of the most dangerous type. She made her so-called home in Detroit, but roved over Michigan to levy blackmail and subsequently extended her raids to Cincinnati, Boston, and other Eastern cities. She was faithless to her husband, and, after his release from Sing Sing, they had a series of bitter quarrels, ending in final separation. Then for some years she roamed over this country and Europe in the pursuit of shoplifting and blackmailing, and once, for the sake of variety, undertaking a lecturing tour. Although she was repeatedly arrested, her craft usually saved her from conviction, even when she joined gangs of notorious bank sneaks as related in a former chapter. She made repeated trips to Europe and under various assumed names reaped harvests of plunder. But with advancing years her remarkable beauty faded away. She became addicted to the opium habit and dissipation marked her face indelibly. Of late years she has had little opportunity for plundering, for her face is so well known in all large cities in this country and Europe that she is constantly watched, if she is not arrested at sight.

She still has considerable means at her command, and her money is fully spent in behalf of her surviving children. Her oldest boy died in Auburn prison, and several other children died in early childhood. But she has two living daughters who have been educated in fine schools in Canada and France. She said a few years ago in regard to them: "They have never known me to use a profane word or allow a drop of liquor in the house. All they know bad about me is what they hear, and as I know I can't always keep them in ignorance of what I am, I don't try to hide anything from them." It appears to be a matter of fact that she has spared no expense in training her daughters to become good and accomplished women. So far as is known her efforts have been successful. If their lives continue to be unsullied by crime, it will surely be a signal testimonial to the preponderant force of environment in determining careers. Moreover, the fact of the exercise of such motherly love and care is a marked exception to the sweeping assumption of Lombroso that women who are criminals usually have little of the maternal instinct. It affords also a specific instance of the weakness particularly noted in the method of this distinguished professor, his neglect to verify the statements which he accepts and announces as if they were indisputable truths. "Sophie Lyons," he says, "though very rich, abandoned her children when she fled from America, leaving them dependent on public charity." He was obviously too ready to adopt a rumor to bolster up a theory.

His general observation touching this remarkable woman is more nearly correct. "She must have possessed a very superior intelligence. She enriched herself by robbery in America and came to Europe to continue the same system out of sheer love of it. Arrested *in flagrante* by the police of Paris, she succeeded in obtaining her liberty through the intercession of the British and American ambassadors."

It is a fact that "Sophie" Lyons was arrested in Paris for picking pockets in July, 1888, and it is also a fact that her artful pretences secured her release, for her masquerade as "Mme. de Varney," was apparently too well sustained to be penetrated even by the keen examining magistrate, although the chief of detectives was not deceived, and identified her soon after her discharge. But for the special intercession of the ambassadors, we must leave Dr. Lombroso to vouch.

Bertha Heyman, who has acquired the title of "The Confidence Queen," by her swindling operations in this country, is another remarkable woman of known criminal parentage. She was born in a village near Posen in Prussia. Her father was a forger with a convict's record. Her family name was Schlesinger, but, when she came to this country twenty years ago, she was married to an immigrant named Karko.

Soon after her arrival she made herself notorious as a so-called "confidence" woman. Her common practice was to obtain loans upon worthless checks, bonds and safe deposit receipts for packages alleged to contain jewelry and other valuables. She was so crafty and ingratiating that she victimized men and women of all classes, from the mechanic with hard earned savings to wealthy brokers and bankers. She was so utterly unscrupulous and grasping that she would set her trap for the poorest immigrant with no less pains, apparently, than the snare for the largest capitalist. After leaving her first husband she married again and acquired the name of Heyman, under which she is most widely known, though she has borrowed the name of Stanley and other imposing fictions for various character parts.

In the conduct of her greater swindles she has spent money lavishly to bolster up her pretences. Her dresses and jewelry have been superb, and of the latest fashion. She has taken the most expensive suites at the best hotels in the country, and used every art to make the acquaintance of people of wealth and social standing. When she had callers, she would contrive to receive exquisite baskets of flowers bearing the counterfeit cards and compliments of various leaders in fashionable society, which would naturally impress her visitors with her exalted standing in the ranks of the "Four Hundred." When the bills for these baskets were sent in by the trustful florists, she was usually masquerading in some distant city.

When her son was old enough to serve as an apprentice in her confidence games, she employed him as a "stool-pigeon"; and, in the negotiations for the disposal of the hand of her heir in marriage, she was able to entrap a number of parents seeking rich sons-in-law. He was accustomed, also, to collect diamond rings and other costly trinkets from the young ladies of his acquaintance, upon his obliging offer to have the jewels reset in the latest fashion; but the owners grew weary of waiting for the return of their jewels. Sometimes the performance was varied by the substitution of the confidence queen for her son, in the negotiation for a marriage. After the engagement of the mother, her rascally son would contrive to borrow enough from his prospective father-in-law to fill his pockets, and then the engagement would be heartlessly broken by the "confidence queen."

This dangerous swindler is now so notorious that her range of fleecing has been greatly restricted. She has been an inmate of several penitentiaries and jails, and has been forced to seek cover, of late years, as the conductress of cheap variety shows and other petty business.

It is to be regretted that it has not been practicable to trace with any certainty the parentage of a third member of the group of noted criminals, whose portraits appear on an accompanying page. Mary Holbrook, alias "Mollie Hoey," has been reckoned the most adroit and sly female thief in this country. It is reported that her maiden name was Mary Williams, and she is said to have been born in Boston, although her first appearance as a criminal was made in Chicago thirty years ago. She was the consort there of a notorious gambler and burglar, named George Holbrook, who was shot dead in the attempt to escape from the jail in Hennepin, Illinois. With two companion prisoners he succeeded in tunnelling under the walls of the jail, and undertook to crawl through the narrow passage. As soon as his head appeared above ground, he was shot by a watchful guard, and his companions prudently crawled back into prison.

Shortly after his funeral "Mary Holbrook" married "Jimmy" Hoey, a young pickpocket, and acquired her familiar name of "Mollie Hoey." She soon became a far more expert thief then her husband, but, in 1870, she was caught in the act of picking the pocket of a woman in Chicago. She was permitted to give a bond which she promptly "jumped." It was learned that she had gone to New York, and she was arrested in that city at the request of the Chicago authorities.

On her return to Chicago, in charge of an officer, she contrived to bolt out of the train, when it stopped, for a moment, at a station in Canada; and raised an outcry that she had been kidnapped on a trumped-up charge. Her ruse succeeded, for the officer had no authority to arrest her in Canada. After her escape she returned to New York and resumed her labors as a pickpocket and shoplifter in close confederacy with "Old Mother Mandelbaum."

In April, 1878, she was arrested in Boston for picking the pocket of a lady, and was placed under bonds, which she "jumped," as a matter of course. Five years later, in the spring of 1883, she was again arrested in Boston, for the theft of pocket books from shopping bags. When she noticed that she was watched, she thrust her hand through the lining of her pocket like a flash, but the movement did not escape the eye of the watching detective. A considerable sum of money and a receipt from an express company were extracted from the lining of her dress skirt. For this performance she was sent to the House of Correction for a year, and as she stepped from the jail in February, 1884, she was arrested upon a requisition from the governor of New York. Two years before she had been convicted of stealing a pocket book in New York and sentenced to five years imprisonment. Her counsel appealed the case and, pending the appeal, she was admitted to bail. As soon as she was released by giving bonds, she made the excursion to Boston which ended in the House of Correction. While in this prison, her sentence in New York had been confirmed by the court of appeals, and New York officers were in readiness to take charge of her as soon as her sentence in Massachusetts expired. She was escorted to the New York state penitentiary to serve out the term of her sentence.

As she suspected that her ally, "Old Mother Maudelbaum," had furnished evidence to convict her, she proceeded to retort from her prison cell by helping to expose the crookedness of the old receiver. In consideration of her service, she was pardoned by the governor, and promptly made use of her liberty to pick pockets in Chicago dry goods stores. She was caught in the act and when she was admitted to bail, she "jumped" her bonds, and departed to Cleveland. Here she was arrested in September, 1886, while carrying off a camel's hair shawl from a leading dry goods store. While awaiting trial she was confined in the county jail.

One evening in October, less than three weeks after her entrance into the jail, the turnkey was pained to observe a hole cut through the wall, at one side of a window, in the women's apartment on the first floor. Some twenty bricks had been taken from the wall and the thick window casing had been roughly cut off for a length of about fifteen inches. There were no bricks or fragments of mortar on the floor, but the missing part of the wall was later discovered in a vacant cell in the fourth tier. The hole was only about 15x8 inches, but it was big enough for Mollie Hoey to crawl through and escape, in company with a boy who helped her. She left lying on the floor a pair of shears with one of the handles broken off. That was not an ideal tool for cutting through a brick wall and a heavy wire netting, but it served her turn. The hole was neatly covered with a piece of dirty, light-gray oil-cloth, which closely matched the color of the walls of the apartment.

There was a hot pursuit, but the lost "Mollie Hoey" had found cover. The latest trace of her was given by a hackman who reported at a city police station that a woman had taken his carriage for a short drive. She had come running up to him, with a shawl wrapped about her head, and told him that she was running away from a drunken husband who had been beating her. Her face and hands were badly bruised and scratched, and the hackman did not question the story. So he drove her to a certain street corner, where she told him to stop. She had some silver tied up in a handkerchief, from which she took a dollar and paid her fare. Then she stepped out of the hack and walked quickly away.

It is reported that she was actually in a house in Cleveland, on the night of her escape, when the police came up to search it. She was having her hair cut when the officers broke in, but she had time to push a plank out of the window to the roof of the next house and scramble across. Then she pulled the plank to the roof and hid herself until the search was over. She then contrived to escape from the city by putting on the suit of a common laborer and coolly walking on board the boat for Detroit, in her disguise. Her hair was cut short and she was smoking a clay pipe with such relish that no looker on suspected that this counterfeit of a man was the notorious "Mollie Hoey." According to the most probable report, this really remarkable thief is now picking pockets on the other side of the Atlantic.

On the same page with these noted criminals appears the portrait of Louise Jourdan, alias "Little Louise," who is discredited by a reputation as a pickpocket that is hardly second to that of "Mollie" Hoey. She was born in England where her father kept a public-house, and was sent to prison for larceny when she was a young girl. Upon her discharge she secured a place as a maid for a wealthy Spanish lady and accompanied her to Brazil. Here she found an opportunity to steal the diamonds of her mistress, but was arrested and sen-

MARION L. DOW.

MARY BUSBY.

MARGARET BROWN.

ELIZABETH DILLON.

tenced to receive forty lashes at the whipping post. From Brazil she came to this country, and soon made herself notorious as a pickpocket and shoplifter in all the principal cities of the Eastern states, in company with "Lizzie" Myers, "Black Amelia" and other expert thieves. She married in succession a number of professional pickpockets, bank sneaks and burglars, and her last known husband was the notorious "Big Tom" Biglow. When he died in 1886, she put in a claim as his widow to property which was estimated to amount to over $100,000. It is not known how this claim was settled, but of late years the widow has contrived to keep under cover. She has always dressed well, and her gentle, quiet manners have enabled her to mingle in crowds without exciting suspicion, and prosecute her dexterous thefts.

Upon a second page are given the portraits of four other typical criminals. Marion L. Dow can probably boast of having assumed more names and characters than any other woman who has not been a professional actress. Her original name as a baby is said to have been Marion Grass, and her birthplace was a town in New Brunswick. Her first appearance in the United States was made in 1870, when she had acquired the name of Warren by marriage. Both her husband and herself had the reputation of being swindlers, in Boston, where they resided for some years; but they contrived to escape conviction.

After a few years the husband died and Marion Warren soon changed her name by marriage to a second husband named Dow. His death soon followed, and the widow took a lodging house as a cover for her swindling operations. In 1875 she attempted to negotiate a loan from a Boston bank upon a "raised" certificate of railroad stock, and when the forgery was detected, she fled to St. John, New Brunswick. Here she was soon arrested for attempting to pass a forged check. There was a disagreement of the jury sitting at her first trial and, before the second came on, she "jumped" her bail and fled to Chicago. Here she took another lodging house to cover her swindling under the name of Ware.

In 1880 she determined to extend her operations by opening a brokerage office in New York, at first in the name of Marion E. Warren, which she expanded by personating the characters of Carrie R. West and Carrie R. McDowell. After swindling her gulls to the extent of about $40,000, she found that New York was becoming so hot that she transferred her brokerage office to Philadelphia, where she furnished a suite of apartments with costly and elegant fittings and all the appurtenances of a wealthy broker. She announced her intention of operating exclusively for the accommodation of speculative ladies, and sent out enticing circulars, guaranteeing her customers against any loss in consideration of one-half the profits of their investments. This assurance was so satisfactory that she reaped a large harvest from confiding women, many of whom put their entire savings into her hands. When the crash came, the widow, Marion L. Dow, as she called herself, failed to clear herself of the charge of swindling and was sent to Moyamensing Prison.

After some months of confinement she secured her release upon some technical error in the proceedings against her. Soon she took a third husband in the person of one Royal La Touche, who had just been discharged from prison. M. La Touche went to Sing Sing in 1883 upon conviction for bigamy, and as his wife desired another husband, she espoused one James E. McDonald.

In the fall of 1883, she opened a "Ladies Investment Bureau" in New York, under the name of Carrie E. Morse. Among her victims was a widow with four children, whom she left completely destitute. In recognition of these swindling operations, Mrs. "Morse" was sent to prison for two years, and as soon as she was discharged she went into the swindling brokerage business again in New York, as "Mme. Marion La Touche." This time she promised a sure return of $50 per month to any lady who would confide to her $300 for investment. She was again arrested, but was ultimately discharged by order of the court. It is not known under what name she is masquerading to-day.

Margaret Brown, better known as "Old Mother Hubbard," has been a thief from her earliest childhood, and her face is now familiar to detectives of every large city in this country. For nearly sixty years she has been roaming from city to city, as a pickpocket and shoplifter, and her successive sentences to prison have been of no avail to deter her from stealing as soon as she was free to use her hands for this purpose. Anything within reach which she could put in her pocket or bag has been a prize to her, and she was apparently willing to run the same risk for a pair of stockings as for a plump pocket book. Her usual dress on the streets has been black silk, which she has carefully kept from any stain or soiling. Once, when arrested in Boston, she wore a plain calico dress under the silk, and, after she had been searched, she coolly requested permission to put on her calico dress over the silk to preserve her professional costume from any defacement when not in actual use. Mary Busby and Elizabeth Dillon are women of the same class and like career, representing the apparently incorrigible professional thieves, who can only be restrained effectually by permanent confinement.

THE TREATMENT OF CRIMINALS.

IN "Le Monde des Prisons," the work of the Abbé Moreau, formerly chaplain of the prison of Grande-Roquette, the author quotes from the letter of a robber this savage prescription for the solution of the criminal problem. "I have little faith in the reformation of professional robbers and thieves. One who has stolen will steal; one who has killed will kill; just as one who has drunk will drink,—and if I should advise the government, it would be to shoot every one of us through the head or to throw us all into the sea with cannon balls tied to our legs—all of us comrades in crime and brothers by blood. Repentance or change in our manner of living almost never takes place."

Our civilization shrinks in horror from this barbaric way of cutting the knot which so many good people have gropingly sought to untie. But it is needful not merely to hold up our hands in protest against barbaric suggestions, but to apply our best brains as well as our hands to a task of imperative public concern—the attainment of the best feasible method for the repression and diminution of crime.

We are glad to recognize the great advances which have been made during the present century in the treatment of criminals in all civilized countries. The hungry child who steals a loaf of bread from the counter of a baker is no longer penned up with burglars and murderers. By the institution of progressive reformatories, houses of correction, and separate prisons for men and women,—the leading countries of the world have gone far toward making adequate provision for the separation, classification and treatment of criminals while actually confined at the charge of the state. Philanthropists to-day can make few just complaints of the inhumanity of prison officials or, even, of callous indifference to the condition of the convicts under their charge. In the fittings of American state prisons, in the quality and quantity of food supplied to prisoners, in the variation of employments and in the interpretation in practice of sentences at hard labor,—such painstaking regard is shown for the comfort of convicts that it is sharply questioned by some experienced observers whether this humane consideration has not overstepped the rational and proper line by making sentences to prison too little dreaded by habitual criminals.

It is certain that the general treatment of criminals in the prisons of Europe is more severe than the course generally followed in American prisons; but it is the judgment of authorities of such undoubted weight as President Brinkerhoff of the National Prison Association, that the results of the severer European method show no advantage over those obtained from our American system of treatment. There has been of late years, however, a marked resolution in a number of the states of this country to emphasize heavily the distinction between the hardened professional criminal and the offender who has yielded to temptation and marred a life of integrity by a single criminal act. It has been judged to be unwise for society and undiscriminating in the treatment of law-breakers, to allot the same penalty for a breach of the law by a person who has otherwise a good record and by one who has repeatedly broken the law and demonstrated his purpose to prey upon his fellow man. The habitual criminal is a continual menace to the just security of law-abiding citizens. He constrains the establishment and maintenance of safeguards which are yearly becoming more costly and burdensome. He conflicts with the elemental purposes of social organization. It seems clearly preposterous to permit such a public enemy to carry on his warfare with occasional brief interruptions as long as he has a plotting brain and molesting hands.

This conclusion has been reached and practically incorporated in the legislation of Ohio, Illinois, Massachusetts and other states touching habitual criminals. Largely through the able advocacy and persistent effort of Hon. Clement K. Fay, one of the prison commissioners of Massachusetts, ten years ago, the legislature of this state passed an act to provide for the punishment of habitual criminals, which became a law by the approval of the governor, June 16, 1887. This act was so carefully and judiciously drawn that it certainly has not operated to imprison any one as an habitual criminal who has not been incontestably a member of that class of public enemies. Its provisions are as follows:

"Section 1. Whoever has been twice convicted of crime, sentenced and committed to prison, in this or any other state, or once in this and once at least in any other state, for terms of not less than three years each, shall, upon conviction of a felony committed in this state after the passage of this act, be deemed to be an habitual criminal, and shall be punished by imprisonment in the state prison for twenty-five years, *provided, however*, that if the person so convicted shall show to the satisfaction of the court before which such conviction was had that he was released from imprisonment upon either of said sentences, upon a pardon granted upon the ground that he was innocent, such conviction and sentence shall not be considered as such under this act.

"Section 2. When it shall appear to the governor and council that any person sentenced to the state prison as an habitual criminal has reformed, they may issue to him a permit to be at liberty during the remainder of his term of sentence, upon such conditions as they deem best; and they may revoke said permit at any time previous to its expiration. The violation by the holder of a permit, granted as aforesaid, of any of the terms or conditions of such permit, or the violation of any of the laws of this Commonwealth, shall of itself make void said permit.

"Section 3. When any permit granted under the provisions of

the preceding section has been revoked, or has become void as aforesaid, the governor shall issue his warrant authorizing the arrest of the holder of said permit and his return to said state prison. Said warrant may be served by any officer authorized to serve criminal process in any county in this Commonwealth. The holder of said permit, when returned to said state prison as aforesaid, shall be detained therein according to the terms of his original sentence; and in computing the period of his confinement the time between his release upon said permit and his return to the state prison shall not be taken to be any part of the term of the sentence."

It is doubtless better to err in legislation affecting criminals on the side of lenity rather than on that of undue severity; and it has been clearly pointed out by Mr. Fay that many notorious professional criminals have escaped indictment under this act by reason of its specification of the terms of previous sentences. A habitual criminal who had a record of several terms of imprisonment could not be prosecuted under this act unless two of the terms were for three years each or longer. But the act has been, nevertheless, of far reaching benefit to the state from the deterrent effect which it has undoubtedly exercised on the commission of felonies as well as on the entrance of criminals from other states. From the point of view of the reformer also, a sentence to a long term, which may be reduced upon the demonstration of amendment of character and conduct, is practically essential to the production of any considerable change in hardened criminals. Dr. E. C. Wines expresses the general judgment when he says that long sentences are "indispensable for reformation."

It is true that this law is very much disliked by habitual criminals, but that fact does not operate to condemn it in the eyes of good citizens, if the criminal has no better justification for his dislike than the consideration that the law may prevent him from robbing his neighbors for a period of twenty-five years. The same criminal is equally disgusted with the application of the Bertillon system to prevent him from concealing his identity from the police and the courts; but the extension of this system has rapidly progressed in spite of his objections. In Ohio and Illinois the punishment of habitual criminals is imprisonment for life; and, if it is certain that these criminals are incorrigible, no solid reason can be urged against a life-long restraint from stealing, robbing, blackmailing or murdering.

In this conclusion it is immaterial whether their criminal proclivities and characteristics are derived from those of the primitive man, as Lombroso contends, or inherited from their parents and grandparents, or acquired through debasing environment or any other source or impulse. Even should it be demonstrated that any such criminal is morally or mentally irresponsible, it is none the less proper and necessary that he should be restrained from preying upon society. The investigations of Dugdale and others who have gone far toward demonstrating that crime is largely the result of a diseased condition of mind and body, do not operate to impair the right of society to protect itself against the commission of crimes by anybody, whether he be insane or sane, diseased or healthy. If expert examiners should determine, for example, that Oliver Curtis Perry, the remarkable train robber, has been of unsound mind for years and is now unquestionably insane, it is none the less certain that he should be strictly confined. An insane criminal is likely to be even more dangerous than a sane criminal, and there should certainly be no less restraint of his freedom to molest society.

It is, however, undoubtedly the duty of our enlightened civilization to pursue the investigation of the causes of crime with the best ability which it can command, and to govern its treatment of criminals in accordance with its advancing knowledge. It has already separated and classified criminals to accord with distinctions of age, sex and degree of criminality. It has further sought to distinguish the insane from the sane criminal, and provided asylums for the treatment of those criminals who are adjudged to be lunatics or idiots. But it has not yet gone far in the extension of its researches along the lines followed by Dugdale nor in any practical application of his conclusions. A criminal may be gravely diseased in mind and constitutionally without exhibiting mania that will ensure his committal to an asylum, or bodily ailment that will send him to a hospital. The treatment of prisoners which is intentionally equitable in its uniformity, may be seriously inequitable and unsuitable in its lack of discrimination.

The Abbé Moreau, who has given particular consideration to the classification and treatment of criminals, advocates the opening of what he terms "penitentiary hospitals" for the reception of criminals who are determined to be constitutionally diseased in mind or body, but are not adjudged to be technically insane. In these hospitals he would have pure air, abundant light, and a moral atmosphere of all good and healing influences. Separation from any depraved companionship is an essential condition for reformation in his theory of treatment. So his ideal hospitals would have a cell for each inmate, whose solitary confinement would be carefully regulated by skilled physicians.

We note this suggestion simply as an instance of advancing discrimination, without undertaking to pass judgment upon its propriety or utility. It may be well to observe, however, that separation from depraved companionship is undoubtedly a good thing for anybody, but the abbé's specific of solitary confinement to secure this separation will be sharply questioned by other authorities. He would apply it with far more rigor to professional thieves. If they are susceptible of reformation, they will reach it, as he holds, only by isolation in separate cells. "Those who are not susceptible will become idiotic or die. Shall we weep for these?" It is certainly remarkable that such a person as the Abbé Georges Moreau should deliberately urge the adoption of a course of treatment that in the cases of hardened habitual criminals would lead to idiocy or premature death.

Besides its advance in the good work of classification and separation of criminals, our modern civilization has addressed itself earnestly to the undertaking of reformation. The provision of separate prisons for men, women and children, and the suppression of vicious intercourse and association are now regarded as simply a basis for the possible upbuilding of good principles and habits. It is considered that youthful criminals, at least, whose vicious propensities are still immature and not hardened, must be susceptible of reformation or improvement to some extent. Our state reformatories are a recognition of the fact that idleness, the lack of instilled habits of industry and thrift, the inability to earn a living by honest, skilled artisanship—are fruitful causes of crime; and their courses of treatment and training are designed to drill their young inmates in useful and honest occupations. And, in general, it is now the design of our criminal laws and establishments to unite reform and punishment.

For the extension of the original separation and classification, at the time of the committal to prison, progressive classification and the systematic offer of incentives for improvement in habits and conduct have been strongly advocated by experienced wardens and other authorities, and these reforms have been already introduced to a considerable extent. "Nothing can be done with men," observes Dr. Wines, "except through the will, and the will can be reached only through the intelligence and the heart. For this, religion in all its freedom and power is necessary; and, in the case of prisoners, progressive classification, whereby the motives which control men in free society and urge them to industry and virtue, may act steadily and effectively upon them, determining to good the choices of their will and the actions of their life." Warden Bridges of the Massachusetts state prison recommended, three years ago, in his report, the classification of prisoners as far as possible. He would make the quality of their food and clothing as well as the enjoyment of privileges, dependent upon their general deportment, to be determined by the warden. He suggested also the propriety of recommending the enactment of a parole system for prisoners.

In a recently published statement the same warden has strongly emphasized the necessity of the employment of prisoners, in order to discharge the obligation of reform imposed by our laws. "Reform," he says, "is an impossibility without work, and that this end of sending men to prison may be best accomplished, labor is a prime necessity." The conclusions reached by the wardens of the principal prisons in other states are in general accord with this position. Employment of some kind is held to be absolutely necessary as a preventive of crime, melancholia and insanity, and it is further essential as a training to enable a convict to make a living honestly after his discharge. The instilling of habits of steady industry, and the healthful exercise and development of the faculties of the body and mind, are regarded as the most stable foundations of reform.

So in some prisons it is designed to carry the education of the convicts considerably beyond the training for some useful trade; and Warden Sage of Sing Sing states that he is now considering the introduction of a university extension course of lectures and instruction. Commissioner Burtis of Kings County, New York, suggests the formation of classes for instruction in mechanical trades and exercise. Warden Thayer of Dannemora prison, New York, and Warden Schneider of Menard prison, Illinois, urge that prisoners should be employed in making articles needed for state and municipal institutions. The building of roads is advocated as an advisable and healthful employment by Warden Grimes of Snake Hill prison, New Jersey.

In view of the intelligent expert consideration that is now directed to the treatment of convicts in the prisons of this country, there is substantial assurance of satisfactory progress toward the goal of feasible reform; but we must expect that this progress will be hampered by the opposition to the conflict of convict labor with that of free workingmen. Committees of the labor unions have warmly protested against even the present limited industrial training in the reformatories for young criminals. It is urged by them that this education operates practically as a handicap to honest apprentices who are obliged to pay or to give their services gratuitously to their employers, for the sake of gaining the same proficiency which the state provides for criminals together with food and lodging. It is further contended that a grave danger to society is involved in the entrance of convicts, after their discharge, into the ranks of workingmen who often have open access to houses in plying their trades. Criminals, it is argued, will make a pretence of reform in order to obtain better openings for plunder; and their thievish practices will seriously discredit the reputation of their honest fellow craftsmen. By such representations and the broad underlying resolution to keep convict labor out of competition with free labor, the undertakings for reform have been embarrassed and restricted.

It is probable, however, that the considerations of humanity toward the convict, the diminution of crime and the welfare of society at large, will secure, before many years, a fairly adequate provision for the useful employment and reform of the criminals in our state prisons and reformatories throughout the country. But this is only a fractional part of a comprehensive undertaking to diminish the spread of crime. It is no less necessary to grapple firmly, intelligently, and unitedly with the problem of the reduction of the number of criminals whom our penal institutions are required to punish and reform. It is obvious that the perplexity and difficulty of adequate reform in our prisons would be greatly diminished if they were not so often over-crowded with convicts. Doubtless these impediments may be largely removed by building more prisons and maintaining more costly establishments; but this remedy is, at best, an unfortunate necessity.

It seems to us that the best efforts of reformers to-day may wisely be directed toward the securing of such environment and training as will nip in the bud the criminal proclivities of the young people who will otherwise furnish a great share of the annual supply to our prisons. It is immaterial to this work of reform whether the budding rascal is largely a product of a diseased or contaminated stock, or whether he is becoming a criminal by force of temptations, idleness, or degraded environment. The method of treatment in individual cases may be fitly varied; but the urgent need of the application of some adequate, systematic treatment appears to us to be obvious.

The establishment in Massachusetts of what are known as probation officers has undoubtedly been of marked service in checking the flow to our state reformatory and houses of correction.

In 1878, a law was enacted by the state requiring the appointment of a probation officer by the city of Boston. His duties, as laid down by the statute, were to attend the sessions of the criminal courts in Suffolk County; to investigate the cases of persons charged with or convicted of crimes and misdemeanors and to recommend to the courts the placing on probation of such persons as might be reasonably expected to reform without imprisonment. He was also required to visit the offenders placed on probation at his suggestion, and to render such assistance and encouragement as would tend to prevent them from again offending.

The working of this enactment was so plainly beneficial that it was extended, in 1880, to authorize the appointment of a probation officer by any city and town in the state; and, in 1891, this provision was made mandatory and the power of appointment was vested in the justices of the municipal, police, or district courts. It is enjoined upon these probation officers to inquire into the nature of every criminal case brought before the courts under whose jurisdiction they act and to recommend the placing upon probation of any convicted person who may, in their judgment, be reformed by this treatment. The courts may place any such person in the care of a probation officer for such time and upon such conditions as may seem proper. The utility of this provision is already well demonstrated. It has operated to diminish considerably the number of prisoners whom the state and the counties would otherwise be required to support; and it has saved thousands of young offenders from contamination and stigma.

There should be, however, some well organized and comprehensive coöperation to anticipate the service of the probation officers. Our churches and schools and public libraries and reading rooms and various associations for humane purposes are all enlisted as helpers in the great work of rearing children to become good citizens. The slums of our great cities have been largely purged and obliterated. With every succeeding year more devotion is given to the diminution of misery, vice and crime. But with all the noble work that has been done, it is obvious that unremitting and greater effort is sorely needed.

Superintendent Brockway of the Elmira reformatory is strongly urging for this end the extension of the service of the public schools. He would have them supply an education for "a definitely determined walk in life, for earning and study and training,—in short, no longer for a general purpose of development to fit children for anything and everything, but to qualify the boys for some thing in particular, for the walks in life they should and probably will follow." This push for physical and industrial training is in the direct line of the design of the present state reformatories, but Mr. Brockway would secure like establishments without waiting for the commission of crimes and the consequent degradation and stigma. This recommendation appears to us to be worthy of the most careful consideration. It may be considered that appropriate physical, mental, moral and manual training of the classes of children, who are now furnishing the chief new supply to our prisons, can properly and advantageously be undertaken by our municipalities.

If the supply of criminals to our prisons is diminished by wise provisions, the outflow will necessarily be decreased and, in so far, it will give less concern to society. But while present conditions continue, the discharged convict is a subject that may well enlist the most careful investigation and consideration. In his Jean Valjean, Victor Hugo has painted with masterly vividness the heart-breaking experience of a released prisoner, roaming from door to door in search of shelter and food. Hugo's convict had some little money in his pocket; but the common shop-keepers and inn keepers shrank from him in fear and loathing, and the outcast could hardly buy bread to eat by the roadside.

There is probably the exaggeration of a poet in this delineation, and in this country a discharged prisoner will find people, without difficulty, who will be pleased to entertain him with meals and lodging while he has money to pay them; and will not annoy him with probing questions. But steady, honest employment—a want scarcely less urgent than food and shelter—is, unfortunately, often beyond his reach, even if he has certificates of good conduct in prison and sanguine assurances of his reformation. While so many men with untarnished records, good education, and skill in the arts are seeking employment, it can hardly be expected that good engagements should be readily found by men whose latest reference is a state prison or, at best, a reformatory.

So it happens that thousands of discharged convicts drift back, disheartened, into their old ways of life, even when they leave prison with good intentions. The habitual criminal may be beyond the control of any reform influences which surround him in prison, and may turn to crime, as soon as he is released, without any effort toward amendment. Still, even such hardened rascals as Chauncey Johnson have repeatedly expressed their bitter regret that they could find no opening of honest employment. "I would rather earn five dollars honestly," said Johnson once, with apparent sincerity, "than get fifty dollars by stealing; but I have wasted my chances and my life. Who wants to hire an old thief while he can get good young men to work for him?"

There should be no fluttering sentimentality in dealing with this grave concern. Anything approaching the coddling of convicts is, in our judgment, a serious misdirection of charity. A discharged prisoner should not be suffered to contract the conceit that he has any more claim upon the charity of the community or the funds of the state than any other member of our common society. Under no circumstances should he be encouraged or sustained in any disposition to roam about in lazy idleness. If he is an incorrigible loafer, he should be promptly committed to a house of correction as a vagabond, and, if practicable, forced to earn his bread. But when discharged convicts are honestly anxious to get their living by honest work, helping hands should be outstretched to them. At best, they are terribly handicapped in their search for employment by the brand of their prison record. No rational or feasible provision will put them on the same footing as that proudly occupied by the poor man who has preserved his integrity through every struggle and temptation. The criminal must expect and endure the penalty of crime, not only in his prison sentence, but in the brand that will not be cast off with his convict's garb. He must form and sustain the resolution to stick to honesty in the face of every discouragement, as the sole plank that can save him from sinking to degradation worse than death.

But while every care should be taken not to sap the manhood of a discharged convict, not to make him feel that he is an object of charity and that his crime has been fully atoned for by his submission to his sentence, it is further the concern of society to diminish the number of discharged convicts who are annually committing new crimes and returning to our prisons. If this can be done by a continuance of oversight and possible provision of work, in extreme cases, it would be cheaper and better than the expenditure for the arrest, conviction and support of such convicts by the county or state.

In the latest report of Massachusetts Commissioners of Prisons, the agent for aiding discharged convicts observes: "When a discharged prisoner loses himself in the community, and does not again appear on the prison records, it is an evidence that he has reformed. A man who is sincere in his desire to reform tries to do this. The right thing to do is to aid him, at this time, not grudgingly, but with all necessary facilities wherewith to make a respectable start in the world." The extent of the appropriate aid is broadly stated, but not precisely defined. It appears to be, in the judgment of the agent, necessarily a matter of discretion and variation. A thorough knowledge of the records and character of discharged convicts is practically essential to the proper administration of any plan of oversight and aid.

After all is done that is proper and feasible for the amelioration of the condition of criminals and the advance of their reform, there will still be forever a great gulf fixed between the position of the criminal and that of the honest man. The rascal can hope, at best, for only a few years of possession of the fruits of his rascality. His anticipated enjoyment will be racked by fears and haunted by shame. He will be driven to hunt for cover with the slinking fox or to fly from the face of civilization with the savage wolf. He will find his dearly bought dissipations palling and sickening. He will be a pariah from whom good men and women will shrink. He will have no true friends, no helpful companionship. His home will be blasted and his children will wish that they had no father, or, still worse, will learn to follow his example. It is for this that he has bartered his good name and all that is really good and pleasant in life, and what more can he reasonably expect beyond a convict's cell and a felon's grave? This experience and this fate have been for generations unnumbered the common lot of the criminals comprised under the head of Our Rival the Rascal.

There is no fascination in unmasked crime. The only risk of allurement is through ignorance and delusion. So it has been our aim to show in the clear, colorless light of truth what a criminal's life really is. Such an exhibit cannot fail to impress the most heedless. Surely no young man who retains a remnant of honest resolution, or even of common sense, would be tempted for a moment to put himself in the place of any one of the rascals whose wretched career has been sketched in our story.

SAFEGUARDS.

IN the preceding pages of this volume we have considered Our Rival the Rascal in his manifold phases. We have seen how he has plotted to outwit the ingenuity of those who have devised methods of protection against his criminal attacks; and how he has striven to undermine or overcome the obstacles which have been successively opposed to him. Interwoven with this story of his struggle is the story of the development of the safeguards, which has followed each step of his advance in skill and equipment for attack.

It has been throughout this work one of the authors' main purposes to indicate the precautions which should be adopted by the community in order to secure the greatest possible protection against the Rascal's alert brain and cunning hand; but the insertion of any detailed or adequate description of the inventions which constitute the chief material safeguards, would have necessarily interrupted the flow of the narrative.

The development of these inventions is, however, of such interest and importance that we cannot fitly dismiss it with such incidental mention as has been made in the foregoing chapters. We propose, therefore, in closing, to give a fairly comprehensive description of the latest and best safeguards, serving to relieve, assist or diminish the labors of the defenders of society in the suppression of crime. It would be manifestly impossible to include within the necessary limits of this chapter every device worthy of commendation, or every variation of an approved device. We have therefore confined ourselves to such devices or systems as seem to present features of special interest to the reader and which are of demonstrated and recognized value in the protection of property. In our mention of safes, vaults, locks, and other devices it must be clearly understood that no reflection is intended upon similar devices of approved merit by other manufacturers which are not herein specifically described.

It is doubtful if the inventive ingenuity of man has been more taxed than in the struggle between the burglar and the safe manufacturer. Certainly nowhere else is the conflict between honesty and dishonesty more thoroughly illustrated. The skilled burglar has compelled the recognition of the fact that what man can construct, man, with sufficient time and skill, can destroy; and the prospective gain from bank burglaries is so large that the really skilled cracksman seems to consider no preliminary effort too great to be undertaken in the hope of such reward. In the Dorchester (England) Bank robbery in the early part of this century, when locks were the only safeguard and before burglars were skilled in the use of explosives, the burglars were in the house ninety-two nights before they succeeded in opening all the locks by false keys which they fitted to lock and relock the doors. The same untiring zeal is a distinguishing mark of the burglar of to-day and although wonderful advances have been made in safe construction, the introduction of powerful explosives as agents for robbery has rendered safe cracking, where possible, much quicker work than the opening of the earlier forms of safes.

DEPOSITORY FOR CROWN JEWELS OF SCOTLAND (1707).

When we look upon the latest triumphs of invention in the burglar proof safe, it seems almost incredible that they are the development of a comparatively short period of time. Even iron safes are of quite modern date and fire-proof safes

THE BURGLAR PROOF SAFE. 393

were not introduced until the beginning of this century. Prior to that time the only safes designed for protection against burglary were oak chests, secured by one or more locks, while the only protection against fire was in brick or stone closets with plain iron doors. The fastenings were secured by common warded locks or with iron bands with hasps, staples, and padlocks. A typical safe of this description is the oak chest manufactured as a depository for the crown jewels of Scotland, in 1707. This was secured by three locks, all of which were forced open in the presence of the royal commissioners in 1818, the keys having been lost. We learn from this that as late as 1818 these simple locks (which could

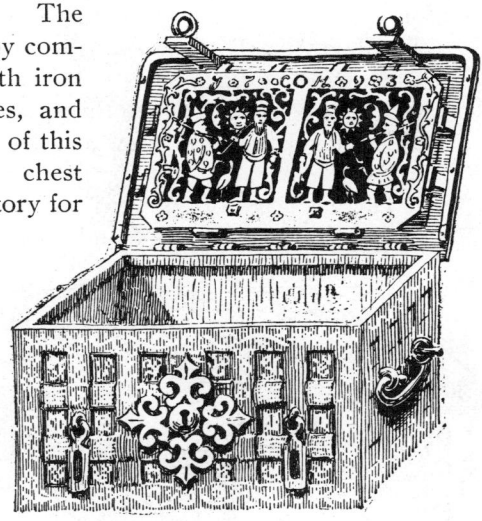

"FOREIGN COFFER."

easily have been picked by a bent skewer) were considered too intricate to be opened by a common locksmith or mechanic. Such safeguards appear puerile in contrast with the intricate lock devices and massive walls of the modern safe, but it must be remembered that, if the construction was simple, the thieves of that day were unskilled and possessed of only rude tools, and the oaken chest of a century ago was fully as secure against robbery as many so-called burglar proof safes of to-day.

The first iron safes were the so-called foreign coffers which were originally brought into England from France and Germany. Those were made of hammered iron, rolled iron not having been introduced at that time. The security of their fastening was only the rude lock of the oaken chests, multiplied by the number of bolts. If there were twenty of these, they could be picked as easily as one. The accompanying illustration shows a fine example of this rudimentary iron safe. It had strong handles, a multiple lock, throwing eight bolts on the inside, two dogs at the back and staples for padlocks. The bolts in the lid were covered by a beautifully chased plate, and the escutcheon over the key-hole had to be moved with a turn screw. When this sprang up, the lock was opened by inserting the turn screw as a lever through the bow of the key.

There is no record of a cast or wrought iron safe being made in England prior to 1800 and they were certainly not in com-

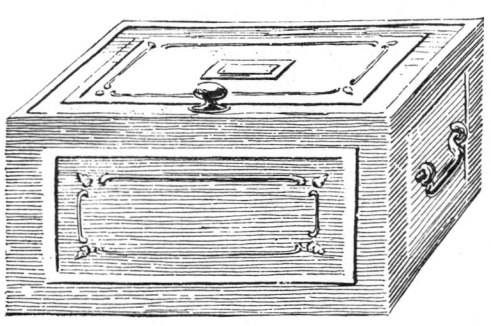

EARLY CAST-IRON SAFE.

mercial use before that time. The first English patent for a safe was issued to Richard Scott, in 1801, and this safe was mainly designed as proof against fire, but, as it consisted of an outer and inner casing of iron, filled with a non-conducting substance, it seems also to have marked an advance in protection against burglars. These safes were known as double chests. In 1829, James Conner, of New York city, constructed a crude safe of this type for the security of his own wealth but not for the benefit of the general public. The long line of improvements in the fire-proof qualities of safes do not enter into the scope of this chapter and it is probably not worth while to enter into a detailed account of the large number of burglar proof devices. Evidently the first progress made by safe breakers beyond the picking or bursting of locks was in the use of tools to cut through the iron walls, for the first improvements in burglar proof devices seem to have been directed against this danger. Many have been the devices patented and at each advance in construction the ingenuity of the burglar proved equal to the genius of the inventor. Hardened iron was cut by better tools, steel was pierced by diamond tipped drills, or shattered by blows, and in 1867, it was demonstrated that Franklinite, a particularly hard form of iron which was supposed to be impenetrable, could, after chemical treatment, be drilled.

The use of gunpowder to blow open the doors was early resorted to and many inventions were patented to guard against this danger; but after safes had been constructed so as to be practically impregnable to this force, came the use of giant powder, then dynamite, and recently high grade liquid nitro-glycerine, which the burglars successively turned to account in their handicraft, and the enormous blasting power of these agents necessitated at once new methods of construction.

Among the various inventions, which were long in use in modified forms in safes of the best construction, may be mentioned Chubb's device (1865), placing the door in a recess and providing an extra bar to prevent its being wedged open; Thompson's (1865) recess door with an interior flange behind which the bolts shot, also to prevent wedging; and Parrish, Thatcher and Glasscock's series of dovetail projections on the door frame for corresponding mortises in the frame, with a bead around the door fitting a groove in the casing. The invention by Chatwood, in 1862, of iron-steel, consisting of a plate of steel welded between two plates of iron, seems to have been the first step toward the chrome steel plate which is to-day considered the most impregnable material for construction. This constant warfare and development should be kept in mind in judging of the merits of safes to-day. Some of the companies now manufacturing safes in this country have been many years in the business and have constantly progressed in their construction. Hence, it will be seen that even the safes of the best companies cannot be relied upon except they are of the latest pattern and contain all the improved devices. It must also be remembered that it is unnecessary to build burglar proof work for security against honest men, and useless to try to deceive skilled burglars by old-fashioned and poorly-constructed vaults.

It is safe to say that many expert bank burglars have had experience in the works of some safe company and know much more about the security or weakness of a safe than the owner can be expected to know. It is the falsest kind of economy to award safe construction to the cheapest bidder, for there are many ways of cheapening construction which simply mean the elimination of the very elements which give security. It is safe to say that many a job is thus awarded which becomes a temptation to an honest workman to turn burglar. He sees the construction of a safe so cheaply made that he knows it can be easily robbed; and the spies of the burglars keep constant watch of the safe factories and are always ready to seize an opportunity for the coöperation of any of its workmen. Until business men learn that no real security can be found in anything other than the best constructed work, safe robberies will continue to be too frequent.

An object lesson of the value of first-class safe work can be found in the attempted robbery of the treasurer's vaults of one of the large Railroad Companies a few years ago. The burglars penetrated without difficulty through the outer doors, which were intended mainly for protection against fire, and then discovered that the inner safe had been recently fitted by the Diebold Safe Company with new doors of chrome steel secured by their latest anti-dynamite device. In disgust they scratched upon the enamel the significant letters "N. G." and departed without wasting further time upon a safe which they knew to be impregnable to their assaults.

The modern burglar proof safe of the best type to-day is

THE BURGLAR PROOF SAFE.

built from the outside inward from alternate sections of welded five-ply chrome steel and iron burglar-proof plate and fibrous iron fastened together by the short screw process. Experience has proven that the weak point of steel lies in the fact that, while its hardened surface gives security against cutting or drilling, the crystallization of the iron into steel, by destroying its fibrous nature, renders it brittle enough to be shattered by sharp blows. Iron, of course, while secure against this method of attack, can be quickly cut or drilled by good tools. The greatest combined strength against drill, chisel and hammer has only been attained in the chrome steel plate originated and manufactured by the Chrome Steel Works of Brooklyn, N. Y., which is used by the leading safe makers in their best work and which has received the unqualified indorsement of the experts of the United States Government. This is made by welding into a solid plate two layers of chrome steel (a tempered alloy of the metals chromium and iron) alternately between three layers of tough fibrous iron. To penetrate such plates it would be necessary to cut each layer of iron and shatter each ply of steel, which cannot be done by the means accessible to the burglar.

In the method of construction used by the Diebold Safe and Lock Company, which we have selected as a

MODERN BURGLAR PROOF BANKER'S SAFE (DIEBOLD).

type to illustrate the burglar proof safe of to-day, the entire outside of the safe is made in four segments of Brooklyn chrome steel known as full angle caps. This form of construction avoids the use of panel plates which might be wedged and stripped off. The edges of these segments are hand-ground to an exact metallic contact and are held together by the next layer of plates (also of five-ply chrome steel), which are screwed firmly to the outer segment and overlap all joints, coming flush with the angles. Next follows another set of chrome steel angles. In this manner the safe can be built to any desired thickness, angles and square plates following each other alternately from the outside to the inside of the safe.

All of these plates are secured by short screws put in at an average of from six to eight inches apart (cèntre to centre), no screw penetrating more than two plates, and no screw or joint in the whole series of plates coming opposite another. These screws are made of twisted seven-ply chrome steel and iron, as impervious to a drill as the plates themselves. The screws which secure the second plate to the outside angles only penetrate through three layers of the chrome steel plate, leaving the ends covered by one ply of steel and iron. The outside screws are thus blind and cannot be located from the surface, but the third plate so covers the head end of the screws that they could not be driven in even if found. Every joint is hand-ground to such a perfect metallic contact that it cannot be penetrated by water.

The door is built, in the same manner, of continuous plates, each the full height and width of the door. It is closed with steps or flanges, tenons and grooves, thus interlocking each plate of the door and jambs when shut. Of necessity each of these plates must be ground, after tempering, to a metallic air-tight joint when the door is closed, in order to prevent the introduction of liquid explosive, now so successfully in use by burglars on old-style work which is file-fitted. In the square door the most vulnerable point is the corner where it

THE BURGLAR PROOF SAFE.   399

might be possible to chip off the steel and cut the iron ply sufficiently to make a small opening for the introduction of explosives, and many successful burglaries have thus been performed. This weakness is obviated by the modern square door with full round corners, of from three and one-half inches to four inches radius, exactly fitting fillets and jambs. All modern safe doors have full tenons and grooves extending entirely around the edges and jambs of the door and are closed by cam or duplex hinges, operated with heavy cam levers or worm gear wheels with linked lever connections, thus seating and closing the door squarely in position and into the tenons and grooves. In addition to this, the grooves into which the tenons project are packed with elastic felt packing, and in safes of the most recent date an elastic metallic packing, which is impervious to the action of acids, has been used. This packing is also used on some of the steps or flanges. The joints are hand ground and fitted so close that a sheet of paper interfering will be cut as smooth as by a razor.

No spindle can be used which will be absolutely burglar proof to the introduction of liquid explosives. Therefore, in the finest safes, the spindle, whether with or without time lock, has given place to an automatic bolt-throwing device. In small chests, however, where the automatic device cannot be worked, the cut-off spindle furnishes reasonable security. This spindle is built half through and offset through the centre of the thickness of the door with a gearing of cogwheels to the inner end which penetrates to the locking device. This construction necessitates two explosions to reach the locking device, whereas spindles built with steps or revolving plates have direct connection through the entire thickness of the door. On safes using the cut-off spindle the Diebold company attach their patent anti-dynamite device by means of which each explosion only locks the bolts tighter. The Diebold Company also manufacture their own time locks and automatic devices, a practice which concentrates upon the makers all responsibility for the proper working of all parts of the safe or vault.

In concluding this brief sketch of the modern burglar proof safe, it may be well to add yet another word of caution to what we have already said here and elsewhere in regard to the choice of a depository for valuables. A burglar proof safe is not designed to be fire-proof and should, of course, be placed within a fire-proof vault or closet. A fire-proof safe does not claim to be burglar proof and should be used only for the preservation of papers against fire. An improperly constructed or out-of-date "burglar proof" safe furnishes little or no protection against fire or burglary. To those who need a burglar-proof safe nothing should be acceptable except the best. To those who cannot afford such a safe, the safe deposit vaults in all our large cities and the bank vaults in smaller places offer the best security at a reasonable price.

The first public safe deposit vaults in the United States were built in 1865 for Col. Francis H. Jenks and were located at 140 and 142 Broadway, New York. The lowest rental charged for safes in these vaults was twenty dollars a year. Two years later Col. Henry Lee built the Union Safe Deposit Vaults, the first of their class in Boston, at 40 State Street. These vaults were opened for the reception of securities on the first of January, 1868, and have since furnished continuous accommodation and protection to depositors.

The main vault is of granite about two feet in thickness, forming an enclosure thirty-eight feet long, twenty-nine feet wide, and nine feet high. Its ceiling is composed of four courses of strongly cemented brick, supported by heavy iron girders set in the granite walls. The only access to this vault is through a single passage-way, closed by double doors of chilled steel with combination locks. This passage opens into a corridor extending completely around the vault, with an entrance into the outer office. A heavy iron door secures this entrance, and watchmen guard the passages and patrol the

SAFE DEPOSIT VAULTS.

corridor night and day. At frequent intervals they are required to register their rounds and test the electric communications leading to the nearest district police station.

Within the main vault five iron vaults or cases are ranged on iron supports between the floor and ceiling. These cases are constructed with chilled steel doors and strong locks, and contain compartments, each of which is closed by an iron door with a double lock. A special, unduplicated key, furnished to each depositor, opens one lock and the other is opened by a special key held by the custodians of the vaults. This provision for security has proved so thorough and practically impenetrable that the only addition required since the construction of the vaults has been the application of the Holmes system of electric protection, which was installed as soon as its merits were demonstrated.

The superior security afforded by vaults of this character was soon realized and numerous additional vaults were constructed in all our large cities to keep pace with the demand for accommodation. In Boston to-day there are not less than nine of these special safe deposit vaults, beside the regular bank vaults, and all are of well approved designs and practically impregnable. To illustrate the most modern methods of construction, we shall describe one of the latest built of these vaults.

In 1875, the Equitable Life Insurance Society of New York built in their building on Milk Street, Boston, one of the most approved vaults of that day, which was leased by a Massachusetts corporation, the Security Safe Deposit Company of Boston. This vault has recently been reconstructed to meet increased demands and to make an advance in safe and vault construction.

The new vault, constructed in 1895, consists of a cage twenty feet wide and forty feet long, built of six-inch steel rails and lined with four inches of welded, five-ply, chrome steel and iron burglar proof plate. This is backed up by a twenty-inch wall of hardest burned brick. Each vestibule and its doors weigh between fifteen and twenty tons. The outer doors weigh about seven tons; are eight feet high by four feet wide, and ten inches thick, and, being locked by an automatic device operated by a three chronometer time-lock, have no holes whatever through the door. The inner door is secured by two locks, the combinations of which are known only to the president and the superintendent of the company. In case of the illness or absence of either, the combination is entrusted to two directors and changed on the return to duty of the regular officials. In this steel vault are six thousand small boxes renting from ten dollars to one hundred dollars a year, according to size.

The foundations of the steel vault extend two feet below the level of the floor and rest upon a lower vault, the floor sides and ends of which are also lined with four inches of chrome steel plate. In this vault are about twenty-five hundred safes of various sizes renting at the same prices as those in the vault above. Inside of each vault are two uniformed custodians whose sole duty is to identify the depositors and admit them to their safes. The locks upon the boxes are manufactured by Messrs. L. L. Bates & Co., of Boston, who have for many years made a specialty of safe deposit locks and who are also experts on bank and safe-lock work.

These locks are so constructed that they can only be opened by the use of two keys, one of which, a master key, is in the possession of the custodian. This key having been inserted and turned, the box can then be unlocked by the depositor's key. The lock is automatic; the key cannot be removed until the bolt has been thrown; and the box, when locked by the depositor's key, cannot be opened without the use of both keys.

Another type of lock made by the same firm and requiring three keys to open is used where the safe is rented to an executor, administrator, or trustee whose bonds are furnished by a surety company. In such cases, the keys are distributed so that it is impossible for the lessee of the safe, or the representative of the surety company, to gain access to the contents except in the presence of each other and the custodian of the vault. In all cases, as soon as a box is given up by the lessee, the lock is changed before the safe is again rented.

The vaults are protected by an electric burglar alarm system which is the invention of the superintendent of the company, Capt. Fred G. Storey, and leads directly to the district police station. On closing at night, the alarm is tested by ringing a signal to the police. If there is any ventilator or door left open or other break in the circuit, it instantly rings an alarm and indicates the location of the omission. The windows of the main room in which the vaults are built, are securely protected by heavy bars and the entrance guarded by a stalwart police officer who admits none except those having business.

Thus much for the security of these vaults; in facilities for the convenience of customers they are equally well equipped. Some one hundred small compartments, called coupon rooms, furnish a convenient place to which patrons may take the tin boxes which occupy the inside of each safe and examine their papers in privacy at their leisure. For the use of ladies renting boxes a special room is reserved, with a young woman in attendance, where facilities for correspondence may be found. A handsomely appointed reading room containing a large assortment of the leading newspapers and magazines, domestic and foreign, a telephone, and stock tickers showing New York and Boston quotations, is furnished for the use of the gentlemen. Not the least important feature of these vaults is their system of ventilation, which, while leaving no weak spots in the construction, maintains a perfect supply of fresh air.

In the consideration of the construction of the burglar proof safe it has been stated that the Chrome Steel Works, Brooklyn, N. Y., were the originators and first in this country to manufacture by a secret formula, laminated, welded chrome steel and iron bars, plates and angles for use in bank safe, vault and prison cell construction. After a time imitations of this material began to creep into the market. These have been manufactured under various names, but the originators maintain that they are the only manufacturers of genuine chrome steel in the United States. Their material has been recognized by the leading experts in this line of business as the only uniformly tool proof material obtainable and, after a most thorough examination, the commissioners appointed for this purpose by the United States Government, gave it their unqualified endorsement as the only material which they could with safety advise to be used in the construction of new vaults and safes for the Treasury Department at Washington.

It can be readily seen that if good for work such as described above, it must be fully as good for use in the construction of prison cells, window guards, etc., and it is extensively used for this purpose; but it appears more expensive to make this class of steel by the Brooklyn process than any other of its various imitations, and consequently the Brooklyn material is sold at a higher price. For this reason there is sometimes a hesitancy on the part of county commissioners and committees acting for the public, to insist upon its use, for fear of being considered in a "job" if chrome steel made by the Chrome Steel Works, Brooklyn, N. Y., should be specifically mentioned as the material to be used. This is to be regretted, for certainly it is short sighted economy to use anything except the best material that can be obtained for this purpose. The first cost of material should not influence those who have under consideration the construction of prison cells, in which the worst class of criminals are to be confined, any more than it should influence a committee in charge of the erection of buildings to be used for financial purposes. The experience of many years has proved that such chrome steel cells cannot be cut or sawed by the prisoners, as has frequently been done with all kinds of cells built of ordinary five ply, laminated, or carbonized steel. The uniform tool proof quality of the material should be the first consideration of all parties interested in guarding themselves

BURGLAR ALARM SYSTEMS.

against an attack or the escape of burglars, after which naturally follows the best and most modern form of construction.

In the chapter upon the bank burglar, we have mentioned the security afforded by proper systems of burglar alarms, especially as a safeguard against the use of powerful electric currents which are indicated by Mr. Rodman's experiments as dangerous agents in safe breaking. It is but another evidence of the wonders of science if greater security may be found in the use of a tiny electric wire than in massive walls of steel and intricate lock devices.

This system of protection originated with Edwin Holmes, who, about 1865, invented and patented the first electric burglar alarm, a model of which he then carried about from house to house and sold in this manner. From this small beginning has grown the burglar alarm business in this country and no better idea of its development can be given than by describing the Holmes system of electric protection which is to-day in operation in the largest cities of the United States and in Canada.

The original burglar alarm of Mr. Holmes was for the protection of houses, connecting the doors and windows in such a manner that, if one was opened, a bell at the head of the bed would be rung. It was a crude device but the burglar alarm has kept pace with the marvellous development in electrical science as will be seen from an examination of the system to-day.

About 1870, the first system of electric protection for bank vaults, safes and business buildings, by what is known as the central office system, was established in New York City by Mr. Holmes, and it has since been steadily improved and perfected.

The system to-day consists of a metallic circuit connecting a patented electric lining and other appliances in the protected premises with a tangent galvanometer and other equally sensitive apparatus, which instantly announces even the most minute change in the workings or interruptions of the circuit, at the nearest central station of the company. Each customer has a complete and distinct metallic circuit in no way connected with that of other protected premises. The electric lining, which completely envelops the vault or safe requiring protection, is so constructed that, if punctured, even by a hole the size of a lead-pencil, the alarm at the station will be immediately sounded.

If a bank vault is to be protected, the entire inside surface of the vault is covered with this lining, and a wooden door lined in the same manner covers the entrance to the vault and completes the circuit. A safe is protected by being completely enclosed in an electrically lined wooden cabinet.

The application of the system to stores or business buildings (commonly known as door and window work) consists in running the circuit through each door and window of the protected premises, and is so perfect that a single door or window cannot be opened, broken, or cut through without instantly giving the alarm. On closing such premises at night a signal is sent to the central station and a reply is instantly given, telling the proprietor whether any door or window has been left open or improperly closed. The signalling instrument in the store also denotes this fact automatically, thus giving double assurance of proper closing of the premises.

At the central stations is maintained at all times a competent force of electricians, inspectors, and call men. Immediately on receipt of an alarm an inspector and a callman, thoroughly armed and equipped and supplied with keys to police signal boxes, go at once to the premises. Their first duty is to announce their safe arrival by signalling back to the central station. If such signal is not received within a reasonable time, another relay is sent to the aid of the first. Each inspector is thoroughly familiar with all parts of the protected premises within his district and knows all persons who can reasonably be expected to be about the place after business hours. As a further means of identification, however, each inspector answering an alarm carries with him an instruction card containing the signature of all persons having authority to visit the premises at such times. Any person thus found must give his signature on a call ticket carried by the inspector. If this exactly corresponds with the signature on the instruction card, and no suspicious circumstances exist, it is considered a proper identification and the matter is merely reported to the proprietor on the following day. Otherwise the suspected person is brought to the central station where he must properly identify himself or be turned over to the police.

This system not only prevents burglary but gives every customer, once a week, a record of every time his store, vault, or safe is opened and the exact opening and closing time of the premises for each day, thus showing any irregularity. Each customer designates who shall open and close his vaults or store, and each of these persons is supplied with a private number by which he can signal to the central station. Immediately upon opening the premises in the morning, the central station responds to the alarm by giving a challenge signal to which the authorized person replies by his private signal. The same method is followed on closing the premises. This challenge signal is sent and its answer accepted only at the regular hours of opening and closing. At any other time no challenge signal is given but an inspector visits the premises. Thus, if an unauthorized person gains knowledge of the signal, it is useless to him and all irregularities of authorized persons are reported. It will be seen that this system furnishes great protection against defalcation or embezzlement as such acts are usually committed outside of business hours.

All fire alarms in the city are sounded at the central station and if, on investigation, any danger threatens a customer's premises, they are guarded and a carriage is sent for the proprietor or his designated representative.

The Holmes system of electric protection has been thoroughly tested by the most expert electricians and has been highly endorsed by United States Government experts. It is extensively used by banks, safety deposit vaults, jewellers, and large business houses in all large cities in this country. This system is also applicable to the safe or vault of the bank in a country town, in which case the alarm apparatus can be located at either a police station, janitor's apartments, or at any point where there is some one on duty who will give attention to an alarm. As the country bank is often selected by the bank burglar as the special object of his attention, it will be seen that such a system of protection is very valuable. The cost of protecting the safe or vault of a country bank in such a manner is small in proportion to the security afforded. It is claimed by the company that no successful burglary has ever occurred upon premises protected by its system and, so far as we have been able to learn, this statement seems justified. It has rendered valuable assistance to the police in the detection and arrest of many criminals and, considering the security of its protection, is not unduly expensive.

The latest system of protection against loss by burglary—and probably one with which many people in this country are not yet familiar—is that of Insurance against Burglary. Our previous chapters have shown fully what burglary is and how desperate are the class of men operating in this branch of crime. While insurance against this great menace to the safety of property is a new thing to this country, it has been carried on in Europe for years by large companies and is there regarded as of equal importance with many other forms of insurance.

The introduction of comprehensive burglary insurance into the United States may fairly be credited to Mr. Howard S. Wheelock, of Boston, who, after studying thoroughly the principles of the system as formulated by the experience of the companies of Europe, secured, in 1890, a charter for a burglary insurance company in Hartford, Connecticut, which, however, was not put into operation. In 1895, Mr. William H. Brewster, of Boston, with the coöperation of Mr. Wheelock, effected the organization of the New England Burglary Insurance Company of Boston, the first company of its kind chartered in Massachusetts, and at the present date the only company authorized to write burglary insurance in this commonwealth, and the only exclusively burglary insurance company operating throughout the United States through agencies established at all important centres.

Although the company's policies are for insurance against burglary, they are not held to the narrow lines of the technical legal definition of burglary, but can be made comprehensive enough to cover all classes of robbery except by defalcation. From an insurance point of view, and as the business is conducted by the "New England," a burglar can enter a bank, warehouse, store, dwelling or stable and damage the building itself and carry off its contents. In the event of loss by burglary the company first satisfies the claim of the policy-holder and then employs special agencies for the capture of the criminal, realizing that a wholesome fear of the company in the mind of the burglar promises the greatest immunity from loss to the clients whose property it insures. On all banks, stores and other business buildings covered by its policies a warning device, giving notice that the premises are protected by the company, must be prominently displayed, and the use of the same device is recommended on private houses, but is left optional with the occupant. It is believed that the notice conveying the assurance of vigorous prosecution will prevent many burglaries.

To illustrate the value of such a system of insurance, tables were recently prepared from estimates given by chiefs of police, heads of fire departments, superintendents of detective agencies, and standard works on criminology, showing the number of arrests for burglary and alarms for fires in seven of the large cities of the United States covering a period of five years, and estimating therefrom the number of burglaries committed and actual fires. It is not necessary to give the full details but is sufficient to state that the average of burglaries to fires thus estimated is in the ratio of nine of the former to ten of the latter.

Although it has been seen from our mention of the bursting of the simple locks on the oak chest containing the crown jewels of Scotland, that, as late as 1818, little progress had been made by burglars in lock picking, yet it was not long before the mechanism of locks became thoroughly known to the criminal fraternity and the burglar, like love, could "laugh at locksmiths." But about forty years ago a lock was put upon the market which has to this day proved unpickable.

In a recent account of the great Northampton Bank robbery, the startling statement has been made that fifty thousand dollars were offered by the thieves for the picking of a Yale door lock, and it is a fact that this obstacle was only overcome after obtaining, by the exercise of great ingenuity and by bribery, a duplicate key. When Linus Yale, jr., in 1865, invented the lock which bears his name, he effected a revolution in the whole art of lock making, both in principle and construction; and a brief account of the lock, now so universally identified with his name, and the conditions before and after its introduction, must be of more than ordinary interest.

Prior to the invention of Mr. Yale the large round key was in universal use, and the idea that the size of the key should be about proportionate to the size of the lock was generally accepted. The length of a key was necessarily such as to enable it to reach through the thickness of the door, and it was clumsy and heavy in proportion. The large old-fashioned keys in use at the time of the introduction of the Yale lock are familiar to all and may still be found in use on some old buildings.

Mr. Yale's invention consisted *first*, in separating the key mechanism of the lock from the case which contains the bolt and enclosing it in a separate compartment, or cylinder, inserted from the front of the door and connected through the door with the lock case behind; and, *second,* in making a small flat key to operate the lock, the key being the same size for all sizes of locks, and all thicknesses of door, and the keyhole being reduced to a narrow slit.

From an examination of Patent Office records, and by the courtesy of the company founded by Mr. Yale, we are enabled to show herewith the earliest form of the Yale cylinder, and also its highest and most recent developments, the Paracentric key and key-way. From these illustrations the construction will be clearly understood. The security and key changes

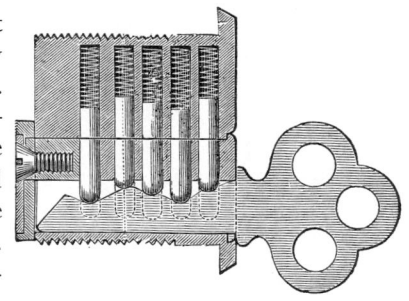

FIG. 1.

are obtained by means of pin tumblers, as shown by the sectional view (Fig. 1) of the lock, as made by Mr. Yale when applying for his original patent. The small key (which was originally made flat) is inserted into a slit in a cylindrical plug, and, as shown, adjusts the height of the pins so that the divisions in them coincide to the division between the plug and the body of the cylinder, thus permitting the plug to be rotated and the bolt mechanism to be operated by a suitable connection with the end of the plug. In Figure 2 is shown the escutcheon or front end of the original Yale cylinder as it appeared from the outside of the door. The facility which this construction offers for the use of a number of tumblers, and the freedom from play and lost motion which the close fitting secures, makes an

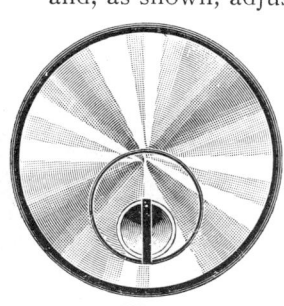

FIG. 2.

enormous number of different keys possible and thus gives the highest security against intentional or accidental interchange of keys.

One point of defect in this construction was the ease with which a duplicate could be obtained either from wax impres-

FIG. 3.

sions or from an outline drawn upon a piece of paper, if a key could be secured, even for a moment, for this purpose. About ten years after the introduction of the first Yale lock, the idea of a corrugated blade and correspondingly shaped key-way developed itself. By interlocking the key and key-way the "tilting" of the key was eliminated, the tumblers were rendered inaccessible, the number of key changes was indefinitely increased, and above all, the duplication of the key was rendered infinitely more difficult. About 1890, however, we find in the Patent Office the "Paracentric" key and corresponding key-way, and this form is now used in all genuine Yale locks and may be said to add another chapter to the history of the art of lock making.

In the Yale Paracentric Lock the pin tumbler mechanism is identical with that of the original and the corrugated forms, the improvement being wholly in the key-way and key. The front view of the cylinder (Fig. 3) shows this new form of key-way and it will at once be seen that the projections extend in such a way and are of such a shape as

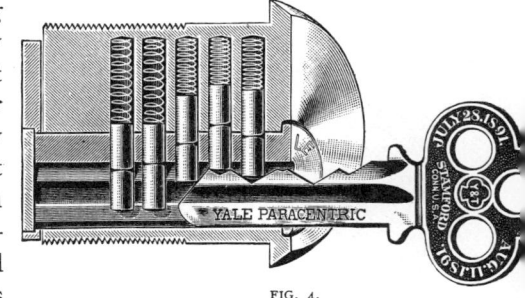
FIG. 4.

to utterly preclude the vertical movement of any instrument which might be introduced with the intention of lifting the pins and so opening the lock. Fig. 4 shows the key partly inserted and it will be seen how the pins are moved up and down, riding upon the bittings of the key as it enters. In Fig. 5 the key is all the way in and the plug partly rotated, thus showing the manner in which the divisions of the pins permit the lock to be opened by use of the proper key. From these illustrations can also be seen the impossibility of operation by any key except one which is "bitted" (or cut) exactly in conformity with the arrangement of the divisions in the pins of the particular cylinder with which it is to be used.

Shortly previous to his death, in 1868, Mr. Yale formed a partnership with Mr. Henry R. Towne, out of which grew the Yale & Towne Mfg. Co., of which for more than twenty-five years Mr. Towne has been president, and which is the sole maker of the Yale locks. Its works are located in Stamford, Conn., and its main office in the city of New York, with branches in other cities. Out of the inventions of Mr. Yale, supplemented by a long series of later improvements and inventions, contributed by others but relating to the same field of industrial activity, has thus grown one of the leading industries of the country whose efforts and products constitute an important element in the defences of society against "Our Rival, The Rascal."

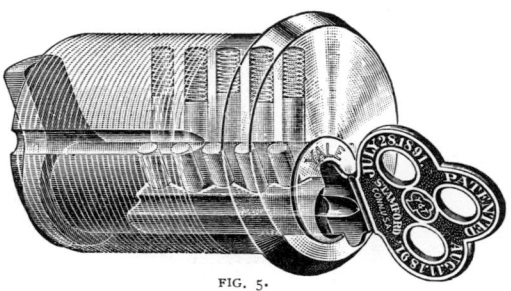

FIG. 5.

It has been duly noted in our chapter upon Forgery that it is far more difficult to guard against the quill in the hand of a skillful operator than to withstand all the assaults which may be made upon vaults and safes by the most effective weapons of the most expert burglar. When one considers what vast amounts of money are transferred by means of a few lines of writing, it is not surprising that many thousands of dollars are annually lost by means of forged instruments. Documents representing wealth may be carefully secured in burglar-proof vaults, but in the transmission of evidences of value from hand to hand, we must rely upon writing ink, which vanishes before the touch of acid or alkali and which can often be fraudulently changed, with almost perfect security against immediate detection, while the document still gives every appearance of being genuine.

Among the many devices perfected to protect the system of exchange by paper, which is so distinctive a feature of our modern business methods, it will be readily seen that none can be better than one whereby the medium itself is rendered incapable of alteration without being so affected as to show instantly the change. Such a medium has been accessible for commercial use for many years in the shape of the National Safety Paper, invented and manufactured by George La Monte of New York, which has a white body, the surfaces of both sides being colored, during the process of manufacture, with chemicals which are derived from the same ingredients as the writing inks used to fill up the documents. The writing thus becomes so incorporated with the color that whatever removes one removes the other and, leaving the white body of the paper exposed, instantly attracts attention to the alteration. The paper is colored in wavy lines, which not only gives an ornamental surface but also renders it proof against artificial coloring after erasure, which might be effected were it merely printed on the surface as a tint. Being alike on both sides it prevents alteration of the endorsements, as well as the face of the document, which is a very important matter, yet frequently overlooked. In short such a paper is protection for every part of a check, amount, date, signatures, and endorsements alike.

This paper is now in use by over 6,000 banks and bankers in this country as well as many large corporations and railway companies, and is largely used abroad as far as Japan and

Australia. A special form of this paper upon heavier stock but equally sensitive in its surface is being manufactured for the coupon tickets of many railroads, it having been found that forgeries of these tickets result in large losses to such corporations. In this paper the colored surface carries with its ornamental lines the name of the issuing company, the same device being in reverse on the back and so exactly registered that, on holding to the light, only one perfect lettering appears. This paper is only sold under contract to the proper officials of the road which uses it, rendering it practically impossible for spurious tickets to be printed.

The necessity of private watchmen for the protection of certain classes of property is generally recognized, but the security of such protection depends, of course, on the fidelity of the employee. It therefore becomes necessary to have some means of determining the watchman's presence and attention to duty. This demand has been met by the invention of various automatic time-registers or watchman's clocks (operated by clockwork or by electricity) which will record exactly the time when the watchman visits his post of duty. Of course it is absolutely necessary to guard against any fictitious record made by the use of false keys or by tampering with the electric wires, for if the watchman can get at the mechanism of the clock, its record is unreliable.

One of the latest devices for this purpose, which is used extensively by the principal financial institutions of New York City, is shown in the accompanying illustration. It consists of a clock movement which will run for eight days, and within which is placed, at the beginning of the week, a paper dial divided into quarter hours for eight consecutive days. The clock being wound and started, the dial travels regularly past a point where a stylus is made to puncture the paper by simply turning a knob at the top of the clock. It is screwed to the wall from the inside and the glass cover, through which the watchman's record is visible at all times, is locked in place by a simple but effective automatic time lock which can not be opened by any key. When the full week has run out, it immediately unlocks itself and the record can be removed and a fresh dial substituted. As there is no way of reaching the mechanism (without breaking the cover) until the lock opens, it is impossible to produce a false record without immediate detection.

Among the most important needs of the police systems in cities has been some method whereby the patrolman on duty could communicate with the station house for assistance or instruction. In 1880, the first regular system for police communication was introduced in Chicago by the Police Telephone and Signal Company of that city. Soon afterwards the Gamewell Fire Alarm Telegraph Company, having large facilities for the manufacture of electrical apparatus, became interested with the Chicago company, and from this starting point has grown the police signal system in use by the Gamewell company to-day.

Prior to 1880, the police departments in some cities had used apparatus of more or less service as a means of communication, such as the dial telegraph; but, with the invention of the telephone and particularly of the transmitter, it became possible to secure new and better results. The original apparatus used by the Chicago company consisted only of a telephone and call box installed in a booth and connected with the station-house. While this marked a great advance in the development of an efficient police service, it was found to be expensive, requiring special operators on duty at all times, who could only sift important from unimportant matter by scanning and recording every message sent in over the line.

To increase the efficiency and economize in the cost of the service a combination was effected whereby anyone of the several calls sent in from a signal box to a police station was not only recorded there by a printing device, but automatically rang a bell on all important calls, while silently recording those not requiring immediate attention.

When the Gamewell system was first introduced, the metallic circuit, as now used on long distance telephones, was not known, and for some time it was necessary to locate the instrument and signal mechanism within a booth into which the officer could retire in order to cut off the disturbing noises of the street. But it was not long before the Gamewell Company put in at Baltimore a system with a large number of what are known as wall boxes which, placed on the side of buildings or on poles, did away with the use of booths. This worked well on quiet streets and, before long, the improvements in telephony made it possible to use wall boxes altogether. This is the form now generally used, although some cities still retain the booths. Among other improvements patented were devices for signalling from the station house to the patrolman at his box, both manually and automatically.

In principle the construction of the essential parts of boxes has varied but little from those first introduced. They contain a pointer which may be placed at any one of six or seven different points, or wants, upon a dial; and, after being thus set, a hook or lever is pulled. This records, at the station-house, not only the number of the box (in practically the same manner that an alarm of fire is sent) but additional characters showing just what is wanted. Patents were also taken out very early in the history of police telegraphs—not later than 1881 or 1882,—for a combination mechanism which registered automatically not only the box number and want but also the exact minute, hour, day, and year when the call was sent in.

Within the past twelve years, the Gamewell company, operating with the Chicago company, have put in a large number of such systems in many of the largest municipalities in the country, including Chicago, Philadelphia, San Francisco, St. Louis, Baltimore, Washington, etc. The New England cities have especially shown great enterprise in thus increasing the efficacy of their police systems. Springfield, Lawrence, Lowell, Waltham, New Bedford, Brookline and Chelsea, Mass.; Portland and Lewiston, Maine; Hartford and New Haven, Conn., and Providence and Pawtucket, R. I.,—are among the places where this system has been in use for a number of years; and it seems to be the general testimony that such a system wonderfully improves the efficiency of the police department, enabling both officials and patrolmen to do work much more rapidly, completely, and satisfactorily. It is doubtless only a question of time when the use of the police signal system will be quite as universal as the fire alarm telegraph.

In the City of Boston, in 1886, the ordinary telephone booths were replaced by the police signal and intercommunicative systems of the Municipal Signal Company of Boston, the workings of which apparatus has been referred to in our chapter entitled "Arrest and Identification." This system enables the patrolman to record, automatically and silently by a printing device at the station-house, the exact moment of his visit to the signal box upon his beat, thus proving his efficiency and keeping him in touch with his superior officer for any needed conference or advice. He can also announce an important or emergency call for patrol wagon, ambulance, or telephone communication by another signal which sounds a continuous alarm at the station-house until the call has received proper attention. These different calls also record themselves by the printing mechanism in distinguishing characters.

Should the officer in charge at the station-house wish to speak to the patrolmen on street duty, he can instantly put himself into telephonic communication with them by manually sounding the gongs in the boxes whenever a patrol signal is received, or he can forestall the arrival of the patrolmen in turn at the street boxes, by merely setting a switch which causes an incoming patrol signal to automatically sound the box gongs and thereby summon them to use their telephones. In the most recent construction of this system a switch may also be set to sound a signal which calls the patrolmen immediately back to the police-station. By the use of this signal, at the time of the riot at the Charlestown State Prison, details of patrolmen from the stations in the central part of the city were recalled from their beats and landed at the prison for duty in less than fifteen minutes, and a large force was thus massed at that place in a very short time.

The system also brings to the assistance of the department a large number of citizens who, being furnished with keys to signal boxes, are enabled to call for police assistance in case of trouble, and thereby, in one sense, constitute an auxiliary police force. When one of these keys is used it becomes locked in place and cannot be released until the officer unlocks the box.

This system was introduced in Boston after a thorough examination of the subject of police signal systems. It has been in continuous use in all parts of the city since its adoption in 1886, and, as in all of the many cities where it has been installed, it has received the complete endorsement of the police authorities.

Among all the other benefits of such systems for police communication, not the least is the fact that they do away with the degrading and offensive spectacle of a prisoner being dragged through the streets to the station-house, and alleviate human suffering by providing an expeditious way of summoning assistance in accident cases, and conveying the injured to their homes or the hospitals.

In pointing out and strongly commending the use of the best modern safeguards, it is not, of course, our design to diminish the responsibility or relax the vigilance of any police organization. We are seeking simply to secure the most thorough coöperation and system of defence against the arts of the rascal, and by so doing to discourage criminal undertakings and reduce the losses of good citizens.

It is already apparent that the application of these safeguards has been greatly disheartening to burglars, "banksneaks" and forgers, and that the actual working range of these criminals is yearly receding. They have been driven to search laboriously for openings where the defences are imperfect or neglected, and every extension of safeguards will make their search more difficult and diminish their possible plunder. We have then a confidence grounded on actual experience that the coöperation for the protection of society will foil more and more completely any possible combination or art of the rascal, and it will be an enduring satisfaction to us if our work in furtherance of such coöperation shall prove to be of substantial service.

INDEXES

INDEX OF CRIMINALS.

	PAGE.
Allen, Charles	125, 140, 328
Allen, Jesse	230
Allen, "The"	230
Anderson, Charles	253
Anderson, Mary (*alias* "Mother Weir")	297
Ballard, Thomas	152
Barracks, William	195
Barrett, William (*alias* Bassett)	104, 111 to 116
"Bassett." *See* William Barrett.	
Becker, Charles	163, 175 to 182
Berkowitz, Gadalia	298
Bernard, John	218
Biglow, "Big Tom"	373
"Black Amelia." *See* Amelia Levy.	
"Black Dan." *See* Daniel Leary.	
"Black Lena." *See* Lena Kleinschmid.	
Borsch, Walter	278
"Bottle Sam." *See* Sam Perry.	
Boyd, Lindsay C.	289
Brady, James ("Big Jim Brady")	53
Brady, John	218
Brockway, William E. ("Old Bill")	163, 182, 183
"Bronson." *See* Charles Spencer.	
"Brooklyn Johnny" (*alias* John Hamilton).	
Brotzki, Samuel	195, 328
Brown, Margaret (*alias* "Old Mother Hubbard")	375
Buck, Frank	127
Bullard, Charles (*alias* "Piano Charley")	44, 49, 50, 53, 54
Burke, John	136
Burke, William ("Billy")	125, 129, 136
Burns, Peter (*alias* "James Joy Julius")	163 to 167
Busby, Mary	375
Butler, Jack	263
Cannon, John H. ("Jack")	236
"Carpenter." *See* William Carroll.	
Carroll, "Patsy"	81
Carroll, William (*alias* "Hayes," *alias* "Carpenter," *alias* "Cole")	10
Carson, George	130, 136 to 138
Chaffee, James H.	115, 296
Chapman, Joseph B.	163, 176
"Cincinnati Red." *See* Red Hyle.	

	PAGE.
Cochran, Bob.	44
Cody, Patrick.	68
Cohen, Rosie (*alias* Annie Levy)	30
"Cole." *See* William Carroll.	
Coleman, William.	137
"Confidence Queen," The. *See* Bertha Heyman.	
Cregan, James.	175 to 182
Cummings, David (Dave).	44, 56 to 58
Curtis, Henry.	241

"Daily, Charles." *See* Edward C. Smith.	
Davis, Henry.	218
Davis, Richard O.	167, 169, 174
"Dayton Sammy," *alias* Samuel Straehler.	
"Dean, A. H." *See* Frank L. Seaver.	
Dennis, John.	276
Dillon, Elizabeth.	375
Dobbs, "Johnny".	68, 107
Dollard, "Joe".	83
"Dorris, Charles H." *See* Jack Strauss.	
Dow, Marion L. (*alias* "Carrie E. Morse").	373 to 375
"Dr. Edward S. West." } *See* Edward Farebrother.	
"Dr. St. Clair."	
Drohan, Richard.	106, 107
Duffy, Frank (*alias* Pete "McCormack").	25
Dunlap, James.	43, 44, 57, 74 to 76
"Dutch Alonzo." *See* Alonzo Henn.	
"Dutch Charley".	98

"Ellicott." *See* Edward Williams.	
Elliott, "Joe".	165
Ellwood, George A. (*alias* "Gentleman George").	116 to 118
Engle, Gottlieb.	163, 167, 176
"English Harry".	5
Evans, George H. (*alias* "Kid Miller," *alias* "Lady Hand George").	126
Evans, Walter.	106, 107
Everhardt, Charles J. (*alias* "Mash Market Jake").	174, 175

Fale, William.	241
Farebrother, Edward (*alias* "Dr. Edward S. West," *alias* "Dr. St. Clair").	241
"Fielding, David H." *See* Max Steele.	
Fields, Kate (*alias* Annie Upton).	33
Figgat, C. M.	326
Fisher, Charles.	167, 169 to 175, 331
Flynn, Arthur.	290
"Frisco Slim".	3
"Funeral" Wells. *See* James Wells.	

| Gardner, George | 44 |

INDEX OF CRIMINALS.

PAGE.

"Gentleman George," *alias* George A. Ellwood.
George, Theophilus 277
Gifford, Charles 218
Gifford, Henry 218
Gleason, James 97, 98
Goldstein, Joseph 30

Hamilton, John (*alias* "Brooklyn Johnny") 88
Hamilton, Sheldon (*alias* "Shell") 141, 163, 165
"Hayes." *See* William Carroll.
Hedspeth, Marion C. . . . . 256 to 259
Henn, Alonzo (*alias* "Henry Morton," *alias* "Dutch Alonzo") 125, 126
Hennessey, George (*alias* "Kid") 25
Heyman, Bertha (*alias* "The Confidence Queen") . . . 368, 369
Hicks, Chas. A 218
Hines, Joshua ("Josh") 25
Hoey, Jimmy 370
Hoffman, Henry (*alias* "Tannis," *alias* "Mug") 90
Hoffman, Henry (*alias* "Carl Schultz") 241
Holbrook, George 369
Holbrook, Mary (*alias* "Mollie Hoey") . . . . 369 to 372
Hope, James (Jimmy) 43, 55
Hope, John 43, 55
Hovan, Horace (*alias* "Little Horace") . . . 121, 125 to 127
Hovan, Robert 127
"Howard, Joe" *See* Joseph Killoran.
Hurley, Michael (*alias* "Pugsey") 108, 109
Hyle, Red (*alias* "Cincinnati Red") 240

"Jack Sheppard," *alias* John Mahoney.
"Jackson, Billy." *See* William E. Stewart.
"Jackstraws." *See* Jack Strauss.
"John Doe." *See* Edward Williams.
Johnson, Chauncey . . . . 131 to 135
Johnson, John C. 157
Jourdan, Louise (*alias* "Little Louise") 372
"Julius, James Joy." *See* Peter Burns.

"Kauffmann, Louise." *See* Rose Stade.
"Keene," *See* Walter Sheridan.
Kelly, Edward ("Eddy") . . . . 73 to 80
Kelly, Harry 278
"Kid Johnson" 4, 7
"Kid" Hennessey. *See* George Hennessey.
"Kid Miller." *See* George H. Evans.
Killoran, Joseph (*alias* "Joe Howard") . . 137, 139 to 141, 328
King, Jack 263
Kleinschmid, Lena (*alias* "Black Lena") 297
Kurtz, Michael (*alias* "Sheeny Mike") . . . . 86 to 88

"Lady Hand George." *See* George H. Evans.
La Libertè, George 264
"Lambert." *See* Charles McLaughlin.
Lavoiye, Edmond (*alias* "Charles E. Marshall") 97
Lawrence, Frederick 278
Leary, Daniel (*alias* "Black Dan") 53
Leary, "Red" 56, 68
Levy, Amelia (*alias* "Black Amelia") 297, 373
"Levy, Annie." *See* Rosie Cohen.
"Levy, Lina." *See* Rosie Vokar.
Lewis, James 218
"Little Adam." *See* Adam Worth.
"Little Dave" (*alias* David Mooney).
"Little Horace." *See* Horace Hovan.
"Little Joe." *See* Joseph McCluskey.
"Little Scotty" 33
Love, John 86
Ludlow, Lewis 195
Lyons, Edward (Ned) . . . . . . 44, 58, 363 to 365
Lyons, James E. . . . . 230 to 235
Lyons, Sophie . . . . 129, 362 to 368

Maher, William (*alias* "Billy Marr") 137, 140
Mahoney, John (*alias* "Jack Sheppard") . . . . 88 to 90
Mandelbaum, Frederica ("Old Mother Mandelbaum ")
                                    294 to 296, 365, 370, 371
Manning, Sidney (*alias* "Sid Yennie") 137, 139
Marsh, "Ike" 44, 54
"Marshall, Charles E." *See* Edmond Lavoiye.
"Marshall, E. R." *See* Albert Wilson.
Martin, John, Jr. 299
Martin, Sam 259
"Mash Market Jake." *See* Charles J. Everhardt.
McCaffrey (*alias* Peters), James. 25
McCartney, John Peter 153
McCluskey, Joseph (*alias* "Little Joe," *alias* "J. M. Shaw") 136, 180
"McCormack, Pete." *See* Frank Duffy.
McCoy, "Big Frank" 68
McDonald, George 161
McKenna, Roxie . . . . 237 to 239
"McLain." *See* Chas. McLaughlin.
McLaughlin, Charles (*alias* "McLain," *alias* "Lambert," *alias*
    "Seaman") 239
McLaughlin, Ellen 33
Meyer, John H. 289
Miles, George (*alias* "George White") . . . 44, 46, 52, 53
Mincheon, James (*alias* "Doc") 195
Minor, Rufus ("Rufe") 130, 137
Mooney, David (*alias* "Little Dave") 96, 97
Morgan, Charles (*alias* "D. M. Speer") . . . . 259 to 261

INDEX OF CRIMINALS 427

	PAGE.
"Morris." *See* Edward Williams.	
"Morse, Carrie E." *See* Marion L. Dow.	
"Morton, Henry." *See* Alonzo Henn.	
Murray, John W.	290
"Myers, Lizzie."	298, 373
"Myers." *See* Caroline Smith.	
O'Brien, Thomas	188, 190, 195
O'Connor, Wallace ("Wally")	137, 139
"Old Mother Hubbard." *See* Margaret Brown.	
"One Eyed Thompson."	153
Perris, Sam (*alias* "Worcester Sam")	44
Perry, George	76
Perry, Oliver Curtis	265 to 275, 327
Perry, Sam (*alias* "Bottle Sam")	239
"Peters, James." *See* James McCaffrey.	
Phearson, Philip	141
"Piano Charley." *See* Charles Bullard.	
Porter, "Billy"	87
Post, George W.	188 to 190, 195
Prior, Joseph (*alias* "Walking Joe")	236, 237
"Pugsey" Hurley. *See* Michael Hurley.	
Quigley, James	88
"Ralston." *See* Walter Sheridan.	
Raymond, Augustus ("Gus")	137, 139
Raymond, William	195
Reilly, "Little Joe."	176
Reno, John	250, 251
Reno, Frank	250 to 254
Reno, Simeon	250 to 254
Reno, William	250 to 254
Rogers, Michael	251
Russell, Harry	140, 328
Scannell, Roger T. (*alias* "R. O'Connell")	325
Schneider, Ernest V.	278
"Schultz, Carl." *See* Henry Hoffman.	
Scott, Robert	44, 57
"Seaman." *See* Charles McLaughlin.	
Searcy, C. J.	259
Sears, Walter	290
Seaver, Frank L. (*alias* "Frederick Stebbins" *alias* "D. W. Woods." *alias* "A. H. Dean")	180
"Shaw, J. M." *See* Joe McCluskey.	
"Sheeny Mike." (*alias* "Michael Kurtz.")	
"Sheeny Si"	5
Sheridan, Walter (*alias* "Stewart," *alias* "Ralston," *alias* "Stanton," *alias* "Keene")	121, 123 to 126

Shinburn, Max . . . . 44, 45 to 51
Sly, Adelbert . . . . 256 to 259
Smaling, William E. 290
Smith, Caroline (*alias* " Myers ") 33
Smith, Edward C. (*alias* " Charles Daily ") . . . 109 to 111
Sondheim, Jacob (*alias* " Al Wise ") 195
" Speer, D. M." *See* Charles Morgan.
" Spence." *See* Charles Spencer.
Spencer, Charles (*alias* " Spence," *alias* " Bronson ") . . . 276
Stack, Joseph (*alias* " Spanish Joe ") 289
Stade, Rose (*alias* " Louise Kaufmann")
" Stanton." *See* Walter Sheridan.
Start, Philip 25
" Stebbins, Frederick." *See* Frank L. Seaver.
Steele, Max (*alias* " Henry T. Woodruff," *alias* " David H. Fielding ") . . . . 167 to 174
" Stewart." *See* Walter Sheridan.
Stewart, William E. (*alias* " Billy Jackson ") . . . 277
Straehler, Samuel (*alias* " Dayton Sammy ") 25
Strauss, " Jack " (*alias* " Charles H. Dorris," *alias* " Jack straws") 239
Susicovitch, Carlo 176
Swain, David 218, 221

Talbot, John 81, 84

Ulrich, Charles 152
" Upton, Annie." *See* Kate Fields.

Vokar, Rosie (*alias* " Lina Levy ") 30
Van Horn, Frank 276

" Walking Joe." *See* Joseph Prior.
Walsh, John (" Jack ") 81, 83, 84
" Watt Jones." *See* Thomas B. Wills.
Wells, James (*alias* " Funeral ") 24
Whalen, Joe 117
" White." *See* George Miles.
Wilkes, Henry Wade (*alias* "George Wilkes," *alias* "Willis") 163 to 167, 177
Williams, Edward (*alias* " Ellicott," *alias* " Morris," *alias* " John Doe " 100
Wills, Thomas B. (*alias* " Watt Jones ") 25
Wilson, Albert (" Al," *alias* " E. R. Marshall ") . . 163, 166, 167
Wilson, Clay 195
" Wise, Al." *See* Jacob Sondheim.
Wols, Jacob 30
" Woodruff, Henry T." *See* Max Steele.
" Woods, D. W." *See* Frank L. Seaver.
" Worcester Sam." *See* Sam Perris.
Worth, Adam (*alias* " Little Adam ") . . 44, 54, 85, 176

" Yennie, Sid." *See* Sidney Manning.

GENERAL INDEX.

	PAGE.
AIR PUMP, THE	57
ALBANY STREET GANG	105
ARREST OF CRIMINALS	306
ARSON. (*See* THE INCENDIARY.)	
BANK BURGLAR, THE	35–63
Old-Fashioned and Modern Contrasted	35
Tools	38–41
Preparation for a Burglary	42
Improvement in Defence Against	61, 62
Dangerous Uses of Electricity	62
BANK SNEAK, THE	120–143
Methods of Operation	122, 129, 131, 136
Precautions Against	134
BANK ROBBERIES.	
Bank of England (Bidwell Forgeries)	161–163
Barre, Vt., Bank of	52
Boylston Bank (of Boston)	43, 47, 49, 53, 54, 60
Covington (Ky.) Bank	43
Dorchester (England) Bank	392
Falls City Tobacco Bank of Louisville, Ky.	56
Italian-American Bank of New York	86
Manhattan Savings Bank of New York	42, 47, 55, 60
Middleburg, N.Y., First National Bank of	51
Northampton (Mass.) Bank	43, 60, 409
Ocean National Bank of New York	43, 47, 52, 60
Plainfield, N. J., First National Bank of	127
Quincy, Ill., First National Bank of	57
Smith's Bank, Perry, N.Y.	55
Traders' Deposit Bank, Mt. Sterling, Ky.	129
Viveres, Belgium, Provincial Bank of	49
Walpole (N. H.) Savings Bank	45
West Maryland Bank	48
BANK VAULTS	66
BATES, L. L. & CO.	401
BEGGARS	1–14
Report of Boston Overseers of the Poor	14
BERTILLON SYSTEM, THE	320–324
BIDWELL, AUSTIN	160–163

BIDWELL, GEORGE	161
BREWSTER, WILLIAM H.	408
BROCKWAY, Z. R.	339, 386
BUREAU OF CRIMINAL INVESTIGATION (Boston)	312–336
BURGLAR ALARM SYSTEMS	63, 402–404
BURGLARS' CORRESPONDENCE	74, 76
BURGLARY. (*See* also BANK BURGLAR, SAFE BREAKER, STORE BREAKER, HOUSE BREAKER, etc.)	
What constitutes	64, 65
Insurance against	408
"BUNCO GAMES"	185–222
The Shell Game. (Thimble rig)	185
Origin of "Bunco"	188
Gold Brick Swindles	191
Cross Roaders	193
"Sweating" Gold Coins	196
Sunken Galleons and Buried Treasure	196
"Green Goods" or "Sawdust" Games	197–203
Horse Sharps	203–211
Flim-Flam Game	212
Bogus Business Investments	215
Advertising Frauds	216
Worthless Checks	217
Swindles on Immigrants	218
"CHOKE PEAR," THE	285
CHROME STEEL	395, 397, 402
COMPOSITE PHOTOGRAPHS OF CRIMINALS	348
COUNTERFEITING. (*See* also FORGERY)	145–153
Definition of	145
Methods used in	146–153
Precautions against	147
Tests for	149
"Sweating," "Plugging" and "Filling"	150
Raising Bank Notes	153
Washing Bills	153
CRIMINALS, THE TREATMENT OF	376–390
Massachusetts Legislation	378
Probation Office	385
DIEBOLD SAFE AND LOCK CO.	397, 399
"DIPS"	23
"DRAG," THE	40
"DUCHESS OF GAINSBOROUGH" PORTRAIT	55
DUGDALE, R. I.	340
EXPLOSIVES FOR SAFE BREAKING	57, 61, 72
EXPRESS THIEF, THE	278
FAY, HON. CLEMENT K.	378

GENERAL INDEX.

PAGE.

FENCE, THE. (*See* THE RECEIVER.)
"FILLING." (*See* COUNTERFEITING.)
FIRE MARSHAL, MASSACHUSETTS STATE 304
FLAT WORKERS 99–101
FOOTPAD, THE 280
FORGER, THE. (*See* also Counterfeiting) 145–184
    Counterfeiting 145–153
    Definition of Forgery 151
    Forged Signatures 154
    Forged Signatures, Detection of 155
    Precautions against 156–160
FRAZER, PERSIFOR, on Forgery 155

GALTON, FRANCIS 348
GAMEWELL FIRE ALARM TELEGRAPH CO. 415
"GRIPPER," THE 39

HAYT, CHIEF JUSTICE 339
HEDSPETH GANG, THE 255–259
HEREDITY IN CRIME 340
HIGHWAYMAN, THE 280–290
"HOISTERS" 29
HOLMES, EDWIN 404
HOLMES'S ELECTRIC PROTECTION 404
HOTEL THIEF, THE 223–247
HOUSE BREAKER, THE 93–119
    Sneak Thieves and Amateurs 94, 101
    Second Story and Flat Workers 95–101
    The Professional Burglar 102–118

IDENTIFICATION OF CRIMINALS 306–320
IDLENESS AS A CAUSE OF CRIME 339
INCENDIARY, THE 299–305
    Definition and Punishments of Arson 300
    Commercial Incendiarism 301
    The Pyromaniac 303
INSURANCE AGAINST BURGLARY LOSS 407
INSURANCE AGAINST FIRE 300

"JACK," THE 39
JAIL CELLS, CHROME STEEL 403
JAMES GANG, THE 255
"JIMMY," THE 38
"JOHNNY DOBBS" GANG 107

KEY NIPPERS 102, 103
KLEPTOMANIA 28
KNOCKOUT DROPS 288

LA MONTE, GEORGE 413
LODGING HOUSE TRAMPS 8

432   OUR RIVAL, THE RASCAL.

	PAGE.
LOMBROSO, CAESARE, Theory of Crime	341, 357, 361
MAKING OF CRIMINALS	337–356
MOORE, LANGDON W.	44
MOREAU, THE ABBE	376–381
MORGAN GANG, THE	255, 259, 261
MUNICIPAL SIGNAL CO. OF BOSTON	417
NATIONAL BANKERS' ASSOCIATION	184
NATIONAL SAFETY PAPER	413
NEW ENGLAND BURGLARY INSURANCE CO.	407
"PENNYWEIGHT THIEVES"	30
PETTIGROVE, FRED. G., Gen. Supt. of Mass. Prisons	320
PETTY THIEVES	84
PICKPOCKET, THE	15–26
Methods of Operation	15–26
Training of Children as	22
Professional Gangs of	23–25
Cover Sought by	25
Precautions Against	26
PINKERTON, ALLAN	251–252
PINKERTON DETECTIVE AGENCY	162, 184, 257, 262, 330
PLATE CUTTER, THE	41
"PLUGGING." (*See* COUNTERFEITING.)	
POCKET BLAST-PIPE	40
POLICE SIGNAL SYSTEMS	310, 415, 418
POLICE SYSTEMS	308, 336
The Boston System	309–336
PROAL, M. LOUIS	339, 348, 357, 359
PYROMANIA	303
RECEIVER, THE	291–298
RENO GANG, THE	250–254
RODMAN, SAMUEL, JR. Experiments in Safe Breaking	62
ROGUES' GALLERY	316, 319, 332, 333
"SAFE BOOKING"	40
SAFE BREAKER, THE	66–84
Methods of Operation	69
Use of Explosives	66–72
Tools	70, 77, 80
SAFE DEPOSIT VAULTS	400–402
SAFE DEPOSIT LOCKS	401
SAFES, BURGLAR PROOF	66, 67, 392, 400
SANDBAG, THE	284
SANFORD, C. E.	414
"SECOND STORY WORKERS"	95–98
SHOPLIFTER, THE	26–33
Dabblers in Shoplifting	27

GENERAL INDEX. 433

	PAGE.
SHOPLIFTER, Guarding Stores in Shopping Districts	27
Professional Shoplifters	29
"Morning Hoisters"	29
Pennyweight Thieves	30
Precautions against	30
SLEDGE, THE BURGLAR'S	40
SLEEPING CAR WORKERS	275–278
SNEAK THIEVES	94–101
"SPREADER," THE	40
"STONE GETTERS"	25
STORE BREAKER, THE	66–85
Safeguards against	90–92
"SWEATING." (See COUNTERFEITING.)	
SWINDLING BEGGAR, THE	1–14
TARDE, M.	346, 347–357
TOPINARD, M.	360
TOWNE, HENRY M.	412
TRAIN ROBBER, THE	248–275
TRAMPS	2, 8, 9, 10
WATCHMAN'S CLOCKS	414
WHEELOCK, HOWARD S.	407
WHITCOMB, CHAS. W., Massachusetts Fire Marshal	304
WINES, DR. E. C.	339, 382
WOMAN, THE CRIMINAL	357–375
YALE, LINUS, JR.	409
"YALE" LOCK, THE	118, 409

ADDENDUM.

Since the pages of this volume, containing the history of Chauncey Johnson (pp. 131-134), went to press, the career of this once noted bank sneak has been ended by death. On February 26, 1897, while serving out his sentence of imprisonment at the penitentiary on Blackwells Island, he died of consumption, being then seventy-five years of age.

PATTERSON SMITH REPRINT SERIES IN CRIMINOLOGY, LAW ENFORCEMENT, AND SOCIAL PROBLEMS

1. *Lewis: *The Development of American Prisons and Prison Customs, 1776–1845*
2. Carpenter: *Reformatory Prison Discipline*
3. Brace: *The Dangerous Classes of New York*
4. *Dix: *Remarks on Prisons and Prison Discipline in the United States*
5. Bruce et al.: *The Workings of the Indeterminate-Sentence Law and the Parole System in Illinois*
6. *Wickersham Commission: *Complete Reports, Including the Mooney-Billings Report.* 14 vols.
7. Livingston: *Complete Works on Criminal Jurisprudence.* 2 vols.
8. Cleveland Foundation: *Criminal Justice in Cleveland*
9. Illinois Association for Criminal Justice: *The Illinois Crime Survey*
10. Missouri Association for Criminal Justice: *The Missouri Crime Survey*
11. Aschaffenburg: *Crime and Its Repression*
12. Garofalo: *Criminology*
13. Gross: *Criminal Psychology*
14. Lombroso: *Crime, Its Causes and Remedies*
15. Saleilles: *The Individualization of Punishment*
16. Tarde: *Penal Philosophy*
17. McKelvey: *American Prisons*
18. Sanders: *Negro Child Welfare in North Carolina*
19. Pike: *A History of Crime in England.* 2 vols.
20. Herring: *Welfare Work in Mill Villages*
21. Barnes: *The Evolution of Penology in Pennsylvania*
22. Puckett: *Folk Beliefs of the Southern Negro*
23. Fernald et al.: *A Study of Women Delinquents in New York State*
24. Wines: *The State of Prisons and of Child-Saving Institutions*
25. *Raper: *The Tragedy of Lynching*
26. Thomas: *The Unadjusted Girl*
27. Jorns: *The Quakers as Pioneers in Social Work*
28. Owings: *Women Police*
29. Woolston: *Prostitution in the United States*
30. Flexner: *Prostitution in Europe*
31. Kelso: *The History of Public Poor Relief in Massachusetts, 1820–1920*
32. Spivak: *Georgia Nigger*
33. Earle: *Curious Punishments of Bygone Days*
34. Bonger: *Race and Crime*
35. Fishman: *Crucibles of Crime*
36. Brearley: *Homicide in the United States*
37. *Graper: *American Police Administration*
38. Hichborn: *"The System"*
39. Steiner & Brown: *The North Carolina Chain Gang*
40. Cherrington: *The Evolution of Prohibition in the United States of America*
41. Colquhoun: *A Treatise on the Commerce and Police of the River Thames*
42. Colquhoun: *A Treatise on the Police of the Metropolis*
43. Abrahamsen: *Crime and the Human Mind*
44. Schneider: *The History of Public Welfare in New York State, 1609–1866*
45. Schneider & Deutsch: *The History of Public Welfare in New York State, 1867–1940*
46. Crapsey: *The Nether Side of New York*
47. Young: *Social Treatment in Probation and Delinquency*
48. Quinn: *Gambling and Gambling Devices*
49. McCord & McCord: *Origins of Crime*
50. Worthington & Topping: *Specialized Courts Dealing with Sex Delinquency*
51. Asbury: *Sucker's Progress*
52. Kneeland: *Commercialized Prostitution in New York City*

* new material added

PATTERSON SMITH REPRINT SERIES IN CRIMINOLOGY, LAW ENFORCEMENT, AND SOCIAL PROBLEMS

53. *Fosdick: *American Police Systems*
54. *Fosdick: *European Police Systems*
55. *Shay: *Judge Lynch: His First Hundred Years*
56. Barnes: *The Repression of Crime*
57. †Cable: *The Silent South*
58. Kammerer: *The Unmarried Mother*
59. Doshay: *The Boy Sex Offender and His Later Career*
60. Spaulding: *An Experimental Study of Psychopathic Delinquent Women*
61. Brockway: *Fifty Years of Prison Service*
62. Lawes: *Man's Judgment of Death*
63. Healy & Healy: *Pathological Lying, Accusation, and Swindling*
64. Smith: *The State Police*
65. Adams: *Interracial Marriage in Hawaii*
66. *Halpern: *A Decade of Probation*
67. Tappan: *Delinquent Girls in Court*
68. Alexander & Healy: *Roots of Crime*
69. *Healy & Bronner: *Delinquents and Criminals*
70. Cutler: *Lynch-Law*
71. Gillin: *Taming the Criminal*
72. Osborne: *Within Prison Walls*
73. Ashton: *The History of Gambling in England*
74. Whitlock: *On the Enforcement of Law in Cities*
75. Goldberg: *Child Offenders*
76. *Cressey: *The Taxi-Dance Hall*
77. Riis: *The Battle with the Slum*
78. Larson: *Lying and Its Detection*
79. Comstock: *Frauds Exposed*
80. Carpenter: *Our Convicts*. 2 vols. in one
81. †Horn: *Invisible Empire: The Story of the Ku Klux Klan, 1866–1871*
82. Faris et al.: *Intelligent Philanthropy*
83. Robinson: *History and Organization of Criminal Statistics in the U. S.*
84. Reckless: *Vice in Chicago*
85. Healy: *The Individual Delinquent*
86. *Bogen: *Jewish Philanthropy*
87. *Clinard: *The Black Market: A Study of White Collar Crime*
88. Healy: *Mental Conflicts and Misconduct*
89. Citizens' Police Committee: *Chicago Police Problems*
90. *Clay: *The Prison Chaplain*
91. *Peirce: *A Half Century with Juvenile Delinquents*
92. *Richmond: *Friendly Visiting Among the Poor*
93. Brasol: *Elements of Crime*
94. Strong: *Public Welfare Administration in Canada*
95. Beard: *Juvenile Probation*
96. Steinmetz: *The Gaming Table*. 2 vols.
97. *Crawford: *Report on the Penitentiaries of the United States*
98. *Kuhlman: *A Guide to Material on Crime and Criminal Justice*
99. Culver: *Bibliography of Crime and Criminal Justice, 1927–1931*
100. Culver: *Bibliography of Crime and Criminal Justice, 1932–1937*
101. Tompkins: *Administration of Criminal Justice, 1938–1948*
102. Tompkins: *Administration of Criminal Justice, 1949–1956*
103. Cumming: *Bibliography Dealing with Crime and Cognate Subjects*
104. *Addams et al.: *Philanthropy and Social Progress*
105. *Powell: *The American Siberia*
106. *Carpenter: *Reformatory Schools*
107. *Carpenter: *Juvenile Delinquents*
108. *Montague: *Sixty Years in Waifdom*

* new material added   † new edition, revised or enlarged

PATTERSON SMITH REPRINT SERIES IN CRIMINOLOGY, LAW ENFORCEMENT, AND SOCIAL PROBLEMS

109. *Mannheim: *Juvenile Delinquency in an English Middletown*
110. Semmes: *Crime and Punishment in Early Maryland*
111. *National Conference of Charities & Correction: *History of Child Saving in the United States*
112. †Barnes: *The Story of Punishment*
113. Phillipson: *Three Criminal Law Reformers*
114. *Drähms: *The Criminal*
115. *Terry & Pellens: *The Opium Problem*
116. *Ewing: *The Morality of Punishment*
117. †Mannheim: *Group Problems in Crime and Punishment*
118. *Michael & Adler: *Crime, Law and Social Science*
119. *Lee: *A History of Police in England*
120. †Schafer: *Compensation and Restitution to Victims of Crime*
121. †Mannheim: *Pioneers in Criminology*
122. Goebel & Naughton: *Law Enforcement in Colonial New York*
123. *Savage: *Police Records and Recollections*
124. Ives: *A History of Penal Methods*
125. *Bernard (ed.): *Americanization Studies*. 10 vols.:
    Thompson: *Schooling of the Immigrant*
    Daniels: *America via the Neighborhood*
    Thomas: *Old World Traits Transplanted*
    Speek: *A Stake in the Land*
    Davis: *Immigrant Health and the Community*
    Breckinridge: *New Homes for Old*
    Park: *The Immigrant Press and Its Control*
    Gavit: *Americans by Choice*
    Claghorn: *The Immigrant's Day in Court*
    Leiserson: *Adjusting Immigrant and Industry*
126. *Dai: *Opium Addiction in Chicago*
127. *Costello: *Our Police Protectors*
128. *Wade: *A Treatise on the Police and Crimes of the Metropolis*
129. *Robison: *Can Delinquency Be Measured?*
130. *Augustus: *John Augustus, First Probation Officer*
131. *Vollmer: *The Police and Modern Society*
132. Jessel & Horr: *Bibliographies of Works on Playing Cards and Gaming*
133. *Walling: *Recollections of a New York Chief of Police;* & Kaufmann: *Supplement on the Denver Police*
134. *Lombroso-Ferrero: *Criminal Man*
135. *Howard: *Prisons and Lazarettos*. 2 vols.:
    The State of the Prisons in England and Wales
    An Account of the Principal Lazarettos in Europe
136. *Fitzgerald: *Chronicles of Bow Street Police-Office*. 2 vols. in one
137. *Goring: *The English Convict*
138. Ribton-Turner: *A History of Vagrants and Vagrancy*
139. *Smith: *Justice and the Poor*
140. *Willard: *Tramping with Tramps*
141. *Fuld: *Police Administration*
142. *Booth: *In Darkest England and the Way Out*
143. *Darrow: *Crime, Its Cause and Treatment*
144. *Henderson (ed.): *Correction and Prevention*. 4 vols.:
    Henderson (ed.): *Prison Reform;* & Smith: *Criminal Law in the U. S.*
    Henderson (ed.): *Penal and Reformatory Institutions*
    Henderson: *Preventive Agencies and Methods*
    Hart: *Preventive Treatment of Neglected Children*
145. *Carpenter: *The Life and Work of Mary Carpenter*
146. *Proal: *Political Crime*

* new material added   † new edition, revised or enlarged